RUMANIA
30°
SOVIET UNION
Black Sea
YUGOSLAVIA
ITALY
Adriatic Sea
BULGARIA
Corsica
ALBANIA
Sardinia
TURKEY
IRAN
GREECE
Aegean Sea
Sicily
Tunis
MALTA
SYRIA
IRAQ
CYPRUS
Crete
TUNISIA
Mediterranean
Sea
LEBANON
Tripoli
ISRAEL
JORDAN
Bengasi
Alexandria
Cairo
Siwa Oasis
Desert
of
Calanscio
LIBYA
QATTARA DEPRESSION
Eastern Desert
SAUDI ARABIA
UNITED
ARAB
REPUBLIC
Western
Desert
Sebha Oasis
Medina
Libyan
Aswan
r
a
of
Cancer
Red
Sea
Mecca
Nile
Nubian
Desert
TIBESTI
Desert
Port Sudan
NIGER
Asmara
Khartoum
Lake Chad
MARRA MTS.
CHAD
El Fasher
Blue Nile
SUDAN
Fort Lamy
CHOKE MTS.
ETHIOPIA
Addis Ababa
White Nile
CENTRAL
AFRICAN
REPUBLIC
Juba
Bangui
CAMEROON
UGANDA
KENYA
CONGO
REPUBLIC OF THE
CONGO
Congo R.
Stanleyville
McDonnell
REPUBLIC
GABON
Lake Victoria

BAAL, CHRIST, AND MOHAMMED

JOHN K. COOLEY

BAAL, CHRIST, AND MOHAMMED

RELIGION AND REVOLUTION IN NORTH AFRICA

WITH MAPS BY
CHARLES McDONNELL

HOLT, RINEHART AND WINSTON

NEW YORK CHICAGO SAN FRANCISCO

Published simultaneously in Canada by Holt, Rinehart and Winston of Canada, Limited.

Library of Congress Catalog Card Number: 64-21922

First Edition

Designer: Ernst Reichl
81552-0115
Printed in the United States of America

ACKNOWLEDGMENTS

Arthur A. Cohen, of Holt, Rinehart and Winston, encouraged me to develop into a book the theme of an article first appearing in *Commonweal,* November 1961, entitled "Cross and Crescent." If he had not believed in the project and patiently aided and encouraged it, the book never would have come into being. I am also indebted to the Editor of *Commonweal,* Edward S. Skillin, for permission to use some elements of the original article.

I wish to thank Dr. James Kritzeck, of the Institute for Advanced Study at Princeton University, for his painstaking reading and criticism of the manuscript. His expert knowledge of Islam and the Arab world and specialist's grasp of the questions of Christian-Moslem relations have been extremely valuable in making this a far better book than it could have been otherwise. Highly valuable was the editorial work of Catherine Oleson, who contributed in a thousand ways to improving the manuscript and the finished book. Seymour Barofsky contributed expert knowledge of the ancient Near East, and William Robert Miller gave me valuable encouragement.

Much credit and special gratitude are due my wife, Edith, for the long weeks she spent in typing, proofreading, and helping with research, especially during the final weeks of work on the book at Toumliline Monastery, Morocco. Her critical judgment was invaluable, as well as her moral support during difficult days.

Carl Brown, of the Middle East Institute at Harvard University, and Stuart Schaer, of the University of Wisconsin, offered useful suggestions. I am indebted to Professor Brown for finding and translating the selection from the proceedings of the Association of Algerian Ulama in 1933 in Chapter XXII, and to Professor Schaer, an expert student of Moroccan political affairs, for passing on to me his notes on a lecture by Allal al-Fassi which I have quoted in Chapters X and XIII.

My special thanks are also due to the Benedictine monks of Toumliline Monastery, in the Middle Atlas Mountains of Morocco, and in particular the Prior, Dom Denis Martin, and Dom Placide Pernot, who opened to me their splendid library of books, manuscripts, and periodicals, and generously allowed me to complete work on the book within their walls.

A number of Protestant and Catholic missionaries and clergymen in North Africa, most of whom are named in the text, gave me much useful information and advice. Among many other people who provided considerable assistance, I should like especially to thank the librarians of the National Library in Rabat, those at the Institut des Belles Lettres Arabe in Tunis, and numerous officials, scholars, fellow journalists, correspondents, and others in North Africa who offered opinions and judgments or who cut red tape, making it possible to reach source material that might have been inaccessible otherwise. Members of the staff of *The Christian Science Monitor,* through their benevolent interest, and The Christian Science Publishing Company, Boston, Massachusetts, by kindly permitting me to include material from several of my articles and dispatches published in *The Christian Science Monitor,* also helped my task.

None of the above bears responsibility for faults of the book or errors which I may have committed. All of them made material contributions to whatever merits or virtues it may have.

I also wish to thank the following for their kind permission to allow me to quote material from the books and articles listed:

The Bond Wheelwright Company, Portland, Maine, for an excerpt from The Prophet's Letter to the Himyarites of Yemen, probably after Al-Tabari, from *Muhammed's People,* by Eric Schroeder (1955).

The Clarendon Press, Oxford, England, for the passage concerning the martyrdom of Saint Perpetua, from E. C. E. Owen's book, *Acts of the Martyrs.*

The Christian Science Publishing Company, Boston, Massachusetts, for permission to use material from several of my articles and dispatches, published in *The Christian Science Monitor,* expecially "Tunisian Interlude," of April 12, 1962 (London edition).

E. P. Dutton & Co., Inc., New York, and Routledge and Kegan Paul Limited, London, England, for excerpts from *Fathers of the Church,* by F. A. Wright.

E. P. Dutton & Co., Inc., New York, and Ernest Benn Limited, London, England, for excerpts from *Private Letters Pagan and Christian,* by Dorothy Brooke.

Éditions Sequoia, S. A., Brussels and Paris, for permission to translate the quotation from an African Christian's description of Paradise and the excerpt from Athanasius' Life of Saint Anthony from *Atlas de L'Antiquité Chrétienne,* by F. van der Meer and C. Mohrmann (1960).

W. Kohlhammer Verlag, Stuttgart, for permission to translate and use the Manichaean texts appearing in *Heilige Schriften,* by Gunter Lanckowsky (1956).

Librairie Plon, Paris, for an excerpt from *Les religions de l'Afrique Antique* by Gilbert Charles-Picard.

The North Africa Mission, London, England, and Upper Darby, Pennsylvania, for permission to quote from Abe Wiebe's article, "A Saviour of Life and Death" in *North Africa* (London, Sept.–Oct., 1963) and from Francis R. Steele's editorial "Tolerance and Truth" in *Cross and Crescent* (Upper Darby, June, 1963).

Oxford University Press, London, under the auspices of the Royal Institute of International Affairs, for permission to include in Chapter III the verse about Jugurtha and Massinissa, taken from *A Survey of North West Africa,* by Nevill Barbour (1959); and quotations about syncretism and Hellenism in the Mediterranean, from *A Study of History,* by A. J. Toynbee, abridged by D. C. Somervell (1949).

Pantheon Books, Inc., New York, for an excerpt from *The Age of Constantine the Great,* by Jacob Burckhardt.

Presses Universitaires de France, Paris, for permission to translate and use a description of the city of Fez from their bilingual (Arabic and French) edition of *Voyages d'Ibn Batoutah* (Ibn Batuta), 1942.

The University of Chicago Press, Chicago, for an excerpt from *Medieval Islam,* by Gustave E. von Grunebaum (1958).

For Edith

and Katherine Anne

CONTENTS

INTRODUCTION

In most parts of Africa, Islam is making enormous headway against both paganism and Christianity. In Africa, and to a somewhat lesser extent in the eastern Arab world, the relationships between the faiths and the reasons for Moslem successes in religion and in politics are a vital part of daily history.

While living and reporting the past decade in North Africa for *The Christian Science Monitor* and others during Algeria's dramatic breakaway from French rule and the social revolution which followed, it occurred to me that some of the keys to Islam's recent triumphs might be found far back in time. In trying to discover them, and in seeking meaningful ties between religion and the revolutions which have repeatedly erupted against imperialist control in North Africa since the time of Carthage, the idea arose for this book.

I have not presumed to attempt a political or social history, or even a definitive history of religion in North Africa. Those are jobs for a professional historian, not a journalist. What I have tried to do is set out some main themes in the relationship between religious faith, alien imperialism, and the native Berber revolutionary spirit which always arose when the rule of Phoenicians, Romans, Arabs, Spanish, French, or any other colonial power pressed the Berbers and their more recent heirs in North Africa, the Arab nationalists, too hard.

Why was Islam, and with it Arabic culture, able to establish a solid base and later a successful society which has survived on the southern shores of the Mediterranean where Christianity was not? What chance might Christianity have for a return? These are some of the questions which dogged me as I undertook the book. To the extent that readers discover the answers with me, or are perhaps stimulated to seek better ones than mine, I shall feel that I have succeeded.

In compiling the material for this book, the formidable problem of transliteration of Arabic words into English characters arose. In general, I have tried to use the method of the *Shorter Encyclopedia of Islam,* edited by H. A. R. Gibb and J. H. Kramers

(Leiden: E. J. Brill, 1953), omitting its diacritical marks. Proper nouns, both names of people and places, have posed an especially difficult problem. Many have filtered into English usage over the years in different manners that seem to defy any system one would impose upon them now; others, of more recent date, have come to be spelled in Latin characters, but in French, Spanish, or Italian forms, depending upon which nation colonized a particular part of the Arab world. Most journalists and newspaper readers, including myself, are the despair of scholars. We are accustomed to these "corrupt" transliterations. In deciding what to change from, or what to leave in its seemingly most current form, a certain amount of random choice necessarily came into play. Always, however, it has been my intention, which I can only hope has been successfully translated into method, that each word or name which a reader may be familiar with or may meet in another spelling, will nonetheless be recognizable to him. In some cases I have reproduced spellings as they appear in copyrighted material.

I have sometimes had to make English translations of Arabic texts from versions already translated into French or Spanish, since the originals were not available to me. I am responsible for these translations and believe I have taken precautions to avoid any serious error. In other cases, I have been helped with some translations from the Arabic, as noted in the Acknowledgments, by persons who read Arabic more easily and with less need to refer to dictionaries than myself.

For the reader who may not be familiar with Arabic terms, a glossary of those words which recur in the text has been appended to the end of the book.

To me, North Africa is a truly fascinating area, certainly more important in the world of today and tomorrow than many of us realize. I can only hope that this glimpse into its past and its present communicates some of this fascination and arouses more interest in it.

JOHN K. COOLEY

Casablanca, 1964

PART ONE

BAAL AND CHRIST

CHAPTER I

THE CROSS FACES THE CRESCENT

> [Christianity's spiritual] victory surpasses the understanding of those grown accustomed to link the Cross with a flag and the Gospel with the Occident. For such last possessors of a primitive mentality, the Church, essentially characterized by human conduct and structures, "retreats" or "advances" with armies, pacts and pipelines. The fact is that the independence of Algeria proclaims the final twilight of all the Crusades.
>
> André Mandouze, 1962

The man on the Louis XVI divan stared me full in the face, his glittering eyes as blue as the Mediterranean visible through the far window of the palace. "The future of the Christians in North Africa?" He repeated my question, seemingly chewing it over with his massive, Roman jaw. "Or, do you mean the future of the Christian churches?"

The speaker was President Habib Bourguiba of Tunisia, one of today's secular heirs of sixteen centuries of Moslem religious hegemony in North Africa, once Christianized by the contemporaries of Septimius Severus and of St. Augustine. He was speaking less than a year after the independence of Algeria had again, after a hundred years of conquest and domination by Christians, placed all of North Africa back under Moslem rule.

"The Moslem invasion of North Africa wiped out the Christian presence here," Bourguiba told me. "Since then, I regret to say, the Christians have always been associated with the colonizers. The Christians, down through our history, have always wanted to evangelize, to Christianize, and to re-Christianize North Africa."

Bourguiba's enthusiasm burned through the film of fatigue over his features, resulting from the cares of governing, sometimes nearly singlehandedly, a small but troublesome nation aspiring to progress —cares which recently included a plot against his life.

"France always saw herself as the continuance of Rome in North Africa," he said, his eyes lighting up again. "Look at Cardinal Lavigerie in the last century—his aim was to evangelize all of North Africa!

"The future of the Roman Church, of the churches, in North Africa? It will be about the same as that of the Europeans themselves. *On the day when the last remnants of colonialism are gone, our relations with the Christian church will be exemplary and ideal.*"

"And the situation now?"

"Now," he said, leaning forward on the divan, "now there are still sequels of the colonial spirit—vestigial remnants, you might say. There are still small pockets of colonialism: some military bases here, some special business interests there. As long as colonialism exists, we cannot be perfectly at ease with the Christians."

Bourguiba warmed to his subject, and his thoughts flowed more easily into words. "I spoke with the Pope about this," he recalled. "I told the Holy Father that Christian presence, the presence of Christians, is welcome among us. We believe that our relations will be worked out, that there can be a friendly coexistence."

"But there were problems?"

"Of course," retorted Bourguiba. "There are still many millions of acres of Church land. They should be growing food for Tunisia, not lying idle. And there are too many churches. They were built when there were hundreds of thousands of Europeans in Tunisia. Now how many are there? Everywhere I go I see churches. This is not necessary! We have discussed this with the Holy See and hope to place our relations on a new basis.

"You must understand," Bourguiba went on, "that the Roman Catholic Church here was a state church—a French state church. France paid subsidies to it under the agreement of 1893. Imagine, their bishops called the French presence here 'the Ninth Crusade'! They dared to use that phrase at their Eucharistic Congress, at Carthage in 1930. They insist on using the old imperial term—the Archdiocese of *Carthage*. Why not the Archdiocese of *Tunis?* Imagine, they were commemorating on our soil the French landings in Algeria in 1830. And their bishops wore surplices with crosses—they made a state occasion of it: they invited our own Moslem religious authorities, including the Mufti of Tunis! It was incredible;

the height of provocation! No, I tell you; this mentality must go."

President Bourguiba's words were a spontaneous reaction to my unexpected questioning. He had not intended them to be a treatment in depth of the vast question of the Christian future in North Africa. But they touched some of the most salient features of the emotional complexities standing between Christians and Moslems, the prides and prejudices, and the glimmer of hope for an understanding which occasionally lights their relations.

He was soon to gain his cause. On June 10, 1964, after long and secret talks, the Roman Catholic Church and the Tunisian Moslem state signed an accord. Officially it was called a *modus vivendi*. It assured the Church religious freedom. But it eliminated the Archdiocese of Carthage and substituted a much lower-ranking "prelature nullius" of Tunis. It turned over seventy-seven churches, chapels, and other real estate to the Tunisian state. It ended French government subsidies to the Church in Tunisia. It gave the Tunisian government something unprecedented in the newly independent Moslem nations: the right to be consulted, instead of the French government, about the naming of bishops. The break with the past had come at last.

President Bourguiba, who is essentially secular minded, and such Moslem religious leaders as Allal al-Fassi in Morocco and Ahmed Tewfik al-Madani in Algeria, though agreeing in their political suspicions of the remaining Christian missionaries in North Africa, are not the only ones aware of the need for a change in Christian mentality. Archbishop Léon-Etienne Duval [1] of Algiers, who was dubbed "Mohammed Duval" and whose churches were plagued with plastic bomb attacks by many of his parishioners because he wished to extend Christian tenets of brotherly love to the Moslem community, suffered perhaps the greatest diminution of his flock of any bishop of the Church since the Roman legions began leaving Africa in the fourth century A.D. In June, 1962, there were still over one million Europeans in Algeria, most of whom were at least nominal Christians. By 1964, the number of Christians in Algeria had dropped to around forty thousand. Christianity had paid dearly for the tragic political errors, not only of the colonial power,

[1] Archbishop Duval was consecrated a cardinal by Pope Paul VI on February 22, 1965.

but of the anti-Moslem terrorism of the European Secret Army Organization, which Archbishop Duval had termed in a pastoral letter of March 3, 1962, "the negation of the Christian ideal and of all human morals."

"More than ever," Archbishop Duval told me, "the Christian presence in North Africa is converting to a spiritual presence, to a work of Christian testimony. The social and charitable work of the Church will go on." On the very day of our meeting, Archbishop Duval and Pastor Chevallier, the leader of the tiny European Protestant community in Algeria, had set an example to their parishioners. To mark the beginning of the Moslem month of fasting, Ramadan, they donated blood to the Moslem hospitals of Algiers. An appeal was made to Christians in all the Algerian churches to do the same.

"The fact that Christians offer their blood during Ramadan," said a pastoral announcement of the Archdiocese of Algiers, "is a symbol of brotherhood and friendship." In any event, the churches astutely chose a moment when the Algiers press, even the Communist daily, *Alger-Republicain,* was extolling the moral benefits of the fast, *al-sawm,* which is one of the five pillars of Islam, and pointing out that Ramadan is a time for charity and brotherhood. Tewfik al-Madani, the Algerian Minister of Religious Property, told me that such gestures by Christian leaders were appreciated and that "there are not likely to be any problems between Christians and Moslems because the bad Christians have nearly all left Algeria anyhow." The Republic of Algeria, he reminded me, was by definition of its founders a lay state where all faiths are welcome.

DISAPPEARING ISLANDS

The social and charitable work of the Christians and their churches in Moslem North Africa does go on, with the limited means at hand. There are still islands, such as the Archdiocese of Algiers, where human contact between the two communities has not been shattered by the latest, century-long episode in the history of encounter between Christianity and Islam on the southern Mediterranean coasts. However, these seem to be disappearing islands, rear posts of Christianity in a great Moslem tide which is sweeping over most of the African continent and which shows no signs of ebbing.

Some estimates, as Kenneth Cragg has observed, are that Islam is spreading ten times faster than the Christian church in pagan Africa, "while the Christian cause by contrast labors under acute disabilities of circumstance and character." [2] More significantly, in many African lands, including Egypt, where the Copts constitute one of the oldest Christian communities in existence, the Sudan, and in "new" countries like Nigeria and the Republic of Mali, Christians, both born and converted, are yielding to a variety of social, political, economic, and psychological pressures, and some of them are becoming Moslems. Even in North Africa, where the religious communities have lived completely apart, there are cases of the conversion of native Jews and of European Christians to Islam, often when they marry Moslems. Most rare, on the other hand, are the cases of Moslems being baptized, and never are such cases given publicity in North Africa. The Catholic Church does not baptize at all, though the Protestants try to.

In Morocco and Tunisia, there is a tiny handful of native Christians; in Libya there are virtually none. Of some six thousand native Roman Catholics in Algeria—most of them Kabylie Mountain Berbers—before the war for independence from France began in 1954, scarcely two thousand remained by the first year of Algeria's freedom. Though a very few of these, in Morocco and Algeria, hold positions of some importance in government, intellectual life, and the arts, they must remain silent about their faith in public or risk losing their standing in the community and becoming Christian pariahs in a Moslem society. Christians, in the north as in the south of Africa, are identified with conquest or the white man's rule.

"The Church feels threatened in North Africa," complained the French right-wing newspaper *Aux Ecoutes,* on August 11, after the battle of Bizerte in 1961. "The princes of the Church in France," it continued, "considered that Catholicism, especially in Islamic countries, would have nothing to suffer from a policy propitious to the rise and consolidation of young nationalisms." What the writer had to say about the exodus of Europeans from Tunisia has since come true for Algeria. He wondered if the Archdiocese of Carthage "may not finally disappear, because its titulary may no longer have a flock

[2] Kenneth Cragg, "Africa: The Challenge of Islam," *The Christian Century* (Feb. 7, 1962), pp. 159–60.

to administer. For, after all, if the sheep all leave, what use are the shepherds? And the sheep are leaving. By boatloads. And without the intention of returning."

In 1964, when the great exodus from Algeria had ended and the European colonies throughout North Africa seemed to be reaching a stable level, less than 250,000 Christians remained in Morocco, 40,000 in Algeria, about 40,000 in Tunisia, and perhaps 15,000 in Libya if one adds the American colony at Wheelus Air Force Base and the personnel of the Western oil companies to the remnants of the once large Italian colony. This leaves scarcely half a million non-Moslems from the Atlantic coast to the Egyptian frontier (excluding 200,000 native North African Jews) in 1965 as against nearly two million in the same zone ten years earlier.

In all the countries of North Africa, however poignant the human problems often are, the problems facing Christianity are essentially the same. They appear under somewhat different lights, depending upon the form of the Islamic establishment: Morocco is a more or less theocratic, though constitutional monarchy, where Islam is the official state religion, though freedom is guaranteed to other faiths; Tunisia and Algeria are both republics. In Algeria, Premier Ahmed ben Bella's ruling team seems eager to give the country the egalitarian flavor of "Islamic socialism," though some Moslem conservatives oppose this. Since it won its independence from France in 1956, Tunisia, like Algeria, has been run as a one-party state which declares in its constitution that Islam is the official state religion, but where President Bourguiba has discouraged Moslem traditionalists, and where relations between Moslems, Christians, and Jews have been generally admirable. Libya, where Italian power collapsed in 1943, with an absolutist monarchy and a history of Islamic particularism, is perhaps the most barren ground of all from the viewpoint of Christian missionaries.

Does the political and military departure of Europe from North Africa entail the same decline of Christendom as that which followed the departure of Rome's prefects and legionnaires? Perhaps it does, but to assess the prospects, it may be useful to examine some of the errors and some of the triumphs of the past, as well as the North African setting of this strange and complex encounter of faiths.

THE BACKGROUND

Islam superseded Christianity in North Africa after A.D. 700 through a combination of stronger faith and superior force. The Roman colonizers, and the Phoenicians before them, subdued the native Berbers through military power, guile, and commercial bribery. The pagan state religions of the Phoenicians and Romans, with Carthage as their seat, seemed to have profound meaning to the Berbers only as long as they were supported by the military force of the occupiers. Though many Berbers embraced them, their effects were not lasting. Christianity infiltrated the Roman Empire in North Africa, almost as an historical afterthought, at a stage when that empire had already entered a state of decay. For three centuries Christianity flourished, and it seemed to be working changes. Then, suddenly, its moribund Byzantine heirs were toppled by the thinly strung-out armies of the Arab caliphate, sweeping out of the East like a great desert sandstorm and eventually carrying all resistance before them.

Islam was ultimately successful because it offered the Berbers a way of life and a civilization which they could assimilate—though some have done so slowly—and a social structure seemingly far better suited to their needs than Latin or Greek Christianity was able to provide. In North Africa of the twentieth century we are suddenly faced with a phenomenon at least superficially like the consolidation of Arabo-Moslem power under the caliphate: the Christian communities are dwindling, disappearing, losing strength. Between the first defeat of Christianity and its allied Greco-Roman civilization in 700 and the new retreat of the Christian faith and its allied Western secular power in the middle part of the twentieth century, there lie centuries of crusades, conquests, and colonizations. Nearly always, during their course, the cross appeared to the Moslems as an ensign of war and an instrument of subjugation, going on before the legions of Christian soldiers not as the emblem of the gentle Christ they had been taught by their Koran to revere but as a symbol of conquest.

Like the Allies of World War II in 1942, when the Romans landed in North Africa about 200 B.C., they came not to conquer or convert the Berbers but to defeat, if they could, an alien enemy operating from African bases. The pagan soldiers of Rome thus had other ideas than St. Louis when he attacked Tunis in 1270 or the Christian soldiers of Charles V of Spain in 1535 or those of France's General de Bourmont when he landed in Algiers in 1830, and whose secretary proclaimed on that occasion:

"The sign of the world's salvation appeared amidst that fortress [the kasbah of Algiers], constructed by the children of Mohammed against the peoples of Christ."

The Romans in the first Punic War had other motives. They wished only to defeat their Mediterranean rival, Carthage, and then go home. But soon they became involved in a process of alliances with African rulers, in recruitment of African mercenaries and, finally, in military and agricultural colonization: the classical pattern of imperialistic conquest as our own age came to know it.

The coming of Christianity to Africa at first seemed only an incident. Not until the reign of Constantine did it become part of the imperial establishment, a *raison d'état*. For France's Cardinal Lavigerie, however, during the consolidation of French military power in nineteenth-century Algeria, the raising of the cross among the "heathen" Arabs was a sacred duty.

THE EPHEMERAL CHRISTIAN ESTABLISHMENT

The crumbling of the Roman Empire's institutions and the internal quarrels and schisms that weakened the African Church after the age of St. Augustine, who died in 430, made it ripe for its eventual decline. Justinian's Byzantine armies and priesthood reinstated a Christian orthodoxy for a short time among the Berbers, only for it to vanish under the great wave of Moslem conquest that rolled in around 650.

The Roman state church in North Africa and its Byzantine revival, like the North African state churches of the French, Spanish (in northern Morocco), and Italians (in Libya) of our own age, were in fact, colonial churches. Praetors, prefects, and minor government officials; army officers and soldiers; and some of the Latin-speaking bourgeoisie and intelligentsia were its communicants. Its missionary drive lacked the vigor and vitality of the church further east in Egypt, where the desert monks of the third and fourth centuries translated the Scriptures and liturgy into local dialects, and their successors carried Christianity far up the Nile into today's Sudan and southeast into the northern half of modern Ethiopia.

The Roman state church in North Africa was at a disadvantage from the start. For about a thousand years before the Romans came, the North Africans, called *Lebou,* or Libyans, by the Greeks, and Berbers by later historians, had already been subject to an Oriental influence: the Phoenicians from Sidon and Tyre. After 814 B.C., much of North Africa came under the direct domination of Carthage, Phoenicia's final seat of colonial power in Africa.

Between the founding of Carthage and its final destruction by Rome in 146 B.C., the culture of Carthage, Punic culture, deeply penetrated the upper North African social strata, perhaps more deeply than Roman culture did later. It left certain traces. However, like that of Rome, it never basically altered the way of life of the Berbers, a rather mysterious people who probably came first from western Asia somewhat more than five thousand years ago. From the Nile Valley to the Atlantic coast, these white men were the dominant race in North Africa from about 2000 B.C. until the Phoenicians began to colonize the Mediterranean coasts. Today, in "Arab" North Africa, there are still at least twenty-nine distinct Berber tribal groups, more or less Islamized, whose people speak, wholly or in part, the dialects of the Berber language which in their pure form are nothing like Arabic. The Berbers have behaved receptively, yet resiliently, toward all the successive foreign invaders and their foreign faiths: Phoenicia, Rome, the Vandals, Christian Byzantium, the Moslem Arabs and, finally, Christian Western Europe.

Why did the culture of Islam permeate most of Berber society? Why is it increasing its hold on it today? Before trying to discover the answers, we should look at the workings of pre-Christian colonialism in North Africa.

CHAPTER II

THE HERITAGE OF TANIT: PHOENICIAN COLONIALISM AND CARTHAGE

> Hamilcar, wearing a red mantle like the priests of Moloch, stood near the image of Baal, beside the toenail of its right foot. When the fourteenth child was brought to be sacrificed, everyone noticed his gesture of horror. But soon, recovering himself, he crossed his arms and looked at the ground. On the other side of the statue, the Grand Pontiff stood motionless like himself. Lowering his head, weighted down with its Assyrian mitre, Hamilcar saw the gold breastplate covered with the stones of destiny, where the flickering flame glowed in lurid tones. He blanched with terror.
>
> GUSTAVE FLAUBERT, *Salammbo,* 1861

The Book of Genesis tells us that "Canaan [son of Ham, son of Noah] begat Sidon, his first-born. . . ." The Phoenicians seem to have been a branch of the biblical Canaanites, and Sidon, by 1250 B.C. or earlier, was one of their principal cities on the eastern Mediterranean coast. They were seafarers who occupied parts of the Fertile Crescent before the coming of the Philistines and the Hebrews. While their adventurous traders took to the sea, the intellectuals who stayed behind evolved the strange Phoenician civilization, a potpourri of Egyptian, Mesopotamian, and other earlier ingredients blended with a Semitic tribal stock. They developed a revolutionary hieratic alphabet, which they eventually took with them to North Africa.

Seeking the gold of West Africa and the silver of fabulous Tarshish, or Tartessus, near present-day Cádiz at the mouth of the Guadalquivir River in Spain, the Phoenicians set sail in their high ships toward the Strait of Gibraltar. Along the way they built landing places at roughly thirty-mile intervals. Often these developed into trading posts and then into permanent settlements on the North African shore. First they grew along the coast of present-day Libya, then west of there in what is now Tunisia, Algeria, and finally in Morocco and Western Europe. Men of Tyre founded Gades (modern Cádiz) about 1100 B.C. and Utica, their largest settlement on the Tunisian coast before Carthage, shortly afterward. Their gods came with them. From archeological excavations at Larache (Morocco) and from the writings of the Roman historian Pliny the Elder we know that at Lixus (Greek Loukkos; modern Larache) there was a temple of Melkarth, the Phoenician forerunner of Hercules, older than the sanctuary of the same god in Gades. The number of Phoenician tombs and some pottery found in places along the Moroccan Atlantic coast like Mulelocha, south of Mazagan, and Al-Khenzira, near Cape Blanc, suggests that the soldiers, bureaucrats, and priests who followed the sailors and traders were not content to organize life in the trading posts, but colonized the hinterland as well.

All accounts agree that the Phoenicians must have been clever colonialists. They seem to have taken no land for farming, and to have traded for their food with the Berbers, occasionally taking Berber women as wives or concubines, and remaining generally on good terms with the local population. The human atmosphere thus was probably propitious for them when they founded Carthage, the great North African metropolis which was eventually to rule about three hundred African cities and lord it over most of the civilized world until eclipsed by Rome.

Carthage, which even to President Bourguiba in 1963 represented a symbol of power, was founded about 814 B.C. on a neck of land between the Lake of Tunis and another salt lake, the Sebkha Ariana, like most Phoenician cities, in a good military position to withstand sieges. The favorite legend of the founding says that Dido, a beautiful Phoenician noblewoman, fled to Africa after the murder of her Tyrian husband and obtained from Iarbas, a Berber prince, the grant of as much land as the hide of an ox would cover. By cleverly cutting the hide into numerous narrow strips, she eked out enough space to found the city of Karthadasht (Phoenician for "the new town"). When Iarbas courted her, then tried to force her to marry him, she took her life on a funeral pyre. In the *Aeneid,* Virgil calls Carthage "Juno's favorite dwelling," destined to become "the metropolis of all nations."

After modest beginnings, during which the city paid both tribute to Tyre and rent to the Berbers, Carthage began to prosper. Its first and most profitable colonial enterprise was the export to the East of Spanish silver, which Carthaginian seafarers obtained in exchange for trinkets. Later it dealt in tin, which, mixed with copper, yielded bronze, much in demand throughout the Mediterranean world. During the sieges of Tyre by such formidable enemies as Shalmaneser, Nebuchadnezzar, and Alexander, wealthy Tyrians came to Africa, mainly to Carthage. The city's commercial and political power grew as that of Tyre and Sidon declined.

As this happened, Carthage stopped paying rent to the Berbers, who were used as serfs or were driven inland. With the conquest of the island of Iviza and probably of the islands of Malta, Gozo, and Pantelleria as well, revenues began to pour in from all parts of the new Punic Empire. One town alone, Leptis Minor, paid the equivalent of over one million dollars yearly into the Carthaginian treasury. Patrician families built great fortunes. Professional colonizer-explorers sailed far down the African coast, and at least one, according to Herodotus, was commissioned by a King of Egypt to circumnavigate Africa and write a report on his trip.

The new colonialism of Carthage had greater commercial vision than its older sea-borne Phoenician version. In 1962, an expedition of the Pennsylvania State Museum discovered evidence in the Punic settlement under the ruins of the Roman city of Leptis Magna (Libya) that this had been the terminus of a land trade route bringing ivory, ostrich feathers, and leopard skins up from the center of Africa over Saharan caravan routes.

From about 600 to 480 B.C., Carthage fought the wars of conquest in Africa, Sicily, and Sardinia which were to prove her later downfall. The Carthaginians recruited African mercenaries for their armies when and where they could. A treaty signed with Rome in 508 B.C. gave Rome equal trading rights, but Carthage political supremacy, in Africa: one of the first geographical partitions of the Mediterranean between the Latin West and the Semitic East, a division which was later to be consecrated in the present-day division between Islam and Christianity.

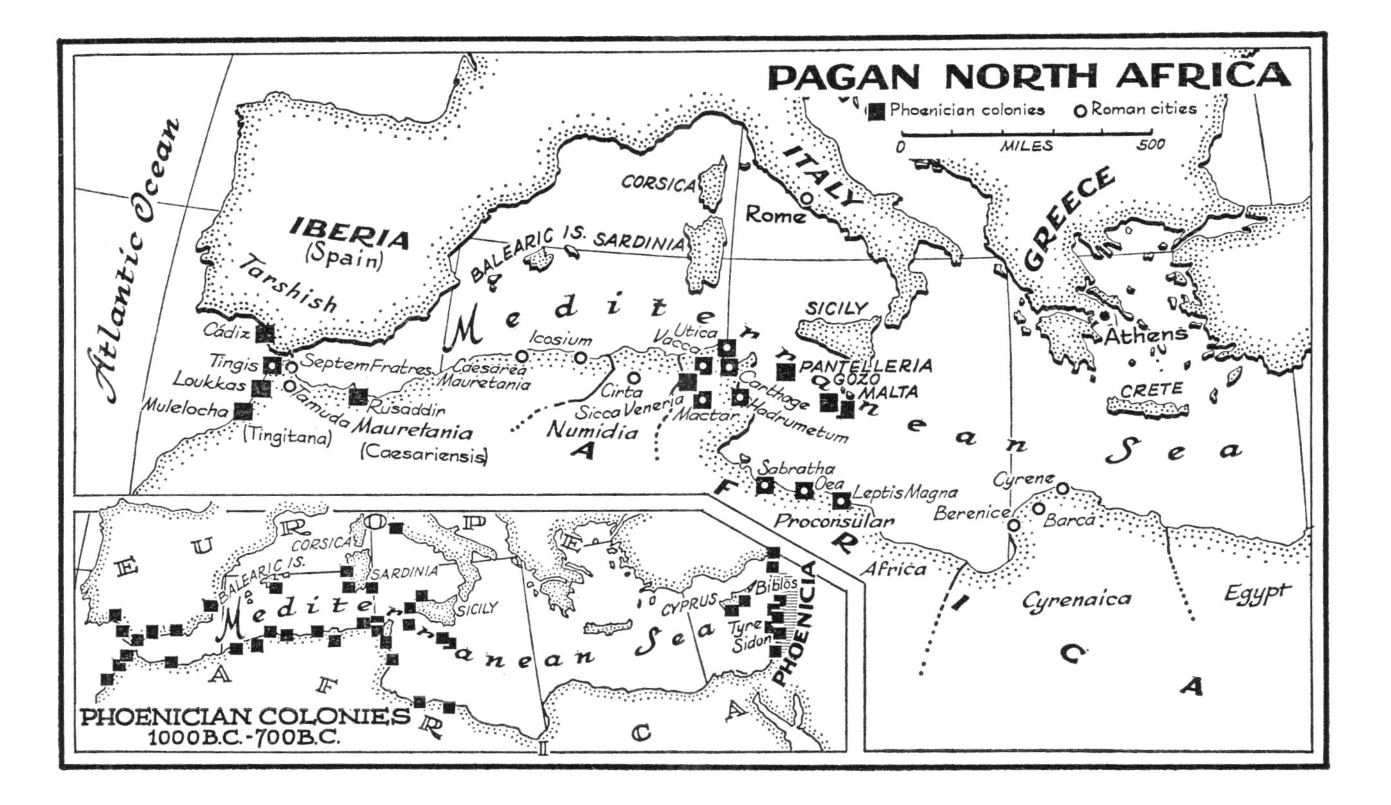
PAGAN NORTH AFRICA
Phoenician colonies
Roman cities
0
MILES
500
Atlantic Ocean
IBERIA
(Spain)
Tarshish
Cádiz
Tingis
Septem Fratres
Loukkas
Tamuda
Mulelocha
(Tingitana)
Rusaddir
Mauretania
(Caesariensis)
Caesarea
Mauretania
Icosium
Cirta
Numidia
Sicca Veneria
Utica
Vacca
Carthage
Mactar
Hadrumetum
CORSICA
SARDINIA
BALEARIC IS.
ITALY
Rome
SICILY
PANTELLERIA
GOZO
MALTA
GREECE
Athens
CRETE
Mediterranean Sea
Sabratha
Oea
Leptis Magna
Proconsular
Africa
Cyrene
Berenice
Barca
Cyrenaica
Egypt
AFRICA
PHOENICIAN COLONIES
1000 B.C.-700 B.C.
EUROPE
CORSICA
BALEARIC IS.
SARDINIA
SICILY
CYPRUS
Biblos
Tyre
Sidon
PHOENICIA

Carthage had to battle the Numidians (Berbers of the area now included in eastern Algeria) and Mauretanians (further west) from 470 to 450 B.C. to protect its supply lines to Spain and the Atlantic coast. By 450, after the subjection of Sicily by the Punic generals Himilco and Hannibal, the secular power of Carthage stood at its height. The Greeks were driven back from Sardinia, Corsica, southern Spain, and all of the African coast west of Cyrenaica. In one of history's crucial decisions, Northwest Africa was thus largely deprived of early Hellenizing influences and further opened to those of the Semites.

Carthage was now a full-fledged colonial power in the modern sense. Berber revolts broke out about 400 B.C., and a rebellion of African mercenaries ensued when a Punic general, Himilco, abandoned his African soldiers in defeat near Syracuse (396 B.C.). Slaves joined the rebels, and the rebellious coalition succeeded in capturing Tunis. But Carthage got help from troops in Sardinia in the nick of time. Special sacrifices were offered in 379 B.C., when the rebels nearly got across the walls. In 367 B.C., an officer who modestly nicknamed himself Hanno the Great tried an unsuccessful military *coup d'état,* with the help of Berbers, against the city's oligarchical government, but was executed for his pains.

THE PUNIC STATE RELIGION

The Phoenicians brought a religion foreign to the Berbers, and one more sophisticated than their own. Their soldiers and priests found, like the sources who reported to Herodotus, that the Berbers offered animal sacrifice "to the sun and moon, the worship of which is common to all the Libyans." They worshiped all manner of nature deities, sometimes concentrated in sanctuaries, called *Mzarra* in the hard, sibilant Berber language, and often provided with megaliths as altars. A tourist may see one today at Mactar in Tunisia. There were tribal totems and innumerable animistic beliefs, many surviving today despite Islam's official disapproval. Some weird animal gods included a local, ram-headed equivalent of the Egyptian god Amen, or Ammon-Ra, which the Greeks and Romans later called Jupiter-Ammon, the lord of the sun.

There were personal gods, too, among some of the more sophisticated tribes. A remarkable pantheon appears in bas-relief on a stone found at Béja in Tunisia (Vacca in ancient times). The names, in Latin characters, probably added by Berbers who learned Latin after the Roman occupation, are Magurtam, Inam, Macurgum, Matilam (who is shown cutting the throat of a sacrificial sheep), Bonchor (who seems to be the senior deity of the group), Vihinam, and the goddess Varssissima.

The chief Punic god was Baal-Ammon, who became identified with the Greek Kronos or with Zeus. On a stele at Sousse (Tunisia), which seems to bear his best-known portrait, he is a rather dignified old man with a beard, wearing a long robe and a tiara, and seated on a throne supported by sphinxes, one of the sure signs of Egypt's influence on the religion of the Maghreb at the time. He probably descended from El, the great Middle Eastern sky god and god of fertility. Melkarth (later Hercules), whom we have already met in the far west of the Maghreb, reigned at Carthage too. So did Eshmun, or Ashmun, identified with Aesculapius, the god of healing and the "blameless physician" in Homer's *Iliad*. There was also Bes, who was often a figurehead on the prows of Phoenician ships: a sinister, bow-legged dwarf with a pot belly.

The patroness of Carthage, normally associated with Baal-Ammon in inscriptions, was the great goddess Tanit, often called *Tanit Pené Baal* (Tanit, the face of Baal). She was the new, North African incarnation of the glamorous and terrible Astarte (sometimes Ashtoreth, or other spellings) of the Orient. Her symbols included an open hand, which has survived in Islamic North Africa as the hand of Fatima, a talisman and a charm. Tanit had another sign, still seen in Berber jewelry today: a triangle surmounted by a horizontal pair of arms and a disc-head. This still has talismanic value to many North Africans.

THE SYNCRETISM OF ROME

It was probably far easier for the Romans to take over this motley assortment of deities when they conquered Carthage than it was for the Berber subjects of Carthage to swallow them. Tanit and Baal were to reappear under the Romans in the guise of Juno Coelestis (the Celestial Goddess) and Saturn. Tanit-Juno was a virgin and a mother-goddess at the same time; she anticipated the cult of Mary in North African Christianity. A remarkable pre-Christian, neo-Punic madonna of the first century A.D. is one of the most striking statues in the Bardo Museum in Tunis. As a goddess of love, sex, and fertility, Tanit-Juno also combines elements of Hera and Venus. Baal-Ammon-Saturn in Punic Carthage, as in the Roman one, was a protector of harvests and of country life.

On the tomb of St. Augustine's mother, the Berber St. Monica, now in the Lavigerie Museum in Carthage, there is a remarkable bas-relief of a guardian goddess. She carries a dove in one hand and seems to be a late, sophisticated version of Tanit. It was probably to an earlier and more bloodthirsty Tanit that the Carthaginian priests offered their sacrifices of human babies, described so luridly by Flaubert in *Salammbo*. James Frazer sketches the ceremony at the Tophet, or place of sacrifice, succinctly in *The Golden Bough*. Children were placed on the sloping hands of an idol from which they slid into a fiery oven. Meanwhile, "people danced to the music of flutes and timbrels to drown the shrieks of the burning victims," [1] and the parents were forbidden to show grief. The first complete Tophet found by archeologists, in 1922, near the ruins of the commercial port of Carthage, contains bones of babies and other proof of systematic sacrifice of first-born children: babies ranging from new-born to two and one-half and three years of age. This Tophet is like one discovered at the Canaanite cemetery at Ge Hinnom, near Jerusalem, which dates from the seventh century B.C.

These grisly sacrifices and the new Punic religion gradually developed by Baal's priests in North Africa appear linked mythologically to the legend of the city's founding by Queen Dido and her burning, since Phoenician mythology regarded the founding of a city as a religious act. The legend of the city's foundation is probably a sacred tale: a queen is sacrificed to assure the safety or prosperity of the city. Dido's sacrifice was intended to assure the community's well-being. Whenever in its earlier years Carthage was hard pressed by its enemies, as after the Sicilian campaigns, the number and tempo of sacrifices increased. The Carthaginian general Hamilcar, after his defeat at Himera, Sicily, in 480 B.C., sacrificed many of his own men

[1] James Frazer, *The Golden Bough*, abridged edition (London, 1954), p. 281.

and then himself, upon learning of the extent of his defeat. Julius Caesar writes of one of North Africa's Romanized Berber kings, Juba I, who told the people of Zama that if he were defeated in battle he would come back and throw them into the royal fires.

In the Punic language a human sacrifice was called a *molk,* which has a Semitic root meaning possession. The Hebrews changed this in their texts to *molok,* and the Biblical conception of Moloch as the name of a god to whom sacrifices were offered seems to be an error arising from this. In the latter days of Carthage, more and more patrician families purchased from priests the right to substitute animals for children, a practice called *molchomor.*

The clergy of the Carthaginian establishment, at least in the parent city, was rich and strongly organized. Religion and the state were inseparably linked. The magistrates, or *sofetim,* supervised the temples and all their practices, including sacred prostitution and sacrifice.

At about the beginning of the sixth century B.C., Carthage seems to have been swept by a revolution in religion, manners, and morals. Flamboyance and license in public and private life gave way to a wave of puritanical reform. At the same time, the form of government evidently changed from a sort of monarchical dictatorship to an aristocratic oligarchy. Carthage and its allies, including the Persian Empire, the Asian Phoenicians, and the Etruscans, combined forces to check Greek expansion into the Mediterranean. But Greek religion infiltrated Carthage just the same. The city began to worship Greek goddesses (mainly Demeter) and to institute Greek funeral practices.

The death of Alexander the Great in 323 B.C. probably saved Carthaginian independence until its eventual destruction by Rome. But Greek supremacy in the Orient appears to have worked profound changes, perhaps revolutionary ones, in North African society and religion, partly through Etruscan, Sicilian, and other intermediaries in contact with Carthage. The old gods, identified with the old political systems, had failed. Just as Athena on the Acropolis of Athens was identified with Periclean democracy, Tanit in Carthage personified the order imposed by the commercial and sacerdotal aristocracy, which was badly shaken by the wars of the third century. The syncretism of the Punic and the Hellenic gods is dramatically evident in accords signed between Philip of Macedon and Hannibal in the third century B.C. They invoke Zeus and Hera but also Heracles (Hercules) and "all the gods Carthage possesses; all the gods which Macedonia and the rest of Greece possess."

Mysticism and mystic movements, both fanatical and otherwise, have always tended to spread among the more humble people of North Africa rather than among the upper classes. Late Hellenic mysticism affected the lower-class Carthaginians and the Berbers subject to their influence. Where previously Egyptian scarabs and even such Oriental trappings as the jagged arrow symbol of the Babylonian god Marduk had been borrowed, the Carthaginians now began to adopt Greek signs and symbols. After Punic troops had profaned and pillaged shrines of Demeter and Ceres in Greek-occupied Sicily, Carthage suffered great economic and military reverses. The superstitious Carthaginians built sanctuaries and installed the cults of Demeter and Ceres, determined to propitiate these Hellenic gods and vainly hoping to put an end to their misfortunes. As in all crumbling societies, hieratic religion weakened, and magic enjoyed a boom. Carthage now entered its decline and headed for destruction. After a brief Punic resurgence in Sicily, there followed the fateful wars with Rome which began in 264 B.C. and ended with the physical annihilation of Carthage by Scipio's Roman legions in 146 B.C.

Phoenicia, as transplanted and transfigured in Carthage, was to North Africans what France, Spain, and the other Christian colonial powers became later to them: it was an alien civilization, equipped with superior military force and a domineering economic and commercial structure. It imposed a religious faith closely identified with its military and political mastery and far better organized in every respect than their own.

SEMITIC LANGUAGE AND SEMITIC CIVILIZATION

Through the use of the Punic language, Punic civilization became, after a fashion, naturalized and spread through certain parts of the Berber world. These included the immediate hinterland of the city of Carthage; such Libyan cities as Leptis Magna; coastal patches of present-day Algeria; and certain enclaves of Morocco, notably Tangier, Melilla (the Phoenician Rusaddir), and Larache, among others. Phoenician colonialism introduced wine grapes and taught the Berbers how to use metal, how to plant cereals and fruit trees. Punic words still are used in North Africa, such as the proper name Abdeshams which, as Nevill Barbour has noted, was as current in Carthage as it is in modern North Africa.[2]

In this way, Carthage left behind certain material advances and a sort of Semitic cultural aura, based on a solid tradition that had persisted for nearly a thousand years in some centers. The Latin, and eventually Christian, system which Rome next imposed on the Berbers seems not to have dissipated this aura: St. Augustine himself found Punic still in use by provincial Berber bishops in the fifth century A.D. This Semitic cultural aura seems to have left the Berbers far more receptive to the Arabic, Islamic tide which was to sweep in from the east than they were to the Latin, Christian one which came from the north.

Punic culture had influenced much of the Mediterranean: southern Spain, the Balearic Islands, Sicily, Sardinia, and Malta as well as North Africa. Arnold Toynbee's description of what happened throughout much of the Oriental and the Mediterranean worlds seems to apply especially well to North Africa: "The cultural conflict between Hellenism and the Oriental civilizations—Syriac and Egyptiac and Babylonic and Indic—likewise reappeared within the bosom of the Hellenic society as an internal crisis in Hellenic, or Hellenized souls: the crisis that declared itself in the emergence of Isis-worship and Astrology and Mithraism and Christianity and a host of other syncretistic religions." [3]

In North Africa the official Punic polytheism of Phoenician and Greek origins, which had no real notion of divine transcendence as we know it in modern Islam, Judaism, or Christianity, seems to have left the Berber population thirsting for something which would be, spiritually, infinitely more satisfying. More than this, nearly a thousand years of domination by foreign soldiers, prefects, and priests had spread among the Berber elite an electrifying slogan: Africa for the Africans.

[2] Nevill Barbour (ed.), *A Survey of North West Africa* (London, 1959), p. 12.

[3] Arnold J. Toynbee, *A Study of History*, abridged by D. C. Somervell (London, 1949), p. 203.

CHAPTER III

ROMAN GODS AND BERBER NATIONALISTS

> Jugurtha hear, your children are awake
> Tell Masinissa, now his vengeance
> he shall take
> Algeria's sons, we'll set our country
> free.
> Frenchmen? No. Frenchmen we will
> never be.
>
> KABYLIE REVOLUTIONARY SONG, 1954

The old gods of Carthage fell, and Tanit herself emerged from the flames of Carthage clothed in the new garments of Juno. Her Berber subjects changed sides, as they have often done under later foreign masters. By 44 B.C., when Julius Caesar had redivided Africa and had begun consolidating Roman power, some of their leaders advocated a new, self-conscious North African nationalism which was later to be taken over by Islam and which remains the chief political current of today. Through these chiefs, whom the Romans educated and in some cases made kings, this feeling had already gained a foothold by the time the Christian faith began to spread in the second century A.D. Like the Berbers themselves, the Christians were at first the underdogs, oppressed by prefects who ruled in the name of Rome's old pagan pantheon. Unfortunately for the future of Christendom in North Africa, the alliances were soon reversed with the reign of Constantine the Great (A.D. 306–337). The Church was converted into an arm of Roman state power, and, in Berber eyes, it tended to become identified with the Roman oppressors.

THE MERCENARY KINGS

Rome ruled in North Africa through alliances with Berber chiefs who received educations, military honors, and worldly riches from the colonial power. Some of these Berbers discovered that the benefits of European civilization might be used by them to make themselves African rulers rather than Roman subjects. Masinissa (*c.* 240–149 B.C.) is the first outstanding Berber figure of North African history. He absorbed Punic culture, then used it to extend civilization and progress to his subjects. In doing so, and in observing how the wars between Rome and Carthage, the foreign rivals, could be turned to his own advantage, he set an example for future Berber rebels. The recent Emir Abd-al-Krim al-Khattabi, who in the 1920's defeated an entire Spanish army and briefly threatened to erase European influence from Morocco for good, was the best known of these in our day.

Syphax (*c.* 250–200 B.C.), a ruler of Numidia (part of modern Tunisia and Algeria), had been given the beautiful Carthaginian lady, Sophonisba, as his wife in return for his services to Carthage. He wore a Greek-type diadem for a crown and used Punic rather than Berber as the official language of his court in Cirta (Constantine). In the name of Carthage, he waged war against a staunch Berber ally of Rome, and his own African rival, Masinissa, King of Massyles. In a battle with the Roman expeditionary forces of Scipio at Campi Magni, Syphax was defeated and his camp was burned. Masinissa captured him as he fled, and Syphax eventually died in prison in Italy, with Sophonisba throwing herself on Masinissa's mercy and asking to be spared from Roman vengeance. According to Livy, she said that if she must die, Masinissa should kill her himself. "If only as the wife of Syphax," she is reported to have said, "I prefer to trust the word of a Numidian, a man born in the same Africa as myself, rather than that of a foreigner by birth and nationality."

Masinissa was entranced, and married her at once, hoping the Roman commander would relent. He did not and told his Berber "ally" to choose between his kingdom and his wife. Masinissa put power before love and sent his Queen a bowl of poison, telling her he had not wanted to make her such a wedding gift, but her feelings left him no other choice. Sophonisba drank the poison and so apparently complied with the old Punic tradition of a sacrifice of honor. Her husband, with the aid of Rome, became the most powerful king the Berbers had ever known.

Masinissa was educated at Carthage and served first against the Romans during the wars in Spain between 212 and 206 B.C., when the persuasiveness and friendship of Scipio seem to have decided him to change camps. He joined the Romans when they landed in North Africa in 204 B.C. Soon Masinissa became the king of all Numidia. His domain was the largest Berber realm North Africa had ever seen. It stretched from the Moulouya River in northeastern Morocco roughly to what is today the Algerian-Tunisian border.

Masinissa undertook the "denomadization" of the desert people. He tried to settle them on good farmland and converted them to the Hellenistic cult of Demeter, the Greek corn goddess. But Masinissa, who called himself king and had an army and a navy, also developed ideas of his own divinity which worked his undoing with the Romans. On coins struck in his kingdom, he appears wearing a diadem and a laurel crown. Before foreigners, whether they were Phoenicians or Romans, he proclaimed the popular doctrine that Africa ought to belong to the Africans.

Masinissa nearly unified the Maghreb. But when he grew too ambitious, the Romans took alarm; they divided his kingdom among his sons. Masinissa had been too African and too nationalistic.

Masinissa's grandson, Jugurtha (*c.* 150–104 B.C.), who commanded the troops of Numidia, tried to drive the Romans out and unite Numidia under his own rule. When the Berbers attacked and killed Italian merchants living in Cirta, the Senate sent a punitive expedition against Jugurtha. After a long war against the Romans, Jugurtha was captured; he eventually died in a Roman prison.

The two last great Berber kings were Juba I, King of Numidia (died 46 B.C.), and Juba II, King of Mauretania (*c.* 50 B.C.–*c.* A.D. 23). Juba I meddled in Roman affairs by supporting the Senate against the Roman dictator, Julius Caesar. In part of the Roman civil war fought in Africa in 47 and 46 B.C., Juba sided with Caesar's rival, Pompey, and killed himself after Caesar's victory. Most of Numidia was made into a Roman province "for security reasons," as would now be said, and those Berbers who had supported Pompey were punished.

Juba II stands out as one of the few Berber rulers in all history who apparently made much more than a superficial adjustment to European culture, civilization, and religion. His wife, Cleopatra

Selene, daughter of Antony and Cleopatra, inspired his adaptation. Sent to Rome to witness Caesar's triumph in 46 B.C., he was educated in Italy and became a Roman citizen. He returned to Africa to take over the western Kingdom of Mauretania, and he probably maintained capitals in both Volubilis (near Meknes in Morocco) and Caesarea (Cherchel in Algeria). He wrote books in Greek on the history of Rome, on Greek and Roman art, on Libya, Arabia, Assyria, and the Canary Islands, and grammatical and literary studies. His son, Ptolemy, was murdered by the mad despot Caligula in A.D. 40 for having dared to wear purple, the imperial color, and a new series of Berber revolts broke out in the wake of his death. People of Algeria's Kabylie Mountains and the Moroccan Atlas still tell folk tales and recite poems of these uprisings.

THE PAGAN ESTABLISHMENT IN NORTH AFRICA

After the fall of Carthage, the Romans quickly organized their rule in Africa. At first they limited their domain to the small Province of Africa, roughly equivalent to present-day Tunisia. Later they moved westward into Numidia and Mauretania. Roman power, Roman culture, and the pantheon of Rome's official gods, headed by Jupiter, gradually extended their sway from Cyrene to Sala Colonia (at present-day Rabat) on the Atlantic coast.

The Roman clergy imposed on Roman citizens and Berber subjects who fell under their control the cults of Juno Coelestis and Saturn, the Latin equivalents of Tanit and Baal. The forms of worship were outwardly Roman; the actual ceremonies were unorthodox and retained many of the old Libyo-Punic characteristics. This "unorthodoxy" was probably reinforced when Julius Caesar restored Carthage to its former place of importance in the Empire in about 50 B.C. The restoration of Carthage proved to be a serious mistake. Jacob Burckhardt, writing of the danger to Rome of "the temple which Dido had founded to the celestial Deity," describes it as having been "fatal to the Empire, less on account of its complaisant prostitutes than by reason of the subversive oracles which it issued and the support which it gave to more than one usurper." [1]

[1] Jacob Burckhardt, *The Age of Constantine the Great* (Garden City, 1956), p. 109.

Just as in the fifth century B.C., the Punic priests, or *kohanim,* transformed their faith to absorb Greek and Oriental traditions, they now absorbed the Hellenic-Roman ones. Aphrodite, for example, had been eclipsed by Tanit in the olden days. Now she was fetched back across the narrow straits from Sicily, and a cult of Aphrodite, or Astarte, complete with gorgeous temple prostitutes, was installed in the colony of Sicca Veneria (today's Le Kef, a Tunisian town near the Algerian border).

Juno Coelestis was represented as the all-powerful mistress of the universe, with lesser divinities as her faithful servitors. Neoplatonism and other exotic doctrines began to seep into North African Roman paganism by the third century A.D. and were likely an ingredient of the African form of Gnosticism born in Christian Egypt at a later date.

Sacrifice retained in Roman times the pre-eminent role it had in the Punic era: the sacrifice of animals—and even of human beings—survived in many corners of the Empire. It was not overly discouraged by the authorities until the coming of Christianity because the Romans feared that to end sacrifice would incur the wrath of Saturn.

THEOCRASY IN NORTH AFRICA

Classical Roman religion in North Africa, as in all subjugated territories, developed in a pattern of theocrasy, or the intermingling of gods. The Aphrodite of Greece was recognized in the Near Eastern Astarte and Ashtoreth; the Hathor of the Egyptians; and Tanit, the Celestial Goddess of Carthage. There seems to be an ancient urge among most religions, especially polytheistic ones, to seek out similarities in other faiths and, where possible, to syncretize them. One of the many derivations of the Phoenician Baal in the Old Testament (Baal-zebub, Baal-peor, Baal-berith) was the name chosen by the mad young Roman priest-emperor, Antoninus (Avitus Bassianus), who decided that he was an incarnation of Baal as the sun god, or Elagabalus (Heliogabalus). About A.D. 220 he brought to Rome a black stone of Emesa (Syria), sacred to Baal and offered the god, whom he identified with himself, a temple, sumptuous sacrifices, and a wife. Elagabalus sent to Carthage for the image of the Celestial Goddess, Tanit, and married her to the Phoenician god in solemn rites celebrated in Rome. This was syncretism carried to its most logical absurdity.

The mixing of religions under the later Roman Empire did much to prepare North Africa for monotheism. The Semitic cultural afterflavor left by Carthage was to favor Islam. Certain pagan rites seemed at times to have anticipated Christianity too. Libyo-Punic and Roman cults celebrated at El-Djem in Tunisia and Tebessa in Algeria practiced immersion of children in water. Belief in the immortality of souls, one of the teachings of Mithraism and some of the other Oriental mystery religions which infiltrated North Africa from the east, is illustrated by an inscription on a gravestone at Mactar (Tunisia), dating from the end of the third or beginning of the fourth century A.D.,though some consider the inscription "crypto-Christian":

JULIA BENENATA

> For I, said the dead one, who always inherited a pious body, I live by Virtue of divine law in the sweet Elysian Fields of Persephone [Greek goddess of fertility] and I gaze down from above on the sun and the constellations.[2]

There was a great gap in North African paganism, as there still is in North African Islam today, between the public establishment and religion as it was practiced by the people.

The high priests of Juno, Saturn, and the other official deities were state functionaries. Priests were trained at African sacerdotal colleges. But just as the rural Moslem in North Africa today makes pilgrimages and worships at local shrines and sanctuaries, usually dedicated to local saints, the unsophisticated Berber folk of Punic and Roman times worshiped at Tophets, shrines often surrounded by steles. A higher level of sophistication came at about the end of the second century A.D. with the temple sanctuary, provided with a high altar for sacrifices. The rural Berbers of those days, like those of today, had to keep up their sanctuaries and temples at their own expense since in the country they were not state supported.

[2] Quoted in Gilbert-Charles Picard, *Les Réligions de l'Afrique Antique* (Paris, 1954), pp. 23 ff.

CHAPTER IV

THE COMING OF THE CROSS

> We are but of yesterday, and we fill all your cities, islands, forts, councils, even the camps themselves, the tribes, the decuries, the palaces, the Senate and the Forum.
>
> TERTULLIAN OF CARTHAGE, *c.* A.D. 210

Many Christians scarcely realize that Jesus Christ is said to have spent some of his infant months in Africa. Mary and Joseph took him to Egypt to escape murder by Herod, the Gospel of Matthew tells us. A visitor to Masr al-Khedim, the oldest quarter of Cairo, can see the Church of St. Sergius which the Coptic Christians of Egypt say is constructed on the site where the Holy Family lived. A Jew of Alexandria named Apollos is mentioned in the Acts of the Apostles as having been "instructed in the way of the Lord" and as having converted Jews there before going to Greece where Paul was preaching at Corinth. A man from North Africa had participated in the Passion of Christ. The Scriptures tell us that Roman soldiers compelled Simon of Cyrene, a town soon to become the first Christian community west of Alexandria, to carry the cross to Calvary.

Christian missionary tradition says that a rescript of the Emperor Claudius, after expelling the Jews from Rome about A.D. 41, forbade the Jews of Alexandria to receive in their city any of their coreligionists who had been in contact with Christians. An Egyptian papyrus published in 1935, referring to the dialogue between Christ and Pontius Pilate, is believed to date from between A.D. 130 and 135, and, at about the same time, the Emperor Hadrian refers to Egypt in a letter saying, "There are Christians . . . bishops of Christ . . . worshipers of Christ." These last two documents show that by the first part of the second century A.D., Christianity had arrived and had spread in the valley of the Nile. From then on,

Christianity, both orthodox and heretical, spread as swiftly in Egypt as it did in the Middle East.

Most of the first Christian communities were in Palestine and Asia Minor. The only recorded Christian community in Africa west of Egypt of the first century is that of Cyrene, or Pentapolis (modern Goureina, in northeastern Libya near Bengasi). However, second-century documents mention churches at Carthage, Sitifis (Sétif, Algeria); Lambaesis (Lambèse, in the Algerian Aurès Mountains); Madaurus (Algeria); Uthma, Thuburbo Minus, and Thysdius (all in Tunisia); and Leptis Magna (Libya). By A.D. 300, Christians were already a majority of the population everywhere in the Province of Africa except on Cape Bon, near Tunis. Both Numidia and the northern tip of Morocco, around Tangier, had become partially Christianized, as had much of the Libyan coast. There were about fifty churches from the province of proconsular Africa, which had by far the largest Christian population, and twenty more from Numidia, all represented at the Synod of Carthage in 256.

It is clear that present-day Tunisia was most intensely Christianized in 256, with eastern Algeria a poor second: Hippo Regius (Bône) was the central episcopate there. Only one episcopate has been discerned with certainty in Morocco: that of Tingis (Tangier). In Libya, churches at Leptis Magna, Sabratha, and Oea (Tripoli) were represented at Carthage in 256. These three were all in what today is Tripolitania and seem to have been the furthest eastward push of Latin Christianity in North Africa at that particular time. It might be possible to see in this pattern one of the reasons why of all today's Maghreb countries, Tunisia, though officially Arab and Moslem, has remained the one most open and sympathetic to Western intellectual currents and probably the most tolerant of both Christians and Jews.

There is some remarkable early Christian art in North Africa, such as a mensa bearing the symbols of eternal life, now in the museum in Cherchel, baptismal fonts discovered at Doura, Timgad, and Djemila in Algeria, and Christian lamps in Tunisia. A sarcophagus found at Tebessa, dating from A.D. 400, shows a female figure which may be either the Church—or Rome.

Christianity seems to have taken hold largely among the Latins in the towns. Only urbanized and Latinized Berbers were very much exposed to it. Even after Constantine had legalized and established it as the official state religion, St. Augustine wrote to Crispin, the Bishop of Guelma, who had tried to convert Berbers in his district to the Donatist heresy, to challenge him to go out among his flock with him to ascertain their true belief. He acknowledged that Latin culture and liturgy had spread so slightly that they would need a Punic interpreter.

To the North African intelligentsia, however, the revelation of Christianity was a thrilling experience. Saint Cyprian of Carthage, who was born a pagan in about 200 and died a martyr in 258, was a Latinized Berber. He acquired fame and riches in Carthage as an orator and pleader of causes before he discovered Christianity. "The doors that had been shut opened, and light shone in the darkness," he wrote.

Cyprian became one of the major Fathers of the North African Church, a perfectionist who aspired to the complete imitation of Christ. He was ordained priest, and in 248 when Donatus, Bishop of Carthage, died, Cyprian was drafted for the post against his will at a time when the Church was showing the effects of persecution and apostasy. His heroic martyrdom by order of the Proconsul Galerius Maximus caused an unprecedented public demonstration of faith and solidarity by the Christian community of Carthage. A basilica was later built at the site of his beheading, where Augustine preached an anniversary sermon two centuries later.

THE PERSECUTIONS

Until the fourth century, Christianity remained an illegal, subversive doctrine. North African Christians, both Roman and Berber, were outlaws, hunted by the Roman prefects and proconsuls. The first general persecution came under the Emperors Marcus Aurelius and his son, Commodus, between 177 and 192. Twelve Christians of Scillium were executed at Carthage in 180, and others doubtless died in the same period. Although Roman officials led the persecutions, there is no available evidence that Berber nationalism played any role whatsoever in the lives or deaths of the martyrs: their stories are part of the spiritual annals of the Church; they are depicted neither as allies nor enemies of European secular power.

One of the worst persecutions seems to have been the work of a man who was a Berber himself: the Emperor Septimius Severus, first African ever to wear the purple, who reigned in Rome from 193 to 211. He was born in Leptis Magna, whose forums and temples became models copied throughout Africa. Various Roman historians describe him as a Berber who learned Latin well, but who never lost his African accent. How did this man, the only Roman Emperor to come from Africa, who died far from home in York, England, in 211, treat the Christians of North Africa? Probably worse than most others. He and his wife Julia Domna were not content to be merely the worldly heads of the official pagan cult. They were venerated by a servile priesthood as Jupiter, the lord of the world, and Juno, his queen. The imperial god offered his disciples in Africa and elsewhere an opportunity to give thanks for the universal order brought to the restless Roman world by his armies, which included many Berber troops. This raising of an African emperor to the rank of virtual divinity greatly antagonized North African Christians. It set a dangerous precedent of absolutism in the blending of religion and state.

Among Severus' first Christian victims in the persecutions that began in 203 were two women of Carthage, a noble-born girl named Perpetua, whose parents were pagans, and Felicitas, a slave who was eight months pregnant when executed. Both had apparently become interested in Christianity, but neither had been baptized at the time of arrest. Perpetua, who had a small baby, described how unexpected their seizure was:

> On another day when we were having our midday meal, we were suddenly hurried off to be examined; and we came to the market place. Forthwith a rumor ran through the neighboring parts of the market place, and a vast crowd gathered. We went up onto the platform. The others, on being questioned, confessed their faith. So it came to my turn.[1]

[1] Anne Fremantle, *A Treasury of Early Christianity* (New York, 1953), p. 189.

Both were thrown to the beasts and killed by gladiators after being mutilated, though not before giving one another a final embrace and reaffirming their faith.

Tertullian, who was born between 150 and 160, and who became the first of the classical Christian writers and theologians of North Africa, was a contemporary of Perpetua and Felicitas and one of the greatest defenders of the Christians of Carthage against the cruelty of Severus.

Tertullian was inspired by Roman law and Roman legalism, in contrast to the Greco-Oriental mystic humanism of Clement of Alexandria, his Eastern contemporary. He studied in Rome, became a priest there, and returned to Carthage while still a young man. There he embraced the new heresy, Montanism, which had already begun to weaken the faith in North Africa. As one of the factors which prepared North African Christianity for the later victorious assault of Islam, it is worth remembering that, like Gnosticism and other major heresies, Montanism came from the East: Montanus came from Phrygia and in 156 proclaimed himself the "one through whom the dispensation of the Holy Spirit had begun." Two feminine prophets, Maximilla and Priscia, joined him in proclaiming the imminence of the Last Judgment.

Tertullian joined the Montanists in 207. He did so because, like many other North Africans, he felt the Church was becoming too worldly. His spirit, which we might call puritanical today, seemed to yearn for the simplicity of the primitive church, and this produced many quarrels with the hierarchy. He roundly denounced in *De fuga* those who fled from the persecutions of Severus and finally broke away from the Montanists to found his own sect of "Tertullianists."

Tertullian was troubled about the wickedness and wiles of contemporary North African womanhood:

> A holy woman may be beautiful by the gift of nature, but she must not give occasion to lust. If beauty be hers, so far from setting it off she ought rather to obscure it. . . . The less you trouble to please other men, the more you will please them [your husbands]. Have no fear, blessed sisters; no wife is ugly to her own husband . . .

> I see that some women change the color of their hair with saffron dye. . . . Evil, most evil is the omen of those flame-colored heads, a defilement imagined to be charm.[2]

When not worrying about morals, Tertullian was a rigorously legal-minded apologist. In later life he conducted polemics against the Jews, who were not persecuted in Roman North Africa, and against the Gnostic sect of Valentinians and the ascetic Marcionites, who aspired to free Christianity from all its blood-ties with Judaism. In theological thought, he was very close to the doctrines of the integral nature of Christ which were to be adopted by the Council of Nicaea in 325.

After the persecutions of Severus, the Church enjoyed a period of peace and consolidation in North Africa. It lasted until Cyprian's episcopate. A synod at Carthage around 200 gathered about seventy bishops from the proconsular province and Numidia. A second, in the time of Pope Fabian (236–250), convoked about ninety. Cyprian called another in the autumn of 256, which about the same number attended, and for the first time some came from far-off Mauretania, where, according to Tertullian, several tribes of Berbers already knew of the Gospels by the beginning of the third century.

In 298, the distant outpost of Tingis, capital of Mauretania Tingitana and today's Tangier, was the scene of the first martyrdom in Morocco of which reliable written records exist: Marcellus, a native of Tingis and a centurion in the army, suddenly threw away his arms and declared himself a Christian. Cassian, a recorder in the court where Marcellus was tried, protested the sentence of death passed on Marcellus as unjust and was executed himself a short time after the soldier's death. It is interesting that both martyrs were apparently judged by Roman officials under the jurisdiction of the Diocese of Spain, to which Mauretania Tingitana had been attached since 285.

At the opposite end of North Africa, Christianity's decisive separation from Judaism was taking place at almost the same time. In the synagogues of the Greek-speaking lands, including Cyrene in Libya, and probably on the island of Djerba, off southern Tunisia,

[2] Fremantle, *A Treasury of Early Christianity*, pp 63–64. The practice of using saffron dye to change hair color is still current in North Africa.

leading rabbis no longer recognized the version of the Septuagint used by the Church and turned to the Hebrew text instead. In Palestine and later in Babylonia, Jewish schools were founded in the second and third centuries which produced the Talmudism that was brought to North Africa by later Jewish immigrants. Christianity in North Africa was thus cut off more and more from direct contact with one of its most vital roots, the Semitic one, another factor which could account for its later collapse before the advancing tide of Islam.

REVOLTS, APOSTASIES, HERETICS, AND PAGAN REMNANTS

Perhaps no other factor weakened North African Christianity as did the schisms and heresies which rent its ranks in the third, fourth, and fifth centuries. Even the persistence of paganism, though it gave North African religion a peculiar favor which it has not entirely lost under Islam today, seems to have been less important in weakening Christianity.

Cyprian seems to have foreseen this, from his vantage point in Carthage. Before his martyrdom in 258 he told his compatriots: "You ought to be aware that the age is now senile. It has not now the stamina that used to make it upstanding, nor the vigor and robustness that used to make it strong. . . . This is the sentence that has been passed upon the world; this is the law of God; that what has been must die, and what has grown up must grow old." [3]

Tribal revolt now flared in all the mountain zones. As soon as the police power of the Third Legion established by Emperor Alexander Severus began to weaken, the Berbers launched attacks against the Roman outposts and settlements. The Berbers, remembering Masinissa and Jugurtha, renounced their superficial collaboration with the Romans and mounted an armed opposition. This revolt at times included all of the Maghreb except Tunisia, where the growth and spread of cities and urban life had made peasant uprisings nearly impossible. To meet the Berber threat,

[3] Quoted in Toynbee, *A Study of History*, p. 247.

Septimius Severus had once advised his son, "Pay the soldier richly and forget about the rest." The result in North Africa was a militaristic state, where *putsches, pronunciamentos,* and the subordination of all else on the part of the Roman occupiers to military needs became common. The same phenomenon reached such proportions in our own time that regimes in Madrid and Paris were made and broken by military men in North Africa. The successful revolt of 1936, when General Francisco Franco used North Africa as his base of departure, and that of May 13, 1958, which brought General Charles de Gaulle back to power in France, have been the most spectacular examples.

The economic and financial crisis sweeping the Empire after about 250 did not spare North Africa. Gold content of the money dropped to the vanishing point; tenant farmers began paying their rents in produce rather than in money, and even soldiers and officials often had to take their salaries in kind. Among Diocletian's reforms in 301 were price ceilings, which could not be maintained.

The Berber revolts which swept over Numidia and Caesarian Mauretania between 250 and 262 had an effect on social classes as well as on religion. The land of Roman colonists was seized, just as was that of many French *colons* in Algeria in 1962 and 1963, after Algerian independence. Cyprian had to send 100,000 sequestras raised by the Bishopric of Carthage to ransom Christian captives, especially young girls whom he feared the Berbers would violate.

Diocletian detached the administration of Tingitania from the rest of the Maghreb and placed it under the administration of Spain. Morocco seems never to have interested the Romans except as a sort of sentry post at the Pillars of Hercules (Gibraltar and Ceuta, the Roman Septem Fratres) to protect the rich provinces of southern Spain from invasions coming from Africa. Most of Morocco's Roman citizens were Berbers. Morocco was a purely military province, where there was little agricultural colonization. As a result the Christian churches, tied to the process of urbanization in Tunisia and Algeria, never achieved more than a toe hold in Morocco. This helps to explain why the Moslem conquest of Morocco was so relatively swift and why it is probable that fewer

Christian remnants survived there than anywhere else in the Maghreb.

The persecutions of Decius, which began in 250, threw the North African Christian community into dismay and confusion. Many Christians at Carthage, to avoid death and torture, lapsed into apostasy. These were called *lapsi.* Cyprian remarked with deep regret that many apostatized even before they were threatened. The *lapsi,* or *sacrificati,* resumed sacrifices to the old, official gods. Others, called *libellatici,* simply purchased certificates saying they had sacrificed, and for them absolution was easier. One Carthaginian bishop, Novatus, an enemy of Cyprian, tried to attract apostates to himself for absolution and threatened those going to Cyprian with excommunication. Far more serious in its weakening of the North African Church was a movement started in Rome by Novatian, or Novatus, a presbyter or elder who opposed the indulgence of Pope Cornelius (251–253) toward the apostates and was chosen bishop by a party of purists who agreed with him. The resulting schism spread through most of the Empire and lasted until the sixth century.

Cyprian tried to block its extension in North Africa. "There is only one head, there is only one source, only one mother," he wrote in his treatise *De lapsis*. "It is from her womb that we are born, it is her milk that nourishes us, it is her spirit which animates us." But the heresy took a firm hold in Africa.

Diocletian (284–305) launched a fresh wave of persecution against the Christians in 303. In Africa, in one small town alone, Abitina, near Carthage, nineteen women and thirty men died in prison because they were suspected of holding illegal Christian meetings. Lactantius and Arnobius were two African writers of Latin who protested the persecutions openly but were not prosecuted for doing so.

In the time of Diocletian and Constantine the Great (306–337) the Church was administratively already closely modeled after Roman secular power, though probably not yet totally associated with it in Berber eyes until its establishment by Constantine in 313. The six ecclesiastical provinces closely coincided with the six civil provinces of Constantine, though the frontiers were not exactly the same. The Bishop of Carthage exercised official control in his province and unofficial control everywhere else in North Africa between Tangier and Bengasi. For North African Christianity, which seemed to have changed the face of the Mediterranean littoral for some time to come, the scene was now set for its greatest triumph—and its greatest defeat.

CHAPTER V

HERESY, ORTHODOXY, AND DECLINE

> So it is that two cities have been made by two loves; the earthly city by love of self to the exclusion of God, the heavenly by love of God to the exclusion of self.
>
> The truth is that these two cities are intertwined in this world, mixed up with each other until they are finally pulled apart at the Last Judgment.
>
> SAINT AUGUSTINE, *De Civitate Dei,* XIV, 28; I, 35

Constantine's Edict of Milan (313) ended the persecution of Christians throughout the Empire, including North Africa. It led to a permanent alliance between the Church and the Roman state. The Emperor sent a messenger to Caecilian, Bishop of Carthage, who was authorized to pay from the imperial treasuries the sum of three thousand folles (about $60,000) and be ready to make further payments to relieve the hard-pressed churches of North Africa.

The Church of martyrs now became the state Church. Its first task was to combat two new heresies, both of which took a firm hold on the Latin Church of Africa. Both weakened it, and both penetrated it with Oriental and local African dogmas which served further to detach it from the Latin Popes and make it easier prey for the later Moslem conquest.

MANICHAEISM

Manichaeism spread rapidly among Christians in the third and fourth centuries. Its founder, Manes, was born in 216 in southern Babylonia and was crucified at Gandishapur, Persia, in 276, after living the life of a zealot and spreading confusion throughout the Christian world. Manes referred to himself as the "Seal of the

Prophets" and the "Apostle of the Last Generation." Like the Zoroastrians of ancient Persia, he taught that life was an eternal struggle between the kingdom of the spirit, represented by light, and that of the flesh, represented by darkness. Redemption was to be achieved not through a single act but through a continued process, with Christ as a sort of "helper toward the light." The Manichaeans believed that in order to escape a cycle of human existence marked by the constant struggle of the realm of light against the demons of material darkness, a man must observe absolute asceticism, extending even into matters of diet—abstaining from meat and wine.

Some specialists have related Manichaeism to Gnostic writings of the Christian East. In one group of Psalms for the festival of Bema, coincidental with Easter and celebrating Manes' passion and death, the master is supposed to have told Bahram, a scornful acquaintance:

> Ask all men about me. I have no master and no teacher, from whom I learned the wisdom or from whom I had these things. But: as I received them, I received them from God, that I should preach them in your realm. . . . Witness of all that I bring lies visible; all that I proclaim already existed in earlier generations. But that is the custom, that the way of truth sometimes is manifest and sometimes is hidden.[1]

Augustine was later to embrace the doctrine briefly, then denounce it. An edict of Diocletian had warned against Manichaean doctrine in 297, and from 382 Manichaeism became punishable by death in the Western Empire. Later, the Moslem (Abbasid) Caliph al-Mahdi (775–785) was to persecute the Manichaeans, after they had achieved spectacular successes in Persia and among the Uigur Turks in China.

But in Carthage and in Hippo Regius (Bône), monastic communities of *electi* (perfect Manichaeans) and wider lay circles of *auditores,* or *catechumeni* (secular Manichaeans), appeared who studied Latin translations of Manichaean writings. After the estab-

[1] Manichaean text quoted in Gunter Lanczkowski (ed.), *Heilige Schriften* (Stuttgart, 1956), p. 60.

lishment of the Catholic Church, the clergy called upon Roman state power to crush the heresy.

THE DONATISTS AND DONATISM

Until the Vandals arrived in 429, North Africa was little affected by the schism provoked by the partisans of Arius (*c.* 256–336). This presbyter of Alexandria, who probably came from Cyrenaica, denied the eternal existence of the Word and the truly divine nature of Christ, insisting on the plural elements in his being. Arius' opponents were led by Bishop Alexander and his successor Athanasius, who upheld the divinity and unitary nature of Christ. The Council of Nicaea, summoned by Constantine in 325, decided for the latter, though the churches in the East, including many in present-day Libya, swung later toward Arianism.

The Berbers were far more affected by Donatism. Its most direct cause was the large number of *lapsi* which the persecutions of Diocletian left behind. Factions formed behind two rival bishops of Carthage, Caecilian and Donatus, each accusing the other of having turned over the Holy Scriptures to officers of Diocletian during the persecution. The Numidian clergy and a large part of the Carthaginian population agreed with Donatus that the imperial authority had been far too soft on the *lapsi*. Constantine decided the dispute in favor of Caecilian. The Donatist clergy, bolstered by popular Berber support, replied by excommunicating Caecilian's followers. They claimed that the apostolic succession had been interrupted. Only the African Donatists, with their doctrine of rebaptism, were right, they said; all the bishops in Europe and Asia who were saying otherwise were wrong.

New riots and uprisings broke out against imperial authority. At this point, the theological battle was compounded by a social revolt of landless peasants, sharecroppers, and agricultural workers like those seen in North Africa in our own day. The so-called *circoncellians* (from *circum cellas,* those who loiter around the farms) massacred city dwellers in Algeria. Imperial troops were sent against them and order was briefly restored. But by 365, the Berber tribes had begun a general uprising which aimed at nothing less than expulsion of Roman—and Catholic—power from North

Africa. Leptis Magna and other points in Tripolitania were threatened.

The corrupt Count Romanus of Africa insisted upon a bribe of four thousand camels before he would send imperial troop reinforcements. When imperial commissioners arrived from Rome to investigate, Romanus bought them off. One Berber rebel, Firmus, conquered Caesarea (Cherchel) and Icosium (Algiers) but was halted at Tipasa, on the Mediterranean coast. A quaint legend, perpetuated in French colonial literature, says the Berbers were halted by the intervention of St. Salsa, a little girl who attained martyrdom under Constantine after having cast into the bay a bronze dragon worshiped by local pagans.

In 375 the Roman cavalry general Theodosius routed Firmus, who strangled himself. His body was sent to the victor draped over a camel's back. But Donatism survived, and Africa seemed likely to go over completely to its fanatical "socialism." There were probably some seeds in it of the savage courage which the Kharidjite Berber schismatics of Islam were to show against their Arab conquerors four centuries later.

Crucial as all of the social and political effects of the heresies were on North Africa, their theological effect was to weaken Christian dogma throughout the Mediterranean world and make it more yielding to the onslaught of Islam. Each of the heresies had somehow undermined the fundamental Christian affirmation that Christ must be both completely divine and completely human. While Arianism had taught that Christ was something less than God, the Nestorian theologians, whose doctrine prevailed among many Asian Christians, said that manhood was so divided from Godhead that the two were really separate persons and separate entities. The Monophysite faiths, which at first reached no further westward into North Africa than Cyrenaica, presented Christ in various ways as not truly God. The first seven general councils of the Church, beginning with Nicaea in 325, combated these various heresies and added new brick and mortar to the dogmatic foundations of both Roman and Orthodox Christianity which the earliest Fathers had already laid. At the same time they may have so confused the minds of Arabs, Berbers, and other men in the Mediterranean basin that these were ready to welcome a new and seemingly simpler faith that proclaimed the oneness of God, excluding the need for a Son or for a Holy Spirit.

THE PERSISTENCE OF PAGANISM

Christianity had to face other persistent foes: paganism and superstition, both perhaps as much the bane of young Moslem reformers now as they were among Christian priests then. By Constantine's time, superstition and the worship of Oriental mystery cults—particularly Mithraism, from Persia, and the adoration of Isis and Osiris, from Egypt—had spread throughout most of the Empire and were especially prevalent in the armed forces.

James Frazer sees Mithraism, widely identified with sun worship but also offering the hope of immortality and aspirations to moral purity, as a "formidable rival" to Christianity of this period. It seems to have been widespread in North Africa: the Antiquities Museum in Rabat has Mithra images, found in Sala and Volubilis, that were used in the Roman army. With its graduated stages of merit, each achieved after formidable initiations, Mithraism was capable of producing tough and hardened men. Tertullian, writing to Christian soldiers, admonished them:

> You, his fellow-warriors, should blush when exposed by any soldier of Mithra. When he is enrolled in the cave, he is offered the crown, which he spurns. And he takes his oath upon this moment, and is to be believed. Through the fidelity of his servants the devil puts us to shame.[2]

A far more enduring effect on North African manners, mores, and religious practice was that of the old Puno-Roman paganisms and their associated superstitions. Popular Islam in North Africa today, as nearly any Christian missionary will tell you, is a many-colored thing, an incredibly polyglot mixture of these many ingredients. Neoplatonism, whose teachings reached North Africa in attenuated form, was one such ingredient. Its doctrine of an immanent divine essence has survived until today in the Berber belief

[2] Quoted in Arkon Daraul, *Secret Societies* (London, 1961), p. 79.

in *baraka* (translatable as "blessing," "beneficence," or simply "white magic"), which can be transmitted by its possessors or absorbed from inanimate objects. Oracles were worshiped well into Christian times, notably the image of the Celestial Goddess in Carthage. Finally, about 380, the main Carthage temple was converted into a Christian church, after being closed and overgrown with brambles.

As during the last generations of Punic Carthage, superstition was rampant in Africa by later Roman times. Amulets, phylacteries, belief in the evil eye, known in Arabic North Africa today as *al-ain* (the eye) and in Roman North Africa as *invidus,* were widespread then, as they are today. An invocation on a Roman mosaic found at El-Haouria (Tunisia), which is now in the museum at Sousse, refers to the evil eye as "envious" and "livid" (*invide livide*). To extend the fingers in an obscene gesture against the evil eye seems to have been just as common then in Carthage or Leptis Magna as it is still in Tunis, Naples, or Tangier. The sign of the phallus, which occurs in so many Roman mosaics and is chiseled on outer walls of buildings is not a signpost pointing to a brothel, as so many Mediterranean tourists are told, but an amulet against the evil eye. Much Berber jewelry, particularly in the Moroccan Rif and Algerian Kabylie Mountains, still uses it.

The fish, symbol of the forces of the sea and of the marine origin of Elat-Tanit, is a universal sign of life and generation which Christianity adopted and Islam preserved. It is most familiar in Tunisia, as anyone knows who has toured the markets of Tunis and bought one of the delightful, grinning fish made out of gingham cloth and velveteen embroidery. In Christianity, some of the symbolism of the fish is founded upon the word play in the Greek letters which spell *ichthus* (fish), the initials of *Iesous Christos Theou Uios Soter* (Jesus Christ Son of God Saviour).

Today, as in Roman times, conjurers in Tunisia and Algeria use a perversion of the Jewish Deity, Yahweh, designated in antiquity as Iao or Iao-Sabaoth, as one of their demons. Jewish sorcerers in North Africa have kept a reputation since Roman times for great power and effectiveness: sometimes they are supposed to employ Egyptian demons or fiends, and even gods like Osiris.

Some of the Christian writers were much impressed by this mumbo jumbo. Lactantius observed that

> These supermundane and earthly *daimones* [supernatural beings] know much of the future but not all; the genuine counsel of God they do not know. It is they who suffer themselves to be conjured by magicians, at whose invocation they deceive the mind of man with blinding jugglery so that he does not see what is but believes that he sees what is not.[3]

AUGUSTINE: THE AFRICAN CHURCH TRIUMPHANT

Into this strange Mediterranean world, where the Berbers stirred restlessly under their Roman masters while the European intelligentsia dabbled with eclectic doctrines and waited for a sign, one truly great man was born. Never did Christianity in Africa reach the heights it attained under St. Augustine, whose writings, teachings, and personality still influence Christians and their beliefs throughout the world. For us, the most fascinating aspect of a man who has inspired whole libraries of theological commentaries, histories, and discourses is that he was a North African and one who became the hope of all Christians in North Africa for ages to come.

To picture what Augustine, the man, must have looked like to his Berber and Roman contemporaries, it would probably be better to forget classical European paintings of him as a modern bishop with mitre, cope, and crosier and see him instead in a simple, North African tunic of the kind worn by people shown in the mosaics now in the Bardo Museum in Tunis. Like most North Africans, he was warm blooded, fond of women, food, and drink, and one modern tradition even is able to assure us that he suffered from hemorrhoids.

The basic facts about Augustine are known from his *Confessions* and are elaborated on by his many biographers. He was born on November 13, 354, to Patricius, a town councilor of Tagaste, and Monica, a Berber Christian. He studied at Tagaste, Madaura, and Carthage, and took a mistress with whom he lived for sixteen years

[3] Quoted in Burckhardt, *The Age of Constantine the Great*, p. 196.

and had a son, Adeodatus. In 373 he became a Manichaean. He left for Italy in 383, where the Prefect Symmachus gave him a chair of rhetoric at Milan. After hearing the sermons of Ambrose and long meditation and study on his own, Augustine abandoned Manichaeism to return to his original Catholic faith and was baptized on Easter Sunday of 387. When Monica died, he returned to Africa and in 391 was ordained a priest at Hippo Regius. He became Bishop of Hippo in 396 and died on August 28, 430, while the invading Vandals, who had swept across North Africa, eastward from Spain, were laying siege to Hippo.

Augustine the African man, as much as Augustine the saint and Christian Father, is the image he has left us in his *Confessions*. Even as Mohammed was to be later, he is vivid and frank about his frailties:

> Meanwhile my sins were being multiplied, and my concubine being torn from my side as a hindrance to my marriage, my heart which clave unto her was torn and wounded and bleeding. And she returned to Africa, vowing unto Thee [God] never to know any other man, leaving with me my son by her. But unhappy I, who could not imitate a very woman, impatient of delay, inasmuch as not till after two years was I to obtain her I sought, not being so much a lover of marriage as a slave to lust, procured another, though no wife, that so by the servitude of an enduring custom, the disease of my soul might be kept up and carried on in its vigour, or even augmented, into the dominion of marriage.[4]

But neither Augustine the sensualist nor Augustine the theologian concern us here so much as Augustine, the champion of Roman orthodoxy in the face of rising Donatism and Berber revolt. The foundation of Constantinople in 330 as the new seat of the Empire had already separated the geographical centers of Church and State, and weakened the co-ordination and consequently the power of both in North Africa.

[4] Edward B. Pusey (trans.), *The Confessions of Saint Augustine* (New York, 1961), VI, 102.

THE DIVISION OF EAST AND WEST

Augustine's chief Donatist foe, the Bishop Primianus, was not equal to Augustine's great capacities: Augustine outtalked, outwrote, and outmaneuvered him. From the time of the Synod of Hippo (393), Augustine pressed the struggle against the Berber schismatics. This took on a distinctly military character with the revolt of Gildo, the brother of Firmus. Gildo had aided the Romans, and as a reward he was made Count of Africa. But after fourteen years of loyal service, he withheld help to Emperor Theodosius against a pretender. When Theodosius died and the Empire was divided into Eastern and Western sections, Gildo broke relations with Honorius, the Western Emperor, and transferred the allegiance of the Diocese of Africa (in 397) to the Eastern Emperor, Arcadius, whose seat in Constantinople was much too distant to exercise any real control. A year later he revolted, and the Vandal chieftain Stilicho, now the real master of the Western Empire, had him proclaimed a public enemy by the Senate and sent against him an army under Mascezel, another Berber mercenary who gained so much glory in defeating Gildo that he was apparently eliminated in his turn by Stilicho, who feared his power.

Augustine now launched a full-scale drive against Donatism and succeeded in having it declared a heresy and outlawed by the Emperor Honorius in 405. By sheer military force, the schismatics were largely wiped out or brought back to the paths of orthodoxy in the proconsular province and probably in Mauretania. Donatism and its accompanying social unrest continued in the rural areas of Numidia: the quarrelsome and separatist nature of the Algerian Berbers and Riffians today is probably partly a vestige of these times. Donatism did not completely disappear until the end of the sixth century, and its earlier repression had left an indelible hate against the Empire, the Church, and the landed aristocracy, who all favored the repression. There was a remarkable similarity between Donatist fanaticism and that of the *Kharidjites,* or "Seceders," which, in the eighth century, was to capture the imagination of the Berbers converted to Islam.

Pelagianism was another heresy which Augustine fought. The Breton monk Pelagius maintained that man could win salvation through his acts alone without the help of divine grace. In a series of writings, Augustine refuted this doctrine, and during a polemic with a disciple of Pelagius, supported the thesis that human beings can do nothing without grace. Augustine and the other African bishops refused to submit to the authority of one pope who supported the Pelagians, and the pope had to give in to them.

Augustine made special efforts to refute the teachings of both the Manichaeans and the Jews (*Contra Judaeos*). He succeeded in giving the Church, even in this time of incipient decay and during the revolts that tore asunder the secular fabric of Roman power in North Africa, a degree of prestige and authority that it had never had before and will almost certainly never have again in North Africa. Its bishops, its councils, and the inner strength of its administrative machine made it possible to resist and, sometimes, to reverse the decisions of emperors and of popes.

One reaction against the worldliness of established religion and the secularization of society was, as at later times in Moslem North Africa, the gesture of withdrawal. The anchorites with their solitary monasticism in Egypt had shown the way. St. Augustine supported the practice in the Maghreb. One of the first anchorites had been Anthony (*c.* 251–*c.* 357). In his life we see, once again, a strong spiritual current entering North Africa from the East. Bishop Athanasius recounts how Anthony, who came of a wealthy family, meditated one day in church on the injunctions in the Gospel of St. Matthew to sell one's worldly goods and give the proceeds to the poor.

> As though he had received the command from God Himself —these words of the holy authors—and as though the text had been fashioned for him, Anthony immediately went out of the church, gave the property he had inherited from his parents to the inhabitants of the village, so that neither he nor his sister should suffer further embarrassment from it. He sold all the other real property he possessed, and having sold it for a handsome sum, he gave the money to the poor, keeping a bit for his sister.[5]

[5] Quoted in F. van der Meer and C. Mohrmann, *Atlas de l'Antiquité Chrétienne* (Paris-Bruxelles, 1960), pp. 168f.

Anthony retired to a rock cave, then to the Egyptian desert east of the Nile. By 386, his fame had already spread to Europe: Roman officers at the Court of Trèves who had read of his life had begun to renounce the world themselves.

The founder of monasticism in communities, as opposed to the solitary life of the hermits, was the Egyptian monk St. Pachomius (*c.* 292–*c.* 346), who instituted monastic communities in the Middle East in about 318. Athanasius brought the cenobitical monastery into the West.

There was a third form of monastic life which was midway between the hermits and the cenobitic communities: a semieremitic organization where a cluster of small settlements, each containing two to six brethren under supervision of an elder, replaced the single, tightly knit community. Nitria and Scetis, both in Egypt, were the centers of this fourth-century movement. Ammon, the founder of a monachal settlement in Nitria, Macarius of Egypt, and Macarius of Alexandria were among its most famous elders.

Through Augustine's encouragement, there were a few monasteries that we know of by 500 in such places as Bône, though the practice never seems to have been widespread west of Egypt. It was only with the return in force of Christianity, in the vanguard of the new European invasions of the nineteenth century, that Christian monasticism returned to the Maghreb on any appreciable scale.

CHAPTER VI

VANDALS AND BYZANTINES

> What is there new, I ask, of delight in this world? Everywhere we observe strife; everywhere we hear groans. Cities are destroyed, fortresses are turned over, fields are depopulated, the land has returned to solitude. . . . And yet the blows of Divine justice have no end, because among the blows those guilty of evil acts are not corrected. . . . See what has befallen Rome, once mistress of the world. She is worn down by great sorrows, by the disappearance of her citizens, by the attacks of her enemies, by numerous ruins. Thus we see brought to fulfillment what the prophet [Ezekiel] long ago pronounced on the city of Samaria.
>
> Pope Gregory I, 593 or 594

When Augustine died in 430, another horde of foreign invaders was swarming across North Africa and forcing their faith on both the Berber natives and Roman settlers. This time they came not from the East but from the West. By 409, the Vandals, Germanic barbarians who had become Arian Christians, controlled much of Spain and were plundering the Moroccan coasts from bases in the Balearic Islands. They entrusted the conquest of Africa to Genseric, their most capable general. Genseric had an ally, Bonifacius, the Roman Count of Africa. Bonifacius had scored some spectacular military successes against Berber rebels, though he had allowed his daughter to be baptized as a Donatist and was at war with Rome himself.

Bonifacius is said to have called upon Genseric for help. Genseric landed somewhere near Tangier or Ceuta in 429, bringing with him all his Arian people, eighty thousand of them, including fifteen thousand soldiers. Tangier and Ceuta became Vandal tributaries, and, though they probably kept most of their Roman political insti-

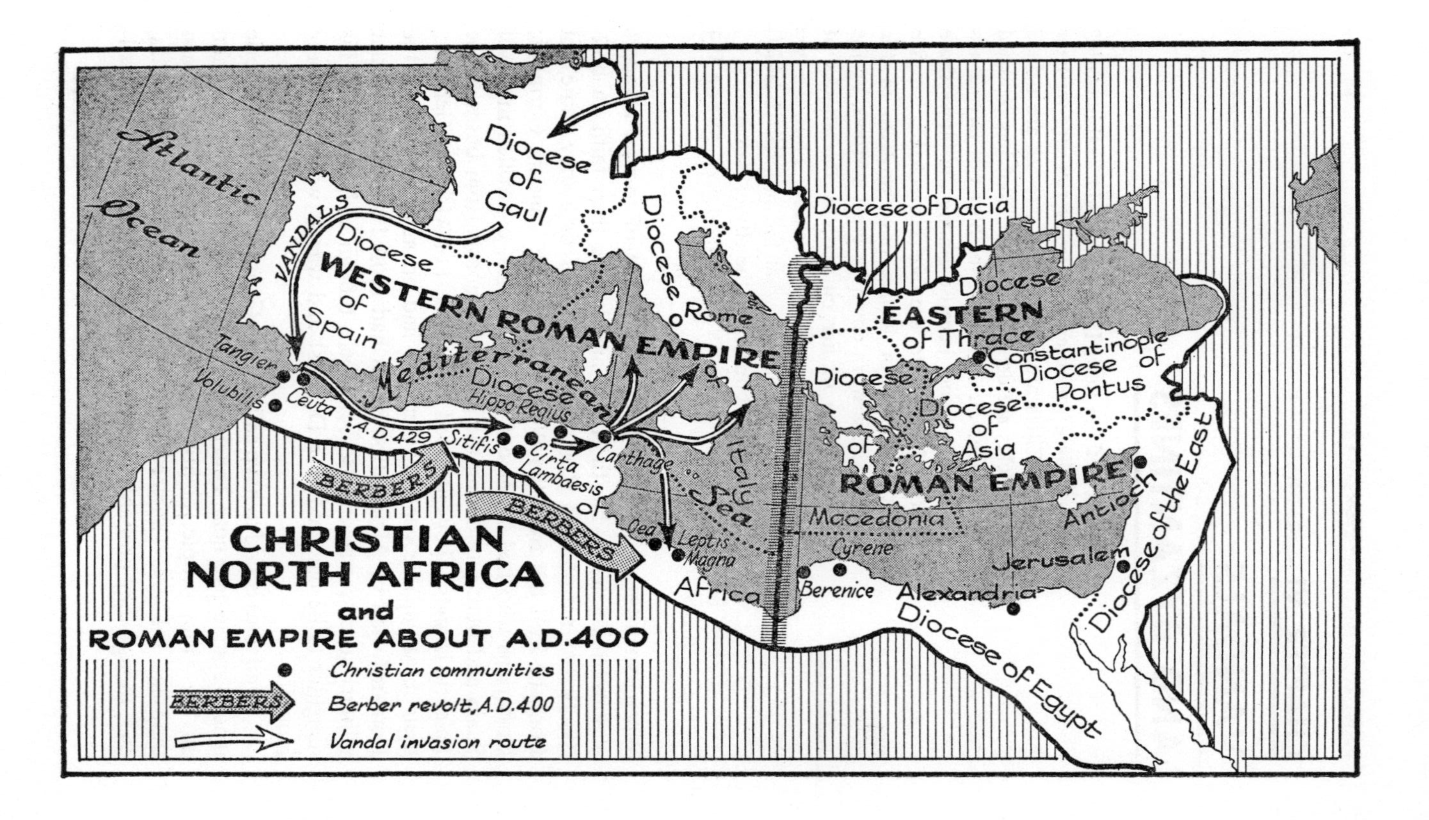
CHRISTIAN
NORTH AFRICA
and
ROMAN EMPIRE ABOUT A.D.400
Christian communities
BERBERS
Berber revolt, A.D.400
Vandal invasion route
Atlantic
Ocean
Diocese
of
Gaul
VANDALS
Diocese
of
Spain
WESTERN ROMAN EMPIRE
Diocese of Rome
Diocese of Dacia
EASTERN ROMAN EMPIRE
Diocese of Thrace
Constantinople
Diocese of Pontus
Diocese of Asia
Diocese of Macedonia
Diocese of the East
Diocese of Egypt
Mediterranean Sea
Diocese of Italy
Diocese of Africa
Tangier
Volubilis
Ceuta
A.D. 429
Sitifis
Hippo Regius
Cirta
Lambaesis
Carthage
Oea
Leptis Magna
Cyrene
Berenice
Alexandria
Jerusalem
Antioch
BERBERS
BERBERS

tutions, they had to adopt the Arian creed. Genseric pushed eastward.

In 435, a convention signed at Hippo made the Vandals officially Roman allies, despite their heretical faith and the threat they represented to both the western and eastern halves of the Empire. In 439, Genseric, not satisfied with Morocco and Algeria, marched on Carthage and captured it while its population indulged in hedonistic delight. Salvianus, an orthodox Christian preacher of Marseilles, described the scene, "Outside the walls, throats are being cut; in the city there is fornication. Those outside are captives of the enemy; the others of infamy."

The Vandals prepared to attack Europe from their African bases by building themselves a fleet with the timber of the Atlas Mountains. By 442, Genseric had control of all of Roman North Africa except the interior of Morocco. He controlled the Strait of Gibraltar and Rome's African grain supply as well.

Genseric's Arian hordes systematically persecuted the orthodox Christians, confiscating their churches and seizing their treasure. Arian rites were instituted in the basilicas that had been built in Carthage to honor St. Cyprian. The Carthaginian orthodox clergy was packed off to Rome aboard old scows. The Vandal army invaded Italy, sacked Rome in 455, and shipped its treasures back to Africa.

Leo I, the emperor of the east, sent a powerful expeditionary force under Count Marcellinus, hoping to save Europe and rescue African orthodoxy by capturing the Vandals' rear base. But he was tricked into an ignominious defeat by Genseric near Cape Bon. The victorious Vandal now agreed to reopen the Catholic churches and recall the bishops in return for official recognition of his rights over Africa, Corsica, Sardinia, Sicily, the Balearic Islands, and Ischia in 476, the year that is usually considered to mark the final collapse of the Western Roman Empire.

The Vandal kingdom which Genseric and his successors set up to rule the Maghreb was yet another example of a foreign politico-religious establishment, imposed on both the natives and the Romans. The king named all state officials, and the Arian clergy, like the earlier orthodox clergy, was given official status. Latin was retained, except for Arian church services which were held in the Vandal language.

Roman persecutions of the earlier Christians in North Africa appear rather mild beside the repressions by Genseric's son and heir, Huneric (477–484), of non-Arians in the Vandal kingdom. Manichaeans were burnt alive. Women of orthodox Roman families were delivered up to pagan Berbers, who abused them badly. Bishops were thrown naked outside the walls of Carthage and forced to work the land: ninety of them died in the space of two years under this treatment. An Arian priest detailed to guard Eugene, the paralyzed orthodox bishop of Carthage, poured vinegar into his mouth. Choir boys and priests of Carthage were beaten and flagellated. Refugees trying to flee from Tipasa had their tongues cut out: orthodox Christian tradition has it that they continued to speak without tongues. Gibbon describes how "respectable citizens, noble matrons and consecrated virgins were suspended naked" and "torn with scourges, or burnt in the most tender parts with red-hot plates of iron."

The next Vandal king, Thrasamund (496–523), was benevolent by comparison with Huneric. He ended the maltreatment of the orthodox, though he continued the exile of their bishops. Thrasamund debated religion with Fulgentius, an orthodox theologian. During his reign there seems to have been a sort of court literature, written in Latin on Vandal themes; and Carthage, that aged and fading trollop among cities, was redecorated once again.

THE BYZANTINE RECONQUEST

Justin I mounted the throne in Constantinople in 518. When Thrasamund saw that Justin had patched up relations with the Roman pope, he quickly sought an alliance with Theodoric, the king of the barbarian Ostrogoths and ruler of Italy.

Thrasamund's successor was an effeminate old man named Hilderic (523–530). Hilderic allowed the orthodox churches to hold a council and exercise some degree of freedom, even though the Emperor Justin had banned Arianism in the Eastern Empire in 523.

By this time, the Carthaginian merchants, whose businesses had been totally ruined by the Vandals, and the orthodox clergy were imploring Justin I and his successor, Justinian I (527–565), to deliver them. The gradual decline of Vandal seapower, noted by Justinian's acute naval and military intelligence services, was an important factor in the successful reconquest of Africa by his greatest general, Belisarius, in 533. Belisarius realized that he had better not antagonize the Berbers if he hoped to have any lasting success in his mission of re-establishing imperial authority and orthodox Christianity. He was aware of the native distaste for Vandal rule and tried to use it to his advantage.

When victory was secure and the Vandals defeated and dispersed, Justinian put a military resident-general, or *magister militum,* in charge of the slim coastal strip of Africa which the Byzantines now controlled. His headquarters was at Carthage. He built chains of fortresses from Libya all the way west to Ceuta, on the Strait of Gibraltar. Authority over the natives was symbolized by the local churches and the fortified military posts which protected them.

Once again, the Arians, the Donatists, and the remaining pagans were suppressed. The wealth and the immunities of the clergy were restored. At first, the Byzantines found a good reception at the hands of all the North African Christians, Roman, Berber, and Oriental.

The new North African Church, physically rebuilt in the form of Byzantine basilicas, whose ruins a traveler sees today in places like Leptis, Sabratha, Tebessa, and Cherchel, was an Oriental Church. The rich mosaics, especially numerous in Tunisia, wove a new note of Eastern color into the graying fabric of North African Christendom. The Mosque of Kairawan in Tunisia, named after North Africa's Arab conqueror, Sidi Ukbah ibn Nafi, is one of the buildings where this color, and the syncretistic nature of Tunisia's past, come through most strongly. The shape of its minaret, like the towers of many of the Byzantine fortresses, recalls the great lighthouse of Pharos at Alexandria. In the prayer hall, the pillars supporting the arches are nearly all taken from the ruins of Byzantine, Roman, and even Punic buildings, transported from Utica, Carthage, and the Orient. Pillars of marble and red porphyry, surmounted by Roman capitals of different periods, resemble those seen in Antioch, Constantinople, and the Byzantine portions of St.

Mark's Cathedral in Venice. The miracle of the pillars, like that of the mosque as a whole, is that these improbably blended elements have produced a striking impression of unity and harmony.

Unfortunately for Christianity, spiritual unity and harmony seemed to have totally deserted its North African churches. The old heresies and schisms and some new ones as well were rampant. The orthodox Christians, resisting the new Oriental influences, found themselves forced more and more to look for support to the popes of Rome, who were enfeebled by the new barbarian power in Europe.

There was one brief revival of Christian missionary work among the Berbers under the praetor, Thomas, during the reign of Justin II (565–578). Thomas extended both the Byzantine secular power and the Byzantine Church into the Fezzan, the far southern province of today's Libya, before the tide of Berber tribal revolt surged around and swallowed it up again.

Pope Gregory the Great (590–604), remarking ruefully that Rome—which still included and relied upon the secular power of Constantinople—was no longer "mistress of the world," and that North African Christians were in a bad way, tried to save what he could. He even called upon the eastern emperor to act against heresy, including Donatism, which was reappearing in North Africa. Gregory, by his insistence that the Church of Africa was a daughter of the Church of Rome and owed it submission, annoyed the Byzantine authorities.

The last major Christian crisis before the Moslem invasion took place when Sergius, the Patriarch of Constantinople who had crowned the African exarch Heraclius emperor at Constantinople, denied that Christ had manifested both of his natures and taught instead that he had a single nature, both human and divine. This grew into the Monothelete heresy and was finally condemned by the sixth great council of the Church at Constantinople in 680–681. In 638 a Monothelete edict called *Ecthesis* was promulgated by Heraclius, causing new outbreaks in North Africa. The effects of this heresy were further aggravated when, about this time, many Monophysite monks and nuns from Egypt arrived in the Maghreb, making more and more converts and antagonizing the orthodox Christians who were thoroughly discouraged by the failure of the Emperor to act against the heretics. In 645, as the Moslem Arabs prepared to attack North Africa, an emperor who was strongly suspect of Monothelete tendencies, Constans II, was on the throne in Constantinople, and a priest named Maximus led a brief Berber revolt which tried unsuccessfully to put the orthodox exarch Gregory on the imperial throne.

One of many Berber revolts against Byzantine power was led by a renegade soldier named Stoza, who at one point fled to Morocco and married the daughter of a Berber prince. Around 545, after some hostages had been executed, the Byzantine exarch, Solomon, led his troops on a foray southwest to Tebessa. When he saw the size of the Berber army, he tried to come to terms. How much respect the Berbers held for Christianity by then emerges from their reaction when he proposed through an emissary to swear a binding oath of peace. Replied the Berber chief, "Will he swear by the Gospels? It was on those books that the faith of his nephew Sergius was pledged to eighty of our innocent and unfortunate brethren!" Solomon was defeated and killed in the battle that followed.

In 587, the Berbers captured Carthage. Meanwhile, the emperor had halted persecution of the Jews and had allowed the Donatists to rise again in Tunisia and Algeria. When these needed protection, they were able to buy it from the corrupt Byzantine officials who were already imposing a crushing tax burden on their subjects.

THE LANGUAGE BARRIER BETWEEN EAST AND WEST

When Paul and the Apostles had first preached in the Mediterranean world, Christianity in North Africa was strongly favored by the fact that the Roman Empire was largely unified in language and culture. Those Berbers who had contact with it shared in this general Greco-Roman *paeduma,* though, for them, Latin was a far more important ingredient than Greek. Punic traces lingered on but the spread of Latin and the fact that many people were bilingual or even trilingual by Augustine's time had greatly aided the missionary work of the Church.

But the precarious unities which Rome had brought now disappeared. Political unity was the first to go, with the foundation of Constantinople and the Eastern Empire. Justinian was the last emperor who briefly made into fact the theory of imperial unity. His triumph was as brilliant as it was ephemeral. The rise and the victory of Islam were soon totally to sever, for all practical purposes, East from West along the Mediterranean. At the same time, the Latin language, dying out in Europe, expired in North Africa. It was not replaced by Greek, now being used in the Eastern Churches and for the affairs of state of the Eastern Empire. The language barrier meant that North African Christianity was cut off from its Greek and Hebrew sources.

Augustine had foreseen this last and great difficulty as early as 403, when he wrote in a letter to St. Jerome, who had advocated importing and using Greek translations from the original Hebrew texts of the Scriptures:

> It will be a grievous thing that, in the reading of Scripture, differences must arise between the Latin Churches and the Greek Churches, especially seeing that the discrepancy is easily condemned in a Latin version by the production of the original in Greek, which is a language very widely known; whereas, if any one has been disturbed by the occurrence of something to which he was not accustomed in the translation taken from the Hebrew, and alleges that the new translation is wrong, it will be found difficult, if not impossible, to get at the Hebrew documents by which the version to which the exception is taken may be defended.[1]

Had North African Christianity, through its schisms and divisions, sealed its own doom? Or had external factors which were out of control of the Christian communities themselves, condemned it? Seemingly by a combination of agencies, the scene had been set for a relatively quick and easy victory by the forces of Islam gathering in Arabia. That their final victory in North Africa, after early success, was neither quick nor easy, as we shall next see, was probably due far more to the nature of the Berbers and their Arab conquerors than to any surviving vitality of the North African Christian community itself.

The fervor of early Christians and the wisdom of the African

[1] Quoted in Fremantle, *A Treasury of Early Christianity,* p. 98.

Church Fathers had taken root in soil already prepared by the early seeking of the Punic priests after divine revelation. The ancestral fear of a terrible, avenging figure like Jehovah, supreme among the gods, was a logical forerunner of the doctrines of Augustine that man as a sinner can be saved from his fate only through divine grace. But by the time the first swift-riding Arab horsemen arrived from the East, the image of the Christian God which had been preached by Cyprian and Augustine, and even the figure of God's Son, had become blurred and crisscrossed in North Africa with the countless arguments and heresies over their natures, their essences, and their manifestations in the Holy Ghost. We can well imagine a Berber thirst to return to simplicity: to achieve direct contact with a God who can only be God when He is One and has no associates. The conquering Arab armies brought a remedy for this thirst: the faith of Islam.

CHAPTER VII

THE VICTORY OF ISLAM

> To be sure, we know that certain *mudjahidun* [fighters for the faith] struggled in our mountains believing they were living back in the time of the Prophet, just as certain Frenchmen cannot think of a revolution without referring to their own in 1789.
>
> ASSIA DJEBAR (Algerian novelist), 1962

Scarcely seven generations after Paul and the Apostles and their followers spread Christianity in the Near East and the northeastern corner of Africa, Mohammed and his followers in Arabia created a faith which was to move the world at least as profoundly as Christianity had and displace Christianity in a major portion of the world.

Islam means surrender: surrender to the will of God. It is terribly wrong to call the faith which Mohammed founded "Mohammedanism," which implies worship of the Prophet as a divine being. The disciples of Mohammed, and his successors, regard him as do all the 435 million Moslems of today as the *rasul,* or messenger of God as well as his Prophet (*nabi*). Like Abraham, Moses, Isaiah, and Christ, he transmitted God's message to men, but he was the last, the Seal of the other prophets, who completed this message.

To dwell upon his life here in detail would be retelling a tale which many others have already told, and still are telling, some of them superbly. But it is useful to glance quickly at some high points of his career.

Mohammed was born in Mecca, perhaps in the Year of the Elephant, A.D. 570 or 571, named after the war elephants of Abraham, the Christian Abyssinian viceroy of Yemen, who in that year led an unsuccessful raid against Mecca. If that raid had succeeded, the fate of the Semitic and Mediterranean worlds might have been quite different, as the Hidjaz, the holy land of Arabia, would have stood a good chance of being converted to Monophysite Christianity.

There were Christians and Jews living among the polytheistic Arabs: according to one Islamic *hadith,* or tradition, Mohammed at the age of twelve, while on a caravan trip out of Mecca with his uncle, was noticed by a Christian hermit named Bahira who lived near Busra in Syria. Bahira remarked how the trees seemed to cross their branches in a miraculous fashion to shade him. He found a prophetic sign between the boy's shoulders and recommended to Mohammed's uncle that he protect his nephew against all dangers, as he had a great mission to perform.

Mohammed recognized the virtues of Christians in the Koran and predicted that "whosoever believeth in God and the Last Day and doeth right—shall not be seized upon by fear nor shall they grieve."

Mohammed's first wife was a rich widow, Khadidja, whom he had served in the caravan trade. He began his prophetic career about A.D. 612, when, in about his fortieth year, he withdrew into the mountains in the fashion of the Christian monks to pray, meditate, and lead an ascetic life.

The *hadiths* and the standard Arabic biographies of Mohammed tell us that the "uncreated word" of the Book (Koran = reading or a recitation) first descended into his heart on a night in the last third of the Arabic month of Ramadan in a cave on Mount Hira, in the Hidjaz. This is now celebrated as the *Lailat al-kadr,* or Night of Destiny. A mysterious being ordered him to

> Read, in the name of thy Lord who hath created,
> Created man from a clot of blood.
> Read: for thy Lord is the Most Beneficent,
> Who teacheth man to use the pen,
> Teacheth man that which he knew not.

After discovering that he had miraculously acquired the power to recite, Mohammed saw the Archangel Gabriel, who began to reveal the early, or Meccan, verses of the Koran to him, little by little, over a period of three years. Only Khadidja and a few other intimate friends and relatives, including his cousin Ali, his future father-in-law Abu Bakr, and his son-in-law Ali, recognized his prophetic mission at first. When he began to preach to the Kuraish, the pagan

Arabian tribe of his region, they persecuted and waged war against him and his clan. Mohammed's sermons violently assailed Hubal, Lat, Uzza, Manat, and the other heathen gods of the Kuraish. In these and in the Koran, he acknowledges the prophetic mission of Jesus Christ but breaks completely with the doctrine of the begotten Son and the Trinity:

> Say: God is One!
> God alone!
> He begetteth not, neither is He begotten.
> There is none resembling Him.

On July 12, 622, the beginning of the "exile" (*hidjra,* or migration), Mohammed and his followers fled to Medina, where he began the organization of his socialistic, yet theocratic community of believers and waged war against the Meccans. Here the nation, or *umma,* implying a community of believers, and occasionally misused, especially in recent times, as a synonym for the political ideal of a pan-Arab nation, first came into being. As Mohammed revealed the second, or didactic and lawgiving portion of the Koran, the community was beset by difficulties similar to those of the early Christians. It had to contend especially with the hypocrites, or *munafikun:* fair-weather Moslems who apostatized when the going got rough.

After successes in debates and in battle against pagans, Christians, and Jews, Mohammed broke completely with Judaic and Christian tradition and ordained Friday (*al-Djamaa,* the Day of the Assembly, probably a market day in Mecca) as the day of prayer. Friday became an official day of rest only quite recently in most Moslem countries: the main North African cities still retain the Sunday business holiday imposed by the French, though purely Moslem districts often close their shops on Friday. During the nationalist resistance to European rule, the closing of shops on Friday became a form of nonviolent protest: I can remember seeing French policemen in Casablanca and Algiers and their Moslem auxiliaries breaking open doors and shutters with crowbars on Friday mornings.

The Medina community became a microcosm of the future world of Islam and the birthplace of "Islamic socialism," about which we hear so much today. It was essentially a tribal socialism, with blood relationships the chief cohesive force. Tribal loyalties came before all others, and this was probably an essential difference between early Islam and the primitive Christian communities. Private property was protected, but all men were expected to behave as brothers. Charity was made one of the Five Pillars of the faith. The others are: (1) profession of God's oneness and the role of Mohammed as God's messenger; (2) the saying of the ritual prayers each day; (3) observance of the dawn-to-twilight fast during Ramadan; and (4) the pilgrimage to Mecca, when this is physically and financially possible for a believer. The *djihad,* or holy war, took on some of the attributes of tribal battles, but the *mudjahada,* or greater holy war, the spiritual struggle against the desires and inclinations of the flesh, was rated as more important.

There are many conflicting and contradictory views, depending upon which passage of the Koran or which *hadith* is cited, concerning how Moslems were expected or are expected to behave toward Christians. Essentially, in a Moslem-ruled state, the only state which is considered entirely just, there is toleration but hardly equality: like the Jews and the Sabaeans (the Old Testament People of Sheba), Christians are classed as peoples of the Book and entitled to protection, provided they are willing to adopt the status of *dhimmi,* or protégés, and pay a tax. This has not been true in North Africa since the European conquest of the nineteenth and twentieth centuries. But one must not forget that it was a set principle of Moslem polity. The Prophet is said to have written to the three Himyarite princes of Yemen:

> If a man cling to his Judaism or Christianity, he shall not be forced from it, but he shall pay the Tribute: a gold dinar of full weight for every grown man or woman, free or slave. . . . And Tribute-Payers are also under the protection of God and His Apostle; but he that shall not pay shall be their enemy.[1]

The document upon which most early relationships between Moslem rulers and their Christian subjects seems to have been based

[1] Quoted in Eric Schroeder, *Muhammed's People* (Portland, Me., 1955), p. 133; probably after al-Tabari.

is the so-called Covenant of Umar. Umar reigned as caliph from 634–644. The Covenant is supposed to be a letter written by Umar in which he quotes a letter from a group of Christian petitioners. In return for safety, he directs the Christians to pay tribute and undergo various humiliations. Upon request, they were to entertain and feed any Moslem guest in their churches for three days. The ringing of bells or the beating of the *nakus,* a wooden board used instead of bells as a call to service by some Eastern Christians, had to be done gently. Singing and chanting were to be soft. They were not to build a church, convent, hermitage, or cell, or repair any that needed repairs, or even assemble in one that was in a Moslem quarter. They could not show a cross in public; they were not allowed to learn the Koran or teach it to their children; to build houses higher than those of the Moslems; to keep or show weapons; or to keep slaves which had been the property of Moslems.

How some of these provisions came to be applied by legalistic minds later in North Africa is shown by the minute details in a *fatwa,* or legal advisory, handed down by a mufti (religious jurist) in Morocco about four centuries after the death of the Prophet:

> The Christians may not increase the height of their churches, nor change the construction if the church is built of dry bricks and they wish to rebuild it of stones. If the outside has not been completed, they will be prevented from finishing it in any case. . . . Neither Christians nor Jews will be prevented from putting finishing touches on any structure which has been built, from raising up a door, if the level of the soil is raised, or to make the necessary arrangements to accommodate worshipers inside the building.[2]

Mohammed died in 632—about the time of the surrender and conversion of Mecca. Under the orthodox caliphs, or successors of Mohammed, the spiritual force of Islam and its electric appeal to the Arabs materialized into a military offensive aimed at nothing less than conquest of the world. The only solid man-made barrier

[2] *Fatwa* of Abu Hafs al-Attar; quoted in *La Pierre de Touche des Fetwas de Ahmad Al-Wansharisi, Choix des Consultations des Faqihs du Maghreb,* in *Archives Marocaines,* XII (Paris, 1908), 223.

standing in the way of conquering the Mediterranean world was the Christian Byzantine Empire, whose subjects in the Middle East, North Africa, and elsewhere groaned under heavy taxes and were beset by religious disputes. Abu Bakr (632–634), Umar (634–644), and Uthman (644–656), the first three orthodox caliphs, waged vigorous war against it.

The extreme sensitivity and adaptability of Arabs served them in good stead in adapting Byzantine and local administrative and agricultural procedures, of which they had no previous knowledge in their primitive desert society, to found settled and sedentary communities. In doing this, they showed high ability to take the advice of Christians, Jews, and almost anyone who had a skill to teach, or an aptitude which they could borrow.

The Arab rout of the Byzantine armies began between Gaza and Jerusalem in 634. It moved swiftly forward after that with incursions into Syria and Iraq. Umar, the first *Amir al-Muminin,* or Prince of the True Believers (still one of the titles of the King of Morocco today), established the primacy of the Arabs over their taxpaying subjects. Palestine fell in 640; Persia in 641, and Egypt in 644, the year in which Umar was murdered and Uthman was chosen caliph by a group of electors.

The Christians were generally given the option of converting or paying the tax. Many seem to have regarded Islamic monotheism as closer to their own Monophysite doctrines than the theology which had been imposed on them by the Council of Chalcedon. By 680, a large number of the Monophysite churches of the Near East had gone over to Islam. In that year, the sixth ecumenical council in Constantinople denounced the Monothelete heresy, one of the latest "compromise versions" of Monophysite doctrine. The Byzantine Empire, though still holding its outposts in North Africa, had lost the three patriarchs of Alexandria, Antioch, and Jerusalem to Moslem secular control. The Patriarch of Constantinople now had no more rival episcopates in the Eastern Empire, but henceforth Constantinople was to be under constant Moslem attack and to be sacked as well by the Latin Crusaders, until its final fall to the Turks in 1453.

In trying to stem the Arab tide, the Byzantines relied heavily on allied troops (*foederati*), often heretic or non-Christian barbarians like those they used against the Vandals. These were a frontier force of hereditary soldiers, paid for their services in grants of land. The professional Greek soldiers themselves were concentrated in the mobile central army, or *comitatenses*. During the campaigns in Egypt, the Near East, and North Africa, the Byzantine intelligence service sought to learn Arab tactics and plans, then employed ruses and stratagems in the field while using tricky diplomatic methods to embroil the Arabs with other North Africans. Perhaps this is one source of the reputation of the *Rumi,* then a term applied to the Greeks, but often extended to all Christians, as being crafty and sly.

THE FIRST RAIDS IN NORTH AFRICA

West of Egypt, the Moslem conquest was to prove a difficult and lengthy task: yet the elimination of Christian elements, compared to the Middle East, where large Christian communities paid the taxes and survived, was to be almost total. On the face of things, the situation in most of North Africa must have looked like a pushover to the Arab commanders. The Byzantines held and controlled far less territory than had the Romans. The graft of Byzantine tissue onto the body of Africa had never been healthy: now it was dying. The Berber tribes had resumed their independent ways. Monophysite refugees had kept Christianity weak and divided since the Vandal invasion. And, perhaps, the aura of a certain Semitic cultural tradition still lingered on from Punic times, making acceptance of the new Semitic invasion all the easier.

Ironically, the sites of the first known Christian communities in the Maghreb, Barca and Pentapolis in Cyrenaica, were the first to fall to the Moslems in 642–643. The Arabs were developing a powerful Mediterranean fleet which captured Cyprus and Aradus in 649–650. Later it was to threaten Constantinople itself. By this time, a strong element of shrewd military and political calculation appeared mixed in Arab motives, along with the pristine religious fervor. The Arab commanders realized that if the Berbers could be converted to Islam, they would make excellent troops to use against the Byzantines. During the early Arab incursions in the Maghreb, al-Tabari tells us, the Caliph Uthman in Medina sent letters to two of his commanders in which he said: "You are not far from Constantinople. Take your arms there, ask the Berbers who have embraced Islam for auxiliaries." When the Berbers had furnished the troops, the Moslem generals left for Constantinople by sea.

In 646, Gregory, the Byzantine governor of Africa, made things easier for the Arabs by clashing with the central power in Constantinople: he revolted and proclaimed himself emperor. The Arabs captured Tripoli just after 647, but Uthman's governor in Egypt was content to collect a tribute there and push no further.

The Arabic name for Tunisia, next goal of the Arab armies, was *Ifrikiya,* simply an Arabized version of the Latin, Africa. A favorite tale of Arab historians is that when the general Ibn Abi Sarh, governor in Egypt, suggested that a spearhead might be pushed westward from Tripoli in order to conquer *Ifrikiya,* Uthman, who had received many unfavorable reports about the Maghreb, indulged in a play of words based on the Arabic root *f·r·k.* "That country," he is supposed to have told the governor, "should be called not *Ifrikiya* but *mufarika*" (that which provokes dissension or disorder). This is what has led some historians to adduce the tradition of the Maghreb, in Eastern Arab eyes, as "the far-off land of perfidy."

The stronghold of the Byzantine patrician Gregory was at Sutefula (today's Sbeitla, Tunisia). In earlier encounters in Tripolitania, Gregory had rejected the option of accepting the Koran or paying tribute. His armies consisted of a host of Berbers and probably assorted Christian riffraff, including Latins and Vandals who still lingered on. Gregory's chief asset, at least from the literary viewpoint of the Arab chroniclers who came after him, was that he is supposed to have had a handsome daughter who could shoot a bow, ride to perfection, wield a mean blade, and who fought at her father's side.

This fine specimen of Christian womanhood apparently fell into the hands of Zubair, the Arab general who defeated and killed Gregory at Sbeitla in 647. Refusing to make her a slave, Zubair is said to have announced to his entourage that his sword was consecrated only to the service of religion and that he fought for a reward "far above the charms of mortal beauty or the riches of this transitory life."

Christian Africa had a few more years of respite. Discord had erupted on Moslem home soil. After the accession of Ali to the caliphate in 656, civil war broke out. This first serious outbreak of strife within the Moslem ranks ousted Ali from the caliphate and gave it to Muawiyah ibn Abi Sufian. He came from the Kuraish, whose conversions were suspected of being dictated by political expediency. Muawiyah remained caliph until 680. He moved the Umaiyad (Ommaid) Caliphate, as it was now called, to Damascus, and it lasted until 750. However, Ali's followers, the Shiites, or simply The Party, insisted on remaining loyal to Ali and his progeny, claiming that God had designated him as caliph through Mohammed and that the caliphate was his by legal, hereditary succession. They recognized neither the Umaiyads nor their successors, the Abbasids. The Shiite schism has affected North Africa in many ways, despite the fact that it follows the orthodox legal and religious code, or *sunna,* today, in opposition to the Shiites.

Muawiyah, a shrewd and calculating man, had a Christian wife and Christian advisers, and he reorganized his armies and navy along Byzantine lines. He pushed the conquests of Islam into Turkey and as far as Central Asia. Most important for us, he took a strong interest in North Africa.

THE FOUNDATION OF KAIRAWAN AND THE "CHRISTIAN" COUNTERATTACK

The general whom Muawiyah chose to lead the Moslem offensive in North Africa was Ukbah ibn Nafi. He was the nephew of Amr, who had conquered Egypt. Ukbah had captured the first Christian stronghold west of Egypt, at Barca. His path into the Maghreb was prepared by Muawiyah's governor of Egypt, Ibn Hudaidj, who in 647 raided Tunisia, defeating a Byzantine army which had landed at Sousse, seizing and sacking the fortress of Jaloula, and then returning to Egypt laden with loot.

Ibn Khaldun, the great judge, writer, and adventurer, who died in 1406 and whose histories are the chief source of all our knowledge about North Africa in this period, tersely sums up the problems that faced Ukbah:

> After the formation of the Islamic community the Arabs set out to propagate their religion among other nations. Their

> armies penetrated into the Maghreb and captured all its camps and cities. They endured much in their struggles with the Berbers, who as Ibn Abi Yazid [one of the early Arab historians] has told us, apostatized twelve times before Islam gained a firm hold over them. These Arabs did not establish themselves in these parts as tent dwellers or as nomadic tribes because the need to maintain their authority did not allow them to occupy the open country, but limited them to the towns and camps.[3]

The Christians in North Africa were more disgruntled than ever by Byzantine rule. A new edict of the Emperor Constans II (641–668), called "The Type," severely sanctioned certain deviations in the Church ritual. As usual, it stirred the strongest sort of opposition in the Maghreb. Gennadius, a Byzantine usurper, appears to have negotiated with the Moslems and may have helped Ukbah's passage into the west: in any case, the emperor backed a rival of Gennadius and the result was more of the usual internal strife, just at the moment when Ukbah's new offensive was to lead to the first permanent Moslem implantation west of Tripolitania.

Ukbah decided to create a great fortress and base of operations in the central Tunisian desert. He may have chosen the site which he called Kairawan (The Place of Arms) because there had been Byzantine garrisons and some Byzantine fortifications there to build on, though this is by no means certain. "I would build a city which can serve as a place of arms for Islam until the end of time," he is said to have proclaimed at the founding in 670. The Great Mosque of Kairawan, Islam's first permanent citadel in the Maghreb, took five years to build.

Ukbah's new Moslem Tunisia became for a while something which it has traditionally tried to avoid being, especially in our own day, a dependency of Moslem Egypt. Ukbah temporarily fell from grace and was replaced as governor of Tunisia by Abu al-Muhadjir. But Ukbah and his armies moved on westward into Algeria with lightning speed. He passed through Bougie, but may have bypassed Cherchel and other Byzantine strong points on his way to Tangier. There is no certain way of knowing how extensive were his first

[3] See Ibn Khaldun, *Prolegomena,* trans. M. de Slane (Paris, 1934), pp. 15–16.

operations in Algeria or Morocco. We do know that Julian, the Byzantine exarch at Tangier (called by Arab historians the "King" of Tangier), and who controlled at least one tribe of Christianized Berbers, the Ghomara, is supposed to have dissuaded Ukbah from attacking the Christian (Arian) Visigoth kingdom in Spain. Their interview, says the Moroccan historian al-Slawi, went like this:

JULIAN: Do you want to ride to your destruction among the Visigoths, cut off from all reinforcement by sea and leaving impious Berbers behind you?

UKBAH: Where are the impious Berbers?

JULIAN: In the Sus Valley. They are men of great bravery and strength.

UKBAH: What is their religion?

JULIAN: They have none; they live like beasts and are ignorant that the existence of God is a truth.[4]

Did Ukbah really push on into southern Morocco, as far as the Sus, traditional abode of witches and sorcerers, to convert the "impious Berbers"? The traditional story is that he arrived somewhere along the Atlantic coast of Morocco. There are as many Moroccan villages claiming this honor today as there are sites of George Washington's overnight stops in the Eastern United States.

Other accounts embroider on this and picture Ukbah as a sort of Arab Alexander, longing for new worlds beyond the western ocean to conquer for Islam.

Even if the North African Byzantines were to a great degree enervated, some of their Christian Berber allies were not. The great hero of the Christian resistance in North Africa, whose importance may have been magnified by nostalgic French historians, was a chief named Kosaila. His Christian tribe, the Awreba, has a curious story. The Awreba apparently constituted a Christian Berber kingdom called Pomaria, near present-day Tlemcen, which has since become a center of Moslem learning and religious conservatism in Algeria. Ibn Khaldun pinned the Christian label on Kosaila, and it has stuck. Kosaila had a lieutenant called Seherdid al-Rumi, a

[4] Ahmed ben Khaled en-Naciri es-Slawi, *Kitab El Istiqça Li Akhbar Dawal El Maghreb el-Aksa,* 3 vols., trans. A. Geraille (Paris, 1923), I, 181.

Christian like himself. According to another Arab historian, Ibn Abd al-Hakam, Kosaila was supported by the "Greeks of North Africa." He had previously been captured by Ukbah and put in chains, but he escaped and led a large allied army of Berbers and Byzantines against Ukbah, who was killed in 683 and buried in the oasis of Sidi Ukbah, near Biskra (Algeria), still a site for Moslem pilgrimages. Kosaila captured Kairawan. For a fleeting instant of history, he seems to have been the master of all the Maghreb. Then, in 686, the new caliph, Abd al-Malik, issued orders in Damascus for a fresh attack. Kosaila met death in battle at the hands of the Moslem General Zohair ibn Kais, at Mems, near Kairawan. Zohair retreated, only to be ambushed and killed by a sea-borne Byzantine raiding force at Barca.

THE JEWISH RESISTANCE: KAHENA

Some oversimplified French accounts of the Arab conquest have often neglected the Byzantines and have pictured the resistance as having been the work of Christianized Berbers entirely. The Awreba tribe, however, when it lost its power seems to have retired to its kingdom near Tlemcen. Then, in 790, when the Arab Idrisid dynasty moved west to establish its power in Fez, the Awreba gave the Moslems a cordial reception. It was from the Awreba that Idris recruited his troops for the final Arab conquest of Morocco; the members of the tribe converted directly from Christianity to Islam. The explanation for the rapid conversion is probably the same one which can be used for the relative success of the Roman conquest and all the other well-organized foreign invasions of Morocco (Ukbah's definitely had *not* been well organized). A population of Christian Berbers, who had been at least superficially "civilized" by Carthaginian and then by Roman colonialism, but was then completely cut off from the Roman and Christian worlds (including their latter-day Byzantine version), found itself faced by a heavily armed and determined force that had the added strength of a powerful new religion and rallied to it at once.

After Kosaila's death the torch of resistance passed to a tribe of Jewish Berbers called the Jerawa, whose stronghold was in the eastern Aurès Mountains. They were apparently camel-riding nomads.

A word may be helpful at this point about the Jewish communities in North Africa, since they played some role then—though they no longer do—in resisting Islamization. North African Jews came in four historic migrations. The first seems to have been about 320 B.C., when the Greek prefect Ptolemy Soter deported 100,000 Jewish captives from Palestine to Africa. These were landed at Carthage and migrated westward, leaving traces at Volubilis in Morocco. Many Moroccan Jews—about 80,000 remained in the modern kingdom in 1964—still call themselves *Plistim,* "Palestinians."

A second migration came to Morocco after 150 B.C. as fugitives from a persecution in Cyrenaica; these settled in the Moroccan Atlas and Rif Mountains. Another wave arrived in Tunisia, Algeria, and Morocco after the great Jewish revolt of Simon bar Khotba against Roman rule in Palestine in A.D. 68. Finally, beginning in the fourth century A.D., the Jews of Spain began to flee the persecutions of the Arian Visigoths: this Jewish emigration from Spain continued by fits and starts until the final persecutions carried out by Christians during their reconquest of Moslem Spain from the thirteenth to the fifteenth centuries.

Kahena was the queen of the Jerawa. Her name, in the Arabic, Hebrew, and Punic languages, denotes a priestess, or perhaps a sorceress. Her Arab adversary was Hasan, the governor of Egypt. The matter-of-fact Arab historian al-Bayan writes:

> After destroying Carthage [about 687–689], Hasan then demanded to know who was the most powerful chief in *Ifrikiya,* and he was told that it was a woman who governed the Berbers and who was generally known by the name of Kahena. She lives, it was said, in the Aurès Mountains. This Jewish woman predicts the future and all that she announces comes to pass. If once she were killed, Hasan would meet neither resistance nor rival again. Hasan marched against her.[5]

Kahena, who was also reported by *hadith* to have "supernatural knowledge which her familiar demons taught her," led her Jewish Berbers against the enemy with a force that resembled the avenging

[5] Al-Bayan, *Histoire de l'Afrique et de l'Espagne,* trans. E. Fagnan (Algiers, 1901), p. 25.

fury of some primitive Haganah. Hasan's troops were expelled from the Gabès region of Tunisia and took refuge in Tripolitania. Finally, about 693, and after defeating three Arab offensives, she was conquered and killed in the Aurès Mountains at a place called Bir al-Kahena (Kahena's Well).

The French historian E. F. Gautier sees in Kahena's final defeat one of the main turning points in the North African drama: the end of organized resistance to Islam. He compares the coalition of Roman remnants, Greeks, and Christian and Jewish Berbers who were defeated with Kosaila and Kahena with the alliance of Gauls and Romans who successfully turned back the Germanic invasions of France around 500, with the vital difference that Kahena and Kosaila failed.

In any case, Kahena seems hardly to have been loved by all her people, some of whom regarded her as a tyrant and dictator. In fact, she may have even been an anti-Semitic Jew. Jewish folklore in eastern Algeria still contains this lament:

> O sons of Yeshurun
> Do not forget your persecutors
> The Chaldeans, Caesar, and Hadrian, and Kahiya [sic].
> This cursed woman, more cruel than all the others combined
> She gave our virgins to her warriors
> She washed her feet in the blood of our children
> God created her to make us expiate our sins
> But God hates those who make His people suffer
> Give me back my children
> So that they may wear mourning for me:
> I have left them
> In the hands of Kahiya.[6]

Legend has it that Kahena had two natural sons, one Berber and one Greek, probably symbolic of the anti-Moslem coalition. After the defeat of Hasan, she is supposed to have adopted a young and handsome Arab prisoner, telling him, "You are the most handsome and the bravest man that I have ever seen. So I wish to give you

[6] Quoted in André Chouraqui, *Les Juifs d'Afrique du Nord* (Paris, 1952), p. 48.

my milk so that you may become the brother of my two sons. Among us Berbers, the kinship of milk gives the right of mutual inheritance." She then took farina mixed with oil, smeared it on her breasts and let all three youths eat from them. The night before her final defeat, she ordered all three to desert and surrender to Hasan.

Her defeat was the signal for the tribes to submit *en masse* to Hasan and to convert to Islam as well. For the first time, there was a core of native Moslems in the Maghreb. According to Ibn Khaldun's version of the legend, Hasan had the good sense to turn command of the Aurès over to Kahena's three sons and then to put the new Moslem warriors to good use. For there were many new tribes and many new lands yet to conquer.

CHAPTER VIII

THE CHRISTIAN DIASPORA

Church work goes on slowly.
SEVENTEENTH-CENTURY
ENGLISH PROVERB

Islam's conquests of 680–1250 split the Mediterranean into Christian and Moslem halves, divided by a line running from the Strait of Gibraltar to the Bosporus. This line has remained, despite aggression and counteraggression by both sides, until 1965. The Christians who lived inside Moslem North Africa were of two sorts. First, they were Berbers who remained in a diaspora until the last vestiges of the native Church were wiped out during the epoch of the Crusades. By 1100, Europeans—merchants, militiamen, adventurers, and missionaries—had begun to appear in the Maghreb. In some cities a few descendants of Byzantine Greeks probably lingered for a few generations after 700.

Of the secret life of the native Christians, severed from Rome, from Constantinople, and often from the Christian portions of Spain, we know little. But the isolation of the Christians within Moslem society is evident.

Around 1150, the Kadi (cadi) of Marrakesh, Musa ibn Hammad, consulted the illustrious physician-philosopher of Córdoba, Ibn Rushd, or Averroës (1126–1198), who had come to the puritanical Marrakesh court of the Almohad sultan, Abu Yakub Yusuf, about a former Christian—we do not know whether he was a native or a European—who had embraced Islam. In public, said the kadi, he professed himself a Moslem, but it was reported that he had secretly remained a Christian. A search of his house revealed a room resembling a chapel, "in which there was a recessed alcove turned toward the East. An oil lamp was suspended there and there were various objects upon which there remained the traces of melted tapers. Books, written in Christian [i.e., Latin] characters, and many candles. A stick with a crosspiece forming a cross and tiny round, flat wafers, imprinted with a seal" were also found, together with a piece of wood resting on four legs which might be used to read the Gospel. Should this suspect, asked the kadi, be condemned as a *zindik*—a dangerous heretic (also applied to Manichaeans)? Suspicion alone, replied Ibn Rushd, and even the grave circumstantial evidence, was not enough.

> The testimony of irreproachable Moslem witnesses would be needed. Do you not see that if the rumor circulates about a Moslem that he drinks wine and if wine is found set before him on several occasions, he will not be subject to the penalty applicable to those who drink wine, even if he is under strong suspicion? A man accused by public rumor of fornicating with a woman of loose morals, notoriously known as such, and who locks himself in his house with her for a length of time, will not incur the penalty of fornication, even if his being together with her for a long time makes the fact of fornication probable. He is subject only to a painful corporal punishment. Likewise, this converted Christian incurs only a painful correction as a result of the suspicion weighing on him following the discovery in his house of the objects you mentioned.[1]

THE LAST LATIN COMMUNITIES

The main center of Roman and of Christian culture in Morocco had been Volubilis. Byzantine power at Ceuta and Tangier probably never penetrated to Volubilis. An eighth-century manuscript shows that there was an episcopate of Tangier until sometime in the eighth century. But Tangier disappears from an episcopal list drawn up by Pope Leo the Wise in 883, leaving only Ceuta, where a church had been dedicated to the Virgin after the Byzantine reconquest in 534. Ceuta was generally treated as a political part of Spain after that, as it is under General Franco today, and we know of no later bishops in Morocco.

In 655, eight years after the defeat of the Byzantine exarch Greg-

[1] Ibn Rushd, quoted by Ahmad al-Wansharisi, *Archives Marocaines,* XII, 271–72.

ory at Sbeitla and Ukbah's march to the west, the city of Volubilis was still using Latin and Roman names and titles. A Christian tribe succeeded the Romans as masters of the city and its hinterland. By the end of the sixth century and during the seventh, Volubilis became a rallying point for Christian refugees fleeing western Algeria and eastern Morocco. In 656, just a year before the outbreak of the first great revolt of Berber Kharidjite heretics against the new Arab conquerors, the death of a prefect named Julius is recorded in an inscription.

By this time the rulers of Volubilis seem to have become a council of Christian chiefs. According to Ibn Khaldun, the remnants of Kosaila's tribe, the Awreba, migrated from Tlemcen westward to Volubilis. Other tribes practicing either Christianity or Judaism were the Fendelulas, the Balula, the Mediuna, and the Fazzaz. Ibn Khaldun says that the Berber confederation called the Bagwata, which held the area between Fez and Tlemcen, supported the heretics and believes that the presence of the Christian Awreba in Volubilis helped to insure their victory. Ibn Khaldun evidently worked on the theory that Moslem heretics and Christians were natural allies against the True Believers.

In Algeria, the last known Christian communities were at Numerus Syrorum (Lalla Marnia, not far from the birthplace of Ahmed ben Bella); Albulae (Ain Temouchent, the domain of wealthy French colonists and stronghold of the "Christian" terrorist Secret Army Organization in 1962); Altava (Larmorciere) and, as mentioned, Pomaria (Tlemcen), which lasted the longest. The evidence is epigraphic: a tomb in Tlemcen mentions a dead man as having been "taken" from his near and dear and describes the tomb as his "house of eternity" (*domum*[*a*] *eternale*[*m*]). The last Christian gravestones there still displayed a chrism.

During the first century after the Arab conquest, coins were struck, probably at Carthage, with purely Latin legends. Some of them carry the inscription: *Muse f*[*ilius*] *Nusir,* the name of Musa ibn Nusair, the Moslem general who followed up Ukbah's drive to the west and invaded Spain.

Sometime in the eleventh century, the Patriarch of Alexandria sent an extraordinary mission of bishops to Kairawan. They were ordained by the patriarch to "cherish and revive the dying embers of Christianity." Gibbon takes this to indicate that Latin Christianity was "decadent" and that the Orthodox clergy was trying to be the agent of resuscitation. A better guess would be founded on the fact that early Islam in North Africa, especially in Kairawan, was tolerant toward eastern Christians—one version says they were Copts—whom Ukbah was said to have installed in the city, along with some Jewish families, and that the bishops sent from Alexandria were merely to minister to the Orthodox flock there.

During the second half of the eleventh century, seven letters were sent from the Roman Curia concerning internal affairs of the Church of Africa. They are written in Latin, and addressed to the local clergy. From them we know that there were only five bishops left in 1050 in the ancient territories where there had been hundreds.

Bishop Servandus of Hippo had to go to Rome to be consecrated by the pope, since the three bishops required for the ceremony were no longer to be found in the area. He returned to Hippo with letters from Gregory VII, at that time occupied with preparing the First Crusade, to the Primate Cyriacus, the people of Hippo, and the Emir En-Nasir. In 1114 there was still a pastor in Bougie, Algeria, where in 1212 the pathetic participants in the Children's Crusade were sold into slavery and where Ramón Lull, the Catalan mystic and luminary, became the first missionary to be martyred by the Algerian Moslems a century later.

In 1076, only three bishops remained. In 963, the Andalusian geographer al-Bakri found a Christian community with a church at Tlemcen. Further and more recent evidence of the diaspora of the Church is provided by discovery of a dozen Latin epitaphs in the necropolis of An-Agila, Tripolitania (tenth century), and two others at Kairawan (eleventh century). Around 1150, the geographer al-Idrisi finds the Latin language still in use at Gafsa, in southern Tunisia.

When the Berber ruler of the Almohad dynasty, Abd al-Mumin, conquered Tunis in July, 1159, he destroyed the episcopate of Carthage and put an end to the formal Church hierarchy in Africa. Native Christians who remained were exiled or forced into apostasy.

LATIN TRACES IN THE MAGHREB

Much has been made by some French historians of the lingering traces of a native Christian Latin culture in North Africa. The most interesting one is perhaps the fact that the Moroccans, both Arabs and Berbers, still use the Julian calendar in agricultural life. The Berber vocabulary and the spoken Arabic used in Morocco, which includes words of Berber origin, employ words with Latin stems for farming terms. This is sometimes presented as evidence of a "certain nostalgia" or a "memory" of Roman Christianity. Perhaps, but a present-day Moroccan historian contends that this Roman terminology is more recent, "because it comes from Moslem Andalusia, which in turn had it from Romanized Iberian dialects. It was the Berber mountaineers, crossing over into Andalusia, who took up agriculture in the Spanish Sierra more than did the others. They rapidly adapted to the local agricultural habits and terminology. Moroccan farmers still celebrate annually the festival al-Ansara [corresponding to Midsummer Day, June 24, sometimes called the Day of St. John the Baptist], as did the Andalusians in the time of the Umaiyads." [2]

Reluctant as the Berbers were to accept Islam, it seems to have been far more to their taste than Christianity. Since the eighth century, North Africa has looked neither to the Latin West nor to Byzantium for its religion, its language, its civilization, and its culture, but to the Arab East. What happened in the Maghreb after the Arab conquest was less the establishment of Arab hegemony than it was the coming of the Arab way of life and of the Islamic religion, adulterated, as it still is, at the popular rural level by the remnants of the ancient religions, superstitions, and cultures of Rome, Carthage, and the pre-Phoenician Libyans.

The appeal of early Islam to North Africans must have been similar to that fascination which it seems to hold today for so many Christians and pagans in Africa and large parts of the Asian world: it is a missionary faith, without hierarchy or priesthood, promising

[2] Abdelazziz Benabdallah, "L'Islam et la Structuration de l'Etat Marocain," *La Nation Africaine* (Rabat, Oct. 7, 1962).

its communicants that contact with God which, to many Afro-Asian minds, does not seem to exist in Christianity. Then as now it seemed both to preach and to practice the natural equality of man. Women and slaves, black and white, sound and infirm, were all supposed to be social equals if they accepted Islam and to be under the protection of God. The North Africans, too, saw in Islam a faith which they thought at first could not be twisted and deviated in its pristine simplicity, as they had seen happen to Christianity in the heresies of Arius, of Donatus, and of scores of others, or in the linguistic, political, and doctrinal barriers they had observed growing up between the Eastern and Western Churches.

For three millennia, the southern coast of the Mediterranean had known a multitude of gods. There had been animal gods and tribal totems; mother goddesses and sex goddesses; thinly disguised Western versions of outlandish Egyptian deities; priests and oracles who were the mouthpieces of a god, but who were nearly always the arms of some oppressing secular power as well. God-kings and god-emperors had taken and turned the sacred texts to their own profane ends.

The largely unlettered rural Berbers of the west were not the sophisticated bourgeois of the Syrian cities. Neither Latin nor Byzantine ways of life had taken hold among them. This, not any greater intolerance on the part of their Arab conquerors, is probably the real reason why no communities of native Christians like the Arab Christians of the East survived or prospered on the soil of the Maghreb. The Berber soul, while capable of assimilating some of the materially advantageous teaching of the Phoenicians, the Romans, and perhaps even the Greeks, remained below the surface as parochial as it had ever been. To the Berbers, it seemed that the new Prophet in the East had been a simple man of plain talk: a rustic man of the outdoors like themselves who had been miraculously endowed with the gift of eloquence, and who, through the Holy Book and through the agency of his successors, had sent the message of God directly to them.

Beginning with the middle of the twelfth century, Christianity in North Africa became a European import, as it had been under Rome. It was preached, propagated, defended, and guarded by Europeans. At first, the expeditions of the Crusaders, who thought they could reconquer by the sword the lands and shrines lost to Islam, barely brushed the shores of the Maghreb. They caused little friction or intolerance in everyday life, except at the time or place military force was applied. The Christians in North Africa, some of whom we meet later, were mainly scattered European missionaries, European militiamen in Moslem service, and peaceful merchants of Venice, Genoa, and Pisa. Like the Jews, they lived in privileged, or at least protected, Christian enclaves within the body politic of North African Islam. Except for the massacre of a few of the more ill-prepared or importunate missionaries, these Europeans lived in relative peace and harmony with their Moslem neighbors. This peace, and the spirit of entente between Christian and Moslem, was to be rudely shattered by the gradual return of Europeans in military force, generally men who sought the things of this world rather than those of the hereafter and who came prepared to fight for them.

PART TWO

THE KINGDOMS OF MOHAMMED

CHAPTER IX

MOSLEM IMPERIALISM AND BERBER REVOLT

> All orthodox Muslims regard the Sharia as setting the perfect standard for human society, although their own practice may fall short of it.
>
> SIR HAMILTON GIBB, *The Structure of Religious Thought in Islam,* 1948

On a sultry spring night, rambling through the bazaars of Cairo with a friend, we paused in one of the little squares near the great Mosque of al-Azhar. It was like being back in Fez or Marrakesh. On a richly colored though slightly frayed rug sat an old storyteller weaving tales of the past for an audience of perhaps a hundred, mainly young folk but some old men too, gathered in a circle around him. His was a traditional tale, which many of the best-known Arab chroniclers wrote down, about the ancient defection of the west from the rule of the East.

"In the days of Ukbah and just afterward," the old man said, "the newly converted Moslems of North Africa had been good and religious subjects of their caliph. But seditious agents from Iraq, that perfidious Oriental land, circulated among them, urging them to rise up and break away from the rule of the Umaiyads. 'Were not their officers,' said the Iraqi dividers, 'as cruel as they were corrupt?'

"At first, the people of the Maghreb were loyal: 'We can scarcely blame the Prince of the True Believers,' they said, 'for the misdeeds of his civil servants.' But it came about that a Moroccan named Maysara and ten companions set out for the court of the caliph to seek an audience and see for themselves how God's kingdom on earth was really administered.

"When they arrived at court, wearied by their long journey from the west, they were kept waiting and not allowed to see the Prince of the True Believers, Hisham. Finally, to cut through the red tape, they told Hisham's secretary to tell his master for them that 'when the caliph commands an expedition against the infidel Christians, he may include us among his own Arab soldiers. But when it comes time to divide the spoil, he may leave us out.

" 'Not only this: our sheep are killed, and unborn lambs are torn from the bellies of our ewes to make white fur cloaks for Hisham. This we have suffered, since it seems not much for the Commander of the Faithful.'

"The secretary promised to pass on their message to Hisham.

"But Maysara and his companions could wait no longer. Their money was nearly gone, and so they wrote down their names on a paper which they gave to a counselor of the court. 'If your master asks who we were,' they said, 'give him this.'

"Then they returned to the Land Furthest West, and when they arrived, they killed Hisham's governor and made themselves the rulers of the province."

The storyteller had summed up well the main reasons why the Berbers rejected rule from the East. These events happened in 741, when Hisham had to send one Syrian army, which was defeated, and then another, commanded by the nephew of the first general, to put down the great revolt which swept North Africa from Tangier to Kairawan. This friction between Arab rulers and their Berber subjects was destined to delay the Islamization of North Africa, the real Islamization in depth, for at least three centuries more. This is perhaps one of the reasons why neither the forlorn pockets of Christians in their diaspora nor the popes concerned for their welfare had given up hope.

It was hard for the Berber converts to Islam to accept the idea of the caliphate. Their resistance to it was one of the reasons why the Abbasid caliphs, who nominally ruled the Moslem world, from Baghdad, between 750 and 1258, were never able to exercise real authority west of Tunisia, except for a short time in 761.

As a universal institution, the caliphate had two great Christian rivals, both of them successors of the Roman Empire: one was the new Holy Roman Empire of the West, which Charlemagne founded in Western Europe on Christmas day, 800, in formal alliance with the Roman Pope. The other was the Byzantine Empire of the east. Like the two Christian empires, the caliphate concerned itself with both temporal power over men's bodies and with the salvation of their souls. But most of the resemblance ends there.

The caliphs were, first and foremost, the successors of the Prophet. The Koran says: "He [God] it is who placed you as successors in the earth and hath raised some of you in rank above the others, that He may try you by [the test of] that which He hath given you."

This idea was developed by the jurist al-Mawardi, who defined the caliph's function as "to look after the welfare of the Moslems, spiritual and temporal, by defending them from internal and external enemies and by seeing that the revealed laws were observed." [1] Ibn Khaldun finds that the caliphate substitutes for the Prophet, "inasmuch as it serves, like him, to protect religion and exercise political leadership of the world," guiding men in conformity with the dictates of the *sharia,* or religious law.[2]

As the caliphate took on more and more of these political overtones, it grew harder for its agents to hold onto their far-flung subjects in the west, crushed by the overpowering weight of taxes. Spain was lost to the Abbasids in 756. The new Umaiyad dynasty which under Abd al-Rahman I began to rule Moslem Spain from Córdoba in 756 and lasted through almost three brilliant centuries until 1031 made only nominal acknowledgment of Abbasid spiritual authority. The Umaiyads mentioned the caliph in their Friday prayers and struck his image on coins.

The first and fundamental challenge to the Umaiyad caliphs of the Orient had been, as we have seen, the revolt of Ali and his companions. But even before Ukbah's armies had ridden across North Africa, another Eastern schism had arisen which was to have grave consequences in the west: the revolt of the Kharidjites, or "Seceders." They claimed that any Moslem in good standing could become imam, or spiritual guide, or even caliph, and that good works, rather than divine grace, was the most important thing in the life of caliphs, imams, or ordinary men.

[1] Abu al-Hasan al-Mawardi, *Al-Akham as-Sultaniyah* (Bonn, 1853), p. 230.

[2] Ibn Khaldun, *Muqadimma,* trans. Franz Rosenthal (London, 1958), I, 388.

The Kharidjite idea that an imam may be deposed if he departs from the pathway of true religion was used against Mohammed V of Morocco when his French enemies and their Berber allies deposed him in 1953, pretending to act in the name of orthodoxy. The Kharidjites thought there was no inherent superiority in any race or tribe, especially the Kuraish of Arabia. They liked to destroy the pretensions of the caliphs to omniscience by quoting the Koranic phrase, "the decision is God's alone" (*La hukm illa li-llah*). The orthodox believers, however, considered that the Kharidjites had placed themselves outside the *sunna,* or "practice" of the Prophet. In their thinking about community life, they were very close to the clannishness of the Berbers and their emphasis on the tribe. Punishment for sins would not be eternal, they believed, provided one were willing to observe the rules of the tribe and the community.

THE HERETIC DYNASTIES

Kharidjism began to spread in North Africa under the last Umaiyads and soon developed three wings: an "extreme left," or Azrakism; a "center left," or Sofrism; and an "extreme right," or Ibadism.

Most of the remaining unorthodox Moslems in North Africa today are the Ibadites of southern Algeria, on the Island of Jerba, and the Jebel Nafusa in Tripolitania—all areas where Berber language and culture are still strong.

Around 740, the caliph's governors in Kairawan decided to force the new Berber converts to pay two taxes, normally paid only by Christians or Jews: the head tax, and a levy on real estate. In Tangier, the governor of Morocco soon found himself with a full-scale proletarian revolt of the Ghomara (onetime Christians), Meknasa, and pagan Bergwata tribes on his hands. They appointed a Sofrite water carrier as "caliph," later deposing and massacring him when they suspected him of being too prone to compromise.

A Bergwata tribesman named Saleh ibn Tarif proclaimed himself the New Prophet; moved the Ramadan fast to the month of Rajab; decreed ten prayers daily instead of five and even changed the date of the sacrifice of al-Adna, when Moslems are supposed to commemorate the offer of Abraham to sacrifice his son Isaac, from the Moslem month of Dhul al-Hidja to that of al-Moharram. Saleh's followers were forbidden to wash after sex relations unless they were illicit ones. A man could have as many wives as he wished (instead of the four specified by the Koran), provided they were not cousins of the husband. Thieves were to be killed wherever encountered.

Saleh went so far as to publish a new "Koran" in the Berber language, though written down in Arabic characters. It had twenty-four chapters (instead of the 114 suras of the Holy Koran), each named after a prophet or something in popular folklore (Adam, Noah, Moses, Aaron, the Devil, the Wonders of the World, etc.). He borrowed an idea from the Shiites, the followers of Ali, and proclaimed that he was the *mahdi,* or Hidden Imam: the supreme being who was to appear at the end of time, and that he would then come marching in behind Jesus (Sidna Isa), praying. This weird Sofrite heresy was not completely stamped out in Morocco, despite all the vigorous military action undertaken against it, until the rise of the Almovarids in the middle of the eleventh century.

The holy city of Kairawan itself was a victim of Sofrite tribesmen from southern Tunisia, who sacked it, and Ibadites from the Jebel Nafusa, who drove the Abbasid governor from Tripoli. The governor of Egypt sent troops who crushed the Sofrite imam, Abu al-Khattab, southwest of Zelten, Tripolitania, after some hard fighting, in 761. In Algeria, a noble of Persian origin named Rostam who had controlled Kairawan for a time withdrew to the mountains near Tiaret, in southwestern Algeria and became imam there around 778. Only in Tunisia did Moslem orthodoxy and Arab order prevail. Just as this part of the Maghreb had been the one most intensely "Europeanized" and Christianized under the Romans, now it became the portion most intensely occupied and "Arabized" by the new invaders.

In the Ibadite kingdom in Algeria, society was puritanical but not intolerant: one Arab historian says there were Christians living in Tahert, the capital, including "a knight who was among the well-known defenders of the city." Shiite attackers destroyed Tahert in 911, but the Ibadites survived.

MOROCCO

In 788, a descendant and a follower of Fatima and Ali, Idris ibn Abdallah, arrived in Morocco, a refugee from an Oriental massacre by the orthodox Abbasids of rebel Shiite elements. Tunisia was under orthodox control and Algeria was held by hostile Kharidjites, so Idris decided to found a kingdom in Morocco. His first allies were none other than the Awreba, the Christian tribe once led by Kosaila. Idris and his lieutenant, Rashid, through eloquence and through their knowledge of Oriental administrative and agricultural techniques, were evidently able to convince the Awreba that the Islamic way of life was best. With the idea of making Morocco his base for the reconquest of the Orient, Idris first tried to found a capital on the remains of Volubilis (Walilia). Finding it too small, he founded a new city at *madinat fas* (the Town of the Pickaxe), on the site of the Andalusian quarter of today's Fez. With his Awreba allies, he attacked the Jewish and Christian tribes still holding out in the mountains and apparently converted them one by one, carving out a new, embryo Berber-Moslem nation in north-central Morocco.

This was the time when Christian, Moslem, Jewish, and even pagan elements that had survived—some Moroccan authors lumped all the non-Moslems together under the name of *majus,* or fire-worshipers—formed a new Moroccan Moslem community.

Idris had a son by Kenza, a Berber concubine. Kenza and the faithful Rashid raised him. In 791 or 792, the Caliph Harun al-Rashid, the ruler of the Arabian Nights who sent an elephant and the keys of the Holy Sepulcher to Charlemagne, dispatched to Fez a secret agent who poisoned Idris. His son took over the kingdom as Idris II. For reasons which are not clear, he executed the chief of the Awreba tribe, his onetime Christian allies, and then founded the new city of Fez on the left bank of the River Fez, across from the older *madinat fas.* It became a refuge for Arabs persecuted in the East, as Idris had been, and others in difficulty in Spain. From Kairawan and from the new Islamic state in Spain, al-Andalus, came men whom Idris enlisted as auxiliary soldiers and who helped him extend his power. Later, his kingdom broke up into separate principalities, which disappeared when a new conquering Shiite dynasty, the Fatimids, arrived and took power in 921.

FEZ

It is not easy to describe the spell which Fez has thrown over visitors ever since it began its existence. Nearly six hundred years after it was founded, the great Moroccan traveler Ibn Batuta, who had traveled into the depths of China and India and had seen and described as many lands as his contemporary, Marco Polo, wrote in praise of the Marinid king who built on the foundations Idris had left, that among "the noblest actions of our master"

> . . . we would mention the following: first, the construction of the new mosque, in the Pure City, the capital of his illustrious kingdom: this is the mosque which stands out through its beauty, the solidity of its structure; its brilliant éclat, and its marvelous arrangement; and second, the building of the great college. . . . It [Fez] has no parallel in all the civilized world in grandeur, in beauty, in magnificence, in the quantity of water, and the advantage of the site.[3]

Though it is the main city of westernmost Islam, Fez is much like some Oriental metropolis. To travelers from the East, it suggests Jerusalem or Damascus. In the secret, labyrinthine streets of the old city, which echo the soft gurgling of springs and underground rivers, no automobiles are permitted to this day, nor could they pass if they were. Despite its proud, snobbish, and cultivated bourgeoisie, its tradition-minded center of learning, the great Kairouyine University, where Ptolemaic cosmology was still being taught in the 1920's, it became the birthplace of twentieth-century Moroccan nationalism. The prestige of its great mosque and the traditions of the city are all part of the aura of Fez as the chief bastion of Oriental Islam in Morocco today.

[3] Ibn Batuta, *Voyages,* Arabic text with French translation by C. Demfremey and B. R. Shanguinetti (Paris: Imprimerie Nationale, 1942), IV, 352.

Yet Christian, Jewish, and probably pagan Berbers all had some part in its creation. Much of its culture and the strength which modern Moroccan culture has drawn from it, might be traced to this diversity in its origin. Sir Hamilton Gibb has concluded that the Berbers of Fez accepted Islam and Idris to reinforce their own power, as they had already done with the Phoenician and Roman cultures and religions, and as some of their latter-day chiefs were to do during the forty-four-year French protectorate in our own century. In other words, Islam was of primary importance to the Berbers at the crucial moment of the founding of Fez because of the prestige attached to it. Today, of course, the prestige of Islam in Morocco, as everywhere else, is being undermined by the secularizing tendencies of our age. But certainly in the intricate streets and windowless houses of Fez, it will hold out the longest.

ISLAM IN THE SAHARA

What has been said about the Islamization of Fez and northern Morocco applies to much of the Sahara desert too. The Roman occupation of North Africa and its various military and exploring missions to the south seem to have left far fewer cultural traces on the great deserts which begin south of the Atlas Mountains than it did in the north, though Christianity did, for a time, penetrate the Fezzan in southern Libya before disappearing completely.

One thing the Romans did bequeath the Arabs was the caravan trade. Using the Roman caravan routes, the Arabs discovered the profit to be made in channeling gold, ivory, and Negro slaves from the south. This trade brought Negro blood and Negro paganism into Moroccan life. The "devil dancers" of the Gnaoua, a religious brotherhood that is Sudanese in origin, whom wealthy Moroccan city dwellers still occasionally invite to their homes on festive occasions to exorcise demons, are an importation from Black Africa, with modifications acquired from Berber paganism.

The Moslem conquest of the Sahara, which reached as far south as Mali and Ghana, continued until about the beginning of the seventeenth century. Here there were no remnants of Hellenistic culture and no Christian religion to contend with—only an animism, generally far more easily absorbed into Islam's flexible ways than Berber animism had been into the rigid framework of Roman or Greek Christianity.

Islam profoundly affected desert society. As in the north, it appeared as a prestigious sociopolitical religious system which above all brought a marvelous new language, Arabic, to the desert people and moved in for a more or less comfortable coexistence with an earlier desert feudalism. The Islamic missionaries were most successful but converted the Berbers more than superficially only in the furthest west, in what is today Mauretania, Rio de Oro, and the Spanish Sahara.

THE INDEPENDENT DYNASTIES: TUNISIA

Relations between the caliphate, the Tunisian Berbers, and their new Arab masters were far better than in Morocco. From 801 to 909, a dynasty founded by Ibrahim ibn Aghlab, called the Aghlabids, ruled *Ifrikiya* in more or less orthodox harmony with the Abbasids. Tunis, after all, was not quite as far away from Baghdad as were Fez or Algiers. The Aghlabids even held the city of Tripoli to the east. Christians, in their shrinking diaspora, seem still to have played an important role in Tunis. The ruling class was composed of about 100,000 descendants of the Arab invaders. Most of their subjects were converted Berbers. But a few remaining Berber Christians, and possibly some of the progeny of the last Romans, were grouped together under the colloquial name of "Africans." These also included some *Rumi,* or Greeks, remaining from the former Byzantine garrisons. The Jews, especially physicians, formed an intellectual elite, as they did throughout most of North African history.

The belief often held in the West that Christian and Jewish minorities always suffer under Moslem governments, which are strongly influenced by religious zealots, is belied by this period of Tunisian history. The real powers behind the Aghlabid rulers were the Islamic theologians, or *fukaha,* of Kairawan. Their influence extended into every walk of life and letters, but they generated no wave of intolerance.

In the new capital of Abbasiyah, outside Kairawan, Sultan Ibn Aghlab received the envoys of Charlemagne, who came under the pretext of seeking the relics of St. Cyprian, but who actually were seeking help against the Arabs in Spain. When the Aghlabids undertook the conquest of Christian Sicily after 813, a jurist, Asad ibn al-Furat, was named commander-in-chief of the army. The campaign had no adverse effect at all on the lives of Christians and Jews living peacefully in Tunisia while the fighting was going on.

The Aghlabid ruler who decided to subdue Christian Sicily, still nominally a Byzantine province, was Ziyadat Allah I. Under Asad's command, an army of mercenaries and adventurers landed in Sicily, which was too distant for the Byzantines or even the Italian city-states to get worried about at first. By 900, the third Ziyadat Allah had practically conquered it, despite sporadic and tardy defense efforts by the Holy Roman Emperor Leo VI, as well as Venice, and even Constantinople. In the meantime, Arab armies had sacked Italian cities, including Rome, and even forced the pope to pay tribute.

THE SHIITE CONQUEST OF THE MAGHREB

Once again, a refugee from the Orient changed North Africa's history. This time he was Ubayd Allah, a Shiite who came to Algeria and won the support of a Kabylie tribe, the Ketama. He was a member of the Ismaelites, who through the centuries have grown to be one of the richest and most powerful of the Shiite sects: the late Agha Khan and his son, the Ali Khan, were its leaders in our own day. They considered that Ismael, the seventh imam, was the last of the visible imams and that his descendants still live on, each as a *mahdi,* or Hidden Imam.

The Ismaelis of North Africa, whose rulers came to be called Fatimids, were not religious obscurantists. Sir Hamilton Gibb has observed that the "reformed" Ismaeli movement wished to integrate Islam with Hellenistic culture, which, as we have seen, has never taken firm roots in North Africa. In this way they hoped to build a new religious establishment with the aid of educated city people, making a concerted missionary drive to win over the more indifferent lower classes. Jewish and Christian scholars worked with the new rulers. But their effort to give Islam a new look remained limited and scarcely penetrated the masses of the people.

Ubayd Allah had himself proclaimed *mahdi* in 910 and attacked Tunisia. In 912 he founded the Tunisian seaport of Al-Mahdiyah (city of the *mahdi*), and his victorious armies captured Tripoli. Under the name of Fatimids (followers of Ali and Fatima), they invaded Egypt in 913–914. For the first and only time in history, a western dynasty was to dominate the East for a while. Although the Fatimids established a protectorate over Morocco, with its strongest points in Sijilmassa, they met orthodox resistance in Tunisia from an unexpected quarter: the same Islamic doctors who had helped to inspire the successful holy war against Sicily now organized clandestine underground resistance.

Ubayd Allah's son, Abu al-Kasim, faced a revolt against his tyranny led by Sudanese-born Abu Yazid, "the man on the donkey" to the Arab historians, who taught the Koran at the south Tunisian oasis of Tozeur. His revolt was drowned in blood at Kairawan in 946, and his corpse "was scorched and his skin, stuffed with straw, was placed in a cage to serve as a plaything for two monkeys especially trained for that purpose." [4]

Fatimid domination in North Africa lasted another generation, during which the orthodox Moslems of Spain campaigned against the Shiite heretics in Morocco and extended their influence as far east as Algiers, where Friday prayers were said in the name of the Caliph of Córdoba. Christian counterpressure mounted in Sicily, which revolted in 947 and called on Constantinople for help. The Fatimid governor put down the Christian uprising and built a mosque at Reggio di Calabria, warning that "a single stone removed from this edifice will be the signal to destroy all of the churches of Sicily and *Ifrikiya*." Finally, under Caliph al-Moiz (953–975) Fatimid rule was transferred from Tunisia to Egypt, where it lasted two centuries.

THE HILLALI ARAB INVASION

Another Berber dynasty, the Zirids, ruled much of Tunisia and part of Algeria from a mountain capital, Achir. Then about 1050 began a mass migration which has marked North Africa more than

[4] Ibn Khaldun, quoted in Charles-André Julien, *Histoire de l'Afrique du Nord* (Paris, 1961), II, 624.

anything since the first Moslem conquest: the invasion of two Arab tribes, the Banu Hillal and the Banu Solaim. Both were warlike Arabian Bedouin tribes that had settled in Egypt and made themselves highly troublesome there: so troublesome that the new Fatimid rulers saw a chance to settle old scores with the Zirid rulers of Tunisia and Algeria and at the same time rid themselves of this nuisance.

The *Sirat banu Hillal* is a cycle of romantic Arabic folktales. It describes the Hillali march westward, which included many amorous adventures and the slaying of innumerable dragons, demons, and other legendary monsters. "Like an army of locusts," wrote Ibn Khaldun, an Arab himself, "they destroy all in their pathway." Kairawan fell and was sacked in 1056–1057. And the great historian used the Hillali migration to prove the point he made in the title of one of the chapters of his *Prolegomena:* "That the Arabs can establish their rule only over plains."

In addition to the Hillali, a Yemeni confederation that traveled a somewhat different path, the Banu Maquil, an entire nation of men, women, children, camels, and domestic animals, perhaps more than a million in all, slowly migrated westward, taking a century to reach Algeria from the Nile Valley.

The Hillali migrations encountered the nomadism of the Maghreb which had already existed among the Berbers since the time of the Phoenicians, or even earlier. The similarity between the habits of the newcomers and those of the Berbers they met, especially the Sanhaja nomads, speeded up the Arabization of the countryside and probably eased and expedited the spread of Islam. No longer were Arabism or Islam the monopoly of the city dwellers of Kairawan, Fez, Bougie, or Tlemcen. Though there seems to have been little direct impact of the new wave of eastern Arabs on the remnants of Christianity, it probably hastened their submergence.

The tribal society of the Berbers was now giving way to kingdoms. Ibn Khaldun often repeats that as a tribe dies, a nation is born. The new Berber kingdoms, especially in Tlemcen and Fez, hired the Arab invaders as mercenary soldiers. The new Berber rulers in Morocco settled entire confederations of them along the Atlantic coast: we are reminded of the *foederati* of the Romans and Byzantines. The Arabs became well-paid military allies, who were given land and told where to live in return for service in the internecine wars that were beginning to rage among the Berber monarchs.

There was another factor, vital in the final demarcation of the Christian-Moslem frontier in the Mediterranean. Christian power began to rise along Europe's southern coasts. The little kingdoms which the Fatimids left behind in Tunisia and Algeria could not cope with it nor prevent the loss of Sicily to the Normans and of Corsica and Sardinia to those Christians they knew much better: the Genoese and the Pisans. The lines were drawn for the next great encounter between the two faiths in the holy wars which, from the Strait of Gibraltar eastward to the tomb of Christ, swept over the Mediterranean world for the next seven centuries.

CHAPTER X

THE SPANISH FRONTIER: ARAB CULTURE AND THE BERBERS

The Hispanic community of nations has the ineluctable duty of interpreting *Hispanidad* [the essence of Spanishness] as a system of principles and norms destined to the better defense of Christian civilization and to the ordering of international life in the service of peace.

OFFICIAL BULLETIN OF THE SPANISH STATE, FEBRUARY 8, 1958, DURING A MOROCCAN GUERILLA UPRISING IN IFNI AND THE SPANISH SAHARA

The Berber troops of Tarik ibn Ziyad, a Moroccan, crossed the Strait of Gibraltar in 711 and carried Islam into Spain. Since then, the captains and the kings of that country down to the time of General Franco have regarded Spain as the most crucial point of contact between the worlds of Christendom and of Islam: a "bridge," in fact, between them. But Spaniards have also regarded themselves as envoys extraordinary to Islam, privileged by an Islamic past which is evident in Spain to this day, and therefore as very special spokesmen for Western Christianity in its encounter with "Eastern" Islam.

A Spanish Foreign Minister of the 1950's, Martin Artajo, was one of many European statesmen who used the "bridge" as a political doctrine. Though Spain had relinquished its role as protector of nearly 100,000 Spanish Catholics still living south of the Mediterranean, a sort of vague Christian mystique surrounded his unsuccessful policy of cultivating the Arab states. This mystique has nearly always been present in Spanish attitudes toward North Africa, and still is today.

Rulers and Christian prelates in Spain have almost consistently

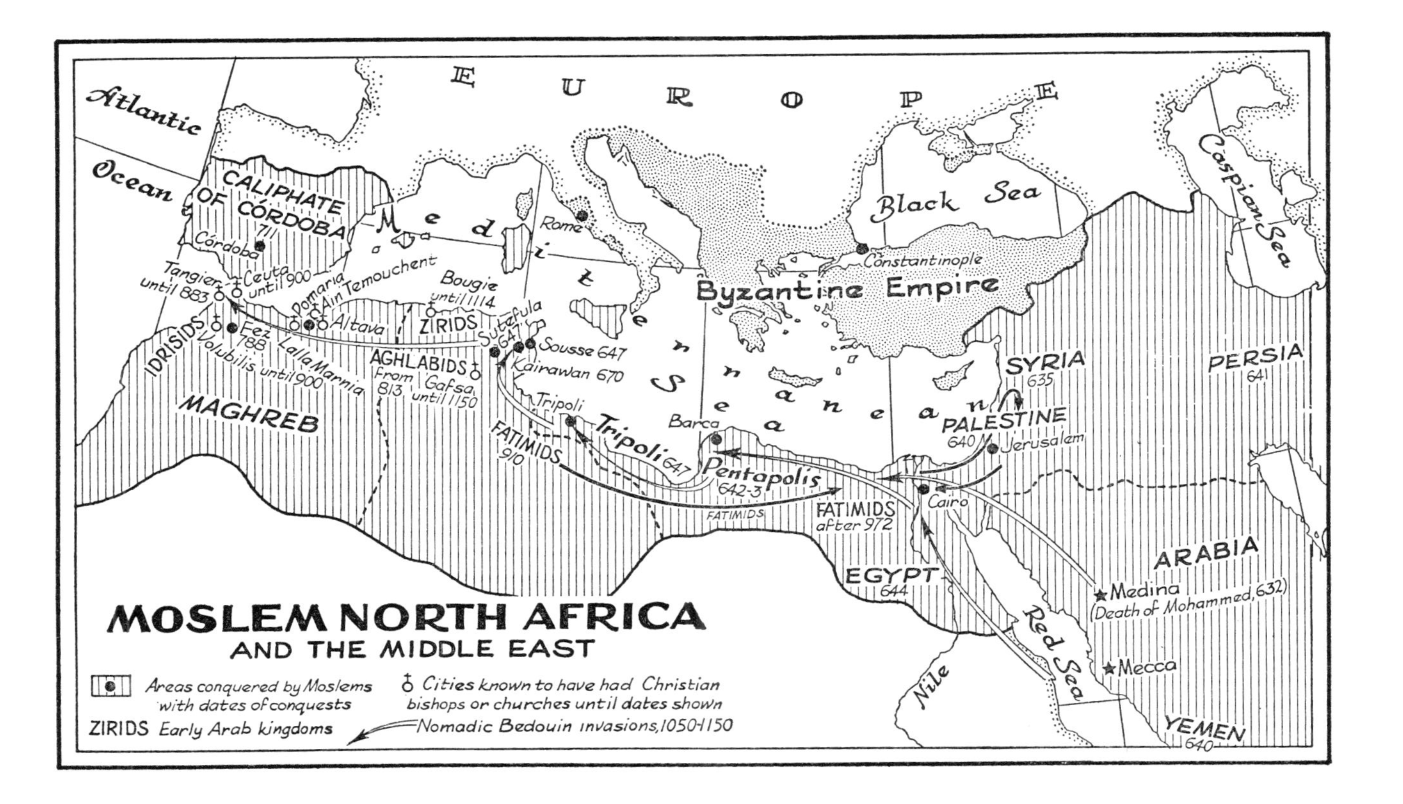

MOSLEM NORTH AFRICA
AND THE MIDDLE EAST
Areas conquered by Moslems with dates of conquests
ZIRIDS Early Arab kingdoms
Cities known to have had Christian bishops or churches until dates shown
Nomadic Bedouin invasions, 1050-1150
EUROPE
Atlantic Ocean
Mediterranean Sea
Black Sea
Caspian Sea
Red Sea
Nile
CALIPHATE OF CÓRDOBA 711
Córdoba
Tangier until 883
Ceuta until 900
Pomaria
Ain Temouchent
Altava
Fez 788
Volubilis until 900
Lalla Marnia
IDRISIDS
MAGHREB
Bougie until 1114
ZIRIDS
Sufetula 647
AGHLABIDS
From 813
Gafsa until 1150
Sousse 647
Kairawan 670
Tripoli
Tripoli 647
FATIMIDS 910
Rome
Byzantine Empire
Constantinople
Barca
Pentapolis 642-3
FATIMIDS
FATIMIDS after 972
Cairo
EGYPT 644
SYRIA 635
PALESTINE 640
Jerusalem
PERSIA 641
ARABIA
Medina (Death of Mohammed, 632)
Mecca
YEMEN 640

looked upon North Africa, especially Morocco, as Spain's back doorstep, both geographically and spiritually. Any hostile power there might launch or support an invasion. For this reason, Spain was reluctant to see the United States leave its air bases in Morocco in 1963, for fear that Russia might move into them or that some new Moslem imperialism, remembering the vanished age of Moslem conquests, might profit by the withdrawal of Washington's restraining hand to embark on adventures against such remaining enclaves of Spanish Christian control as Ceuta, Melilla, and the Spanish-occupied territories of Ifni and the Sahara. Spain's slow and reluctant military evacuation of her former protectorate in northern Morocco, which won its independence along with the much larger French protectorate in 1956, caused many a Spanish general and historian to look nostalgically backward. The mythical image of Franco, who had used about ten divisions of Moroccan Moslem troops in his "Christian" campaign against the Spanish Republic, as a sort of prophet bridging the gap between Islam and Christianity, was dissolved at the time he disbanded, for security reasons, his famed Moroccan bodyguard. Its incongruousness was perhaps never better illustrated than when the official printing presses turned out, for use in the Spanish Sahara, a series of stamps showing Franco dressed in a desert burnoose and mounted on a camel. Such stamps were given me by a Spanish officer when I visited there in 1956.

THE CONQUEST OF SPAIN

Tarik's crossing to Gibraltar had a prelude which is often forgotten. At least one of the Berber revolts against Byzantium assumed overtones of greater aggressiveness when pagan Berbers under a king named Gasmul defeated and killed three Byzantine generals (568–570) and apparently planned or attempted to cross the Strait with the intention of invading Europe. In 621, the Visigothic Christians, like their forebears, the Vandals, invaded North Africa from Spain and captured Tangier. By 700, Ceuta was the only Byzantine possession left. The Visigothic king helped Count Julian repulse Musa ibn Nusair before Ceuta's walls in 706. Then he took the king's side against Roderick, a usurper, giving Ceuta to the Moslems in 706 and perhaps taking nominal possession of Sala, abandoned by the Romans three centuries before but never occupied by the Byzantines.

Before leaving for Spain, Musa ibn Nusair charged seventeen Arab scholars with the task of teaching those Berbers he controlled the language of the Koran and the dogma of Islam. Tarik was one of the new Berber vassals of the Arab rulers. Musa had sent him ahead for the conquest of Spain. His conquering Moslem army advanced with lightning speed from their initial bases on and near the Rock of Gibraltar (*Djebel al-Tarik* = Tarik's Mountain). The Visigoths were badly beaten at Wadi Bekka in July, 711, and Moslem spearheads at first bypassed, then subdued, the more stubborn bastions of Christian resistance, such as Toledo. Tarik and Musa joined forces and together they pushed on to conquer the north. Musa returned to Africa in 714, laden with loot, and then went home to Syria.

Abd al-Rahman I governed the conquered portions of Spain and vanquished rebellious Berbers and their Christian ally, Eudo, the Duke of Acquitaine, deep inside Frankish territory. But the Moslem drive to the north was finally smashed by the warmly dressed Frankish infantry of Charles Martel (the Hammer) between Tours and Poitiers in October, 732, while the Moslems shivered in their light clothes. This spelled the end of the Moslem threat north of the Pyrenees.

In Spain, Musa's Arab troops were conciliatory at first toward their new Christian subjects, called *mustaribun,* or Mozarabs. They and the Jews, who had suffered terribly under the Visigothic persecutions which had driven many to Morocco, were treated with the full traditional rights of *dhimmi,* or protégés, and there was little, if any, persecution. But the Arabs themselves were torn by Middle Eastern blood feuds.

The son of Abd al-Rahman I, who died in 788, was the pious Emir Hisham I (788–796), a cruel military despot who oppressed his Christian subjects. The authority of the Oriental Abbasid Caliphate had ended, and with it, apparently, the strict observance of rules about Christian protégés. The Moslem theologians saw to it that the prescriptions of the *sunna,* the orthodox rite, were strictly observed by Moslems. They also persecuted the Christian renegades, then settled in Córdoba. The Mozarabs, provided they kept quiet about theological questions and did not attack the Moslem order in public, were generally left in peace. However, in eighth-, ninth-, and tenth-century Spain they were already what the Christians were to become at various later times in North Africa: a potentially restless enclave which might seek the help of Christian renegade soldiers or call on the help of Christian Europe.

Between 850 and 859 there were some Mozarab martyrdoms, culminating in that of the zealous Archbishop Eulogio of Toledo. A kind of embryo Spanish nationalism, which at first cut across confessional lines, arose in some places. In Andalusia, a Moslem, Umar ibn Hafsun, who later became a Christian, led a revolt in the Sierra Nevada Mountains in 879. Christian-Moslem divisions ran right through families at the time of a Christian uprising in Córdoba, when some Christian converts of Moslem origin were condemned as renegades to Islam.

The *hadjib,* or prime minister, of the child Caliph Hisham II hired Berbers and even Spanish Christians from the north for his court. He made his Christian prisoners enlarge the Mosque of Córdoba, using the captured bells of the Christian holy place of Santiago de Compostela as braziers. Later, the Berbers sacked and ruined it.

The separatist caliphate of Spain ended in 1061 when the last caliph, Hisham III, was deposed. Spain split into warring Christian and Moslem kingdoms. The Christian counteroffensive from the north now gathered force and cast its shadow—a shadow soon to take substance in the Crusades—over Spain and the Maghreb.

When Charlemagne unsuccessfully besieged Saragossa in 778, he was as much the ally of Yemenite Arabs against the tyrannical Umaiyad caliphs established at Córdoba since 756 as he was a champion of Christendom. Advancing Christian kings often permitted enclaves of tribute-paying Moslems to keep the faith of the Prophet. Papal ordinances regulated the separation of Jews and Moslems in Christian territory. Generally speaking, the rulers were more tolerant than their troops, and even the rulers of Castile, who became the chief standard-bearers of Christian reconquest, allowed Moslem vassal states to exist in their rear, as the main Christian spearhead pushed into Andalusia, toward Córdoba and Seville. The largest of the vassals were to be the Emirate of Niebla and the Kingdoms of Granada and Seville. Some Moslem rulers even took part in person in the wars of Christian reconquest, sometimes encouraging at the same time Moslem revolts against Christian rule.

Even as the tide of war turned slowly but inexorably against the Moslems, learning and the arts reached a height they have never attained since in Spain or North Africa. Scholars and statesmen in Europe and Africa in those days had relatively free access to Christian, Jewish, and Islamic works, in contrast to the book burnings which followed the era of the Crusades, when every Islamic book and manuscript that could be tracked down was burned by order of the Inquisition in Spanish cities. The Arab culture of Spain often drew the grudging admiration of the rest of the civilized world. Emigrants and the flow of scholars, merchants, spies, and adventurers between Spain and North Africa eventually brought Andalusian culture to North African cities like Fez and Kairawan, the great centers of Arab humanism. It seemed for a time that Arabic culture, and the Arab transmutations of classical culture, preserved and translated from the Greek, might permeate Western Europe. The lament of the Christian writer Alvaro in 854 is often quoted:

> My fellow Christians delight in the poems and romances of the Arabs; they study the works of Mohammedan theologians and philosophers, not in order to refute them, but to acquire a correct and elegant Arabic style. Where today can a layman be found who reads the Latin commentaries on Holy Scriptures? Who is there that studies the Gospels, the Prophets, the Apostles? Alas! the young Christians who are most conspicuous for their talents have no knowledge of any literature or language except the Arabic; they read and study with avidity Arabian books; they amass whole libraries of them at vast cost; and they everywhere sing the praises of Arabian lore. On the other hand, at the mention of Christian books they disdainfully protest that such works are unworthy of their notice. The pity of it. Christians have forgotten their own tongue and scarce one in a thousand can be found able to compose in fair Latin a letter to a friend! But when it comes to writing Arabic, how many are there

> who can express themselves in that language with the greatest elegance, and even compose verses which surpass in formal correctness those of the Arabs themselves.[1]

Allal al-Fassi, the most prominent living spokesman for conservative Islamic trends in North Africa today, alluded to Alvaro in a lecture sponsored by the Moroccan Ministry of Education in October, 1959. Al-Fassi is one of those contemporary Moslem leaders who associate the Western penetration of Islamic culture with the Christian religion to the point, at times, of complete identification. Bitterly, he found that

> the Moslems have awakened now. They have found that the overwhelming majority of their sons are very far from any knowledge of Islam or of all the Arabic language. Rather they have reached the same state which the Spaniards were in during the ninth century, described by Father Alvaro. . . . Is it not a catastrophic irony of history that this role is now reversed and that the Moslems have become more deserving of these insults which Father Alvaro uttered to his coreligionists? Everything has changed in our Christian [sic] world. Will we be able to change our works as the Christians changed theirs? [2]

RECONQUISTA AND THE CRUSADES

Before 1500, the clash and the interplay of North African Islam and European Christianity took place largely in Spain and Portugal. Historians of the Crusades, which in their strictest military sense were simply a European military adventure to end Moslem power in and around the Holy Land, too often neglect the Moslem conquest of Spain as a stimulus to this adventure. The *reconquista,* as Christian historians came to call it, was in some sense a part, if only a subsidiary one, of the main drama of faith, fanaticism, avarice,

[1] Indiculus Alvaro, quoted by Gustave E. von Grunebaum, *Medieval Islam* (Chicago, 1958), p. 57.

[2] Unpublished lecture by Allal al-Fassi, "The Role of the Islamic Ulama" (October, 1959), quoted by the author from lecture notes made available to him by Prof. Stuart Schaer, University of Wisconsin.

and bloodshed which were the Crusades proper. The traditional seven Crusades touched North African soil in only a few episodes which we shall look at later. But the Spanish frontier shared largely in the general state of mind of the Crusades, during their incubation, their advance, and their aftermath.

Like the Crusades themselves, the Christian counteroffensive in Spain and Portugal, which three dynasties of Moroccan rulers tried to help stem, was nourished ideologically by one of the most fantastic collections of misconceptions of Islam that has ever existed in history. During the martyrs' movement in Spain, such absurdities were written about Mohammed's life as the assurance of St. Eulogius that he was expected to rise again on the third day after his death; that Islam was a heretical sect of Christianity (a fundamental medieval belief which has persisted in some quarters down to our own day); that Mohammed was possessed by demons; that Moslems were heathen who worshiped a pantheon of gods, including "Mahomet, Apollon, Jupin, Tervagant" and even including "Alkoran" (the Koran) as one of them. Piers Plowman, probably written by William Langland as late as 1360, pictures Mohammed as a demon.

The ideas widely held by Moslems about Christians and the type of reaction they engendered were sometimes equally far-fetched. The following is a *fatwa,* or legal advisory, rendered by a post-Crusades *kadi,* or judge, named Abu l-Musab Az-Awari, dealing with the subject of blasphemy:

> What decision should be taken about a Christian who says, "Jesus created Mohammed?" He shall be put to death.
>
> Once a Christian was brought to me who had said: "By Him [God] who chose Jesus in preference to Mohammed. . . ." Hesitating about what decision to take, I beat him to death; I believe that he still remained alive one day and one night. Then I ordered someone to drag him by the foot to a garbage heap, where the dogs devoured him.[3]

In 1063, Pope Alexander II gave solemn sanction to the Christian reconquest by granting a special indulgence to Christian warriors in Spain. As a result, many French knights joined the movement.

[3] Al-Wansharisi, *op. cit.,* p. 337.

France and French arms have played major roles in the encounter between the Christian and Moslem worlds ever since. Vikings, settled in Normandy, ousted the Moslems from Italy and Sicily in the eleventh century. French nobles and knights led the First Crusade and founded the short-lived Latin Kingdom of Jerusalem in 1099. In later centuries, France often claimed to be the lawful protector of Oriental Christendom against the exactions of the Turks.

During the confused wars between the great and petty Christian and Moslem monarchs, the legendary hero of Spanish literature, the *condottiere* Rodrigo Diaz de Vivar, the "Champion" (*campeador*) of the Christian Spaniards and *saiyidi,* or *sidi* ("my master") or *mio Cid* to the Moslems, became one of the most written-about mercenary soldiers of all time. The Cid's constant quarrels with Alfonso VI of León probably did much to retard the speed of victory of Christian arms. But this victory, bitter and ambiguous though it was, came closer as the weakness of Islam grew.

CHAPTER XI

THE SPANISH FRONTIER: MONKS AND MERCENARIES

> The message of Islam is to create an Arab humanism.
>
> MICHEL AFLAQ, 1943

Outside help soon came from an unexpected quarter: the veiled Sanhaja Berbers of the Sahara. Among nomads who wore veils all their lives and ate the meat of their herds, a Moslem chieftain named al-Jaddali had subjugated the Negroes of Senegal. Later he met a theologian at Naffis, near Marrakesh, who was equally interested in reform and conquest. Together they founded a monastery, or *ribat,* on an island near present-day Mauretania and Senegal. Here the "people of the *ribat*" (*al-murabitun*), or Almoravids, as the Spaniards Latinized their name, built a tough, fanatical military community. They conquered the heretical Berber Bergwata of the Moroccan coast and by 1087 an Almoravid ruler, Yusuf ibn Tashfin, was in strong control of the western Maghreb, from the Sahara to Tangier. The fighting monks were next to move east to capture Tlemcen, Oran, and the suburbs of Algiers.

Ibn Tashfin sent his army of zealots across the Strait of Gibraltar in 1083. Advancing north, he summoned Alfonso to convert to Islam and nearly captured him after routing the Christians near Badajoz. Ibn Tashfin made two expeditions into Spain. When he died he left to his son Ali, whose mother had been a Christian slave, an empire which included a large chunk of Moslem Spain, North Africa east to Algiers, and the Balearic Islands.

Ali's rigid doctrines killed artistic endeavor and religious sentiment. All deviations from the strict, fundamentalist interpretation of the Koran were severely punished. Casuists calling themselves doctors of the law published opinions on various subjects which sometimes took the force of law and which were often aimed against Christians and Jews. Religious tension seems to have kept pace with, or even outstripped, political strife. A contemporary *fatwa* clearly shows the spirit of the times:

QUESTION: During the entire month of Ramadan, a community had for imam, in all the offices, an individual who carried a Koran with him. When the month of Ramadan had ended, this individual told them, "I have led all your prayers and I am a Christian." Then the man disappeared. What was to be done?

ANSWER: Obligatory canonical prayers will be repeated, whether or not it is time for them. . . . If anyone succeeds in catching the Christian, he will be asked to return and make amends. If he refuses, he will be put to death.[1]

CHRISTIAN MILITIA, THE NEW *MAHDI,* AND THE ALMOHADS

While the Christians were winning victory after victory in Spain, Spanish Moslem culture under the Almoravids began to flow south into North Africa. The doctrines of great philosopher-jurists like Ghazzali and philosopher-musicians like Ibn Bajjah (Avempace) spread the refinements of Arab humanism in North Africa, which had few direct relations with the Orient. Mosques in Morocco built in the twelfth century, with heavy pillars rather than the old and more slender columns inside, are like those of Córdoba and Granada, with the arches cut into lobes. The Kairouyine Mosque in Fez was enlarged, and the foundations of today's Grand Mosques of Tlemcen and Algiers were laid. The essential parts of all these cities and of Marrakesh, heavily influenced by Andalusia, date from the time of the Almoravids (1056–1147). Spain and Tunisia also influenced each other under the rule of the Aghlabids in Tunis.

European Christians returned to North Africa as mercenary soldiers recruited in Spain. Originally, they were probably adventurers like the Cid who would fight for anyone who paid them enough. In 978, the steward of the estates and the lover of a Basque lady named Aurora Subh, mother of the Caliph Hakim II, reorganized the Spanish Moslem army. He replaced unreliable Slavs with Berber mercenaries from Africa and Christian ones from northern Spain, where he completely destroyed the shrine of Santiago de Compostela.

These mercenaries served various Moslem rulers in Spain

[1] *Fatwa* of Abu Said ibn-Laubb, quoted by Al-Wansharisi, *Archives Marocaines,* XII, 65.

through their ups and downs until deported to Salé and Meknes in Morocco after the Moslem defeat of Arnisol, for which they were blamed.

By 1120, the Berbers were in an uproar again: a new *mahdi* had appeared. This time it was a strict-minded zealot named Mohammed ibn Tumart of the Masmuda tribe, a man from the Sus Valley of southwestern Morocco whom his early companions had nicknamed "The Torch" because of his burning religious fervor. He studied in Córdoba around the time Ghazzali's books were burned and then had a strong orthodox indoctrination in Baghdad. On the way home he paused to give puritanical sermons and lectures to unreceptive ears in places like Tunis, Constantine, and Bougie, where the easy-going ways of Moslem Spain had begun to catch on. Later, his writings were passed on to Christian Europe by one of the great medieval translators, Mark of Toledo.

Ibn Tumart and his successor, Abd al-Mumin, collected an army which began to whittle down Almoravid power in one campaign after another. They came to be called *muwahhidun*, or Almohads (unitarians). They were based among the Atlas Mountain Berbers, who had a tightly knit religious-military organization, founded on republican habits and knitted together through an iron disciplinary system. The Almoravid King Ali threw the Christian militias, commanded by a chief named Reverter, against the Almohads. Reverter was killed in battle in 1144–1145, and Abd al-Mumin reportedly had the pleasure of crucifying him. Ali's son, Tashfin ibn Ali, brought with him from Spain reinforcements in the form of a bodyguard of four thousand top-flight Moslem cavalrymen and sixteen hundred Christian prisoners. One of the prisoners was a bishop named Miguel, who during a long captivity in Morocco copied and dated in Fez a manuscript of the Gospels in Arabic.

After the Almohads captured Marrakesh in 1147, some of the Christian militiamen returned to Toledo with "their clergy and bishop," according to a Latin chronicle of the time of King Alfonso VII. The bishop was probably a Mozarab from Spain who had been deported earlier with his charges. Though they had no jurisdiction on African soil, the priests who ministered to the Christian prisoners continued to exercise their ministry.

When in about 1230 King Ferdinand III of Castile provided

twelve thousand Christian knights to help Sultan al-Mamun of Morocco to defeat his rival and nephew Yahia ibn Nasir, Ferdinand tied strings to his aid: Mass should be celebrated publicly; the militiamen should have their own church in Marrakesh, and they should even have the right to ring its bells. The church, Notre Dame, was destroyed soon after it was built, but there was an episcopate in Marrakesh until the fourteenth century. The fortunes of war went so badly for al-Mamun that he even made a commitment to prevent Christians serving in his army from converting to Islam, while permitting any conversions to Christianity made on his territory.

Mamun's sympathy for Christianity seems to have been dictated largely by politics: it had a strongly anti-Almohad slant. When he arrived in Marrakesh, Mamun is supposed to have solemnly cursed the memory of Ibn Tumart in the Mosque of al-Mansur. "I tell you," he shouted, "that the story of your *mahdi* is only a swindle . . . there is no *mahdi,* unless it be Jesus, the son of Mary." An Arab chronicle reports that in 1232, when Mamun laid siege to Ceuta, his old enemy, Yahia, captured Marrakesh, devastated the Church of Notre Dame, "and also massacred a number of Jews and Banu Farkhan." This was a contemptuous term for the Christian militiamen: *farkh* denotes a small bird or a young boy, but also a bastard.

In 1246, Pope Innocent IV expressed concern about the dangers to the Christians and asked the Almohad power to provide fortified places near the coast where they could find refuge. The pope's messenger was Lope Fernando d'Ayn, a Franciscan monk. The pope had made him what amounted to Vicar of Africa, with jurisdiction over the faithful of the Diocese of Marrakesh and all other Christians in Africa as well. Innocent IV recommended him to the rulers of Tunis, Ceuta, and Bougie. The pope's main concern seems to have been the spiritual welfare of those Christians living as free men in Moslem territory; the merchants and mercenaries, rather than the slaves or prisoners.

The Almohad ruler, Murtada, could not resist opening his reply with a bit of polemic:

> We know that superior intelligences are repugnant to admit that He [God] had a Son or that He should be called the Father; in any case, the Compassionate Sovereign is above the opinions

> professed by the Trinitarians [Christians], idolators and atheists. The echelons and the degrees of God are high, but he who wears around his neck the chain of the doctrine of His unity is manifestly the possessor of a jewel.[2]

Murtada told Innocent that he might indeed send a man to minister to the Christians, "a man who will concern himself with their religious interests and prod them to observe their habitual laws. Choose one of superior intelligence and good conduct," which of course, remains good advice for clergy or missionaries being chosen for delicate missions in Islamic countries today.

The militiamen, a sort of Christian Foreign Legion, existed as an organized body until about 1386 and did much fighting for a number of Moroccan rulers. Always they were allowed to have their own chaplains. In 1220, they were stationed in Marrakesh under the orders of the Infante of Portugal and were involved, as we shall see later, in the first misadventures of European Catholic missionaries in Morocco. By 1248, they were fighting against a new power-hungry dynasty, the Banu Marin, or Marinids, who were to rule Morocco between 1296 and 1470. Gonsalvo and Garcia were two of the most illustrious chiefs of the militiamen. Garcia, to his own grief, became involved in palace intrigues at Fez. The "Chronicle of the Kings of Castile" discloses that fifty Christian knights "of the line of those who came in the time of the Goths" had asked to return to Seville. The King of Castile granted them noble titles in 1394.

These militiamen lived in privileged enclaves as *dhimmi,* or protégés. They seem rarely if ever to have had any sort of religious trouble with their employers or with the Moslem population around them. When they could, they acted to curb the rash acts of some of the more zealous and ill-prepared of the early Christian missionaries. The Crusades had made the existence of such a community all but impossible in the Middle East. But real deep-seated distrust and systematic intolerance of Christians, militiamen or otherwise, appeared in North Africa only after the expulsion of the Moors from Spain in 1492 following the fall of Granada and the final collapse of Moslem power there.

[2] Eugène (Cardinal) Tisserant, and G. Wiet, "Une Lettre de L'Almohade Murtada au Pape Innocent IV," *Hesperis,* VI (1926), pp. 69–83.

THE FALL OF SPAIN

The Almohads intervened in Spain as their predecessors had done, but halted the Christian advance only briefly. Crusaders on their way to the Holy Land helped Sancho I of Portugal to capture part of the Algarve from the Moslems: a separate Christian kingdom of Portugal was already established by 1143, when Alfonso VII of Portugal became a vassal of the pope. But Yakub al-Mansur, the builder of Marrakesh and of the three great mosques of western Islam, the Koutoubia in Marrakesh, Hasan's Tower in Rabat, and the Giralda in Seville, came up from Africa to defeat Alfonso VIII in 1196. So serious was the brief resurgence of Moslem power that Pope Innocent IV decreed a special Crusade. In 1212, Alfonso ended the threat by routing the Moroccans and their allies in the decisive battle of Las Naves de Tolosa.

In the midst of war some Christian rulers, like Alfonso X, the Learned, protected and encouraged Moslem and Jewish culture. Between 1276 and 1410, Christian Aragon, Castile, Portugal, and the shrinking Moslem state of Granada—a jewel of Arab civilization—fought each other and the newest dynasty ruling Morocco. This was the Marinid dynasty (1296–1470), Berbers from the Biskra region of Algeria. These wars often contained incidents of terrible savagery, as when the Christian king, Pedro the Cruel, killed the defeated King of Granada with his own hand.

So many battles and adventures gave the Moslem and Christian Spaniards a common heritage, a sort of ancestral memory of common experience, good times and bad. This has survived in a lack of religious bigotry or "racist" feelings between Spaniards and Arabs as such and has often in the past contributed to the optimism of Spanish imperialists and advocates of the "bridge" policy in their efforts for gain in Morocco and other parts of the Arab world. In Spanish Morocco there was never, for example, any segregation of the sort practiced in French Morocco between Europeans and Arabs. Even before Moroccan independence in 1956, I often saw Spaniards and Arabs eating together in the same restaurants in Tetuan or Tangier. There were mixed Christian-Moslem marriages; something almost unheard of between the French and the Moroccans. All this explains much of the easy familiarity, not unmixed with contempt, but occasionally tinged with great cordiality, which still exists on both sides, wherever Spaniards have daily contacts with Arabs.

The final battles for Granada had a shameful epilogue, which certainly contributed to the rancor and nostalgia still lingering in North Africa today over Granada's loss to the Christians. Most tourists who visit Morocco see, or at least hear about, the Arab families of Fez, Tetuan, or Chauen, who will ruefully display a great rusty key, telling you: "This is the key to my house in Granada."

The terms offered to Boabdil, last Moslem King of Granada, were such that the Moslems would have been allowed to remain and practice their faith, if not all aspects of their previous lives, in peace. These terms were not kept, owing to the evangelical zeal of Cardinal Jiménez Cisneros, Archbishop of Toledo, and one of the leading heroes in today's Spanish-Catholic pantheon of the past. There was a terrible repression and persecution in Spain of Moslems, who were forced to convert or emigrate to North Africa.

The commitments made by the Spaniards not to occupy Moroccan territory were not honored either. After reconnoitering the Moroccan coast and obtaining the agreement of the Portuguese, with whom Spain had concluded treaties allotting them "the Kingdom of Fez," the Duke of Medina Sidonia in 1497 occupied Melilla with the fleet which was later to be used by Christopher Columbus for his second voyage to America. In 1965, Melilla, like Ceuta, was still held securely by General Franco and ruled as a *presidio* of peninsular Spain.

The unassimilated Moriscos, as secret or open Moslems of Spain came to be called, revolted in 1568, and Philip II expelled them from Granada Province, though not from Spain, still hoping they could be assimilated. Finally, between 1609 and 1614, Philip III hounded them to North Africa where they settled chiefly in Tunis, Tetuan, Rabat, and Salé. In Rabat and Salé, close together at the mouth of the Regreg River, they set up what came to be called a "pirate republic," the base of many buccaneering raids. They nourished a fierce hatred for Christian Spain, which had expelled them, but also found it hard to adjust to the ruder life around them in Morocco.

THE AFTERMATH IN MOSLEM EYES

How all this was seen by North Africans is told by an anonymous Arab historian. His facts are fuzzy in some respects, but he probably sets forth accurately the state of mind, including the internal division and lack of self-confidence, of North African Islam on the eve of a new wave of Christian aggression:

> The inhabitants of Spain, after being reduced by the Christian king and seeing all their territories taken from them, spent a few years as tributaries, oppressed by the amount of taxes, compelled to allow free access to their women and to have their children of both sexes taken from them; and finally ordered to change their religion. So they decided to turn to the various Moslem princes of the East and west and adjure them to come to their aid. Sultan Mulay Abdallah of Morocco fallaciously advised them to begin revolting against the Christians so that he could have confidence in their plan, but when they had done this, he reneged on his promises, also lying treacherously to his own faithful and to the divine religion for the passing advantage of his authority.
>
> He undertook correspondence with the Christians and agreed with them that the Moslems of Spain should be transported to the Maghreb to populate the coast, Fez, and Marrakesh, and that a large corps of troops should be raised from among them. When the uprising in Spain had broken out, in connivance with him, and the battles with the Christians had begun, the chiefs, the elders, and the old men were sent to him. Leaving their brethren entrenched in the mountains of Granada and fighting against the Christians, they came to ask his aid but they received only evasive replies, while being made to wait. . . . [Finally they came to terms with the Christians after it became apparent that Mulay Abdallah was in correspondence with the latter.] The majority of the rebels crossed the sea. Mulay Abdallah then imposed painful service upon them and raised an important corps of troops among them.
>
> The Christians of Spain, seeing all the Moslems asking to emigrate, imposed on them the abandonment of their property,

> which they consented to, and the exodus continued; but these accursed ones told those who remained to go and leave behind their children, a requirement which the unfortunates refused. . . . The Spaniards distributed them in regions which offered no means of resistance, and the majority settled in the countryside. The impious [Christians] then forced them to apostatize, which they did despite themselves, and to intermarry with them; they burned all their books, and everyone who let be seen, in prayer or fast, any trace of our religion, they added to all this the confiscation of his goods.[3]

In 1955, at the height of General Franco's flirtation with the Arab world, the publishing house of the official Falange Party in Madrid issued an interesting little volume which touches on Moslem-Catholic relations. It speaks of Spain's twin Catholic and Moslem traditions and mentions "the mystic depths of a Christianized Islam (*un Islam cristianizado*) which would be in keeping with the most genuine, believing, and pious Catholic Spanish spirituality of all time." [4]

[3] Ms. No. 5429, Arabic Collection, Bibliothèque Nationale (Paris). In E. Fagnan (ed.), *Extraits Inédits Relatifs au Maghreb* (Algiers, 1924), p. 391.

[4] Rodolfo Gil Benumeya, *España y el Mundo Arabe* (Madrid, 1955), p. 225.

CHAPTER XII

THE MEDITERRANEAN FRONTIER: CRUSADES AND COEXISTENCE

> Christus vincit, Christus regnat,
> Christus imperat!
> FIRST WORDS OF AN ANCIENT HYMN AND CRY OF THE FRENCH AT TUNIS, AUGUST, 1270

To Mediterranean Christianity, holy war against the Moslems in Spain, North Africa, Palestine, or anywhere else, was a relatively new idea. The first Christians had been taught to abhor war in all its forms, and Tertullian of Carthage and Origen of Alexandria had forbidden military service. Augustine moved a step closer to modern times when he postulated that "war is legitimate if it is a just war"—that is, one fought against the enemies of God. Western Christianity accepted this concept much more readily than did the Eastern Church. Pope Nicholas I (858–867) felt that war was permissible in case of absolute necessity to defend one's life or country but that war in itself was "the work of the Devil."

By the time the barbarian invasions from Europe were menacing the Roman Empire, the Church was more and more prepared to accept military operations to defend, or even extend, its own faith. Liturgical texts of the seventh and eighth centuries invoke divine protection for warriors who defend the Church against its enemies. Pope Leo IV ordered the Christian armies to repulse Moslem invaders landing at the mouth of the Tiber in 849; while Pope John X himself led an expedition against North African invaders at Garigliano in 915, promising eternal life to those who fell in battle. The deterioration of mutual Moslem-Christian tolerance eventually reached a low point which is reflected by many medieval writers, such as Robert Holcot, a Dominican scholastic (died 1349), who included Moslems along with pagans, Jews, idolators, and heretics in the general category of infidels. Holcot proposed for Moslems who do not submit: "despoil them and kill them and devote their goods to the faithful." [1]

After the Moslems captured Jerusalem in 683, they permitted Christians to make pilgrimages to the Holy City. Some of the North African Christians probably participated in these. In this way and through occasional commerce and travel, the East and the West maintained contact, even after the military expeditions of both sides had begun.

In Christian Europe, a new approach to crusading and Islam began in the tenth century. Its beginning was the foundation in 910 of the Order of Congregation of Cluny, at the Benedictine Monastery of Cluny. The Cluniacs applied the Rule of St. Benedict, but with greater discipline and elaboration than ever before. Soon they branched out into more worldly pursuits, such as papal politics and literary studies.

In 1142, Peter the Venerable, ninth Abbot of Cluny, left on a visit to the Cluniac establishments in Christian Spain. By this time, the Crusades were well under way, and Peter was in complete disagreement with their fundamentally military orientation. In order to combat Islam, said he, we must know something about it. While in Spain, Peter had a certain Peter of Toledo, with the help of Peter of Poitiers, translate for him the classical Christian *Risalah* (Apology) of the Arab Christian Abd al-Masih ibn Ishaq al-Kindi, which has been a handbook of innumerable Christian missions ever since. Using a collection of fundamental Moslem books translated for him by several other scholars, Peter prepared a short and concise manual of Islamic doctrine entitled *Summa totius heresis Saracenorum.* He meant to leave the task of trying to refute what Christians consider error in Islamic teachings to a friend, Bernard of Clairvaux. But the latter was too busy preaching the Second Crusade. European rulers like Conrad III and Henry VII were already preparing a large, well-equipped army to defend the new Christian Kingdom of Jerusalem from Moslem attack and if possible, wrest new territory from the Moslems.

Employing, for the first time in Moslem-Christian polemics,

[1] C. Erdmann, *Die Entstehung des Kreuzzugsgedanken* (Stuttgart, 1935), pp. 1–35; also unsigned review in *Hesperis,* XXIV (1937), pp. 205–215.

solid theological arguments, Peter wrote a long, two-volume book called *Liber contra sectam Saracenorum.* He wrote:

> I do not approach you as our Christians often do, with arms, but with words; not with force, but with reason . . . not with hate, but with love . . . a love which should exist between the worshipers of Christ and those who have turned away from Christ, such as existed between our Apostles and the Gentiles of their time, whom they tried to draw to the law of Christ.

"It appears," writes James Kritzeck, who has collected and analyzed the writings by and about Peter, "that his most eloquent testimony is simply that of intelligence, the zeal and the imagination of a great Christian of the Middle Ages." [2] Peter could well be a model to Christians of the twentieth century.

This revolutionary concept of relations between Christians and Moslems is important for North Africa because it guided the first Christian missionary effort there, decided upon by Francis of Assisi, who was probably familiar with Peter's work, and inscribed in the Franciscan Rule approved in 1223. This was a new kind of peaceful crusade. Beginning in 1225, the Almohad rulers and after them the Marinids permitted both Franciscans and Dominicans to establish missions in Morocco. This led to a Christian presence, nearly continuous, even though it was an alien and European one, down to our own day. How these missions fared will be seen later. The initial impetus to this pacific crusade, however, which was to be based not on warlike or political motives but on reviving the active and contemplative life in Christ, was built on the principle of work. St. Francis founded the Order of Friars Minor, or Franciscans, in 1208. The Christian victory at Las Naves de Tolosa in 1212 seems to have made up his mind to concentrate on both North Africa and the Middle East at the same time. In 1219, Francis

[2] James Kritzeck, "Pierre le Vénérable et l'Islam," adapt. by Dom Placide Pernot in *Images de Toumliline* (January, 1962). For a complete study of Peter, cf. J. Kritzeck, *Peter the Venerable and Islam* (Princeton, 1964).

decided to send six monks to Morocco, while he joined the Crusader army then fighting a hopeless battle against Moslem forces at Damietta, Egypt. Before leaving he told them: "My dear sons, God has ordered me to send you to the country of the Saracens to preach Jesus Christ there and destroy the cult of Mohammed." For the first time, Christian friars were being sent to "the country of the Saracens" with only God for an escort, instead of as an adjunct of an army or a bureaucracy.

THE SEA FRONTIER

Sicily had become a Mediterranean stronghold for the Arab fleet and for Moslem land raids into Italy, which threatened Rome in 846. Arabs sacked the two cathedrals of St. Peter and St. Paul and desecrated tombs of the pontiffs. But Moslem sea power declined as Italian naval successes increased. On several occasions, the pope gave his sanction to war at sea by blessing the Christian fleet. In the meantime, the Tunisians fortified their coast and made it almost impregnable with a fortified monastery, or *ribat,* every few miles. The best known such fortress today is at Monastir, President Bourguiba's home town. Later, the *ribat* became centers of religious studies when Sufi mysticism swept over North Africa (after 1100).

Just as in Spain, some of Italy's Christian rulers were not adverse to using the Moslems in Sicily as allies against their own enemies, as Duke Andrew of Naples did against Benevento in 837. Pope John X (914–928) gave the Christian defense the character of a holy war in 915. Under the Fatimid rulers, European Christendom was seriously frightened by North African raids that reached as far as the Alps, where St. Maiolus, one of Peter the Venerable's predecessors as Abbot of Cluny, was ambushed and kidnaped in 972. The Cluniac monks raised a ransom for him. The incident served to arouse some more of the northern Italian princes to the Moslem threat.

In 948, the Fatimid caliph appointed a governor in Sicily who founded an independent dynasty, the Kalbites. This lasted a century. Under them, Christian and Jewish subjects were *dhimmi,* or protégés, who could keep their land. The Fatimid fleet raided as far north as Genoa. An Arab chronicler who joined one of these expeditions found that

> Genoa is one of the great cities of the Franks [a generic term commonly used by Arab writers to describe all Christian Europeans] and has for its inhabitants the overlords of the Christians. These inhabitants, it is said, are Christianized Arabs . . . they do not physically resemble the *Rumi* [European Christians], who are generally blonde or red-haired. These are brown-haired and have straight and well-formed noses. They take part in trade and are good and vigorous sailors.

Of Pisa, the same writer observed that

> its arches are provided with gates of wood armored with iron, open during the day but closed at night for fear of enemies, that is, the Moslems. This was done at a time when the latter, the masters of Sicily, Sardinia, and Messina [sic] gave cause to fear that they might bring in vessels under cover of night.[3]

In 1016, a band of Norman pilgrims from the Holy Land went home to recruit mercenaries to support the Christian Prince of Salerno. In 1072, Count Roger de Hauteville and Duke Robert Guiscard reconquered Sicily for Christendom. King Roger I of Sicily organized a feudal state which had elements of both Islam and Byzantium in its organization, and much of the former Arab bureaucracy as well. In 1098, Pope Urban II gave Roger hereditary legateship, making him the head of both the Latin and Greek churches. Roger tolerated and even cultivated Islam, and his court soon filled up with Arab astrologers, mathematicians, astronomers, philosophers and writers. Later, Roger II (1105–1154) even had a harem. The great Arab geographer al-Idrisi published his description of the earth in 1154 at Roger's court and showed that he knew the earth was round, more than three centuries before Columbus. He also indicated the sources of the Nile River, which no one else knew. Roger had one guard of Christian knights, another of Moslem Negroes, and wore Byzantine robes at court. Norman, Byzantine,

[3] Mahalli Ahmad ibn Ali, *Tonfat al-Muluk;* in Fagnan, *op. cit.*, ms. No. 370, pp. 123 f.

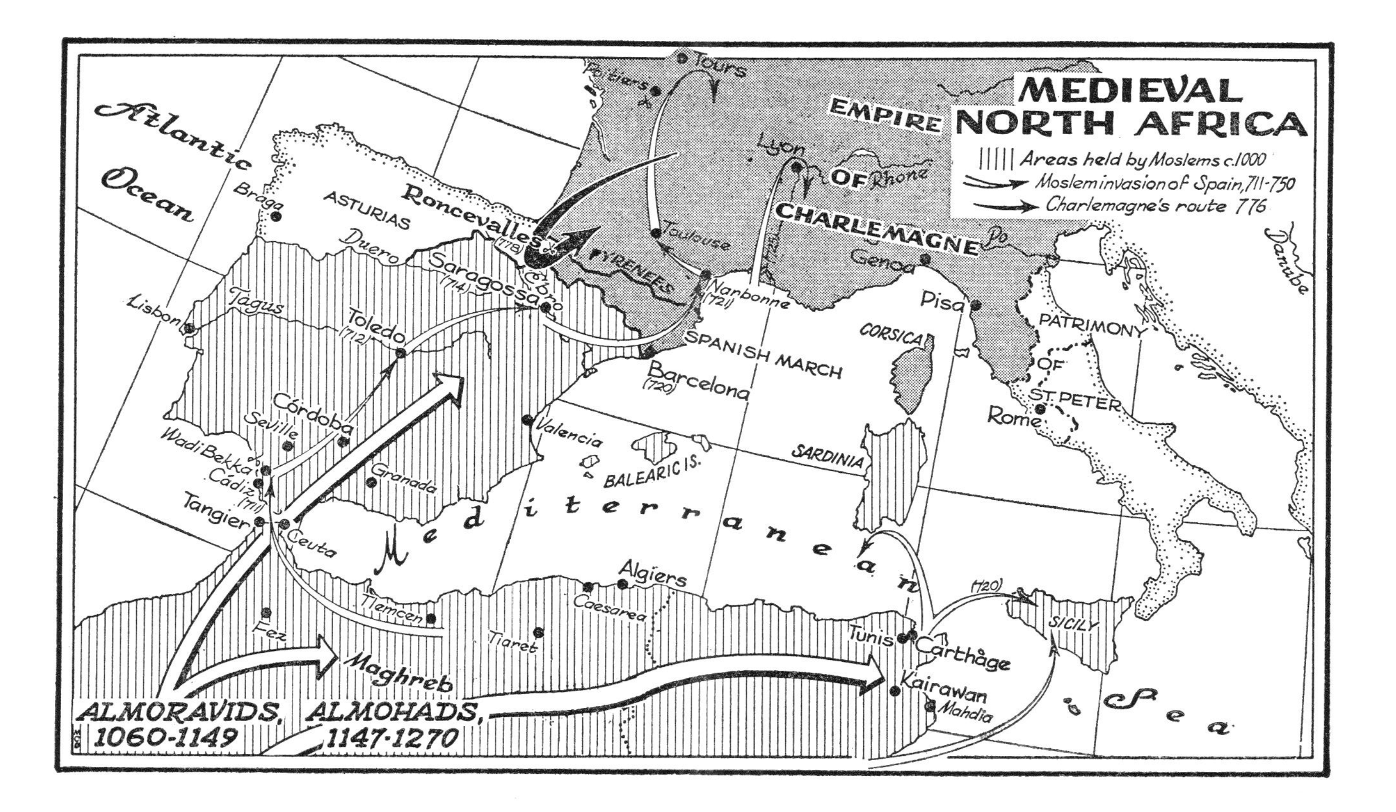
MEDIEVAL NORTH AFRICA
Areas held by Moslems c.1000
Moslem invasion of Spain, 711-750
Charlemagne's route 776
EMPIRE OF CHARLEMAGNE
Atlantic Ocean
Mediterranean Sea
Tours
Poitiers
Lyon
Rhone
Po
Danube
Toulouse
Genoa
Pisa
Narbonne (721)
PYRENEES
Roncevalles (778)
Braga
ASTURIAS
Duero
Saragossa (714)
Ebro
Tagus
Lisbon
Toledo (712)
SPANISH MARCH
Barcelona (720)
CORSICA
PATRIMONY OF ST. PETER
Rome
Córdoba
Seville
Wadi Bekka
Cádiz (711)
Granada
Valencia
BALEARIC IS.
SARDINIA
Tangier
Ceuta
Algiers
Caesarea
Tlemcen
Fez
Tiaret
Maghreb
Tunis
Carthage
Kairawan
Mahdia
(720)
SICILY
ALMORAVIDS, 1060-1149
ALMOHADS, 1147-1270

and Moslem forms combined in art and architecture, as in the Capella Palatina of Palermo and the Cathedrals of Cefalu and Monreale. In disgust, Roger's critics called him the "half-heathen" king, and both Roger and his great-grandson Frederick II (1215–1250) were called the "two baptized Sultans of Sicily."

Pope Victor III had already given his approval for a crusading raid against Mahdiyah by Genoese and Pisans in 1087. The North African coast, so temptingly close at hand, now became Roger's grandiose goal. Between 1134 and 1153, aided by his minister, Admiral George of Antioch, he raided and occupied Mahdiyah, Sousse, and Sfax on the Tunisian coast, then Bône, Gabès and the Island of Jerba, plundering Corfu and Thebes in Greece just for good measure. After Roger and George died, their Norman empire, through combined revolts and Almohad action, melted away even more rapidly than it had been won.

After destroying the Archbishopric of Carthage, Abd al-Mumin drove the Normans out of Mahdiyah and received the visit there of the Sheikh of Sfax, Umar ibn Abu al-Hasan Feryani, who as one Arab historian gleefully asserts, "through treachery got rid of the Christians of that city, which was henceforth added to his possessions." The same step was accomplished by Ibn Matruh, Sheikh of Tripoli, who revolted against the Franks installed in that city. Abd al-Mumin received them well and rewarded them generously. Tolerant in peace, the Almohad rulers were merciless toward their Christian enemies in war, and the aftermath of the conflict with Roger at first kept all Christian influence away.

"PEACEFUL COEXISTENCE"

Despite the vicissitudes of war in Spain and Morocco, the Almoravids, Almohads, and later dynasties kept up generally good relations with the papacy, and this helped to start and keep profitable trade flowing in both directions. A modern Moroccan historian insists that such ties were "constant and friendly" and that "racist and confessional considerations did not enter the Maghreb conception of diplomacy and foreign policy." [4] In general, North Afri-

[4] Abdelazziz Benabdallah, *Les Grands Courants de la Civilization du Maghreb* (Casablanca, 1958), p. 34.

can rulers, politicians, and religious leaders have wished to remain on good terms with the Vatican even during their many conflicts with Europe's secular rulers and have often succeeded in doing so. They have usually distinguished between the acts and attitudes of those Roman pontiffs who were not well disposed and individual bishops or priests who were. In our own time, the same distinction was constantly made during the 1954–1962 revolution in Algeria. North African cordiality toward the Holy See probably reached new heights during the reign of the late Pope John XXIII. The eulogies of Morocco's official state radio when John died in June, 1963, and the accolade it gave to Pope Paul VI far surpassed those it usually gave to leaders of the Arab world.

One early friendly exchange was a letter sent by Pope Gregory VII to the Hammadid King al-Nasir ibn Alnas in 1076, in which the pope expresses admiration for "the elevation of your heart" and prays that "God bring you to the bosom of blessedness of the most holy Patriarch Abraham" and observes that "we believe and confess one God, admittedly in a different manner." Even during the white heat of the Crusades, when Emperor Frederick II, that great admirer of Islam, fought Saladin's nephew, Sultan Malik al-Kamil, and then signed a ten-year truce with him, relations between North African rulers and Pope Gregory IX (1227–1241) were good. St. Francis actually met and talked with Kamil in Egypt.

In 1246, after the Church of Notre Dame of Marrakesh had been built for the Christian militiamen, Innocent IV wrote to the sultan in Marrakesh that he was pleased by his defense of the Church against "ill-intentioned people" and for the "new favors and considerable benefits" he had accorded it.

THE MERCHANT ENCLAVES

If religious relations "at the summit" were good during this period, so was trade. Foreign merchants and traders began to enter North African cities, from Tripoli all the way west to Safi, in the eleventh century. Generally, they lived in special enclaves where they were permitted to store their goods and often have chapels. These Christian merchants, unlike indigenous Jewish ones, do not seem to have had *dhimmi* status, and in some cases they had their own consuls and consular jurisdictions, a custom that continued in Morocco up until independence in 1956.

In 1133, two Moroccan ships arrived in Pisa with envoys of the Almohad Sultan Yahya, who signed a commercial treaty giving Pisan merchants rights in Moroccan ports, and vice versa. Twenty years later, another Almohad ruler concluded peace with Genoa, and, in observation of the agreement, eight Almohad vessels which had surrounded a Genoese vessel at Cagliari, Sicily, broke off an attack when they saw its nationality, and this at a time when piracy and privateering by both Moslem and Christian vessels were spreading throughout the Mediterranean. Under the conventions, Christian rulers were obliged to punish any subjects who committed acts of piracy against the sultan, using the same punishments inflicted on Moslem pirates.

The Christian merchants in Moroccan, Algerian, and Tunisian ports lived a generally tranquil life. Relations were so good that during the early Crusades, North African rulers often refused to pay subsidies which the sultans of Cairo and Damascus demanded. Christians in Morocco, we are assured, were allowed to use the *hammam* (the Moorish bath). In Ceuta, merchants and their families from Genoa, Pisa, and Marseilles lived in compounds, or *fonduks,* with their own consuls, customs inspectors, chaplains, churches, and cemeteries. The Royal Customs Service, in the time of the Almohads, is said to have taken care of expenses for construction and upkeep of the homes, shops, and churches of the merchants. Their own police forces kept order. If the sultan's officers desired to act against a member of the Christian colony, they made preliminary arrangements with the consul first and, under a treaty concluded between Pisa and Morocco in 1358, would do nothing without his participation "unless there were a formal refusal of justice and assistance." A dead Christian's property was placed under guard of the sultan's officers until surrendered to his legitimate heirs.

The situation in Tunisia was much the same. Christian merchants came to settle in Tunis in the twelfth and early thirteenth centuries, once the fury of Abd al-Mumin's vengeance had died down. They bought the hides of sheep and goats, and wax, exported them to

Europe, and sold European fabrics, Oriental products and even wine, for which many North Africans developed a fondness, despite the Koranic prohibition, during the time of Andalusian influence. The Pisans were the most active, and in 1157, even before Abd al-Mumin had finally settled accounts with the Normans, they obtained treaty rights for their persons and their goods.

Around 1200, Christian merchants of Tunis wrote to a Pisan who had left the city following the loss of some of his goods, "Don't hesitate to come back. You will find an excellent reception everywhere, and anyone who comes with you will too. Merchandise prices are right, and you can buy all you want." A Moslem business agent reassuringly appended to the letter, "Tranquillity and business are good, even better than when you left. You will be received and treated here even better than before." Mutual confidence ran so high that at times Moslems are even reported to have given Pisans credit.

In the time of the Hafsids (1228–1574), who succeeded the Almohads in Tunis, trade ties with Mediterranean Europe were even more important. The Christian merchants were grouped by nationalities in *fonduks,* each under the authority of a consul accredited to the Hafsid monarch. The Christian militias of Morocco inspired the Hafsid sultans to recruit their own Christian mercenary bodyguard of several hundred men, often entirely Catalans, who lived in a separate compound all to themselves. Other foreign residents of Tunis included former slaves of both sexes taken by pirates, some of whom converted to Islam; priests ministering to the Christian communities (in Morocco these were mainly Spanish and Portuguese; in Tunis they were Italian); Dominican and Franciscan missionaries, and agents charged with the ransom of Christian captives.

Venetians, Florentines, and Aragonese soon joined the Genoese and the Pisans in Tunis. The Acciauoli and Peruzzi families of Florence installed permanent offices and wielded great political influence at the Hafsid court. Special treaties, regularly renewed, regulated all conditions of Christian-Moslem commerce and established legal relations with Venice in 1231, with Pisa in 1234, and with Genoa in 1236. In 1353, Pisans obtained new guarantees of security, freedom of trade, and recognition of the principle that if an individual Christian merchant caused trouble, only he and not the entire community would be held responsible. On the rare occasions when there was trouble—they became less rare as European military forces intervened more and more often in Moslem affairs—the Christian residents could take refuge from rioters in the *fonduk*. These were built in Tunis, Bône, Bougie, Sfax, Gabès, and on the Island of Jerba. But Jerba became the scene of various attacks, raids, and sieges by Catalans, Arabs, Venetians, and Genoese, especially when the rivalry of Christian and Mahdiyan freebooters grew after 1300.

THE CHILDREN'S CRUSADE

Instead of destroying Islam, the struggle in the Holy Land had only fatally weakened the Eastern Church in Constantinople. Two dark episodes arising from this struggle contributed to ending the rather fragile Mediterranean tolerance. In 1212, some thirty thousand French children led by Stephen of Cloyes were gathered together at Vendôme, France, for a Crusade to the Holy Land. Without adequate food, clothing, or any idea of what a Crusade was all about or even where Palestine was, they marched overland to Marseilles. From here, as some of the unscrupulous men who exploited the whole affair told them, they would walk dryshod over the waters, thanks to divine intercession, all the way to the Holy Land.

Two Marseilles thugs, called Hugh the Iron and William the Pig, who were apparently in the pay of Moslem slave traders and were later hanged for attempting to kidnap Emperor Frederick II, offered to take them to Palestine free of charge on seven ships. Two of the ships were wrecked on San Pietro island off Sardinia. Most of the children were hustled ashore at Bougie (Algeria) and sold into slavery. Some ended up in Egypt, where Sultan al-Kamil, Saladin's nephew, gave them decent jobs as interpreter-secretaries and made no attempt to convert them to Islam. Others were sent all the way to Baghdad, where eighteen were beheaded for refusing Islam. Only one of the thirty thousand children is said to have returned home, after eighteen years of wandering.

ST. LOUIS AT TUNIS

The final and fatal medieval attempt of Europe to bring the cross back to North African shores in force came in 1270. It is remembered, and has deeply colored the attitudes of both Tunisian Moslems and French Christians, even in our own time. King Louis IX of France was the last of Europe's Crusader kings. He had already tasted defeat and imprisonment in the Middle East, after first taking up the cross in 1250. What were the motives of Louis in tempting fate again? The traditional Western view is that he was a truly devout man, dedicated to the best principles of Christianity and sincerely convinced of the justness of the Crusaders' cause, however lost it might appear to be. All the pathos of his Tunisian expedition is brought out in a recent account of his farewell, as he rode away from his beloved chateau at Joinville and his family, not looking back, thinking, "lest my heart should melt within me for the fair castle that I was leaving, and for my two children." Some historians have said that Louis had reports that "the Bey of Tunis" (meaning, apparently, the ruling Hafsid sultan, al-Mustansir) wished to be baptized as a Christian. If Louis really believed this he seems to have been indeed pathetically misinformed. Al-Mustansir was one of the worst possible rulers to approach on religious grounds. For a few years of his reign, his assumption of the caliphate was recognized as far away as Fez and Tlemcen. The Sharif of Mecca and the Mameluke rulers of Egypt recognized him as caliph.

There were, however, strong commercial reasons behind Louis' Crusade. Al-Mustansir had ended the custom of other Hafsid monarchs of paying tribute to the Norman and Hohenstaufen rulers of Sicily in return for security against attacks by Sicilian Christian pirates and the right to sell grain freely in Sicily's profitable markets. Charles of Anjou, Louis' brother, became King of Sicily in 1266. Soon after, al-Mustansir refused to pay any more tribute and began to lend a sympathetic ear to Charles' enemies.

European merchants, probably Marseilles traders living in Tunis, had advanced money to one Luliani, an intellectual who tried unsuccessfully to live from his writing and took a job as tax collector. Luliani was killed by Hillal, chief of al-Mustansir's Christian guard, because he was suspected of wanting to abscond to Sicily with some of his more or less ill-gotten gains. The European merchants demanded payment of Luliani's debts. Al-Mustansir rejected their requests, saying that they were not backed by sufficient proof. The merchants complained to Louis. Al-Mustansir, learning that a major expedition against him was brewing, sent envoys to Louis with a bribe of 80,000 gold pieces to buy him off. Ibn Khaldun says Louis accepted the money, then told them he was sticking to his original plans for the expedition, and refused to refund the bribe, claiming he had never received it.

The attitude of Charles of Anjou is one of the major mysteries of this Crusade. The papacy was vacant, and the absence of a pope's restraining hand provided Charles with an excellent chance to realize an old ambition of moving against Constantinople. However, Louis ordered his brother to join him with his forces. Obediently, Charles turned aside from his Oriental projects and sailed for Tunis with his troops to join the Crusader army. Acting on information or advice which may have been furnished by Friar Raymond Martin, a French Dominican of Tunis who was a friend of al-Mustansir, Louis probably envisaged turning Tunis into a Christian base on African soil from which he might avenge his own earlier defeat in Egypt. Originally outfitted for a new expedition against Palestine, the Christian fleet reached Tunis on July 18, 1270, after a stop at Cagliari, Sicily.

Al-Mustansir did not oppose the landing of six thousand knights and thirty thousand foot soldiers. Apparently he thought he could contain them inside Carthage. Soon the Sultan regretted bitterly that he had left the walls of Carthage standing and that he had not opposed the landing. In any case, he now proclaimed the *djihad* throughout North Africa. Relief armies converged on Carthage from Bougie, from the Berber kingdoms of Morocco, and probably from other parts of Tunisia. Almohad chiefs were the principal commanders. The presence of holy men, doctors of the law, and other noncombatant zealots of Islam added seasoning to the flavor of Holy War.

After a pitched battle between the troops of Charles of Anjou and Yahya ibn Salah, one of the Almohad chiefs, in which both sides suffered severe losses, al-Mustansir grew discouraged. He even considered abandoning Tunis to the Christians and withdrawing to Kairawan. "This was the state of things," says Ibn Khaldun, "when God struck the enemy, and on the morrow, the world learned that the King of the French lived no more." On the hill of Byrsa, from which Phoenicians had once ruled the known Western world, Louis had died of fever, aggravated by the heat, thirst, and possibly by polluted wells, after losing his son Tristram and while the Tunisians, according to one European account, blew hot sand clouds and catapulted corpses over the walls.

The new French commander, a knight named Philip the Hardy, proposed to the Sultan that the Crusaders withdraw, provided the Tunisians reimburse them for the costs of the expedition. Al-Mustansir, knowing that his Arab troops would soon be leaving for winter quarters, agreed. A peace treaty including a fifteen-year truce was signed on November 22, 1270. A separate accord initialed by Charles of Anjou provided that Sicily would remain at peace with Tunis. As the Crusaders' fleet sailed out of the Gulf of Tunis, an unseasonable Mediterranean storm, which the Moslems regarded as the final manifestation of God's wrath, sank some of the ships and badly damaged the rest. The Sultan collected from his people the sums he had to pay the Christians: six mule-loads of silver. All that the Crusader army left behind was ninety catapults.

THE LEGEND OF SIDI-BU-SAID

Carthage today, like the neighboring village of Sidi-bu-Said, is a charming residential suburb, dominated by its cathedral built in a strange style the French call "Byzantine-Mauresque." Cardinal Lavigerie, the would-be evangelizer of Africa, ordered it constructed after the French protectorate was established in 1881 on the site of an earlier commemorative chapel built in 1841. The cardinal's tomb is inside. Near the cathedral is the present monastery of the order of the White Fathers of Africa, who excavated many of the ruins of ancient Carthage and who operate a museum and library. The spirit of fantasy which one finds among the secular-minded younger generation in Tunisia today is well illustrated by a curious legend which a foreigner may hear told in the blue-and-white café at Sidi-bu-Said or from a casual Tunisian acquaintance at Carthage.

Louis did not die of fever, so runs this story. During the epidemic of plague which decimated the ranks of the Crusaders, he took to taking solitary walks near the confines of the walls. Wandering among the ruins one day, he met a wise and thoughtful holy man. Louis explained his cares: the Crusade was going from bad to worse. Return to France, where the treasury was impoverished and the barons were fighting among themselves, was distasteful, if not impossible.

"King," said the holy man, "I believe I have the solution. In Tunis, there is a young man of high birth who is dying of the plague. He looks exactly like you. This must be a sign from God. Bring this unfortunate one secretly to your camp; place him in the royal tent, and he will die in the honor of your name and fame. Your army can then sail home."

"How about me?" asked Louis.

"Look over there," said the holy man, pointing. Louis saw the splendid village of Sidi-bu-Said, gleaming white on its promontory over the Gulf of Tunis, where there was a palace surrounded by flowers and palms. At that moment, a beautiful Tunisian girl passed by, heading for the village. On the same evening, the ailing youth was brought to St. Louis' tent, where he died. The fleet sailed, and St. Louis moved into his palace, where he spent the rest of his days. The holy man taught him the Koran in exchange for instruction in the wisdom of the West.

A MODERN SEQUEL

Europeans and Arabs were to fight for Tunisia many more times, and there was often a lingering flavor of St. Louis' Crusade about most of the later Christian attempts. A mixed European expedition arrived at Mahdiyah in 1389 but was driven away after fighting broke out between the French and the Genoese. The Turkish adventurer Khair ed-Din Barbarossa defeated the last Hafsid ruler in 1533 but was soon beaten himself by the Christian forces of the Emperor Charles V. In 1569, the Bey of Algiers, Uldj Ali, recovered Algiers for Islam but was driven out in his turn in 1573 by a fresh Spanish expedition headed by Don Juan of Austria. In the following year, the Turks managed to establish stable Moslem rule. Turkish control, in its last stages purely nominal, was broken only by an Algerian expedition in 1689 and the French occupation of 1881. This ended with the formation of modern Tunisia in 1956.

The International Eucharistic Congress of 1930, to which President Bourguiba alluded in our conversation related at the beginning of this book, was held at Carthage by agreement of the ecclesiastical and French protectorate authorities. The occasion, which made it doubly injurious in Tunisian eyes, was to commemorate the French landings at Algiers in 1830. The ceremonies were held publicly, with great fanfare. Not only was the Grand Mufti of Tunis invited, but the costs were charged to the Tunisian national budget. The young generation of Tunisian nationalists, like Habib Bourguiba, who was soon to found the Neo-Destour (New Constitution) Party, saw a connection with an ill-fated attempt to evangelize the Berbers then going on in the French protectorate of Morocco. The memory of the Eucharistic Congress still rankles in Tunisia. Habib Boulares, the Secretary of State for Information told me in 1963, "It was incredible. It was as though we were being taken back to the time of St. Louis and living through another Crusade!" Memories, especially when nourished by political need, are slow in dying.

CHAPTER XIII

PORTUGUESE, POWDER MERCHANTS, AND PROTESTANTS

> One of the masters whom the Moslems heed most, lecturing one day more than thirty years ago at the Kairouyine University, heard a church bell ringing. "There is the enemy," he cried. "This is what we must battle against without mercy." This person became our friend. "I believed then," he explained to me, "that the Catholic Church proposed to conquer our souls by native force. I saw in it the religious form of Western imperialism."
>
> DOM DENIS MARTIN, PRIOR OF TOUMLILINE MONASTERY, MOROCCO, 1962

Early on a fall morning in 1415, the Moroccan garrison of Ceuta was astonished to see a Portuguese caravel putting into the harbor. Though war was ravaging Spain and Portugal, Morocco was then at peace. There was no need to fear the Nazarenes, the garrison thought. Squinting in the morning sunlight on the quay, the Moroccans made out a small group of Portuguese in a longboat rowing to shore. They received them kindly. "We are an embassy en route to the Frankish Kingdom in Sicily," the officer in charge told them. "We are in need of water and stores and would like to buy them here."

As the Moroccans unsuspectingly offered their hospitality, a fleet of about ten Portuguese transports and some British ships was creeping stealthily along the mountainous southern coast of the Strait of Gibraltar, just to the west of the narrow neck of land where Ceuta is perched. Aboard one of them was King João (John) I of Portugal, husband of the English princess Philippa of Lancaster, daughter of John of Gaunt.

The Portuguese had been in correspondence with some English

and German merchants established in Ceuta and knew the lay of the land. Before the Moroccans realized what was happening, the Portuguese transports had entered the harbor and thousands of knights, archers, and pikemen were pouring ashore. By all Western accounts, the Moslems put up little resistance to the treacherous attack. At nightfall, Ceuta and all its forts were in the hands of King John. An English chronicler of the day, Thomas Walsingham, says that John "overcame the Moores in the dominion of the King of Barbarie, putting many thousands of them to the sworde." An Arab version is that the garrison resisted like heroes, but the odds were too overwhelming. "The Moslems," says al-Djannabi, "then fled the city, taking with them their families and taking their goods and everything they could, even their scientific books, of which they had an enormous quantity; they also carried everything they found: marble, merchandise, leaving everything empty when the Franks entered." [1]

The capture of the fortress of Ceuta, the southern Pillar of Hercules, where the Portuguese left a garrison of only twenty-five hundred men, was more than just another incident in the Christian *reconquista.* John I had wanted to head off Castilian intervention in Morocco. Instead, he helped provoke it. More important, he established a tiny bridgehead which was to set off a slow chain reaction of religious resistance throughout Morocco. Ceuta withstood every siege the Moroccans could mount against it. Spain won control of it in 1580, when the Spanish and Portuguese crowns were united, and has kept it ever since.

There is no doubt that John I had wanted to strike a blow for the glory of Christendom. By so doing, he had pulled Portugal out of its backseat role as a small country on the western rim of the Iberian Peninsula. His son, Prince Henry the Navigator, who was twenty-one when Ceuta fell, was about to lead Portugal into a fantastic series of overseas adventures. He carried the coat of arms of John's family, the Avis, to all corners of the earth and made Portugal for a time the leading colonial power on earth, a past reputation of which it is bearing the consequences now. Portugal's motives in this and all its colonial ventures were frankly set forth by the government of Dr. Antonio de Oliveira Salazar in 1962, in a statement

[1] Quoted in Fagnan, *op. cit.*, pp. 299–300.

of colonial policy which was as much official dogma in 1455 as it is now:

> The principles of Portuguese colonization stem from the country's traditional faith. From our beginnings as a nation, Christianity has shaped our laws and customs and so firmly is the national character moulded by Catholic doctrine that a religious ethos, generally pointing to Rome, is characteristic of Portuguese thought. Because of this, the sense of mission has always been preserved. Sheer necessity or commercial interests have sometimes dimmed this ideal but they have never extinguished it. . . .
>
> The primary aim of our native policy was conversion, and the royal orders protecting the missionaries are in themselves a proof of sympathy for the natives of those Continents where the sword and the cross went together. The missionaries were there to restrain the violence of the soldiers. They also strove to instruct the natives so that they could be received into the Church, considered the greatest of possessions.[2]

Moroccan prisoners in Ceuta told young Prince Henry about the caravan routes which brought the gold, ivory, and slaves of Senegal and the Gold Coast from Timbuktu to Tunis. He had already heard the legends of the mysterious Prester John, the mythical Christian potentate of the East whose empire was supposed to contain fabulous treasures and who had been sought in vain in Ethiopia in 1316 by eight Dominicans sent by the pope. Henry resolved then and there to "deal a body-blow to Islam." He returned to Ceuta in 1418 and repulsed the first serious Moslem attempt to regain the city.

How did the papacy, which by now was developing further the practice adopted during the Crusades of sanctioning certain enterprises against unbelievers, feel about a new raid against Morocco, perhaps the conquest of Tangier? In 1437, Pope Eugene IV gave King Edward of Portugal his answer: war should not be made against countries which were not Christian but were also not idola-

[2] Antonio Alberto de Andrade, *Many Races—One Nation* (Lisbon: Agencia-Geral do Ultramar, 1961).

trous, unless they launched aggression against Christian states. A king, said Eugene, should not expose his people unnecessarily to the dangers of war, and this was not a project for which he could order prayers.

One of the main motives for the long series of European attacks on North African seaports was the rise of piracy and privateering. With some exceptions, the Moslem ships did no more than English ships did in the time of Sir Francis Drake: they raided the shipping of countries with which they were in a technical, if not legal state of war. They did this for motives of profit; to capture the cargoes and enslave the crews and passengers or hold them for ransom. At times the idea of *djihad,* or holy war, appears too, but nearly always mixed up with the profit motive.

What is much less known in the West is that Christian ships began raiding Moslem shipping in force, especially near Sicily, around 1200, as soon as the European powers had fleets that were sufficiently powerful. One of the first of hundreds of instances recorded by Arab historians is a raid on Tunis about 1200 by two Pisan vessels, which seized three Moslem ships by surprise during a period of peace, putting the crew in irons, helping themselves to the women, and making off with the cargoes. Italian and other European privateers were also attacking Byzantine shipping at this time, though they preferred Arab ships when they were available.

Among the Christian raids on North Africa which preceded the capture of Ceuta, and which contemporary Arab historians seem especially to have resented, was the seizure of Tripoli in 1354. Genoese, some of whom passed themselves off as merchants, were involved here. A few of them had formed a fifth column inside the city after its governor had trustingly admitted them. They aided a sea-borne raiding force which "removed everything to transport it to Genoa, their country, leaving only an absolute emptiness" when they departed four months later. In 1389, another mixed Italian-French expedition raided Mahdiyah but broke up when the Genoese apparently tried some treachery against the French: the Moslems saw this as a sign of divine protection for them. In 1423, a Catalan force of ten thousand seized the Kerkenna Islands off the Tunisian coast from a defending force of two thousand Arabs. Four years later, Catalans laid siege to Jerba for twenty-seven days and tried to surprise the sultan's army during the siesta hour but were driven off.

THE NEW CRUSADE

North Africans are highly sensitive about charges of Western historians that Europe had to carry the war to the coasts of Barbary in order to exterminate the pirates, many of whom were Moslems from Spain, Albania, or Turkey. One present-day Moroccan historian comments:

> Certainly, the inhabitants of the Moroccan coasts sheltered the miserable Andalusian pirates, but the fact, already anodyne in itself, was justified at that time by Iberian enterprises against the Maghreb. The least one could expect of the Moroccans under the circumstances was to remain passive—which was considered later on as a tacit encouragement to the Moriscos [unconverted Moslems expelled from Spain in 1610, who settled in Salé and became the famous "Sallee Rovers," among the most dreaded pirates operating in the Atlantic or Mediterranean] in their legitimate reaction toward the Christian navy [sic]. But better to judge the situation, the general state of spirit reigning at the time, especially in the Christian camp, should be kept in mind. . . . Christian piracy took on the aspect of a veritable crusade against Islam.[3]

The Portuguese phase of the new crusade developed rapidly. As early as 1270, Lisbon had begun to explore the African coast. Now the tempo increased. In 1433, the Portuguese explorer Gil Eannes pushed beyond Cape Bojador. Three years later, Christian knights of Portugal landed on the desolate coast of what is now the Spanish Sahara. Camoëns described this in his *Lusiads,* the Portuguese national epic, as "a country ill-disposed to bear any fruit." Prince Henry tried without success to capture Tangier in 1437. His brother Fernando was captured, and the shock killed King Edward.

Instead of finding the fabled gold of the Rio de Oro, the Portu-

[3] Benabdallah, *Les Grands Courants de la Civilization du Maghreb* (Casablanca, 1958), pp. 101–102.

guese adventurers Antão Goncalves and Nune Tristão captured Moslem slaves for the first time in 1441. Slave trading among these men of the sea was very soon to become a vital part of the "Christian ethos" of the day. Many of the slaves were taken back to Lisbon, baptized and "assimilated," as the Portuguese colonial literature likes to put it, into the population. In the first five years of the slave trade, nearly one thousand slaves were bought or caught between Cape Bojador and the Bay of Arguin, where the first European settlement in West Africa was founded in 1448.

On July 2, 1509, after the Moroccan coastal port of Safi had been captured and a Portuguese bishop had been appointed to look after the spiritual welfare of its Moslem inhabitants, a group of the latter sent a pathetic letter to Diego de Azambuja, the governor, noting that Moslems were being deported as slaves to Madeira. In desperation, the inhabitants were destroying their own houses and fleeing. The Christians had raised the mosque of the cemetery and the *zawiya,* or monastery, of Sidi Ali, a local patron saint, and pillaged the Grand Mosque, which was partially destroyed and desecrated. The letter reports depredations in other mosques and the confiscation of *habus,* or religious property, belonging to the mosques. The Portuguese were also said to have been making free with Safi's womanhood. "If the King wished the population to return to Safi," said the letter, "order your men to descend from our minaret, which is the Moslem safeguard of our religion, for as long as your men are there, no Moslem will return to Safi to live." Those remaining behind would be nothing but Christians in the eyes of the other Moslems. The signers also asked the Portuguese to halt their export of slaves and appoint an intermediary "between Moslems and Christians" to make peace.

The Jews of Safi probably feared the Portuguese even more than the Moslems did. It was no wonder: King Manuel I (1495–1521) had mercilessly expelled the Jews from Portugal in 1496. He tried to reassure them in a letter which promised never to force them to adopt Christianity against their will (*nem isso mesmo os mandaremos tornar christos por constrangimento*), and if he was compelled to expel them "for official reasons," he would give them two years' notice. This generosity was reinforced by a promise to collect only one payment of tribute from every Jewish home.

Agadir, Azzemour, Mogador, and Mazagan were also captured by the Portuguese during the early sixteenth century. By the late eighteenth century all had been recaptured by the holy warriors of the Moroccan *shurafa* (plural of *sharif,* chiefs of more or less noble lineage who claimed direct descent from the Prophet), who were usurping central power in Morocco by this time. Near Mogador, a tourist who is curious enough may still see tombs visited by pilgrims which are said to be those of *mudjahidun,* or fighters for the faith, who perished in the war against the Portuguese.

Ten Christian artisans and merchants lived in Azzemour when the city fell to the Portuguese. The military governor, Rui Barreto, wrote Manuel I that he had better things to do than build three monasteries in the town as the king had suggested. There were no houses available, and the meager funds were better used to other purposes. It would be enough, felt Barreto, to build a small monastery to St. Augustine—in a mosque.

The goal of Manuel in taking Azzemour was to make it a point of departure for conquering and, if he could, converting the Kingdom of Marrakesh. Pope Leo X congratulated him on the early Portuguese successes and in 1514 granted a special crusading indulgence to all Christians of Portugal who went to war against the infidels of Africa. At this time the papacy was reverting to an old medieval custom of dividing up the spoils of the non-Christian world among the strongest Christian powers, which now happened to be Spain and Portugal. The Spanish had settled the Canary Islands in 1424 and were conducting slave raids from there along the African coast that continued through the sixteenth century. As the Hispano-Portuguese rivalry in Africa and on the trade routes to the East grew, Pope Nicholas V issued a bull in 1454 declaring that Ceuta and other Portuguese acquisitions, both past and future, in the surrounding territory and on the coast of Africa from Cape Bojador and Cape Nam southward belonged to the Portuguese crown. This was only the first in a long series of treaties and papal grants which partitioned the non-Christian world between Spain and Portugal.

With the "Bull of the Holy Crusade" (*La Santa Cruzada*), the papacy authorized the granting of indulgences, renewable every five years. Such indulgences had previously been granted to the faithful of Spain and Portugal in recognition of their struggle against the Moors. The new bull was in conflict with the cautious policy announced to King Edward in 1437; it permitted the use of eggs and milk during Lent and the eating of meat on certain days of abstinence, as long as the "Holy Crusade" was being pursued against the Moors.

The kings of Spain and Portugal regularly sold these indulgences to knights, nobles, and clergy who could afford to pay the rates, and it became a major source of royal revenue. In Portugal a special Council of the Crusade administered them. When the struggle ended in the peninsula with the fall of Granada in 1492, the popes indicated they would not reissue the bull. However, the Spanish and Portuguese courts insisted that since they were continuing the war against the infidels in Africa, they had a right to go on enjoying it.

In their enclave at Mazagan, the Portuguese maintained a point of contact with North African Islam where there was occasional strife. This gave them a pretext to continue using the privileges of the bull until they lost Mazagan. For the same reason, the Spaniards retained their own enclaves, or *presidios* (administrative units), of Ceuta and Melilla and several smaller places. The bull, according to an official report made by the Spanish Governor of Melilla in 1715, provided "immense benefits." Ceuta and Melilla also proved valuable as penal colonies for political prisoners from mainland Spain.[4]

The cross not only followed the sword of Portugal, in some cases it went on before it. Pope Alexander VI (1492–1503), who consecrated the division of infidel territory, appointed a Bishop John over the Moroccan diocese, six years before Safi had been conquered. In 1509, Manuel I ordered all Christians living in Safi and other places within jurisdiction of his episcopate to follow the bishop's instruction and pay the tithes which were to finance the upkeep of vicars and parish priests. At about the same time, Manuel

[4] H. de Castries and P. Cenival, *Les Sources Inédites de l'Histoire du Maroc* (Paris and London, 1918), "Spain, First Series," I, pp. 55, 72, 82. The *Sources Inédites* are a large corpus of previously unpublished documents of all sorts concerning Morocco. They are a rich and still largely unnoticed mountain of source material.

concluded a secret financial arrangement with the "infidel" Caid (local military and civil administrator) of Safi, Abd al-Rahman, to favor imports of Portuguese merchandise.

Even though the papacy had taken a negative attitude toward such ventures as King Edward's raid against Tangier, it rigorously prohibited arms traffic with Islamic states and frequently renewed the prohibition, especially as the Turkish threat loomed larger and larger in the East. These decrees were justified by reference to Islamic precepts which supposedly established the *djihad* as a permanent state of hostility against Christendom. But England and France, at that time still the have-not nations in the colonial race, violated the prescription again and again in their own scramble for the good things of Africa, America, and the Orient. After the loss of their *fronteira,* or mercantile military base of Agadir, to the Sharif of Tagmadret in 1541, the Portuguese bitterly blamed English and French arms merchants who aided "the Sharif, against divine and human laws," as one Portuguese intelligence report put it. Nicholas Throckmorton, a British diplomatic agent, reported to William Cecil, Lord Treasurer of England under Queen Elizabeth, that profitable business could be done with the infidels in North Africa, finding "these commodities in great store: gold, copper of the reddist and best for artyllery than is fownde anywher, sugar, dates, gomme arabic for clothiers, amber, wax, skynnes dressed for wearinge and horses better than Spaine," but urging great caution lest the Spaniards and Portuguese become aware of the great possibilities. This was naïve: they already had been for over a century. The British traders had trouble buying horses, because religious law forbade their sale or export to the infidel.

In 1562, the Portuguese ambassador in London protested indignantly that an English ship had arrived secretly at Larache "with offensive and defensive arms and full of Bibles and other books in Hebrew for the Jews of these countries." In her reply, Elizabeth, whose interest in Morocco was growing, asked indignantly how so many Bibles in Hebrew could be found when there were so few in the country. Good Queen Bess could also not understand why one should not sell Bibles to Jews or Moslems or any other nation when they contain the true Commandments of God.

DON SEBASTIAN'S DISASTER

The fortunes of war had already begun to turn against Portugal in Morocco when Jesuit influence began to operate in Lisbon. St. Ignatius Loyola, with five associates, had founded the ultramilitant Society of Jesus in Rome, principally to combat the Protestant Reformation in Europe. Pope Paul III approved it in his bull, *Regimini militantis ecclesiae,* of September, 1540.

Some Jesuits felt that the battle against the infidel in Africa was equally as important as that against the followers of Luther in Europe. Among these were teachers and confessors of King Sebastian (1557–1578), who ascended the Portuguese throne at the age of fourteen. Sebastian "combined headstrong self-will and morbid religiosity." [5] After one false start with an ill-equipped expedition, he crossed to Tangier, which had been captured in 1471, and Ceuta. He had no solid support from Philip II of Spain and had collected a motley army of twenty thousand Portuguese, Spaniards, Germans, and Italians, plus some Moroccan collaborators under a prince named al-Mutawakil. From bases at Tangier and Arzila, the new band of would-be Crusaders marched southward. The Saadid sultan, Abd al-Malik, was a much traveled man who knew Europe, its languages, and its strategy; his army included Moriscos seething with resentment against the Christians who had expelled them from their homes. He drew them further and further into a trap between the Loukkos River, near Larache, and one of its tributary streams, the Wadi Makhassin.

After the landings, Abd al-Malik sent a messenger to Sebastian with a letter which played on Sebastian's anti-Jewish sentiments as well as his sense of chivalry. In it he wrote that if Sebastian held the positions he had taken and waited for the Moslems, he was "a true and valorous Christian, but if you push into the interior and lower yourself by attacking some of my subjects before a prince of your own rank can face up to you, you are only a Jew, the son of a Jew." [6]

[5] William C. Atkinson, *A History of Spain and Portugal* (London, 1960), p. 159.

[6] Quoted in al-Wansharisi, *op. cit.,* pp. 408–411.

Abd al-Malik's numerically superior forces launched an attack as the flood tide came up the river and cut off the Christian retreat. Don Sebastian and al-Mutawakil were drowned. Abd al-Malik himself died of illness during the battle, but his lieutenants kept the news from the Moslem troops until victory was theirs. This "Battle of the Three Kings," as Western historians call it, ended the major Christian threat to Morocco and weakened Portugal, as the blind poet Camoëns had predicted. Spain was now able to dominate its rival, and in 1580 Philip II took the Portuguese Throne. In Morocco, this was a time of peace, prosperity, and Islamic revival under the Saadid Sultan Ahmad al-Mansur (1578–1603), called "The Golden" (al-Dhahabi) because he was so rich that European kings tried to borrow money from him.

MOROCCAN MYSTICISM AND THE RELIGIOUS REVIVAL

From 1524 until the present, Morocco has been ruled by a line of kings who have made the religious unity of their realm as important a matter as is geographical integrity. Nearly all of them have had to defend it against both constant Christian pressure from outside and dissidents, sometimes religious, sometimes tribal, and often a mixture of both, from within. These kings are *shurafa,* or descendants of the Prophet, and their forebears came originally from Arabia. Down to the present ruler, Hasan II, they base their legitimacy on this fact; they could appropriately be called Alids (those descended from Ali), and hence Shiites. However, the Moroccan Alids have completely disassociated themselves from Eastern Shiism. Morocco, like Algeria, Tunisia, and Libya, is completely dominated by the orthodox Sunnite code of Malik, which is equally tolerated in the Islamic world with the three other legal schools, Hanafi, Shafii, and Hanbali.

The House of Sad, sometimes called Saadians, which ruled Morocco until the House of Hasani Filali (more usually called the Alawites) replaced it in 1664, drew much of its early spiritual force from currents of Eastern mysticism. The main current was Sufism, which may come from *suf,* the robe of rough wool worn by Moslems who have withdrawn from the world and retired to a life of contemplation. Born in the Orient, Sufism spread throughout North Africa.

Ibn Tumart, founder of the ascetic Almohad doctrine, was its most successful exponent in the Maghreb. It took root among the nascent religious brotherhoods, or *tarikas,* and the *zawiyas* of the Almohad period. It flourished under the Marinids, and began to take on anti-Christian aspects with the first European attacks.

Sufism received some stimulus from Christian mysticism and from Gnosticism. It used as much Christian experience and Gnostic imagery as could be adapted to Islam's basic doctrines. The old saint worship which the heathen Berbers had known before Carthage and which had never died out came back to the Maghreb. From local saints, who possessed the sacred power called *baraka* and under the doctrine called *karamet* were able to perform saintly miracles, it was only a step back down to the animistic superstitions which the Berbers had so loved in the days of Herodotus. Divinations, spells, and all the other apparatus of trickery provided a means of livelihood for vast numbers of derwishes (dervishes), Sufi adepts who performed religious exercises, sometimes in violent trances.

In some ways, the Sufi revivalists (*marabouts*) in North Africa were like Christian revivalists of our own day. Orthodox rulers, hard-pressed by invasions of Turks, the Hillali Arabs, or Saharan Berbers in the eleventh and twelfth centuries found that the "back to Islam" Sufi preachers, especially among the modest folk, could be useful in reviving patriotic feeling. Some of the Sufi orders extended their influence into the guilds of merchants and artisans. In the *zawiyas,* the Sufi monks taught not only prayer and contemplation but also such subjects as magic and alchemy, as they still do today in some out-of-the-way places in Rio de Oro and Mauretania.

Europeans only casually acquainted with North Africa often tend to regard the *marabouts* as fanatics—wild-eyed men who dance on jagged glass and play with serpents. The other aspect of "maraboutism," which was the main agency through which Islam penetrated animist peoples in West Africa, was related by an unknown seventeenth-century Englishman, who signed his published account of experiences in Morocco "Ro. C." Since he termed Islam "the damnable Religion of the Incredulous More or Barbarian," he could scarcely be accused of being an Islamophile. "Fokers [sic] or Saints," he wrote, "dwell in the best places of the country, keep great hospitality for all travellers. . . . Much good these doe in the country by their example of morall living." [7]

Orthodox rulers like the Marinids and the sultans of Marrakesh regarded the Sufis as dangerous. Against them they built up the strength of the *ulama,* or doctors of the law, who taught orthodox doctrines and gave the stamp of religious approval to the acts of the rulers where it was needed. They also built orthodox colleges (*madrasa*) to combat Sufi influences. Both the Marinid rulers in Fez and the Wattasids, who followed them, tended to use the *marabout* as a religious and political propagandist to preach the holy war against the Christians. At the same time they tried to keep down *marabout* political power which in the time of the Saadids grew strong and sapped the authority of the central government. Most of the secular-minded Arab nationalists of today regard the *marabout* as a reactionary charlatan who is more of a nuisance than a threat.

Under the Marinids, early *marabout* influence had done away with the puritanical rigors and the rigid hierarchy of the Almohad administration. A dynasty which ruled in Tlemcen from 1235 until the Turks destroyed it in 1554, the Abd al-Wadids, made western Algeria into a center of Islamic studies carried on in five *madrasas.*

During the Algerian revolution of 1954–1962, Tlemcen, in the relative seclusion of its mountain fastness, was a quiet center of the religious opposition to French rule. There, during the crisis of the new Algerian leadership in the summer of 1962, Ahmed ben Bella rallied his supporters, including some of the *ulama,* before maneuvering himself into power in Algiers.

One of innumerable examples of early political "maraboutism" was reported to the King of Spain by Pedro Venegas of Córdoba, governor of Melilla. The astounded governor wrote that a *marabout* calling himself "al-Fatimi," a synonym for *the mahdi,* had proposed to capture Melilla through enchantment, without recourse to force, though an attacking army was being made ready. The spells of "al-

[7] Castries, *Sources Inédites,* "England, First Series," British Museum, Press Mark 1198, C 20, *A True Historical Discourse* (London, 1609), pp. 400–401.

Fatimi" were not put to the test, since the governor set a trap for him and captured him.

In the twentieth century, French colonists and reactionary Moroccan *marabouts,* chief among them Sharif al-Kitanni of Fez, head of the influential Kittaniya brotherhood, cooked up a bogus "appeal in the name of Islam" to oust the supposedly heretical King Mohammed V of Morocco from the throne and exile him in August, 1953. This launched Morocco's modern nationalist revolution and discredited "maraboutism" for a time, though it seemed to gain some strength again under Hasan II after 1963.

NORTH AFRICA AND THE REFORMATION

Protestant missionaries working in North Africa have usually felt that they enjoy a certain advantage over their Roman Catholic colleagues. First of all, they do not belong to one of the erstwhile colonial powers, with the exception of a few French Protestant pastors and perhaps here and there a lone Spanish or Italian one who is as much an exile from his own country as he is a missionary to another. Britons and Americans, in the words of one American missionary in Morocco in 1963, "certainly enjoy the advantages of their nationality."

Modern Protestant writers like Kenneth Cragg have approached Islam from a vastly more intelligent viewpoint than the Reformation's founders. Martin Luther (1483–1546) lived in the time of the Turkish military threat to the West. In his eyes, the Church of Rome "might be thought the head and Islam the body, of Antichrist." However, as Norman Daniel notes, Luther is inconsistent here, since "out of God's Church" Luther sees no Antichrist and therefore the Turks could not consistently fill the bill. "On the one hand, certain prophecies, notably the Apocalypse, 'he shall make war against the Saints,' applied strictly to the Turk, and not properly to the Pope at all." [8]

Luther's contemporary, the German reformer and theologian, Melanchthon (1497–1560), felt much more strongly that the name of Antichrist was applicable to Mohammed as the "devastator" and

[8] Norman Daniel, *Islam and the West* (Edinburgh, 1962), p. 280.

"tyrant" of the Christian religion. For Melanchthon, Islam denied Christ's role as mediator or peacemaker and rejected the witness of the Apostles and Prophets by breaking the rules of monogamous marriage. This kind of thinking is still translated into twentieth-century dogma for Protestant workers of the North Africa Mission, as a recent editorial in the North Africa bulletin indicates:

> The truth of the matter is that Islam is an arrogant deception contrived by the master deceiver, Satan, to defeat the Christian Gospel and enslave millions of souls by its lies. This fact is established once and for all by the blatant, consistent denial of the deity and death of the Lord Jesus Christ. Apparent similarities are deliberate camouflage, not innocent glimpses of truth.[9]

Queen Elizabeth I's special ambassador to the Marrakesh court of Sultan Abd al-Malik, Edmund Hogan, was quite taken with the religious views of his host, who wined, dined, and entertained him with traditional Moroccan hospitality. Hogan reported to Elizabeth on June 11, 1577, that Abd al-Malik had told him concerning their Catholic enemy, Philip II of Spain, that the king could not rule his own country but was under the thumb of the pope and the Inquisition. He found that Abd al-Malik disliked Catholics and was "a vearie earnest Protestant . . . and well experimented as well in the Old Testament as New, bering great affection to God's trew religion used in your Highnes realm." [10] This was neither the first nor the last time that a North African ruler would pull the wool over the eyes of a visitor so ignorant of Islam that he did not realize that most of the Old and New Testament stories could be found, in one form or another, in the Koran.

During a secret mission to London, in 1600, a Moroccan agent, Abd al-Wahad, proposed an alliance between Elizabeth and the sultan to wage a sort of holy war against Spain. England, he suggested, could take over the territories held by Spain in Morocco, and England and Morocco together would take "both the East and

[9] Francis Rue Steele, "Tolerance and Truth," *Cross and Crescent* (Upper Darby, Pa., June, 1963), pp. 1–2.

[10] Castries, *Sources Inédites,* "England, First Series," British Museum, Cotton mss., Nero, B, XI, f. 297, p. 226.

the West Indies" from Spain.[11] There was great rejoicing among England's new pro-Protestant friends in Morocco when Spain's Invincible Armada was defeated and scattered in 1588. Elizabeth, prompted by the glowing reports of Hogan and others, continued to dream until her death and Abd al-Malik's, both in 1603, of an Islamic-Protestant axis against Catholic Spain and Portugal. Evidently Elizabeth's ideas were not widespread: the scholar John Chamberlain wrote to a friend in the Foreign Office that "our merchants and mariners will not carry" Moroccans "into Turkie, because they thinck yt a matter odious and scandalous to the world to be too friendly or familiar with Infidels." [12]

Even the hardheaded English of Elizabeth's time were not wholly without their wild fantasies of wholesale conversions in North Africa which would also entail great commercial gain. A British agent named Henry Roberts, who had spent three years in Morocco, wrote to James I in 1603 that Morocco was "verie great and riche . . . and how Godly and Christianlike yt weare to subdue the same from Mahomet to the knowledge of Christ." Roberts suggested that if England made war on Morocco, all Moslem captives should be set free and encouraged, though not forced, to embrace Christianity "that they shal bee better governed by Christian government than ever they weare before." He was astonished by the number "which weare Christians and turned Moores which wee call Runnagates [renegades]. . . . For theis people bee very unstable and changeable in their mynde, and will bee drawne with faire words and good promises." [13]

Another British spy, John Harrison, who in 1581 masqueraded in Tetuan as a ransom agent buying back Christian captives in order to fool some suspicious Spanish friars, used his spare time to write religious tracts to "Spaniards, Jews and Moors," urging all three to convert to the true faith of England. He found the Jews and the Moriscos "already Christians at heart, most of them." The Moriscos especially, he felt, would make good Protestants since they hated Spain. Harrison recommended that both commerce and the Protes-

[11] *Ibid.*, Public Record Office, State Papers, Foreign, Spain, VII, 177–79.

[12] *Ibid.*, Public Record Office, State Papers, No. 94, Domestic, Elizabeth, CCLXXV, 192.

[13] *Ibid.*, British Museum, Additional Mss., 38/39, f. 33, p. 225.

tant faith would profit if England seized Ceuta. As policy, he advised what other colonial powers, more successful in North Africa than England, later adopted as articles of diplomatic faith: keep good relations with the trading cities on the coast; encourage trouble in the interior, and, if possible, take over the Spanish enclaves.[14]

Almost exactly the same sort of reasoning is to be found in the reflections of modern Protestant missionaries. One of the founders of the North Africa Mission, writing in 1900 on the first twenty years of the Mission's labors, found that

> Mohammedanism, Romanism and infidelity are the great anti-Christian forces we have to face. These are not merely systems of error, but systems of error especially devised to obstruct and overthrow the Gospel. . . . Added to the religious difficulties are the political ones, which the zealously religious, whether Moslem, Romanist, infidel or Jew, are ever ready to call to their aid.[15]

Reformation, Counter Reformation, and the wars of religion in Europe came at a time when the new imperialistic Christian offensive against North Africa was beginning to gather momentum. They also coincided with the beginnings of the scientific revolution and the revival of learning under Erasmus and the new scholars. How at least one Moslem leader sees this in retrospect is revealed by remarks of Allal al-Fassi in 1959:

> It is unfortunate that the imperialist campaign against the Islamic world coincided with the moment when materialism in the West reached its highest degree and that the differences which arose between Western schoolmen at the beginning of the Renaissance and between churchmen led to a schism in the Christian religion. Since then, all manifestations of modern civilization and the effect of the Inquisition's religious court were strong on the Christian religion. More than that, it was a severe blow against all religious beliefs because the struggle between the men of religion and the men of science was transformed

[14] *Ibid.*, British Museum, Harein Mss., ff. 320–328, pp. 573–582.

[15] J. Rutherford and Edward H. Glenny, *The Gospel in North Africa* (London, 1900), Part I, p. 242.

into a struggle between what was named the scientific method and the so-called religious method. And although Islam never resisted and never feared scientific study in all its different forms, the Moslems have not freed themselves as yet from *judging Islamic thought in analogy with Christian ideas* [italics mine], attaching to it the faults which Islam and its scholars never committed.[16]

[16] Unpublished lecture by Allal al-Fassi, quoted from lecture notes of Prof. S. Schaer.

CHAPTER XIV

TURKS AND SLAVE TRADERS

> Set you down this;
> And say besides, that in Aleppo once,
> Where a malignant and a turban'd Turk
> Beat a Venetian and traduc'd the state,
> I took by the throat the circumcised dog,
> And smote him, thus.
>
> SHAKESPEARE, 1604 (*Othello*)

By about 1550 many Moroccans believed, in contrast to some of their North African neighbors and in agreement with European Christians, that the advance of the Ottoman Turks represented a major threat to the Western world. Most of the Christian powers saw the drive of the Turks into Central Europe and the Mediterranean as the most serious threat to Western civilization since the Huns. This did not stop one French king, Francis I (1515–1547), from making them his occasional allies against the Hapsburg Empire. The military, naval, and political menace alarmed the West more than the spiritual one. In 1569, a British agent in Cádiz reported to Queen Elizabeth that the Moriscos, then engaged in the revolt against Philip II that led to their exile, were getting more and more aid from the Turks, as well as from the Moroccans. Sebastian of Portugal wrote to his ambassador at the Spanish court that the King of Spain was obliged to intervene in Morocco "to halt the progress of the Turks . . . an obligation connected with the very conservation of Christianity."[1]

The fall of Cairo in 1517 to Sultan Salim, who called himself caliph, had led Pope Leo X to consider a new crusade. Five years later, Salim's son Sulaiman captured the Island of Rhodes, Western Christianity's easternmost outpost, from the Knights of St. John, who had been assisting Christian buccaneers in raids on Moslem shipping. A Greek potter's son from Mytilene, on the island of Les-

[1] Castries, *Sources Inédites*, British Museum, Additional Mss., 28360, f. 26, p. 164.

bos, Khair ed-Din Barbarossa, and his brother, Aruj, emerged as the champions of Islam by daring attacks on Christian ships, especially Spanish ones, and by transporting thousands of Moriscos from Spain to North Africa between 1504 and 1510. Hundreds of treasure-hungry adventurers flocked to join Barbarossa. The Hafsid Sultan permitted the use of Tunisian ports as bases for Khair ed-Din and gave the governorship of the Island of Jerba to Aruj.

The new "crusade" turned out to be simply a series of Spanish raids against North African cities, aimed at suppressing piracy, but also meant as a sort of counterattack against Barbarossa and against the Turks, who were advancing in Europe and who stood behind him. Ottoman diplomats, in fact, had succeeded in convincing many Christian diplomats that the Ottoman sultan was just as much the supreme spiritual leader of all the Moslems, in North Africa and everywhere else, as the pope was of Catholicism.

What had actually happened, and what especially tempted the Turks, was that the relative political and spiritual unity the Maghreb had often known in the Middle Ages was falling apart. Only in Morocco was there a semblance left, and even there the *shurafa* were engaged in a constant power struggle. The rulers of Tlemcen had lost their influence elsewhere in Algeria and had trouble keeping control even in Tlemcen. In Tunisia, the Hafsid monarchs dared not venture outside the gates of the capital: anarchy and the Arab bedouin usually controlled the rest. From Jerba all the way west to Mogador, little pirate republics armed their own galleys and pursued the *djihad* against Christian shipping. In these encounters, both Christians and Moslems enslaved many of their captives: Roger Marbeck, a British doctor who accompanied Lord Howard on a naval expedition to Cádiz in 1596, reported finding and setting free thirty-eight Moroccan captives of the Spaniards "that had beene a longe tyme galley slaves." [2]

Many thousands of other Moslem slaves were taken to Malta by the Knights of St. John and sold in that island's infamous slave markets and in those of Genoa and Pisa. The accounts of European historians tend to skim over these things, of course. From Moslem sources, we know that the capture and mass enslavement of thousands of Christian captives became widespread, after the renewal

[2] *Ibid.*, British Museum, Sloane Mss., 226 f., p. 94.

of European aggression by the Spaniards and Portuguese. Some accounts come from the much-traveled Leo Africanus, one of the most celebrated Moslem converts to Christianity. His given name was actually al-Hasan ibn Mohammed al-Wazzan. He was captured by a Christian corsair, probably from Malta. Instead of selling him, his captors took him to Pope Leo X, and he was baptized. In his *Description of Africa,* Hasan, or Leo, tells of a visit to Tetuan, where he saw "three thousand Christian slaves, all clad in woolen blouses who slept at night chained together at the bottom of ditches." Despite this treatment of Christian captives, Leo is able in the next paragraph to describe the ruler of Tetuan as "an extremely generous man who showed hospitality to every foreigner who passed through the city." [3]

CHARLES V: *CUIUS REGIO, EIUS RELIGIO*

The Spaniards had been retaliating against African corsairs since about 1390. The new element in the sixteenth-century Spanish "crusade" against North Africa was the quickening flame of religious fanaticism on both sides of the Moslem-Christian sea frontier. On the Spanish side, the Inquisition was growing stronger. Mainly, it was intended to coerce Christians, not convert Moslems, and the Jesuits were already pitting the idea of conversion by the fervor of faith against the idea of stamping out heresy by coercion. However, the influence of Cardinal Jiménez de Cisneros, who was no admirer of Islam, was probably the determining one.

One present-day Moroccan historian is anxious to stress how many European renegades there were among the North African pirates, whereas the others "were hardly Moslems at all, properly speaking"; they adhered to a schismatic sect (the Kharidjites of Jerba and of the mountains around Bougie) who "believed themselves to be doing a meritorious thing." [4]

In the time of the Catholic monarchs, Ferdinand and Isabella of Castile (1474–1504), Cardinal Jiménez de Cisneros, after reforming the Spanish Church, planned, organized, and led the

[3] Leo Africanus, *Description de l'Afrique,* French trans. Apaulard (Paris, 1956), p. 268.

[4] Benabdallah, *op. cit.,* p. 101.

attacks against Oran, Bougie, and Tripoli, aided by Count Pedro Navarro. Cisneros' influence extended to the time when Charles, founder of the Hapsburgs, took the throne in 1516.

Oran, in 1509, in the eyes of Leo Africanus, was the home of a "friendly, benevolent, and hospitable population where many Genoese, Venetian, and Catalan merchants lived." The city was full of Christian slaves captured in raids on the Catalonian coast and in the Balearics. A first expedition by Ferdinand to North Africa failed, mainly due to poor navigation, but Cisneros collected a larger fleet. Through some clever tactics, the Spaniards lured most of the garrison outside the city walls, then fell upon their rear. "Even as the Moors began their retreat toward the city," writes Leo, "they saw the Christian ensigns floating on the walls": the Spaniards had already captured it.[5] The pious cardinal personally presided over the massacre of four thousand Moslems, the capture of eight thousand prisoners, and the Catholic consecration of two mosques.

The squadrons of Navarro, who had won his sea legs in pirate raids against Moslem and Christian ships, had already captured Mers-al-Kebir, the best anchorage on the North African coast, where the French still lease a naval base today from Algeria. Bougie, whose people were found by Leo to be "fond of music and dancing," scarcely drew a sword in their own defense when Navarro arrived. Other points along the Algerian coast soon fell, and the Spaniards repulsed a combined attack by Khair ed-Din and the mountain Berbers in 1515. Khair ed-Din fled to Jejelli, a rocky, inaccessible peninsula sixty miles east of Bougie. The Spaniards then decided on the policy they still apply today in holding their Moroccan possessions: they secured fortified strongholds along the coast with protected communication lines at sea, without trying to push inland. By 1512, even Tripoli was in Spanish hands and paying tribute into the coffers of Cisneros.

When Ferdinand died, the Algerian tribute payers revolted and appealed for Turkish aid. The Spaniards had not captured Algiers, by now a thriving city where the influx of many Moriscos nourished a hate of the Christians, but they had seized the four small offshore islands (al-Djazair, "the islands," from which we get Algiers) and placed their artillery. In response to a call for help in the name of

[5] Africanus, *op. cit.*, pp. 341–342.

Islam, Aruj occupied Algiers but was unable to dislodge the Spaniards from their island fortress. At Tlemcen he was killed in battle against the Spaniards, who had been called in as allies by the Arabs there against their Turkish coreligionists, leaving his brother Khair ed-Din as governor of Algiers.

In a decision which changed all of North African history, because it put the Turks in Algiers and Tunis, Khair ed-Din decided to throw in his lot with the orthodox power of the Ottoman Porte. He offered his unconditional allegiance to Constantinople. In return, he got the title of Bey of Beys and two thousand Turkish troops, who helped him oust the Spaniards in 1529. With Turkish power behind him, Khair ed-Din built Algiers and its immediate hinterland into a strong military machine, living from both piracy and legitimate trade, until the French arrived in 1830 to destroy the power of the beys forever and begin their own conquest.

THE HAPSBURG CRUSADE

Thus far, neither the papacy nor the Italian princes had reacted strongly to the new Moslem threat in the Mediterranean. But when Khair ed-Din, not content to consolidate his Algiers regime, pushed east and occupied Tunis and Kairawan in 1534, Rome encouraged Charles V to embark upon a new crusade to Tunis. According to Salvador de Madariaga, the greatest twentieth-century Spanish historian, Charles hoped to save Christian unity while remaining true to the purity of his faith; "hence while uncompromising as to dogma, he tried to compromise as much as he could in every other way." [6]

Back to Carthage came the fleet of the Christians; the same Carthage which had seen the ships of Louis IX foundering in disarray. On July 14, 1535, Charles' allied armies captured La Goulette, which controls the entry to the Lake of Tunis, and then the city itself. Charles personally led his forces into the city, liberated twenty thousand Christian captives, restored Sultan Hasan, whom Khair ed-Din had dethroned, and for a fleeting moment appeared as the champion of Western Christendom, pausing in his triumph to note

[6] Salvador de Madariaga, *Spain, A Modern History* (New York, 1958), p. 43.

that the cannon he captured were supplied to the Turks by the King of France, their Christian ally.

While France and the Turks repeatedly forced Charles to concede the principle that each prince should decide the official religion of his principality, Khair ed-Din laid the foundations of a future Algerian state. Janizaries were recruited in the slums of Constantinople and brought to Algiers where they became a privileged corps of elite troops. Khair ed-Din and the beys who followed him governed by means of a corporative council, or divan, which, however, was soon to be a constant source of palace revolutions and *coup d'état*. On the high seas they made war against Catholic Spain, now the hereditary enemy of the Algerian cities. Their swift ships were manned by an international band of brigands unlike anything yet seen in the Mediterranean, with the corsair captains in command. Renegade Christians formed a corps of "technical advisors" who informed the Turkish officers of the best raiding sites, the most suitable landing beaches, and the richest and most vulnerable of the European coastal towns to plunder. Slaves and condemned criminals manned the oars of the galleys. Algiers prospered on the plunder, and the beys co-operated with France to chase the Spaniards out of the central Mediterranean.

The French used the opportunity to install their first consul amid the new polyglot society in Algiers, where Turks, Arabs, Spaniards, Kabylie Berbers, Maltese, Frenchmen, and Italians all lived. It was a period in which guns and money talked louder than either Bibles or Korans. At the same time, the fact that the Turks shared a common religion with their Arab and the Berber subjects softened their impact as foreign invaders and made it relatively easy for them to exploit the country and penetrate into the interior, where they set up their garrisons. More than once, the uneasy Porte intervened to prevent an independent and unorthodox Algerian state from breaking out of its control.

In 1541, Charles decided to strike what he regarded as the octopus of Moslem power at its head. He launched an expedition against Algiers. With an armada of more than five hundred ships carrying more than twelve thousand marines and twenty-four thousand soldiers, the army of imperial Christendom waited until autumn, when the Ottoman fleet was not likely to venture onto the treacherous Mediterranean. They landed at the mouth of the Harrach River and reached the heights that dominated Algiers. Suddenly a terrific gale, lashed with rain, broke upon them and the Arabo-Turkish defenders forced them to retreat, with the Knights of St. John covering their withdrawal to the ships, now wallowing in the wash of mighty seas. Most of the ships were lost.

Charles returned to Spain, his days of crusading over. The Turks seized Tripoli from the Knights of St. John in 1556, the year that Charles abdicated and the crown passed to his son Philip II (1556–1598). Philip decided to close the Mediterranean to Islam at its narrowest point if he could. In 1559, he sent an allied naval force eastward, but it was completely wiped out by the Turks when it settled down to winter on the Island of Las Gelves.

In 1565, the Spanish fleet repaid the Knights of St. John for past favors by raising the siege of Malta. The Turkish governor in Algiers, Ali, a Venetian captured by a Turkish galley off the Calabrian coast, was, according to one version, converted to Islam in order to have freedom to revenge himself on a Turk who had struck him. His melancholy air led Europeans, especially the French ambassador at Constantinople who knew him, to assert he had remained a secret Christian, but he was unresponsive to advances which Philip, at the behest of Pope Pius V, made to him.

As the British agent in Cádiz had warned, the Turks decided to aid the Morisco uprising against Philip. Philip's struggle against the Turkish sultans, first Sulaiman the Magnificent (1520–1566) and then Salim II (1566–1574), who violated the Prophet's precepts by drowning his intelligence in drink, was rich in battles and violent episodes which reached a climax in the great naval engagement of Lepanto. In 1571, a Catholic alliance of Spain, Venice, and the papacy raised a great fleet led by Don Juan of Austria, which encountered the Turkish ships near Greece and despite their fierce fighting swept them from the Mediterranean. The naval threat of Islam had ended. To Catholic Europe, this seemed as the end of a long nightmare and as the divine sanction of a righteous cause, like the fall of Granada in 1492.

CHAPTER XV

THE RETREAT OF ISLAM

> Sleep in the beds of Christians, but don't eat their food; eat the food of Jews but don't sleep in their beds.
>
> MOROCCAN PROVERB OF TANGIER

One observer at the Battle of Lepanto was Miguel de Cervantes, the greatest author and dramatist that Catholic Spain ever produced. Like thousands of others on that day, he was taken prisoner in the battle and, after serving as a galley slave in the Turkish fleet and in captivity in Constantinople and Algiers, managed to make his way home. During his captivity he met Hasan Agha, whom in the Captive's Tale in *Don Quixote* he calls the scabby renegade. Hasan, a literary prototype of a Christian apostate, was a Venetian who became Pasha of Algiers. He tried to induce King Mulay Abd al-Malik in Morocco to conclude an alliance with Philip to attack Algiers and drive out the Turks.

There were many such renegades in all stations of life on both sides of the Moslem-Christian frontier, and the motives behind their conversions varied from torture to love. Often they became quite influential, even the advisers of kings. An Englishman connected with an expedition against the Morisco pirates of Salé in 1638 described several renegades he met in Morocco. One, the "Caid Jauder," was an Irishman of a noble family whose Christian name had been Edmund Darrow and who had been a volunteer in Sir Walter Raleigh's expedition to Guiana, escaping a shipwreck near Salé. He was "of gallant personage, aboute fifty yeares of age, and of civil behaviour, arguing his descent and suiting his place." Another was "Caid Ali," the King's falconer, who was a man from Somersetshire named Martin Woolfall. He had been a merchant in Safi and "the occasion of his turning More was for love of a Moorish woman." Woolfall was still a secret Christian and had left a letter to this effect in the hands of another English merchant in Safi, placing himself by so doing "in imminent danger of losing his head." Therefore he was eager to escape from Morocco as quickly as he could.[1]

If a Christian in seventeenth-century Morocco wanted to convert to Islam, the standard procedure was to convoke a mixed tribunal of Christians and Moors. The would-be convert would stand between the rows of judges, and the Christian members of the court were allowed to use any and all arguments to dissuade him. He had three chances: each time the Moslems asked whether he wished to renounce the law of his own religion and embrace theirs. One unfortunate convert killed a man shortly after embracing Islam. Instead of being sentenced to death, he was cast out and died, since no one, Moor or Christian, would feed or shelter him: he had become a man without a society.

A Saadid ruler in Marrakesh, Mulay al-Walid (1631–1636) was reported by Christian sources to have treated his Christian captives and the converts of his court with great cruelty. The plight of some Christian captives was truly pitiful, and many in Europe were aware of it. As early as 1198, Pope Innocent III, certainly as cognizant of the missionary possibilities as he was of the humanitarian need, had given papal approval to the formation of the Order of the Holy Trinity. This order was founded expressly to secure release of Christian prisoners. The founder was St. John of Matha (died about 1213), a doctor of theology from Provence, who after becoming a priest reported a vision he had seen: Christ the Redeemer stood between two slaves—a Moor and a European, whose feet were also chained. The order founded monasteries, hospices, and often served as intermediary in delicate negotiations between Moslem and Christian authorities. One-third of its income, whether from work or from donations, was reserved for paying the sums, often fantastically high, which the Moroccan, Algerian, Tunisian, Tripolitanian, and Turkish rulers demanded for redemption of the Christian captives.

On March 9, 1625, the wives of two thousand English sailors enslaved by the Moriscos of Salé sent a collective petition to the House of Lords. Some of these women were already being exploited by merchants of various nationalities who would offer to buy back

[1] Castries, *Sources Inédites*, "England, First Series," Petworth House, Sussex, Lord Leconfield, ms. 73, p. 482.

their men and collect the funds which were supposedly to be used for that purpose but which they often pocketed. The women imagined the captives as "undergoing most unspeakable tormentes and want of food through the merciless crueltie of their manifolde masters, and which is the worst of all, the extreame want of the spiritual foode of theire soules." [2] John Harrison, who often ransomed captives with funds from his own pocket, begged King Charles I as Defender of the Faith to protect the captives. To act otherwise, he said, "were the most unchristian act that ever was heard or read of to banish so many Christians and baptized souls into the hands of the enemies of the Christian religion, Turks and Moors."

Harrison, devout Protestant that he was, resolved to take "a minister or two" with him to Morocco, both to preach to Christian merchants and "to worke some good among that barbarous people, both the Mores and the Jewes, whose conversion we daylie expect." He was annoyed by meeting three Franciscans, "Popish priests and friars" who "willingly expose themselves to all travels and dangers, not only in Barbary . . . but also in the East and West Indies" to make converts.[3] This idea of converting the North African Jews to Protestantism still persists in England. One of the first British missions to begin work in Morocco in the nineteenth century was the "Gospel Mission to the Jews," which had some success in Tangier among Spanish-speaking Jews. The Mission still existed in 1964.

There were some curious Moslem conversions to Christianity. Philip II never seems to have favored forced conversion. For example, in one draft treaty he proposed in 1577 with a Moroccan sharif, he inserted a clause often seen in later accords between Catholic and Moslem rulers, that no one could force a member of either faith to deny his religion. There is almost a note of contempt in a letter of instruction which the Spanish governor of Penon de Velez, in Morocco, sent to ecclesiastical authorities in Spain concerning the "son of the King of Fez and his mother, who are to comply with instructions of the Bishop of Malaga or of Cartagena concerning their conversion to Christianity." [4]

One of the most fascinating stories of conversion of all time

[2] Castries, *Sources Inédites,* House of Lords Papers, Bundle 27, p. 42.
[3] *Ibid.,* Fol. 221, 222, p. 112.
[4] *Ibid.,* British Museum, Egerton Mss., 2047, f. 327, p. 122.

began with an incident at sea.[5] At the end of the fifteenth century, a group of Sanhaja Berbers had started a Moslem monastery at Dilai, near Khenifra, at the edge of the Middle Atlas Mountains in Morocco. They created their own army and at one time controlled most of northern Morocco. In 1654, a galley of the Knights of Malta, commanded by a Provençal named Balthazar de Mandols, surprised a shipload of pilgrims on their way to Mecca near Cape Bon. Among them was one of the Dilai holy men, a certain Sidi Mohammed. He was a young man of about twenty-one, of aristocratic bearing and extremely pallid. The Knights set his ransom at forty thousand crowns or its equivalent in corn, which was critically short in Malta at the time. After first scorning anything to do with Catholicism, Sidi Mohammed asked to attend Mass and did so.

When his ransom had been paid, Sidi Mohammed sailed from Malta. On the first night he dreamed that a violent storm arose and the ship threatened to founder in a sea of fire. The flames of hell seemed to surround his bed, and then the vision of a young man or a beautiful young woman—the various versions do not agree on this—told him solemnly that the only remedy was baptism. When he awoke he ordered the ship to return to Valetta on a pretext and immediately hurried to the cathedral where he threw himself before an image of the Virgin, whose features are supposed to have resembled those of the being of his dream. Next he asked the Grand Master of the Knights of Malta to be converted.

Delighted with this prize catch, though sorry he had not asked for ten times the ransom, the Master charged the Father Rector of the Jesuits to instruct Sidi Mohammed, who called himself the son of the ruler of Morocco and who chose to be christened Balthazar Loyola Mendez, after his captor and the feast day of St. Ignatius Loyola, which fell on the day of his baptism. Once his tendency to brag and boast had been smothered, Balthazar, who became a priest in 1663, astonished all of European Catholicism with his intellectual

[5] This seemingly fantastic tale of a conversion is told in Georges Drague, *Esquisse d'Histoire Religieuse du Maroc, Confréries et Zaouias,* "Cahiers de l'Afrique et l'Asie" (Paris, n.d.), pp. 40–43, and also by Wilfred Blunt in his book *Black Sunrise* (London, 1951), pp. 157–166. Both authors used as their original source a series of documents in Castries, *Sources Inédites,* "France, First Series," pp. 203 ff.

gifts. He is said to have mastered fourteen or fifteen languages, mathematics, and other natural sciences. By 1661, he had moved to Rome to become a novice in the Jesuit College of St. Andrew of the Quirinal. Father Brunacci, the Master of the Novices, found his pupil "impetuous, haughty and headstrong," but he passed his tests and was ordained a Jesuit priest in 1663. Balthazar's first assignment was Genoa, where he converted hundreds of North African galley slaves to Christianity. One of the slaves, an unwilling convert, tried to kill him by offering him a bouquet of flowers dipped in corrosive acid, over which he had mumbled some deadly incantations. Balthazar saw this and got the Moor to agree to be baptized if the flowers did no harm. The man fell on his knees, according to a Spanish-Jesuit witness, asked forgiveness—and was baptized.

One of Balthazar's most spectacular converts at Genoa was no one less than the Grand Mufti of Tunis, who was baptized in Florence, with the Duke of Tuscany acting as his godfather. Pope Alexander VII chose him for a delicate mission to the Great Mogul (Aurangzeb) of Moslem India, who had asked the Vatican for the services of a man who knew Arabic and who could explain Christian doctrine to the *ulama*. Balthazar was showered with attentions and honors in Italy, then went to France on foot with the intention of a short stopover in Morocco before proceeding to Agra. At Beziers a Frenchman who had been a slave in Fez recognized him and said he had sketched him at the head of his Berber troops. In Toulouse, he dined with the archbishop and preached in the cathedral. At Bayonne, he met a French Huguenot, with whom he argued dogma. Finally he reached Madrid, where the boy king Charles II received him, but he fell ill of fever, converting the Moroccan boy servant who attended him just before he died.

The Catholic revival in France produced a fresh outburst of quasi-missionary activity in Morocco, largely by the Capuchin Order. It was skillfully guided from afar, first by Cardinal Armand Jean du Plessis Richelieu and his confidant, Father Joseph; then by Cardinal Jules Mazarin, who ran Louis XIV's affairs of state. Around 1630, a Turk named Mustapha was captured and sponsored for baptism by Richelieu, whose name he took. Jean Armand Mustapha left behind a journal which clearly shows his feelings for his former coreligionists. "The ferocious and uncivil humor of those who inhabit the Western coast of Barbary," he noted in French, "makes our people lose the desire to go to those places, where courtesy seems dead." [6]

THE SHARIFIAN EMPIRE OF ISMAIL

In seventeenth-century Morocco, of all the *shurafa* who were contending for the privilege of fighting the Christians, holding the Turks back, and trying to build some semblance of central power on the ruins of the Sadid structure, the most important were the Filali, or Alawites, who had come from Arabia and settled in the great eastern Moroccan oasis of Tafilalet at the beginning of the thirteenth century. When the last Sadid ruler died, the Kingdom of Marrakesh was left in the hands of a mere caid. Other rulers divided up the Sus and other parts of southern Morocco, while the Dilai *marabouts* ruled Fez and the north. In 1659, an Alawite sharif named Mulay Rashid left the Tafilalet and embarked on the conquest of eastern Morocco, where he pillaged the Jews and based his power on a *tarik,* or Sufi order, probably the Lawati. In 1661, the marriage of Charles II of England to Catherine of Portugal gave Tangier to England. Mazarin was carefully watching for an opportunity to establish French influence in northern Morocco to counterbalance this new British move. He ordered a reconnaissance expedition to the Chafferine Islands. He also attempted to play Rashid off against the English in Tangier. Rashid took Fez in 1666 and got himself proclaimed Sultan. He successfully chased Ghailan, whom the English called "Gayland," war lord of the northern Rharb Plain, out of Morocco to Algiers. Rashid tried to use the Morisco pirates of Salé to further his conquests but was killed when he fractured his skull against an orange tree while riding in the Agdal Gardens of Marrakesh.

Rashid's brother, Mulay Ismail (1672–1727), the most famous North African monarch of all time, succeeded him. Many books have been written about Ismail's spectacular career as the unifier of modern Morocco, mentioning his vast harems, where thousands

[6] Castries, *Sources Inédites,* "France, Third Series," *Chronique de Jean Armand Mustapha,* III, 309.

of women including many Europeans languished, awaiting his pleasure, and about his savage character and appearance.

Ismail was the real founder of the Alawite dynasty; the late Mohammed V, who led Morocco away from French and Spanish domination and into the modern era of independence, and his son, Hasan II, are its most recent representatives. Ismail was a contemporary of Charles II of Spain and James II of England, to whom he wrote in February, 1698, reproaching his conversion to Catholicism, "Even though, in general, all your [Christian] religions are tissues of error and blunders, your best religion is that of Henry [the Eighth], more reasonable than the others, which are steeped in infidelity." [7]

This bloodthirsty and rapacious king was also pious. Occasionally he received with marks of kindness the Trinitarians who had come to ransom some of the thousands of Christian slaves, and others he used in building his splendid new capital at Meknes. "Voluptuous, covetous, passionate, treacherous, more than a tyrant, he tamed the natural savagery of his subjects by showing himself more savage than they," was a view of Ismail set down by a British slave named Thomas Pellow. Another, named Ockley, described how some prisoners had to pull knifelike palmettos out of the ground and how "fifty slaves died 'by the Stink of the Bodies newly bury'd' when the Emperor decided to dig up the Christian cemetery." [8] Any captive who wished could pronounce the *shahada,* the profession of the Moslem creed, be circumcised, and be carried in a triumphal procession through Meknes carrying a small stick pointing heavenward to signify that he "recognized and adored not three persons [the Trinity] but one God."

The French Trinitarians and other missionaries who came to Meknes in attempts to redeem Christian captives were able to take back with them the news that Ismail performed mass murders in the name of Islam, often on Friday, but that he combined such propensities with an astonishing degree of piety in his own faith. He observed all of the ritual fasts, performed his ablutions, and

[7] *Ibid.,* "England, First Series," *Moulay Ismail et Jacques,* II, 97 and note 4.

[8] Wilfred Blunt, *Black Sunrise* (London, 1951), p. 42.

often made the Ramadan fast last for three or four months instead of only one. When several courageous *talabah* (plural of *talib,* Moslem scholars) dared rebuke him for his un-Islamic ways, he threw them into a pit with fourteen lions in which, previously, according to the testimony of two Trinitarians, two French merchants, and fifteen slaves, and a French captive had been cast and miraculously spared. A Jew named Joseph Maimaran, who had helped Ismail secure the throne and had enjoyed great influence at court for a time, fared no better when he was so imprudent as to remind the King of his debt.

It is easy to see that Ismail, whose name and fame spread throughout Europe, especially after he unsuccessfully sought the hand of a French princess of Louis XIV's court, largely contributed to the European idea of North African Moslem rulers as embodiments of savagery and barbarism, a living renewal of the old medieval Christian stereotype about Moslem behavior.

THE SHARIFIAN EMPIRE AND THE HOLY WARS

It was in Ismail's time that Morocco began the most vigorous counterattack it was ever able to mount against European imperialism. First, Ismail reduced the Spanish fortress of Marmora; then he turned northward. Tangier, under British occupation, proved more difficult, though by 1681 the garrison was in trouble, the soldiers hungry and deserting, and the governors corrupt. The British community charter of 1668 had assimilated Tangier into the English community system, permitting its city councilors to enjoy great trading privileges. But a siege by Ismail in 1679 ruined their trade. The House of Commons feared that Catholic influence was growing among the troops and might provide Charles II with forces to try a *coup d'état* against Parliament. For this reason it did not accede to his request for help, seeing, as usual, "the menace of Papism." After Parliament was dissolved, Charles II was reduced to living from subsidies paid him by Louis XIV, and so he decided to abandon Tangier in 1684. The English forces scorched the earth behind them, and a local sharif and Riffian tribesmen entered and wiped out the last organized stronghold of Protestantism in North Africa.

Ismail's "holy warriors" captured Larache in 1689 and Arcila in 1691, leaving only Mazagan in Portuguese hands on the Atlantic, and Ceuta and the smaller Mediterranean coastal provinces in the possession of the Spaniards. Ismail built a *ribat* facing the fortress of Ceuta, but was never able to capture that city. His reign also saw an end of the Turkish threat to Morocco. He fought the corsair captains as fiercely as he fought the Christians and launched deep counterattacks into Algeria which did not end well: the Turks were reported to have taken three thousand Moroccan heads with them back to Algiers in 1701.

Despite his military victories, Ismail was not able to stop the inexorable advance of Christian commerce. European merchants, especially Frenchmen, including many Huguenot refugees, settled in Salé, Tetuan, and elsewhere; a treaty Ismail signed with France in 1682 guaranteed their right to protection by consuls. Except for one forty-year break, this was the beginning of a continuous presence of French consuls in Morocco until its final conquest by France in 1912. Under the 1682 agreement, any French consul could "exercise in freedom in his house the Christian religion—he and other Christians who wish to participate [in services]." Moslems in France were given the same rights.

The French were told they might repurchase slaves and many attempts were made to arrange exchanges. Ismail once offered one Christian slave and three hundred pounds for each Moroccan slave held by the French, but this was not accepted since Colbert, Louis' minister, needed galley slaves for his vessels. Ismail's ambassador at the royal court of France had to return to Meknes without settling the slave question. When Ismail tried to obtain the hand of the Princess of Conti, a royal bastard, he guaranteed that she would be free to exercise her own religion. Louis' court, in an insolent reply, suggested instead that Ismail convert to Christianity. The royal suit ended there.

One of the minor ironies of Ismail's reign was that he never was able to finish the final project of his slave builders at Meknes, the Bab Mansur al-Uldj (Gate of the Converted Christian). His personal government and the sharifian administration had been built entirely by his iron will. It collapsed after he died, and, under most of his eighteenth-century successors, Moroccan central power and Moroccan influence in the world declined steadily. Christian emissaries continued their negotiations, sometimes successful and sometimes not, for trading privileges and the ransom of captives. The *abid,* or black palace guard which Ismail had created from tribes of Sudanese slaves, often revolted and their officers were constantly leading rebellions.

Occasionally, there were attempts at religious reform and even puritanical revival. Wahabism, the mid-eighteenth-century puritanical movement from Arabia, swept into Morocco during the reign of Sultan Mulay Abdallah who died in 1757. It was encouraged by Atlas Berbers. Alcohol, smoking, dancing, music, luxurious dressing and living, and even the adornment of mosques were all forbidden for a time. This was not enforced for long. Sultan Mulay Yazid (1790–1792), who was one of the first rulers to recognize American independence, relaxed Wahabist strictures. He was a piratical ruler who could not resist pillage, even of *shurafa* on pilgrimages to Mecca or returning from them. He oppressed the Christian and Jewish communities and got into serious trouble with Spain because he arrested Spanish consuls in Mogador and Larache and two friars in Tangier. His successor, Mulay Sulaiman (or Slimane; 1792–1822), eased the burdens of foreigners and in 1817, after almost going to war with the United States, finally ended piracy.

All of this, however, was one of the darkest periods in Morocco's history, and the least interesting for us. No special religious or intellectual currents enlightened it. Outwardly, the country's religious and political unity, which had largely been a function of its resistance to the earlier challenges from Europe, appeared intact. Inwardly, it had begun to erode. The French push into Algeria in 1830 exposed Morocco to new perils. The once free interchange between Islamic and Christian culture of Morocco's medieval days seemed far, far away, if not lost forever.

CHAPTER XVI

EUROPE RETURNS: THE CONQUEST OF ALGERIA

> Nowhere does Mohammed have as fervent worshipers as in Algiers.
>
> RAYNAL DE CHAUDRU, 1832

What was Moslem Algeria, the geopolitical if not the spiritual center of Moslem North Africa, really like before France brought "Christian civilization" to its shores once again in 1830? Western accounts of chaos and corruption, personal savagery, and economic decay in the Regency, the period of Turkish rule, were constantly used as apologies for the French conquest both by French and other Western historians. Some French visitors of that day saw Algeria differently. One Frenchman, who carried out various missions for the government of King Charles X, found Algeria was

> not, as believed, inhabited solely by barbarians. The population was divided into very distinct classes; in the cities the Turks, the Colouglis [sons and daughters of mixed marriages between Turks and Algerian Moslems], the Moors [Algerians], and the Jews; in the countryside, the Bedouin and the Kabylies. . . . The Turks occupied all of the posts in the Regency; they had not adopted the language of the Moors and the Moors had not adopted theirs. . . . Far from being hostile to us, the Moors are friends of our civilization. By treating them well, by according them liberty and security, we will find the most useful support among them.[1]

Unfortunately for the future of both France and Algeria, his advice was not heeded in high places.

Nevill Barbour notes the testimony of General W. Shaler,

[1] Raynal de Chaudru, *De la Domination Française en Afrique et des Principales Questions que fait naître l'Occupation de ce Pays* (Paris, 1832), pp. 5–6, 28–29.

United States Consul-General in Algiers after 1775, that the lot of the Christian captives held then "was not generally worse than that of prisoners of war in many civilized, Christian countries," and that Algerians in general "are . . . civil, courteous and humane." He found no "extraordinary bigotry, fanaticism or hatred of those who profess a different religion." [2]

Though all of North African Islam had by this time entered a spiritual decline, its outward and material culture still flourished in Algeria. Seventeenth-century Algiers, a city of 100,000, prospered under a military regime from the proceeds of piracy and honest commerce. In the eighteenth century, Algiers' prosperity ebbed. The deys, the governors of Algiers, became sporadically more despotic. Dey Mohammed ibn Uthman (1766–1791), the leading Algerian ruler of his century, was a builder of mosques and palaces, as was his successor, Baba Hasan, who built the Ketchawa Mosque. This mosque was turned into a church by order of General de Bourmont in 1830, and later was made the seat of the Archdiocese of Algiers. It became a mosque again when Archbishop Léon Etienne Duval ordered it evacuated after Algerian independence in 1962.

The Turks had numerous politico-religious troubles with both the Arabs and the Kabylie Berbers, less because of their status as foreign rulers than because of the particularistic nature of Algerian Islam, still subject to old Berber superstitions and cults. The Kabylie Berbers showed aggressiveness. The Sufi orders, especially the Darkawa, who were strongly inspired by Sultan Mulay Sulaiman of Morocco, were no less troublesome. Shortly before the French landings, one *marabout* named Ben Sharif stirred up the region of Oran, while a Darkawa sharif from Morocco preached revolt among the Kabylie peoples. The Tidjaniya, another powerful Sufi order which had spread into Mauretania and the Sudan after taking root in Morocco, were also active. In 1827, when the conflict with France erupted, the dey's power was so weakened by these schisms that Algeria could present no united front. But soon afterward, the Sufi orders united, relatively speaking, against the French invaders.

[2] General W. Shaler, *Sketches of Algiers,* p. 76; quoted in Barbour (ed.), *A Survey of North West Africa* (London, 1959), p. 38.

THE DIPLOMATIC PRELUDE

Relations between the deys and all of the European powers had wavered between total indifference, more or less peaceful coexistence, and warfare. Peace with one power which stopped profitable raiding of its shipping, often spelled for Algiers a new war with another. At various times, the Dutch, English, and French all found it necessary to bombard Algiers, and there was a long series of naval wars between the regency and the United States, the youngest of the Christian powers, beginning in 1793. They evoked Benjamin Franklin's acid observation that if Algiers had not existed, it would have been desirable for Britain to create it, in order to limit Mediterranean trade competition from its late colony.

The dey's relations with Napoleon had been good, but Bonaparte's reign and his expedition to Egypt signaled the re-entry of France into Mediterranean politics. One French ministry had even planned a landing at Algiers in 1808. Napoleon purchased grain for his Egyptian expedition in Algeria but had not reached agreement on payment. The Algerian Jewish firms of Bakri and Busnach had handled the transaction, despite the dey's hope for direct payment, and creditors had attached the money in France. The dey's navy began to harass French shipping again, and he struck the French consul in Algiers, Duval, with either a cane or a fly swatter on April 30, 1820, at a diplomatic reception. The French blockaded the Algerian coast for two years when the dey refused to apologize and in 1824 supplied the rebel Kabylie Berbers through the ports of Bône and La Calle.

The Darkawa, encouraged from the Moroccan capital in Fez, backed a quasi-religious, anti-Turkish movement among the Hashim tribesmen where the Emir Abd al-Kadir of Mascara (1807–1883), a new Algerian religious hero, was shortly to appear to lead the fight against the French invaders. The Darkawa were aided by the Kadiriya, another Sufi order, against the large conservative Algerian landowners, many of whom remained pro-French as long as there was any hope that the French could stay in Algeria.

Charles X formally declared war on June 11, 1827. The Algerians tried unsuccessfully to destroy the French base at Cape Cascine and succeeded in eliminating the French installations at Bône and La Calle in 1830. Napoleon's disastrous adventure in the Middle East, in some ways a repetition of St. Louis' expedition to Egypt, convinced Charles X that France should have a Moslem ally so as to forestall, if possible, a holy war.

In September, 1829, the king's minister, the Prince de Polignac, accepted a suggestion of the French consul in Alexandria that Mehemet Ali (1809–1849), the Albanian adventurer who had become absolute master of Egypt, should be persuaded to give up his projected attack on Syria and join France in a move against the regency of Algiers. Polignac offered a ten-million-franc loan to Mehemet Ali if he would simultaneously attack the regencies of Tunis and Tripoli with twenty-five thousand men and leave the French a free hand in Algeria. Mehemet Ali refused, partly on grounds of Islamic solidarity, and partly because Great Britain objected.

General de Bourmont, the French Minister of War, decided to go it alone. On May 25, 1830, he left Marseilles with six hundred sailing ships and seven small steamers, transporting thirty thousand men. The initial landing was at Sidi Ferruch, west of Algiers, where after independence in the summer of 1962 the monument commemorating the event was blown up and special prayers of thanks were said in Algerian mosques. Algiers fell after a short fight, and Hussein, the reigning dey, surrendered to Bourmont. Oran and Bône were attacked from the sea, and the French troops at Algiers pressed on through the rich plain of the Mitidja to Blida, at the foot of the Atlas Mountains. "We French," said a propaganda leaflet distributed by the French army before the expedition, "are going to drive out your tyrants, the Turks, who persecute you, steal your goods and never cease threatening your lives." [3]

In a pact Bourmont signed with Hussein, promises were made to respect the Islamic faith and the property of all Algerians. Instead, several of Algeria's best mosques were turned into churches, Moslem feast days were no longer legal holidays (the French ones were instead), and some of the best farmland in the country was confiscated and given to the flood of immigrants that began to arrive from France. De Bourmont, acting on his own, at first claimed only the Mitidja Plain for France. He offered the Beylic of Con-

[3] Quoted by Barbour, *A Survey of North West Africa,* p. 41.

stantine to the Bey of Tunis. The bey seemed first inclined to accept, then abandoned his plans in the face of disapproval from his political and religious advisors. Paris was irritated. This was an irritation with its administrators in Algeria that was to be nearly continuous and was destined to last for over a hundred years—until Algerian independence in 1962.

THE RELIGIOUS RESISTANCE MOVEMENT

As could be expected, resistance to the French penetration had a strongly Islamic flavor. It began in the west. The Emir Abd al-Kadir, son of a *marabout* of the Kadiriya Order, took command of the tribes of Hashim and Amir. Sick of fighting among themselves and with the Turks, they gave Abd al-Kadir the title of Prince of the True Believers in November, 1832, making him their supreme leader. He organized a sort of government-in-exile, complete with law courts and a school system, somewhat similar to the "rebel" republic of the Rif Mountains set up by the Emir Abd al-Krim in Morocco during the Rif War of 1921–1926. Drawing his support from religious chiefs, Sufi and otherwise, Abd al-Kadir divided Algeria up into little "caliphates," stressing religious unity. He proclaimed the holy war. His army of nine thousand men, chiefly infantry, defended his Algerian state between 1832 and 1839, sometimes winning considerable victories and even briefly threatening Algiers in 1837. This was shortly after General Bugeaud, the most dogged and skillful of the successive French commanders, had been forced to sign with him the Treaty of Tafna, granting Abd al-Kadir Mascara and much of Algiers province.

After new hostilities, including a heavy French bombardment of Constantine, Abd al-Kadir proclaimed the treaty broken and marched eastward, capturing the Saharan fort of Mohammed Tijani, whose Sufi order had now been bought and persuaded to fight on the side of the French.

Algeria's neighbors, the Bey of Tunis and the Sultan of Morocco, at first showed something less than brotherly Islamic solidarity. In 1844, the sultan did send his son with sixty-five thousand ill-trained troops against six thousand Frenchmen, who beat them badly at the Battle of Isly. A present-day Algerian historian, Kouriba Nabhami, notes that Algeria had not enjoyed serious support from Tunisia and Morocco. The bey, under French threats, prevented Turkish reinforcements destined for Constantine from crossing Tunisia. The Sultan of Morocco gave an inept son the command of his faltering contingents, while in the interior, the Algerian feudal chiefs made common cause with the French.

By 1845, as a contemporary French historian of that day recorded, "it was against an entire nation, inspired by the double fanaticism of patriotism and religion, that the war had to be waged." Again and again, until 1884, one uprising followed another. The Sultan of Morocco, pressured by the French to hand over Abd al-Kadir after the Moroccan defeat at Isly, was prevented from doing so by the pressure of the Darkawa, some of the other Sufi brotherhoods, and many of the Berber chiefs of the Algerian-Moroccan border area.

In 1846, Abd al-Kadir attacked again, then retreated into his privileged sanctuary in Morocco. This time, under heavy French pressure, the Moroccans expelled him by force, and he was caught in a trap between two hostile armies, the Moroccans and the French, and captured. Despite initial French promises, Abd al-Kadir was first held prisoner in Toulon, then freed on orders from Napoleon III in 1852 and eventually allowed to settle in Damascus. Here, he showed his humanity by saving the lives of thousands of Syrian Christians and others in Damascus during a series of massacres by the Druzes, who are neither Moslem nor Christian. In 1862, France awarded him a medal struck with the words, "Emir of North Africa, Defender of Arab Nationality, Protector of oppressed Christians."

Others took up where Abd al-Kadir left off. In 1845, the first of a new series of self-styled *mahdis* appeared. He was Bu Maza, the man with the goat, a sort of rustic *marabout* who led the Dahra tribe in revolt, calling himself Mul es-Saa, or master of the hour. In Algerian holy war parlance, he was roughly the equivalent of the *mahdi,* or Hidden Imam, of another time. A number of other Algerian national leaders after him adopted the same title.

There was even a new Kahena in the Kabylie Mountains: a prophetess named Lalla Fatima of the Yenni tribe, who was finally subdued and captured by a thirty-thousand-man army led in person by Governor-General Randon. Beginning in 1867, the year of a terrible famine, Mokrani, another "master of the hour," allied himself with two *marabouts*. They stirred up a fresh revolt by exploiting the unrest along the Tunisian border caused when the French tried to recruit Moslem soldiers for the French army. Sheikh al-Haddad, master of the Sufi order of the Rahmaniya, joined this one. The defeated Kabylie tribesmen had to pay the war costs and give up 453,000 hectares of their precious farmland to French *colons,* who were now busily installing their little isles of European civilization in the mountains as well as on the plains along the coast.

Bugeaud himself was aware of the tragic errors France was committing, even if other French statesmen and military men were not. In 1844, he wrote to General MacMahon that the French had always posed as more just and capable governors than the Turks. They had assured the Algerians that the French would preserve their "laws, their property, their religion, and their customs. We owe it to them, and to ourselves, to keep our word in every respect." [4]

Once again, brave words that were lost on the wind.

RELIGION AND EDUCATION: THE "DE-ARABIZATION" OF FRENCH ALGERIA

Outside of the Sufi orders, the intellectual and religious resistance to European penetration of Arab Africa has been based rather on reason than on fanaticism. Certainly, the secular tendencies of French thought had already made an impression in the Moslem world. Al-Jabarti, an Arab chronicler of Egypt during Napoleon's occupation, remarked wonderingly that the French, who had scarcely been seen in Egypt since St. Louis' Crusade, "make their judgments according to reason [*al-akl*] without having a precise religion." [5] The pre-conquest attitude of most Algerians, perhaps not including those of the Sufi orders, toward Europeans and especially toward the Christian religion, was well described by de Chaudru in 1832:

[4] Quoted by Barbour, *A Survey of North West Africa,* p. 221.

[5] Al-Jabarti, quoted in Henri Peres, "L'Institut de l'Egypte et l'Oeuvre de Bonaparte jugés par deux Historiens Arabes Contemporains," *Arabica,* IV (May, 1957), Fasc. 2, p. 128.

Nowhere does Mohammed have as fervent worshipers as in Algiers. The city is divided into numerous parishes [sic], which all have their mosques and their *ulama:* these latter receive only a modest fee for upkeep. The mufti, a sort of supreme bishop and judge, is chosen among them. He continues to minister at his mosque and is no better treated than his colleagues from the financial viewpoint. . . . The religious and political influence which he enjoyed, the respects payed to him when he passes through the city streets, the profound veneration showed him by Moslems come to kiss the hem of his caftan seem to repay him sufficiently for a dignity which one does not attain except through an austere life and the science of the Koran.

The Koran is the only book cited or read [in the Moslem primary schools]. The verses are copied and learned by heart. This is assuredly one of the most powerful causes of the Moslem fervor. The Moors do not pronounce a single phrase, not even a thought, which does not recall to them one of these verses which they learned in their infancy. . . .

This love of the Algerians for their religion does not exclude tolerance among them. One day when I was with Sidi Jali, a venerable old man who knew France and who had made the voyage to Mecca three times; the muezzin having announced the hour of prayer, he sat down to say his with an unction which one would have admired in Europe. I followed his movements with curiosity; he saw me doing so, and when he had finished, he approached me with courtesy and said to me, indicating the heavens, "You and I, Monsieur, we still both worship God." Let us profit from this lesson in tolerance: may access to the temples [sic] remain barred to our troops; may religious ceremonies be respected and protected on all occasions; let there be no more razing of mosques under the pretext of urbanism or beautifying the city [of Algiers], thus casting indignation and pain into the souls of these believers.[6]

Contrast this with the attitude of another French writer ninety years later, after three generations of wars and massacres. His views became those of the majority of his fellow countrymen in Algeria:

[6] De Chaudru, *De la Domination Française,* pp. 44–45.

> Whatever the danger which the cosmopolitan element poses to our [French] nationality [in Algeria], it is no less true that as regards the natives, the French and foreigners—naturalized or not—can be considered as a homogeneous whole, because the Moslems confuse us with the latter under the spiteful name of *Rumi*. . . . In the scale of criminality, it is always the native Moslem who occupies the first rank. . . . The [non-French] foreigner comes next and the Frenchman comes in third place. But our nationals are first among the victims.[7]

Official French policy between 1830 and independence in 1962 was always a curious and vacillating mixture of toleration of Islamic society, attempts at its suppression, and efforts at its assimilation into the French way of life. Generally speaking, every attempt at granting the Algerians full equality with Frenchmen foundered against the determined opposition of the *pieds noirs* (black feet), the new class of Europeans whose lives, fortunes, and families had been completely transplanted to Algeria and who feared total equality for the Moslems with the same kind of fear, often pathological in its depth and proportions, as that with which many "poor whites" in our own American deep South regard the Negro.

Legal opportunities to become Frenchmen, or "French Moslems of Algeria," as the official French euphemism put it, as in the Blum-Violet reforms of 1936, placed the Algerian who was interested in "equality" in a terrible dilemma. He could escape from the humiliating status of "native" (*indigène*), regulated by the *Code de l'Indigènat,* only by naturalization—which most Algerian Jews chose to do after the Crémieux Decree of 1870 gave them the opportunity—but by so doing he would remove himself from jurisdiction of the Islamic law, the *sharia*. Only twenty-five hundred Moslems chose to do this between 1866 and 1934.

The Paris government in the Statute of 1947 made a brave attempt to "integrate" Algeria into the Republic and make all Algerians into Frenchmen, equal before the law, regardless of their faith. In effect, the statute would have returned Algeria to the situation after the Bourmont-Hussein Pact of 1830. It would have estab-

[7] Camille Brunel, *La Question Indigène en Algérie* (Paris, 1906), pp. iii–iv.

lished a regime with a new two-chamber assembly, where all Moslems could keep their Koranic status under the *sharia.* Parliament in Paris ratified this, but the Europeans of Algeria sabotaged the statute when Governor-General Jacques Soustelle tried to apply it in 1955.

A century earlier, Abdallah Nadim (1843–1896), an Egyptian journalist who was a disciple of the great Islamic reformer Jamal al-Din al-Afghani, blamed the phenomenon, which seems to me most appropriate to call the "de-Arabization" of Algeria, on factors which then affected, and still in some measure do affect, all of the Islamic countries. They included: lack of a single language; diversity of dialects—often encouraged by the French as a divisive factor; ethnic diversity (Arabs and Berbers); the flourishing of Christianity and Judaism (in the case of North Africa he could have added pagan survivals in Islam); the lack of either unity or freedom of expression; the lack of the means to raise the standard of living; limited education; and the lack of popular assemblies.

Napoleon III for a time dreamed vaguely of encouraging a sort of "Arab Kingdom of Algeria" under French protection. He allowed some Arabic-language instruction in mixed primary schools and in three official *madrasas,* in Constantine, Medea, and Oran. But the ascendancy of civil authority over the military in 1871 and later attempts of Paris to apply a policy of "assimilation" gradually turned primary education into an instrument to serve the ends of the rapidly growing European colony.

As of 1871, there were two thousand Moslem religious schools. They taught a religious and secular culture transmitted from generation to generation. This system of education faced general and growing hostility from the Europeans, but it gave a basic education to twenty-eight thousand or more Algerians each year. By 1878, as we shall see in more detail when we consider the missionary movement, a system of Catholic missionary schools had replaced the official government schools for Moslems. In 1901 there were twenty-one mission schools run by the White Fathers in the Kabylie country with more than a thousand pupils. The instruction they offered was practical. It included both what we would call liberal arts and practical training. In the Sahara, at Wargla (Ouargla) and Oulad Sidi Sheikh (Geryville) they were not a success, because, according to one Algerian Moslem view, they were attended by so many Jewish students that Moslem families mistrusted the schools.

ANTI-SEMITISM: OFFICIAL AND OTHERWISE

A word should be said here about the threat of latent anti-Jewish feeling, often encouraged by the more retrograde elements among the European population and French administration.

Anti-Jewish feeling has always plagued Algeria. It is an ugly aspect of life in most Arab countries, but in Algeria it was often encouraged to support French rule. During World War II, particularly in 1940–1942 when the Vichy regime ruled in France and controlled Algeria, many Algerian Jews, along with European liberals, were interned in concentration camps. There is strong reason to believe that Israeli groups, though possibly not officially sanctioned by the authorities of the State of Israel, actively supported the quasi-fascist Secret Army Organization (OAS) in its terrorist activities against the Arab nationalists.

De Chaudru, himself a spokesman for French anti-Semitism, wrote:

> One must know the degree to which, for three centuries, the Jews of the Regency have suffered to understand the degree of abjection to which they have sunk. . . . Other causes also explain the dislike of the Moors [sic] for the degenerate race [sic] of the Hebrews. The Israelite cult is much more odious than our own to the Mohammedans. It is known that if a Jew wishes to convert to Islam, he must first confess the divinity of Christ. Only then is he permitted to move into the ranks of the True Believers. A singular requirement, this, which makes him twice over a renegade. . . . Finally, the Jews, because of their adroitness, and through adulation, succeeded in finding protectors among the Turks, and often the favor which they enjoyed there was the object of jealousy of the Moors. Thus there exists between the two races a profound antipathy. We must not fight it: for us, it is a cause of power and security.[8]

[8] De Chaudru, *op. cit.*, pp. 33–34.

By 1850, the French administration was again trying to establish official *madrasas* in order to win Moslem allegiance away from the religious schools (including the Christian ones) and create a Moslem class which would be sympathetic to the aims of the French authorities. The *madrasas* were intended to train candidates for religious positions. There were also Arab-French schools set up in 1850 which were supposed to give mixed instruction. The *colons* blamed the uprisings of 1871, 1876, 1879, and 1881 on Moslem religious instruction: actually, they were popular Moslem reactions against French repression and French attempts to encourage assimilation. The official view was that the *marabout* and Sufi orders were largely to blame, and this was true. This is the way the public prosecutor described the actions of Yakub, a *marabout* defendant in one of the trials following the 1871 rebellion:

> Kneeling near him, he covered an initiate [in his order] with his burnoose and placed his mouth in contact with the other's. A convulsive trembling suddenly stirred the limbs of the initiate and strange hallucinations obsessed him. . . . At this point, he went out to fight [our] soldiers. Such ecstasies, of which a few are as warlike as this, are repeated only too often. Every week on Tuesday nights, a group of fervent initiates meets around the illumined one at the tomb of Sidi Mohammed ben Yahya, celebrated in the region. Yakub, the prey of a sacred frenzy, inspires them with the epileptic dances of the whirling dervish. . . . The European inhabitants (of the region) sometimes hear phrases, the ironical tone of which badly disguises the threat, such as *"Chouia, rumi makash commander"* [Franco-Algerian dialect for "soon, the Christians won't give the orders"]. And again: "Abd al-Kadir will return; you will all be like Arabs then and your throats will be cut!" . . .
>
> At the moment of the outbreak of the rebellion, the defendants . . . announced the arrival of the Master of the Hour. At the Jenoudet farm, when the action began, the defendant explained that the holy war had been proclaimed and that all Algeria would soon become Moslem.[9]

[9] Brunel, *op. cit.*, pp. 7–8.

Most Europeans believed that such exhibitions of mystical excess, which the orthodox religious authorities and especially the Islamic reformers have generally done their best to discourage, were typical consequences of allowing the North Africans to go to their own schools.

In 1901, only 3.8 per cent of Moslem children of school age were actually in school, as opposed to 84 per cent of the Europeans. Special preference was shown to the children of major feudal Moslem families. This was the major exception to the general French rule that "the educated Algerian becomes an enemy." As Franck Chaveau, a French counselor of state, observed in 1901, the Arab chiefs were useful to France "because they were neutralizing another influence much more dangerous; that of the *marabout,* who will always be hostile to us."

Though in 1882 the French compulsory education laws were applied to Algeria, the Algerians—both the intellectual elite and others—were mistrustful. An Algerian working for the French administration as professor at the Constantine Lycée and Normal School wrote in a French educational journal that Algerian Moslem parents who sent their children to French schools believed the French teachers were fanatics who tried to convert their Moslem pupils to Christianity.

Moslem religious leaders began to regard with suspicion the "evolved" *(evolué)* or "Frenchified" Moslem minority. This was the group which after 1920 gave rise to the modern nationalist movement throughout North Africa. But religious leaders felt these Algerians to be actual or potential collaborators of the colonial regime, which of course is exactly what the French had intended them to be. Soon, the *madrasa* began to play a political role in forming nuclei of Arab nationalist thought, and later of political resistance. Since these were supposed to train loyal civil servants, many of them for purely religious functions, they were protected by the administration from the attacks of the European *colons*. This made the cities, especially Algiers (where the Medea *madrasa* was transferred), Constantine, and Oran, into centers of Islamic thought and, after about 1935, nationalist sentiment.

ISLAMIC REFORM AND ARAB NATIONALISM

The impact of the West's armed power on Near Eastern Islam, emphasized by Napoleon's drive into the Near East, had helped to shatter the earlier complacent conviction of many Arab leaders that Islam was innately superior to Christianity in all respects. The coming of American Protestant missionaries to the Near and Middle East in the early nineteenth century—to the Arabs, a new form of Christianity which today's visitor to Arab lands may still hear described as "American religion"—added to the general uneasiness within the Islamic *umma*.

This uneasiness was a challenge which helped produce the response of reform movements in all the Islamic countries and the specifically religious reaction of pan-Islamism. Pan-Islamism is largely discredited in the Arab states and especially in North Africa today, but it still has followers here and there. The pan-Islamists, such as Tewfik al-Madani in Algeria and Allal al-Fassi in Morocco, though they no longer often publicly admit it, would like to see a return to pure Islamic tradition in a unified Islamic society. Direct Western rule in countries such as Algeria produced still another form of reaction—political nationalism.

In Algeria, European incursions into the Near East after 1880 stirred both the European and Moslem populations. Of particular influence among Moslems was the Egyptian magazine *Al-Manar* ("The Lighthouse"), edited by Mohammed Rashid Reda (1865–1935). Reda shared with Jamal ad-Din al-Afghani and Sheikh Mohammed Abduh, another great reformer of the Middle East, the conviction that Islam must learn and adopt the positive points of modern European technology and civilization. Reda saw the current state of Islam as one of stagnation. He and his contemporaries were the prime movers of the great reform movement which came to be called Salafiya. This may be interpreted as a desire to return to the ways of the *salaf* (ancestors, or precursors) and so bring Islam back to a position of world power. Few of these ideologies saw in such a return any threat to Christianity as a religion, in so far as it was dissociated from politics or imperialism.

Nevertheless, those Europeans of Algeria who noticed such things took fright. A visit of Farid Bey, chief of the new Egyptian national party, to Algeria and Tunisia in 1902 stirred much concern among the Europeans and great curiosity among the Moslems. A year later, Sheikh Mohammed Abduh went to France, then to Tunisia and Algeria, attracting much interest among the Algerian elite. The Young Turk revolt of 1908 in the Ottoman Empire caused brief emulation by a short-lived "Young Algerian" movement; a somewhat similar one occurred in Tunisia. Added to this was the fact that there was a constant and permanent state of war in some part of the country, such as fighting in the Mzab in 1882. The Mozabites, though heretical Moslems, were no more anxious to accept French domination than their more orthodox countrymen elsewhere, despite French efforts to promote separatist feeling among them.

MODERN POLITICAL SUFISM: THE SANUSIYA

The rise of the powerful Sufi brotherhood of the Sanusiya was a spectacular manifestation of religious resistance influenced by the new currents from the Middle East. Though it became largely associated with developments in Libya, and gave rise to the dynasty of King Idris of the Sanusi, independent Libya's first ruler, it actually had its roots in the village of Mazouna, a Berber village on the Wadi Warizan (Ouarizane) in western Algeria. This was the birthplace of Sheikh Mohammed ibn Ali al-Sanusi, founder of the order.

In 1837 Sheikh Mohammed returned from a Mecca pilgrimage to settle in the oasis of Al-Bayda, Cyrenaica, which King Idris decided to make his new administrative capital in 1960. It is not far from the ancient Cyrene or Barca, which had been the first Christian center of Libya. In order to purify the faith of superstition and strengthen resistance to European encroachment, Sheikh Mohammed built a network of *zawiyas* in Cyrenaica, each directed by a "father superior," or *khuwan,* known for piety and courage. Sheikh Mohammed died in 1859 and was succeeded by the second master of the order, Mohammed al-Mahdi, who turned his attention to missionary work in the Sudan and Black Africa. By 1867, there were about fifty such *zawiyas* on the Barca Plateau.

The Sanusiya did much to purify and revive Islam as a social force in Libya, especially Cyrenaica. In the far south of the Sahara, they moved in to block the advance of the French toward the Sudan. By 1897, they had established a *zawiya* in the Chad region, at Bir Allali. Al-Mahdi was killed when the French captured Bir Allali in 1902. A French officer of the Arab Bureau had written about this time:

> Islam has brought immense progress to all of the [central African] populations. It develops with the greatest rapidity. But it is a serious danger for us: never will a Moslem accept, without serious reservations, Christian domination, and this truth appears more certain because, in the center of Africa, the influence of the Sheikh al-Mahdi ibn Sanusi is considerable. As distinguished from other Moslem brotherhoods, which mix with their religious ideal only local political considerations, this one has pan-Islamic dreams. It wishes and pursues above all else the expulsion of the infidel from the Dar al-Islam, and for a long time it has been preparing for this goal.[10]

The original religious role had indeed become a political one by 1914. The Italians, in 1911, had driven the Turks out of Libya. The Sanusi, persuaded by both Islamic solidarity and some substantial sums of money, were fighting with Turkey, Germany, and the other Central Powers against the Western Allies. One of their chiefs, Sheikh Sarf al-Nasir, left Tripoli in a German submarine for Pola as the Allies advanced.

The Sanusiya began to decline in numbers and spiritual influence as their military power was gradually crushed by Marshals Bongiovanni and Badoglio between 1921 and 1932. When World War II broke out in 1939, they agreed to fight for the British army against the Axis. Their reward was the new Libyan Kingdom, which became independent, under the rule of the last master of the Sanusiya, King Idris, in 1951.

Paradoxically, the Sanusiya in their original home in Algeria adapted themselves to French rule and ultimately became strongly pro-French. I spoke with the last of the Algerian Sanusi masters, Sheikh Bentekkouk es-Sanusiya, in the bar of the Grand Hotel in

[10] Lamotte, Capitaine de Mission Gentil, "Auchari," *Revue de Cercle Militaire* (1902), p. 12.

Oran in March, 1962, shortly before he disappeared, probably killed by the nationalist FLN. He was truly a figure out of another age—like a Victorian engraving of a Sheikh of Araby with his handle-bar mustache, turban wrapped around a red tarboosh, baggy Turkish trousers, and a wide sash with a curved dagger and an automatic pistol stuck in it. One of the Europeans in the bar, a center of the Secret Army Organization, then fighting a last-ditch battle against the Moslem FLN nationalists, introduced him to me as a "great religious chief."

"What can I do but hope that France will win?" he asked me plaintively, as he sipped his Pernod. "The FLN killed my father and brother at our *zawiya* in 1957. There is no salvation for Algeria except in France. We can never enter the modern age without her." Strange words coming from a Sanusi! This seemingly comic-opera figure tried to fill a role which has, I believe, remained undisclosed until now. In July, 1961, the French authorities encouraged him to visit his cousin, King Idris, in an attempt to influence the old man favorably toward French policy in Algeria.

"The Sheikh was well received at Tobruk," according to a French intelligence report I saw later on. "He was invited to two luncheons with the King and Queen, and our Embassy in Tripoli considers that he was a good influence on the King," who gave him a letter recognizing him as the legal successor of his father. All this time, the Libyan desert was serving as a nationalist military base, and its caravans were moving arms to the FLN guerilla fighters. A few weeks after I talked with the sheikh, he disappeared. His disappearance put an end to the Algerian chapter of the strange story of the Sanusiya.

THE REFORMIST *ULAMA* AND THE NEW ALGERIAN CONSCIOUSNESS

Algerian Moslem troops had already served France in her war with Prussia in 1870. They were to serve again in Europe in 1939–45 and in Indochina, where they absorbed the revolutionary guerilla tactics and some of the Marxist ideology of Mao Tse-tung. But it was probably the war of 1914–18 which, intellectually speaking, made the biggest breach in the colonial system. It enabled the

Algerians to perceive for the first time their own considerable role in maintaining French power in the world and, even more, to see and admire the accomplishments of Turkish and Arab reformers in the Near and Middle East.

By the time of the pompous French celebration of the centennial of the conquest of Algeria in 1930, certain religious and educational leaders such as Sheikh Abd al-Hamid ibn Badis (1889–1940) began to take alarm at the excessive influence of European education. The answer of the Moslem elite to this challenge was the foundation, in May, 1931, of the Association of Reformist *Ulama,* in which Ibn Badis was the driving force and Constantine the initial center of activity. Though it could draw on no state funds and had difficulty raising private financial support, its system of "free schools" offering both religious instruction and sound training in the Arabic language was the pride of Algerian Islam. By 1954, when it became a target of French political repression, the association operated one hundred fifty schools with forty-five thousand students. It also managed to send some students to Middle Eastern universities. But though Ibn Badis, up to the time of his death in 1940, was dreaming of an Arab university, there were only 15 per cent of all Moslems of school age in any kind of school at the outbreak of the nationalist revolution in 1954.

In a conversation I had with Ahmed Tewfik al-Madani, then Algeria's Minister of *Habus* (religious property), in Algiers in January of 1963, he spelled out for me the goals and accomplishments of the association, in which he had been active. He termed them "integral parts of the Salafiya movement."

"We struggled," he told me, "to revive the true Moslem religion and rid Algeria of superstition and obscurantism. We fought the influence of the *marabouts* who aided the French. In every possible way we sought to revive the Arabic language in Algeria and make it a living force. This was the threefold aim of the early phase of Algerian nationalism. From 1930 to 1954, it took on so much scope, added so many mosques and *madrasas* to the Algerian scene, that it became an indispensable moral support for the revolution which was to follow."

It was nearly impossible for most of Algeria's million Europeans to grasp, in 1954, or even in 1962, when their mass exodus began, the importance of the Arabic language. Few of them had mastered it. A bitter private letter written by an Algerian educator in 1955 reflects the Algerian attitude toward Arabic. He writes that it is the "most beautiful language in the world" and that it is "capable of clearly expressing all human concepts." He goes on to explain that " 'The Algerian nation is Moslem and it is part of the Arab world,' said ibn Badis. 'Algeria is our fatherland, Arabic our language, Islam our doctrine,' repeat the *ulama*." [11]

Independent Algeria, where in 1965 hardly fifty thousand non-Moslems remain, adopted a constitution in 1963 giving a primary role to Islam in education and in the state itself, though without granting it a monopoly, for its central idea was still that of a double culture.

[11] M'hammed Hadj Sadek, Inspector General of Education, August 19, 1955. Sadek wrote his letter in French. Quoted by A.M., "Regards sur l'enseignement les Musulmans en Algérie," *Confluent* (June–July, 1963), p. 640.

CHAPTER XVII

EUROPE RETURNS: MOROCCO, TUNISIA, AND LIBYA

French presence never showed the North African peoples anything but an abstract image of liberty.

MICHEL ZERAIFA, IN *Tunisie,* 1955

All through the nineteenth century, the Sharifian Empire struggled to preserve its inner unity and ward off the new and persistent encroachments of Europe. The sultans were constantly obliged either to fight the powerful religious chiefs or to rely upon alliances with them to defeat the invading Europeans or the recalcitrant Berber tribes. Morocco was divided between the *bilad al-makhzen,* the strip of territory along the Atlantic coast and the central plains where a sultan's word was law and his taxes, relatively speaking, were collected, and the vastly larger *bilad es-siba,* or "dissident country," in permanent revolt against central authority.

At times, the zone of Berber dissidence extended to the gates of Rabat. This cut the loyal territories in two parts, obliging the sultan to travel by the Atlantic coastal road when he wanted to go from Fez, his usual capital, to Marrakesh. The Sus Valley, most of the Atlas Mountains, the Rif, and the countryside around Tangier were, as often as not, the hunting grounds of robbers whose principal occupations were pillaging caravans, raiding towns, or kidnaping and holding for ransom European travelers or wealthy Moroccans.

The brief but disastrous clash with France that brought Morocco's defeat at Isly had one predictable effect: it accentuated the activities of the Sufi orders and their anti-Christian propaganda. One of the most powerful of these were the Wazzaniya, led by the Sharif of Wazzan, Mulay al-Hadj al-Arabi. His son, Hadj Abd es-Salim, was not a chip off the old block. He married Emily Keene, a pretty English governess working for an American family in

Tangier, where by 1850 there was already a sizeable international colony.

Spain, nervous at mounting British influence in Morocco, eagerly seized an occasion to attack in 1859. A tribe in the Andjera country, around Tangier and Ceuta, had soiled a Spanish flag at Ceuta. The local representative of the sultan, fearful of Spanish reprisals, wanted to hand over Andjera tribesmen as hostages to Spain, with Britain guaranteeing their lives. Sharif Abd es-Salim intervened to prevent this, and the war was on. The Spaniards, led by a general with the questionable Castilian name of O'Donnell, crushed the Moroccan forces and occupied Tetuan, but made peace and evacuated the city again when the British, fearful about letting Madrid get a foothold opposite Gibraltar, interceded.

The last great sultan before the new European occupation, Mulay al-Hasan (1873–94), or Hasan I, was energetic, devout, and courageous. He managed to hold his tottering empire together. Moroccans remember him as a ruler who reduced the amount of "protection" accorded to Europeans and their Moroccan friends, agents, and business associates under regular treaties concluded with a number of powers, including the United States. One Moroccan historian says that while Hasan was still crown prince, he never let state business or pleasure distract him from prayer and devotion. Ostentatious piety is still often politically rewarding in Morocco, where in the past it was a popular means of judging a ruler.

Hasan I began sending students abroad and inviting foreigners to come and serve as his advisors—a timid beginning to the immense task of lifting Morocco out of centuries of stagnation and isolation. Europe was closing in. The Madrid Convention of July, 1880, had extended commercial and legal "most-favored-nation" clauses, formerly granted only to England and France, to a number of other powers. In 1892, the threat of an attack upon Tangier by the tribes had brought European fleets into the Strait in a threatening naval demonstration. Hasan showed diplomatic skill in playing the intrigues of each European power off against those of the others, and he had much strength of character. But he lacked the means to liberate Morocco from the heavy hand of tradition.

The split between the "official" Moroccan Islam of the *ulama* and the *shurafa* of Fez and the far more independent and unorthodox Islam of the powerful Sufi orders grew wider and wider. Some of the orders, such as the Tidjaniya, who had come from Algeria, more or less supported the sultan and the central administration, called the *makhzen*. Many others did not. Through well-timed alliances with the throne, the powerful Berber clans of the southern mountains, who later became mainstays of French power, grew stronger and stronger. A Krupp cannon provided by the *makhzen* enabled the Glawa family to destroy, one by one, the mud kasbahs of their enemies in the Atlas and build their own empire in the south.

Intellectual life shrank largely into the narrow formalism of jurisprudence, interpreting the *sharia* and the *fatwas*. Under Hasan I there were the beginnings of a literary revival: the master of the Kittaniya Order wrote a hagiography, *Salwat al-Anfas,* and Ahmed ibn Khalid al-Nasiri of Salé produced his history of Morocco.

ELECTRIC BOATS, CUCKOO CLOCKS, AND CHRISTIANS

The next sultan, Mulay Abd al-Aziz (1894–1907), was the bright and well-intentioned son of a beautiful Circassian slave girl. He was a favorite child of his father, who in the traditional manner appointed him heir. The boy was thirteen when he ascended the throne. For a time, the country was governed by a regent, a Negro palace slave named Ba Ahmed, who by intrigue and aggressiveness rose to become Grand Vizier. Ruling as a dictator, he kept the tribes in check, maintained the treasury in reasonably good shape, and resisted European intrigues. When he died in 1900, the war minister, Mahdi al-Menhebi, a member of one of the wealthiest Tangier families, became the young sultan's favorite.

Abd al-Aziz surrounded himself with European adventurers, who flattered him and pandered to his inordinate delight in European gadgets. Instead of tending to affairs of state, he played with cuckoo clocks and fancy toys. Learning that he was fascinated by everything electrical, the French Foreign Office sent him an elaborate electric boat and a mechanic to assemble and service it. The young sultan's favorite was the "Caid" Henry Maclean, a picturesque Scottish convert to Islam and onetime staunch Presbyterian, who had been an officer of the Gibraltar garrison before entering the sultan's service about 1875. The people of Fez, who have never had special love for foreigners in general or Christians in particular, began to accuse the sultan of preferring the company of Christians to that of Moslems. A tax reform provided a pretext for an uprising by a pretender, the "Rogui Bu Hamara" (the man of the she-donkey). This threw the region of Oujda and Taza into ferment for many years to come and provided one of many pretexts for the impending French intervention.

Suddenly, in 1905, Morocco found itself caught up in the treacherous crosscurrents of pre-World War I European diplomatic intrigues. The country was already in debt to several foreign powers, chiefly France. In 1904, the Anglo-French *entente cordiale* gave France a free hand in Morocco, and Britain a free hand in Egypt. Secret articles envisaged the likelihood that Morocco would lose its independence and be partitioned between France and Spain. But Delcassé, the French foreign minister, neglected to consult Germany, which also had various commercial and possibly political projects afoot in Morocco. Kaiser Wilhelm I landed at Tangier on May 31, 1905, and proclaimed his support for the sultan's independence and sovereignty and equal opportunity for all nations in Morocco. As for the reforms which the sultan wished to carry out, he added—referring to reforms which French advisers were already planning and which would give France a strangle hold on Morocco—"it seems to me that he should proceed with many precautions and take into account the religious sentiments of the people so that public order is not disturbed."

There was panic in Paris. Delcassé offered to buy off German opposition to the French plans for Morocco, and the Premier, Rouvier, was even willing to grant the Germans a southern Moroccan port. But the Kaiser insisted on a general international conference to settle what was already being called "The Moroccan Question."

It was held at Algeciras (Spain) in early 1906. The resulting Act of Algeciras, signed April 7, 1906, performed the neat and statesmanlike trick of both assuring and taking away Morocco's political, religious, and economic independence. Independence and territorial integrity were guaranteed, and so was "economic liberty without inequality" for all the powers signing the convention. But at the same time Morocco conceded numerous basic activities of government to her "guarantors." Belgian, French, and Spanish officers were to organize the police. A new state bank, with majority French participation, was formed. A tobacco monopoly, which still existed in 1964, eight years after Morocco regained its independence, and which was still controlled by French capital, was created. Other financial reforms were to be instituted.

REACTION AND EUROPEAN INTERVENTION

Almost simultaneously, Moroccan religious resistance against the sultan, now thoroughly discredited through his compromises and concessions with the Europeans, and against the Europeans themselves, began at numerous points in and around the country's territory. In the western Sahara, a *marabout* named Ma al-Ainin led the blue-veiled Reguibat nomads in a holy war against the French and also the Spaniards, who had begun to establish coastal settlements. He was believed to be a sorcerer who could travel great distances with the speed of light or maneuver armies by means of occult powers. His followers extended their influence and built *zawiyas* as far north as Fez. In 1907, several of them, possibly encouraged by the local German consul, murdered Dr. Emile Mauchamp, a French doctor whose dispensary and humanitarianism—as well as his opposition to sorcery and witchcraft, about which he wrote a remarkable book, *La Sorcellerie au Maroc*—had gained him fame in Marrakesh. This was the signal for French forces to move into the Oujda region of eastern Morocco, where they stayed until after Moroccan independence was restored in 1956. Other French forces landed at Casablanca and moved inland, spreading out over the Shawia Plain, after seven European workmen had been murdered by a tribe which objected to a railroad line being built near a *marabout's* tomb.

A northern chief, Raissuli, harassed the Spaniards in Ceuta and the hinterland of Tangier. He managed to kidnap the "Caid" Maclean, holding him for a ransom of 25,000 pounds sterling.

Mulay Hafid, the brother of Abd al-Aziz, proclaimed himself sultan on August 16, 1907, and civil war broke out. The *ulama* recognized Hafid's sultanate at Fez in June, 1908, and the European powers gave him diplomatic recognition—he already had French military support—in January, 1909. German diplomatic and propaganda activity increased, playing wherever possible on the growing anti-French feeling.

By 1911, the Moroccan crisis was threatening to provoke a world war. After Germany sent the gunboat Panther to Agadir, the Germans agreed to a free hand in Morocco for France, which was now backed by Britain, in return for concessions in equatorial Africa, provided there was economic liberty in Morocco. At the same time, the Spaniards began military offensives from their strongholds in Ceuta and Melilla. One by one, Mulay Hafid, with French diplomatic support, eliminated contenders for his throne, including Sharif Kittani, master of the powerful Kittaniya brotherhood, who was put to death in a horrible fashion. His son, Sharif Abd al-Hai Kittani, took his revenge on France later, as we shall see.

With Germany no longer in the picture, Mulay Hafid was forced, on March 30, 1912, to sign the Treaty of Fez granting France a protectorate over Morocco. A separate convention allotted a small zone of "influence" to Spain in the north. Nominally, the sultan's authority was safeguarded in both French and Spanish zones. Actually it was rarely exercised effectively in the Spanish zone because the authority was permanently delegated to a *khalifa* (caliph), or "Lord Lieutenant," in Tetuan, which became the "capital" of the Northern zone. This arrangement was valuable to General Franco at numerous times, as when he used Spanish Morocco as a staging area in 1936 for his offensive against the Spanish Republic, and when, in 1953, he refused to recognize France's exile of Sultan Mohammed V and turned the Spanish zone into a base of operations for the Moroccan nationalist "Liberation Army."

Tangier became an "international zone" where the sultan's representative, the mandub, was "advised" by twelve nations, including the United States. This statute was settled in 1923 and again in 1945, then revoked after Morocco was reunified in 1957.

Signature of the protectorate agreements provoked the most violent reaction yet seen. The northern tribes revolted and marched on Fez. An anti-sultan Mulay az-Zin, proclaimed himself *mahdi* in Meknes. Mulay Hafid appealed for the aid of the French army to raise the siege of Fez, and the French "pacification" of Morocco began in earnest.

"LYAUTEY THE MOROCCAN"

Mulay Hafid abdicated in August, 1912. Sultan Mulay Yusef (1912–1927) allied himself with the first French resident-general, Marshal Lyautey, against the dissidents. One of the first of these was al-Hiba, son of the *marabout* Ma al-Ainin who was marching northward. A long series of French campaigns ensued, usually aided by feudal chieftains. The resistance finally ended in the Anti-Atlas Mountains in 1934. Meanwhile a French general, who in the eyes of orthodox Moslems was also a representative of Christianity, had become the ally of the Sultan of Morocco, who is believed to be God's representative on earth. This was a situation to the taste of Lyautey, who had already served the French Empire in Indochina, Madagascar, and Algeria. The distinguished French historian and diplomat, Roger Le Tourneau, summed up Lyautey well: he found the protectorate idea much better than annexing Morocco outright because he thought it preserved Islamic and Moroccan dignity.

Lyautey was a rather eclectic Roman Catholic who by no means subscribed to the theories of Cardinal Lavigerie about civilization and the cross marching hand in hand. His knowledge of and respect for Islam, at least its outward forms, became almost legendary among the French immigrants who now began pouring into Morocco, and it earned him much opposition and even enmity among them. "Lyautey le Marocain," a term of admiration in the army, was sometimes one of contempt among the settlers. Lyautey translated his respect for Islam into an absolute prohibition against putting up any European buildings in the old cities of Fez, Marrakesh, Meknes, or Rabat, the four "imperial" cities regarded as capitals by the sultan. Nor did Lyautey ever permit mosques to be converted into churches nor any other interference with Islam. However, he did cultivate the chiefs of the more powerful Sufi orders rather than the orthodox, "official" hierarchy of *ulama* and *shurafa*.

Lyautey's forces defeated al-Hiba in 1913 on the Plain of Ben Guerir. They entered Marrakesh, which al-Hiba's *mudjahidun* had captured on their march northward. The help of Hadj Thami al-Glawi, the Pasha of Marrakesh, was essential to the French operation. Al-Glawi, France's staunchest ally in the south, became a millionaire on the gifts he received from influential French interests and the taxes which a vast network of prostitutes paid on their earnings.

When World War I broke out in 1914, Paris ordered Lyautey to withdraw to the coast and send most of his expeditionary forces to France. Lyautey withdrew, but by astutely leaving skeleton forces at key points and continuing his policy of alliances with the more powerful mountain caids, he managed to hold all he had taken. "By this brilliant and bold decision," observes Nevill Barbour, "he saved the Protectorate." [1]

Lyautey built an elite corps of intelligence officers, the *Service des Affaires Indigènes*. Some of them were used in Algeria during the nationalist revolution of 1954–1962 after long service in Morocco. I made the personal acquaintance of one or two. Their knowledge of Arabic and Berber dialects and of the details of village and country life and even of Islam was often profound, always considerable. But their attitude toward the Moroccans was usually paternalistic. Most of these officers relished the exotic and colorful aspects of their life in Morocco. Many enjoyed being judge, jury, police chief, and supreme sage in their districts. Only a few seemed interested in helping the Moroccans out of their dependent state. The mentality they encouraged strongly affected the Moroccans themselves. It makes many of them still reliant upon "advice" and control of foreigners, whether soldiers, engineers, or men of God.

ABD AL-KRIM AND THE RIF REPUBLIC

The political and military aspects of the spectacular revolt of Abd al-Krim al-Khattabi, a Riffian of the tribe of the Banu Uriaghal, have been told and retold by scores of journalists, historians, and novelists. By wiping out General Sylvester's Spanish army in 1921, this self-educated former clerk shook the Spanish monarchy and dictatorship of Primo de Rivera to their foundations, caused

[1] Nevill Barbour (ed.), *A Survey of North West Africa* (London, 1959), p. 91.

acute tension between France and Spain for a time, and attracted adventurers from all over the world. Abd al-Krim's mountain offensive, which aimed at driving all Europeans out of Morocco, and which nearly did drive out the Spaniards, gave both Francisco Franco and Marshal Lyautey some of the toughest military experience of their careers.

Emir Abd al-Krim interests us because of what he tried to establish: an egalitarian Islamic republic, organized along the lines of a modern state with cabinet ministers and a sort of rural assembly of elected representatives. For balance and contact with the outside world, the Emir even hired a few foreign advisers. The republic's basis, during the years when the Emir and his partisans were able to hold the Spaniards at bay, was both tribal and Koranic. It was supported by the European Communists, especially Jacques Doriot and the French Communist Party.

Léon Gabrielli, a former French administrator in Morocco, was sent by Lyautey on a mission to the emir to sound out peace possibilities and look into the fate of his prisoners. Gabrielli had vainly suggested to Lyautey that he send Jacques Doriot to the Rif to make him lose his illusions about Islam's solidarity with Communism. This was a period when the North African nationalists in Paris, such as Messali Hadj, an Algerian leader who later developed a messianic complex, were flirting with Communism. Abd al-Krim told Gabrielli that he was not a fanatic but a nationalist, "for though I am proud of being a Moslem, other peoples' religion does not interest me." He also stated that though he was a rebel, he was one only "until the hour comes when I have to submit." [2] That hour came in 1926, after he encountered the French army.

Abd al-Krim had never openly backed the sultan. Perhaps he intended to march on Fez and proclaim himself sultan. Marshal Pétain intervened with ten French divisions, supported by aircraft and armor, to turn back al-Krim's threat to the French zone. Abd al-Krim's failure to support Sultan Mulay Yusef helped Lyautey to preserve the myth of French "legitimacy" in Morocco. Rather than surrender to the Spaniards, whom he was sure would execute him in barbarous fashion, the emir submitted to the French when

[2] Léon Gabrielli, *Abd el-Krim et les événements du Rif* (Casablanca, 1953); quoted by V. Monteil, *Maroc* (Paris, 1962), p. 55.

the two armies finally pinned him between the mountains and the sea. He was exiled to Reunion Island. In 1947, at Port Said, he escaped from a French ship bringing him back to France, with the connivance of the Egyptian police. In Cairo during the 1950's he was a member of the Maghreb Liberation Bureau that also included Allal al-Fassi and other North African nationalists, backed first by the regime of King Faruk, then by the Free Officers of Gamal Abdel Nasser. When Mohammed V invited him to return to Morocco, and restored to him his family property in the Rif in 1958, Abd al-Krim replied that he would come back only when the last foreign soldier had left the Maghreb. His name was whispered again during a brief Riffian revolt in 1958–59. His idea of "total liberation" was far from being achieved when he died, probably a very disappointed old man, in Cairo in 1963.

After Lyautey resigned in 1925, the ideal of the protectorate as a purely "guiding" institution rapidly disappeared. More and more, Morocco came to be administered by a growing French bureaucracy. Just as in Algeria, the French civil servants, technicians, teachers, and administrators were far more efficient than the old regime had been. An economic boom was generated for the European community by the phenomenal expansion of Casablanca as a seaport and industrial city. Billions of French francs and hundreds of thousands of French careers were invested in Morocco—to say nothing of thirty-five thousand Frenchmen killed in combat between 1907 and 1935. Morocco offered to many Frenchmen the mirage of a land of unbridled opportunity. The real Morocco—the Morocco of centuries of Islam and of traditions more ancient than Islam—remained as an almost invisible and unobtrusive backdrop.

TUNISIA: THE OPEN SOCIETY

If Morocco had remained a closed Moslem society, with its Jews living as *dhimmi* and its Christians either as privileged counselors or unnoticed tradesmen, Tunisia, by the middle of the nineteenth century, was rapidly becoming an open society. Since Phoenician times, it had been receptive to the trade winds and the crosscurrents of Mediterranean civilization. In its cities, particularly Tunis, Arabs, Turks, and Berbers rubbed elbows in business relationships and sometimes even made lasting friendships with Maltese, Jews, Sardinians, Venetians, Frenchmen, Spaniards. Since 1574, the Turkish military regime in Tunisia had been independent of the Ottoman Porte, omitting many of the more oppressive features of Constantinople's rule elsewhere. A regular dynasty developed after Bey Hussein was recognized by the Porte in 1708 as hereditary ruler of Tunisia. This laid the groundwork for a fairly stable political situation, in sharp contrast to the succession of rebellions and purges in Algeria.

As early as 1665, Louis XIV and Bey Mohammed had concluded a treaty which gave France a sort of religious stewardship—protectorate is probably too strong a term—over the Christian residents. Thus, unlike Morocco and Algeria, where the only Christian presence was the token one of a few missionaries, Tunisia had enough Christian residents in 1844 to justify, in the eyes of the Church hierarchy, the establishment of a Diocese of Tunis. It remained for Cardinal Lavigerie, forty years later, to move the seat to Carthage, elevate it to an archdiocese, and add the imperial connotations.

During an era when Italy seemed to be getting the upper hand in the French-Italian rivalry for predominance in commercial and political, as well as spiritual affairs (the Bishop of Tunis was an Italian), Bey Mohammed (1853–1859) was forced by the pressure of the European consuls to promulgate a "Fundamental Pact" guaranteeing the liberties of all the regency's subjects. The immediate cause of the consul's pressure had been the beheading of a Jew, Batto Sfez, accused by Moslems of blaspheming Islam. Both the liberal ideas of the Tunisian general Khair al-Din and the opportune arrival of a French fleet speeded the bey's acceptance of the pact. The revolutionary thing about the pact was that it recognized, for the first time in North African history, the equality before the law of Moslems and non-Moslems. In the preamble, the pact abolished all discrimination between Moslems and non-Moslems and spelled out specific rights of Tunisian Jews. Appendices recognized the right of every subject not only to profess the religion of his choice *but also to change it,* provided no constraint was used in conversion or to prevent conversion. This was of crucial importance, since apostasy had been punishable by death. Another article protested against religious discrimination in employment.

The next bey, Mohammed es-Saddok (1859–1882), went a step further by granting what was then an extremely liberal, European-style constitution. It provided for a responsible ministry and separation of powers. The civil and religious liberties guaranteed by the pact continued in force. But the new constitution, granted under the diplomatic, if not the military, pressure of France, Italy, and Great Britain, was far too advanced for the mass of Tunisians to understand or approve. A revolution broke out in central Tunisia in 1864, fanned by the *marabouts;* it was not unlike the peasant risings of Roman times. Both constitution and pact were wiped out in the severe repression that followed, and the country sank back into its old autocratic ways. It remained in that condition until the French arrived in 1881. But a tradition of Western, if not to say secular, constitutional rule had begun. The later Tunisian nationalists remembered it, and it certainly affected the liberal, quasi-secular Tunisia of today.

By 1869, the bey, who had been borrowing in Europe, especially in France, was heavily in debt. Since he could not pay, he had to accept an international financial control commission of Britain, France, and Italy. The French and Italians in Tunis, between 1879 and 1881, spied and intrigued at a furious pace to win the juciest concessions of farmland, public utilities, and communications. Finally, in March, 1881, one of the usual raids of the Krumirs, a mountain Berber clan, into Algeria gave the French a convenient pretext for settling accounts with the bey and excluding Italy once and for all. French troops invaded Tunisia from Algeria and landed at several Tunisian ports. There was some heavy resistance, mainly among tribes under the influence of Sufi orders in the south, though not only there.

The Treaty of Bardo, or Kasr-es-Said, signed with the bey on May 12, 1881, gave the French the right to occupy the country temporarily, until order was restored, control the regency's foreign relations, and restore its finances to a sound footing. This was not a protectorate. There was heavy opposition in Paris to Jules Ferry, the leader of the procolonial faction, who together with some of the military, the big banking and business interests, favored "protecting Algeria's tender eastern flank" by a full-scale takeover in Tunisia. Ferry's hopes were realized by the new Convention of La Marsa on June 8, 1883, which gave France effective control, through a resident-general and a corps of "advisers," of all Tunisian affairs. This was a real Protectorate. Though a Tunisian Prime Minister and a Tunisian cabinet continued to function nominally, such key ministries as posts and telegraphs, security and agriculture, as well as foreign affairs and finances were taken over by French administrators.

Tunisia's drift into direct administration by its French civil servants was similar to that in Morocco. There were two important exceptions, both of which have had fortunate consequences for the independent republic: many Tunisian policemen were trained, which enabled the young state in 1956 to quickly get rid of French influence in the police (this was not so in Morocco); and the educational authorities recruited many Tunisian teachers for both elementary and secondary schools, not only for Arabic language and literature and Islamic religious instruction, but also for modern disciplines taught in French. This naturally sped the formation of a nationalist elite, impatient to shake off French rule.

YOUNG TURKS AND YOUNG TUNISIANS

After twenty-five years of fairly peaceful coexistence between the growing mass of European immigrants, both French and Italian, and the Tunisians, the first expressions of nationalism arose among the young Arab generation that had studied in France or in French or Italian schools. Bashir Sfar, President of the Administration of *Habus,* or religious property, suggested in a relatively mild speech in 1906 that Tunisians ought to have more hand in administering their country. This was the starting signal. The new Young Tunisian Party, like the Young Turks in the Ottoman Empire which inspired it, wanted to separate religion from politics. Their obsession was to draft a constitution for the country. *Destour* (constitution) became the watchword of the nationalists and the name of the first real nationalist party in 1920.

When the Italians attacked Tripolitania in 1911, young Tunisian intellectuals, both those of Turkish origin, like Ali Bash Hamba, and Arabs, like Abd al-Aziz Taalibi, were alarmed. This was an attack on the Libyans, Tunisia's Arab neighbors. But it was also a threat to the Ottoman sultan, the last Islamic power in Europe, who was still encouraging pan-Islamic doctrines. The religious nervousness this stirred in Tunisia erupted in a riot at a Moslem cemetery. The rumor spread that French surveyors were "taking over" the cemetery, and Moslems demonstrated. French troops fired, and there were dead and wounded on both sides (September, 1911). There was more widespread violence during a dispute between Europeans and Moslems after an Italian tramway motorman ran over a child.

Tunisia's religious moderation was never more clearly shown than during World War I. All the appeals of the Sanusiya in neighboring Libya to join the war against the Western Allies, backed by the call of the Turkish sultan, who also claimed to speak as caliph of the Islamic *umma,* fell on deaf ears except among a few nomad tribes of the far south. When Italy joined the war on the Allied side, the Sanusiya pushed the Italians back to the Tripolitanian coast. In 1915 and 1916 they were repulsed by French troops when they attacked some of the fortified oases in southern Tunisia.

The awakening of the Moslem world, the end of the Ottoman caliphate, and the ideas of President Woodrow Wilson all had profound echoes in Tunisia after 1918. Tunisia had contributed to the Allied war effort. Sheikh Taalibi, with the support of some of the *ulama* of the Zitouna University in Tunis and of Kairawan, founded the Destour Party. It demanded the emancipation of Tunisia as a nation and appealed vainly to Wilson for support. After 1918, new words came into the Tunisian vocabulary: *watan* (nation) in the sense of fatherland, and *watani* (patriot), though *mudjahid* (fighter for the faith) was still used during the final armed phases of resistance in 1954–1956 in its old sense of someone fighting the holy war.

The new national propaganda caused more incidents with the authorities and more repression. It was in this context that Lemaître, the Archbishop of Carthage, decided upon a number of incredibly maladroit gestures, including the placing of a giant statue of Cardinal Lavigerie, holding up the cross, at the gateway to the *medina* (Arab quarter) of Tunis and the holding of the Eucharistic Congress of

1930 at Carthage. The results were to be grist for the mill of an ambitious and secular-minded young politician named Habib Bourguiba.

THE LAND OF THE SANUSI

"Rome," recalled a jingoist Italian author in 1911, the year of the Italian attack on Libya, "was able to extend its domination to all of Mediterranean Africa, from Mauretania to Egypt, holding the natives as its subjects. The natives were able to reconquer their independence with the aid of the Arabs, but when they lost their liberty again under the Turkish yoke, another Latin nation presented herself to reap the heritage of the great antique mother: Italy." [3] This quaint interpretation of history failed to take into account the fact that the Turkish "yoke" in Libya had long been little more than a nominal power, and an Islamic one at that; therefore not especially objectionable to Libyan Arabs.

Greek, Sardinian, Cretan, and other Mediterranean adventurers had often seized power in either Tripoli or Bengasi, and the Knights of Malta had even ruled in Tripoli for a time. Privateering flourished, and European powers sent the same sort of raiding and punitive expeditions as elsewhere into the Maghreb. About 1740, the Caramanli family became predominant when Ahmed Caramanli murdered most of his Arab and Turkish rivals and sent a large tribute, probably his victims' property, to the Porte in Constantinople. During a general Arab revolt in 1774, Ahmed received the beylic, and the family stayed in power until the Porte removed them and instituted direct Turkish rule in 1835. Yusuf, who was bey at the turn of the century, backed Napoleon's expedition against Egypt, but got into a four-year naval war with the United States when Thomas Jefferson refused to increase protection money for American shipping. The Tripolitanians captured the American frigate Philadelphia in Tripoli harbor and her captain and crew. In a daredevil raid by sea, Lieutenant Stephen Decatur succeeded in destroying the frigate before she could be reoutfitted by the Tripolitanians.

Nevill Barbour relates how William Eaton, a tough-minded American consul in Tripoli who had never served in an Arab coun-

[3] G. Castelloni, *Tunisi e Tripoli* (Torino, 1911), p. 108.

try before, was presented to the Dey of Algiers. He flew into a rage when the senior American diplomat in North Africa, a former captive named R. O'Brien, directed him to remove his shoes and to kiss the dey's hand. Eaton advocated rough and energetic action to end the paying of tribute to rulers of what he called "the Barbary dog kennel." He liked to talk religion with Arabs, and reported that during a conversation with the ruler of Egypt, he had discussed similarities between Islam and "American religion." During his overland expedition to Derna, with a mixed volunteer force of about five hundred men, including some American Marines, to try to install a pretender on the Tripolitanian throne, he told some Arab sheikhs that God had promised a separate heaven to Americans. They would be free, if they wished, to "make up parties and visit the Paradise of Mohammed or the heaven of the Papists." His Arab listeners laughed and expressed doubts that it would be possible for him to visit the Paradise of Mohammed unless he had become a "sincere Moslem."

The Porte intervened in a civil war in 1835, sent the Turkish fleet to pack off the entire Caramanli family, and installed direct rule, which in theory extended all the way down to Ghadames and the desert territory of Fezzan. But a new force was stirring in Cyrenaica: the Sanusiya. Sayyid Mohammed al-Sanusi, son of the order's founder, moved the seat of the order from Jaghbub, near the Egyptian border, to the Oasis of Kufra, deep in the Libyan Sahara. The Turks were far less enthusiastic about this return of strict Islam than were the Bedouins of Cyrenaica, who joined the order in droves.

The supposed anti-Christian bias of the Sanusiya was probably a figment of the imagination of the colonial propagandists of various European countries. In 1878, there were Franciscan Fathers and Sisters of the Order of St. Joseph working in Tripoli, and a few other Italian missionaries in other Libyan towns. However, Cardinal Lavigerie warned some of his White Fathers setting out on an expedition to Ghadames and points south to disguise themselves as commercial travelers investigating the possibilities of French trade with the interior of Africa.

A Tunisian sheikh who performed intelligence missions for the French visited Sayyid Mohammed in Jaghbub in 1895. He reported finding "great scholars" there—"more than three hundred from different countries" and an eight-thousand-volume library.

The Porte gradually began to deal with the Sanusi as with a sovereign nation. The Bedouin were scarcely touched by Turkish rule: what taxes they paid went to their own chiefs, who in turn paid the Turks when necessary. The Sanusi brand of Islam was congenial to the Bedouin. It was so orthodox that the Sanusiya became the only Sufi order to win recognition of the puritanical Wahabis in Saudi Arabia.

"THE FOURTH SHORE OF OUR SEA"

In 1881, the Italians had been badly disappointed by the French success in Tunisia. For decades, various Italian soldiers and publicists had envisaged an expedition to conquer and colonize at least Tripolitania, if not all Libya. Italian schools already educated the European colony and a tiny minority of Arabs. Italian priests ministered to their small flock of European parishioners.

The same sort of secret diplomacy which had prepared the way for the French push into Morocco came into play. An Anglo-French convention of 1899 mentioned Tripolitania. In the Russian-Italian agreement of 1909, Czar Nicholas agreed not to oppose Italian designs. Debates raged in the Italian Parliament among politicians like Riccioti Garabaldi, who wished to send millions of Italian emigrants to Tripolitania to relieve southern Italy's population pressures, and socialists or liberals like Ricchieri, who opposed the project, even doubting that Tripoli had any strategic value. The Italian arguments for the conquest sound startlingly familiar to those of the French empire builders in Algeria. Like the arguments of French in Algeria, the Italians based their intervention on what they saw as the inability of the local populations to live together peacefully. One wrote,

> The Arab and the Jew of this country [Tripolitania] do not love the Turk. The Jews nearly all know the Italian language; the Arabs have a radical antipathy for the Turks. . . . The Tripolitanians do not feel themselves legally bound by the laws of the Ottoman Empire and jealously maintain the privilege of

> not serving in the Turkish Army. . . . All we need do is study Turkish constitutional history a bit to understand how Christians [meaning Italians, of course], Arabs, and Turks cannot, in the long run, sit alongside one another in a parliament.[4]

In 1908, when the Young Turk revolt ended the oppressions of Sultan Abd al-Hamid, the Arabs of Libya opposed the new constitution. There were anti-Turkish demonstrations. However, what the Italians took for Arab eagerness to end Turkish rule was really opposition to the liberal heresies of the Young Turks, such as relative emancipation of women: it was a religious, rather than a nationalistic reaction.

In September, 1911, the Italians sent Tripoli an ultimatum demanding protection for their nationals and their enterprises there. Then they quickly attacked Tripoli, Derna, Homs, Misurata, and Tobruk with powerful forces. Before the year was out they had announced the annexation—on paper—of all of Tripolitania and Cyrenaica, though their forces held only a few coastal points. "If any nation of Europe has the right of possession or protectorate in this land, that nation is Italy" thundered the Roman propagandists, terming their invasion—just as the French had at Algiers in 1830—a "liberation" from Turkish rule.

The Turkish resistance soon collapsed. In October, 1912, the Turkish sultan signed a peace treaty with Italy at Lausanne, in which he managed to give up his rights in Libya without recognizing the Italian claim of sovereignty. After they left, the Turks continued to supply the Sanusiya, who now united virtually all of the Bedouin tribes against the *Rumi* invader in a good old-fashioned holy war, with arms, advisers, and some soldiers. When war broke out in Europe in 1914 there was a great insurrection which forced the Italians back to Tripoli, Homs, Zuara, and the Cyrenaican ports. Under the alliance between the Sanusiya and the Central Powers, the Germans used Misurata as a submarine base. The Sanusi offensive was intensified when Italy entered the war on the Allied side in May, 1915.

The Italians wanted the British, their new allies, to conquer Libya for them, but the British limited their operations to the desert

[4] Castelloni, *Tunisi e Tripoli,* pp. 194–95.

confines of Egypt and Libya. By 1918, Sayyid Idris, the new Master of the Sanusyia Order, was well in control of a regularly constituted state which Rome was forced to recognize in 1920. To counter Idris' growing religious and political authority over the Bedouin, in 1919, a sort of representative assembly was set up in Tripoli by the Italians. Then, between 1921 and 1923, the year that Benito Mussolini came to power in Rome, the Italians struck hard. They disarmed the Libyan army and Marshal Badoglio began a grinding desert offensive against the Sanusi. In 1928, the Sanusiya surrendered in Cyrenaica and the war ended there. Kufra Oasis finally fell in 1932, and leading nationalists were captured and hanged.

To make Libya the "fourth shore" of what Mussolini called *mare nostrum,* "our sea," the Italian government began mass colonization, settling upwards of fifty thousand Italians, mainly farmers, on the narrow coastal strip of good farmland. Mussolini visited "the new Roman Empire" in 1937. He had himself proclaimed "Protector of Islam" and arranged to be presented with a "Sword of Islam." This was a maneuver to annoy Britain and France, already in deep difficulty in the Middle East, and it was probably taken even less seriously by Moslems everywhere than the "bridge" policy of General Franco was to be in later years. In any case, the "Protector of Islam" relied very heavily for garrisoning his desert forts and protecting Italian colonies—always subject to Sanusi harassment—on Eritrean Christian troops.

Meanwhile, the Sanusi leadership remained abroad until World War II. They supported the Allied cause and raised a Libyan desert legion to fight with the British against Marshal Graziani and German Field-Marshal Erwin Rommel. Their reward was the monarchy over the new United Kingdom of Libya in 1951.

PART THREE

CHRISTIAN MISSIONARIES AND MOSLEM RULERS

CHAPTER XVIII
THE EARLY MISSIONARIES

O Tingis! Demente Tingis!
O Marrochium, Marrochium,
illusa civitas!
SAINT FRANCIS OF ASSISI, *c.* 1210

The eager young Christian missionary who arrives in North Africa today from England, the United States, or France, bewildered and perhaps disgusted by the poverty and misery he sees about him, has been taught to blame all this on Islam as a social system. "In many ways," commented a missionary in 1963, "Morocco is a land of death. The pall of Islam is heavy, and its blight that blinds hearts and blinds eyes has ruled for centuries. Rejecting the death and resurrection of Christ, they walk in death. Notice that beggar, all rags and filth. . . . Jesus died for him." [1] To appreciate missionary thinking about North Africa today we may refer to the record of past attempts, often pathetic and tragic, but nearly always tenacious.

MOROCCO: THE MARTYRS OF MARRAKESH

The Franciscans were the first Christian order to worry about the souls of North Africans. They were still doing so in 1964. For the reasons we saw earlier, St. Francis, who had founded his Order of Friars Minor in 1208, selected six Italian friars for a mission to Morocco, where he believed a mysterious monarch named "King Miramolin" (*Amir al-Muminin,* title of the caliph) reigned. The six were Vital, Othon, Berard, Pietro, Accurse, and Adjustus. Vital and Berard knew little Arabic, and they warned Francis when he chose them, "We are young and we are ignorant of the tongue of the people." Their companions apparently had at least a smattering of Arabic.

[1] Abe Wiebe, "A Saviour of Life and Death," *North Africa* (Sept.–Oct., 1963), p. 151.

After many adventures in Spain and Portugal, they landed at Ceuta and made their way overland to the sultan's capital.

Scarcely had they arrived when they began to preach the Gospel on the great public square of Marrakesh. As in Spain, they were taken for lunatics and expelled to Ceuta, but they came back and began preaching again, this time in the market places. The sultan sentenced them to twenty days in prison. Again he expelled them to Ceuta; again they came back, to the embarrassment of the Christian colony in Marrakesh. The militia arrested them and took them along when it rode out to do battle for the Almohads against the Banu Marin. During its mission its water stores ran out and the entire army seemed likely to perish of thirst; Berard prayed for help and then dug with a stick and found a spring.

One Friday he escaped the militia and began to preach in the markets again. The sultan was furious when he saw him and embarrassed when he learned that this was the man who had performed the water miracle. Tension rose in the city. Guards were posted at the doors of all Christians. The friars were thrown into the prison for common criminals near the Koutoubia Mosque and in prison preached to heretics who were their cellmates. They were brought before a judge and quizzed on their beliefs. Othon replied with the profession of faith. "How do you know all this?" asked the judge.

"I know it," replied Othon, "by the testimony of Abraham, of Isaac and Jacob, of all the Patriarchs and Prophets, and our Lord Jesus Christ who is the pathway without which man errs and deviates, the truth without which he is betrayed, the life without which one dies forever. And this is why Mohammed leads you by a false path and by lies, to eternal death, where with his followers he is eternally tormented."

The judge had been impressed and interested up to the last sentence, which spoiled everything. They were locked in individual cells, beaten, and tortured. The sultan sent for them. Othon spat on the ground when he pronounced the name of Mohammed, as the government and women of the court looked on. When a minister of the sultan struck him, Othon literally offered his other cheek.

The final exchange between the sultan and Othon went like this:

SULTAN: It is you who scorn our law and the Faith and blaspheme the Messenger of God.

OTHON: We do not scorn any true faith, for your faith is not a true one, it is false: only the faith of Christians is true because it is most sure. . . .

SULTAN: Convert to our faith, and I will give you these women for wives, money and honors in my kingdom.

OTHON: We want neither women, nor money, and we scorn all for Christ.

SULTAN: My arm and my sword will punish you roundly for these follies! [2]

He split the skull of each friar with his sword. The women dragged the bodies out, and they were thrown to a sizeable mob which had gathered and which played with the heads and organs. This was January 16, 1220. When Dom Pedro Fernandez, a Portuguese knight in the sultan's service, sent two officers to recover the relics, the populace rioted and killed them. The other Christians locked their doors tight for three days. Franciscan tradition has it that when the sultan tried to destroy the remains by fire, the bodies would not burn. Through bribery and personal contacts, João Roberto of Coimbra, Dom Pedro's chaplain, managed to get the bones, embalm them, and place them in silver chests. Dom Pedro, pursued by the troops of Sultan al-Mustansir, got them to Ceuta and then to Portugal, where the relics were duly delivered in Coimbra.

The Spanish preachers who were assigned to the Christian *fonduks* were acquainted with Moslem manners and mores. They knew better than to proselytize in the market place. But in 1227, when three Italian Franciscans, Daniel, Agnello, and Leon, came to Ceuta and established a mission where they were later joined by four converted friars, they did preach in public and were beheaded after imprisonment and the usual offers.

In 1221, only a few months after the martyrdom at Marrakesh, Pope Honorius III wrote to the bishops and archbishops of all the world, calling upon them to appoint two missionaries from each diocese for work in "infidel or Saracen" lands. They were permitted

[2] *Analecta Franciscana,* III, pp. 581–582.

to solicit alms in the form of money but were told not to shave their heads, to wear secular garments, and to avoid any unusual behavior so as to be better able to minister to Christian captives. In 1225, a Dominican priest named Domingo was consecrated Bishop of "Miramolin," with missionary jurisdiction over Morocco, but he probably never left Spain. Missionaries were directed to "conduct themselves with caution among the Infidel and not in rash, indiscreet or precipitate fashion." [3]

The mission to Morocco was placed in the hands of the Archdiocese of Toledo, which also had jurisdiction over southern Spain, Algeria, and Tunisia. In 1226, the sultan offered freedom for Christians in Morocco provided their bishop be a Franciscan. This was evidence of the good impression which some of the Spanish Franciscans had made upon him. Andalusian *émigrés,* slaves, militiamen, and merchants constituted what might have been the nucleus of a native Moroccan Church, had there been any mass conversions and had Western European military power not interfered—the two major "ifs," perhaps of all North African history. By 1250, Trinitarian friars and the so-called Mercederians, or Brothers of Mercy, had begun their efforts to redeem Christian captives.

St. Ramón Peñaforte warned Franciscans in Morocco that they must not engage in any arms traffic. They also had to avoid helping any Moslem at war with any Christian or selling Christians as slaves, even if the slaves were Jewish or Moslem women who were falsely represented as Christians. The penalty for any missionary who violated these precepts of the Rule was excommunication. However, the relatives of Christian renegades, especially parents, might live with the renegade in an attempt to reconvert him, just as spouses in a mixed marriage could live together.

St. Ramón reported some of the early endeavors of missionary work in Spain and Africa to the Master-General of the Franciscan Order. These included the care of Christian knights, "who thirsted for the word of God"; ministry to a few indigenous Arabic-speaking Christians—almost certainly recent converts, unless some clandestine ones remained from an earlier time—who "desired the friars with a great desire"; recovery of apostates who suffered from great

[3] Pierre de Cenival, "L'Eglise Chrétienne de Marrakesh au XIIIe Siècle." *Hesperis,* VII (1937), p. 63.

poverty or "seduction of the Moslems"; refutation of the idea current among the North Africans that all Latins were idol worshipers; the instruction and consolation of Christian prisoners; and, finally, preserving the excellent impression created among Moslems, especially in Murcia, Spain. With exemplary realism, St. Ramón relegated proselytism to secondary importance.

TUNISIA AND LIBYA

After the failure of St. Louis' Crusade at Tunis in 1270 and Louis' death, Charles of Anjou signed a treaty with al-Mustansir, the sultan, which allowed Christian churches to be maintained—and even permitted Franciscans to preach and make conversions. One friar of the time commented that although merchants and other Christians living in Tunis were able to receive the sacraments regularly as a result, only a very modest number of Moslems were converted.[4]

Franciscan missions had already worked in Tunis in 1219 and 1227. They were no more popular with the Christian merchants than those in Marrakesh had been with the European traders there. The Tunis merchants succeeded in having the missionaries expelled, though not before they had converted at least one Tunisian prince. Nor were they inactive in Libya. In the second half of the thirteenth century, beginning the tradition of Italian missionary work there, a Franciscan named Conrado de Ascoli devoted his career to the mission. One present-day Spanish source claims that his work led to 6,400 conversions,[5] though the figure seems incredible and may have actually been something more like sixty-four—which in itself would be a relatively high figure.

RAMÓN LULL: THE "ENLIGHTENED DOCTOR"

There is no more spectacular and, in many ways, enigmatic figure in all world missionary work than the Catalan Ramón Lull, or Raymond Lully (*c.* 1232–1315). Nearly all missionaries of

[4] Norman Daniel, *Islam and the West* (Edinburgh, 1962), pp. 115–119.

[5] Bernardino Llorca, S. J., *Nueva Visione de la Historia del Christianismo,* 2 vols. (Barcelona, 1956), I, 5; 7.

today, whether Catholic or Protestant, regard him as the pioneer. He was the first missionary to acquire a thorough working knowledge of the Arabic language and a very solid and serious knowledge of Islamic doctrine. He used both assets to meet the Moslems of North Africa on their own ground, seeking to convince their intellectual elite in theological controversy and their masses by preaching in the market place. If all his life was in one sense a deliberate search for the martyrdom which was his final destiny, it was also a hard-working, inspired dedication to the principle that Moslems, like schismatic Christians, could and must be brought to the fold of Latin unity.

Largely as a result of Lull's intervention, the Council of Vienna (1311–1312), shortly before Lull's strange death, decided to found five colleges to teach Hebrew, Arabic, and Chaldean in Rome, Bologna, Paris, Oxford, and Salamanca. The foundation of the first Dominican school in Toledo in 1250 and Lull's Franciscan College in 1276 for missionary linguistics had already marked the beginning of regular Oriental studies in Western Europe.

There was far more to Lull than just his vast energy as a scholar, missionary, and apologist. Professor R. W. Southern, one of the latest Western scholars to deal with the West's medieval views of Islam, sees in "all this torrential energy" behind Lull's production of over two hundred books "a streak of madness" and in his life a suggestion that the Christian West, after an age of reason and hope, had begun to grow more desperate over the magnitude of the problem of Moslem-Christian relations.[6]

Born in Majorca, Lull was, at various times, besides a missionary, a poet and novelist in the Catalan language; a mystic fascinated by cabbalism; a reformer; and a world traveler. After having been reared in an atmosphere of luxury, he decided to become a Franciscan and withdrew to live a hermit's life. To learn Arabic, he bought a Moslem slave who carefully tutored him. One day the slave was imprisoned as a thief. The slave's suicide in prison probably did more than anything to produce Lull's "streak of madness."

The Abbé Berenger regards Lull's ideas as presenting "one of the strangest paradoxes of history" and says Lull "felt that

[6] R. W. Southern, *Western Views of Islam in the Middle Ages* (Cambridge, Mass., 1962), note pp. 78 f.

Islam should be thoroughly understood by Christians, but that once they won this understanding, they should use this knowledge to destroy it." Lull hoped to secure both the return of the Orthodox Churches to the Roman fold and the conversion of the Tartars to Christianity, in which he placed great hope. He was certain that Moslems and others could be converted through reasoned arguments suited to their particular social and educational status. He felt that learned Moslems tended to have doubts about the validity of Islamic doctrinal points anyway and that this doubt would serve as a basis for attack.

In 1307, he went to Bougie (Algeria) saying that he intended to defend the Trinity. He was arrested for preaching in the market place and brought before the town kadi, who arranged for a public debate with several Moslem doctors. His relentless arguments got him thrown into prison, and the Bougie mob demanded his death; but a Catalan and Genoese military force managed to rescue him. Later he went to Tunis.

One of Lull's most famous discussions was with Hamar, a scholar of Tunis. Lull had argued earlier that "in the most simple Divine Essence there is Trinity of Persons." Lull taught that God the Father generates the Son and both expire the Holy Ghost. In the debate with Hamar, he applied this principle to the "seven conditions" and "eleven qualities" which Hamar attributed to God. Lull tried to show that the Trinity and Incarnation were better explanations of the attributes of God which Moslems admit than the Moslem principles. Lull admitted at one point that he was less interested in actual Moslem objections to Christian dogma than in other objections which he himself considered plausible.

Complaining that Christian merchants in North Africa could not hold up their end in religious arguments with Moslems, he wrote down for them some arguments they could use to demonstrate the truth of the Trinity in arguments with Jews, as well as with Moslems. In this treatise, God is represented as the generator of goodness which is transmitted on through the Son and the Holy Ghost. Lull's arguments were probably a bit too complicated for most of the down-to-earth merchants.[7]

In his works, Lull always carefully arranges the speeches he

[7] Daniel, *op. cit.*, pp. 178–180.

puts into the mouths of his Moslem debating partners and makes sure that the Christian side has the last word. Here is a sample from his *Book of the Gentile:*

> MOSLEM SAGE: Since Mohammed is honored so greatly in the world and by so many people, it follows that in him justice accords with the charity of God; for if this were not so, then would God not suffer him to be honored as he is, and if He suffers it, wrong and honor would accord with charity, against charity and honor and justice, which is impossible. Whence it follows that, by reason of the honor wherewith Mohammed is honored by God, Mohammed is a prophet.
>
> GENTILE: From what thou sayest, it follows that Jesus Christ, who is so greatly honored in this world, is God; and that His apostles, and the other martyrs, who are so greatly honored likewise, died in the way of truth. For, if God suffered not the dead that died in falsehood to be honored in this world, then that which is said of Christ would not be true, neither would Mohammed be worthy of honor nor a prophet.[8]

A recurring theme in Lull's dispute with Hamar and in other writings was the difference between the Christian heaven of angels and seraphim and the voluptuous Moslem one of beautiful women and fleshly delights. Lull seemed to feel that the allurements of the Islamic paradise were not important in making conversions to Islam, and he shows one of his fictional Tartars as recoiling from the idea. "What will Paradise be," he makes him say, "but a tavern of unwearied gorging and a brothel of perpetual turpitude?"[9]

Conversion of the Tartars, or Mongols, who as invading enemies of Islam might prove to be the saviors of Christendom—their King was thought by many to be the persistent but legendary figure of Prester John—was a dominant thought of the time. Mongol embassies led by Nestorian Christians even came to the West between 1285 and 1290 to discuss joint operations against Islam, and the leader of one attended Mass in St. Peter's. Before Lull's death,

[8] See von Grunebaum, *Medieval Islam,* p. 52.

[9] Daniel, *op. cit.,* p. 45.

the Mongols had become Moslems and Christian hopes for a second front in the Middle East had been dashed.

North Africa, thought Lull, would only be one fragment of the great Moslem empire which might be reclaimed for Christianity without the need to conquer it by force of arms. To carry out this conversion, one must first approach the elite. Lull's chief obsession in this approach was his desire to refute the philosophy of Averroës, whose ideas had permeated Islam and deeply influenced Christian philosophy. Averroës' teaching of a radical Aristotelianism which challenged the immortality of the individual soul, having only the intellect participate in immortality through the union of intellect with active intellect, became one of Lull's targets. (St. Thomas Aquinas (1226–1274) and the other schoolmen were showing that Reason and God are completely compatible to a Christian.)

Despite warnings of friends and colleagues, Lull returned to North Africa a third time in about 1314. Accounts of his death differ in details. All agree, however, that he sought martyrdom by once again preaching in the public square of some city, probably Bougie, and that this time his wish was satisfied. He was stoned to death by a crowd which he seems to have deliberately provoked. Nonetheless, Lull probably understood the Moslems better than any European of his own age and most in ours.

LATER MINISTRIES

After Lull, no single missionary stands out for centuries. Spanish Franciscans, now permanently established in Marrakesh and later in Fez and Tunis, continued their generally discreet ministry among the Christian captives and merchants. They probably made an occasional conversion among the Moslems. In 1289, Pope Nicholas IV appointed Friar Rodrigo de Gudal, the former superior of the Franciscans at Saragossa, first as bishop, then as papal legate for all of Africa. The pope exhorted him to visit his diocese "so as to see to the defense of his Order, or better, of all Christendom," but it is not certain that Gudal obeyed. The Trinitarians, Redemptorists, and others were already at work among Christian prisoners. Often their perilous lives ended in violent deaths, as was the case of two

English Trinitarians, Firmy and Silvester, who were hanged at Marrakesh in 1326 while trying to ransom captives.

In 1310, the Dominicans included southern Spain and Africa in a province of their order governed by a vicar. The Prior of Murcia sent two of the rare Arabic-speaking friars to Seville to train "those who live among the infidel." In the same year, the Bishop of Marrakesh, who apparently lived there, since this was a time of relative toleration, asked permission to wear the Dominican habit. During this era of toleration, an intellectual elite developed, and there was a brief semblance of the old interfaith contacts. But in 1325, Pope John XXII had to ask the Bishop of Marrakesh to end "free-lance" missionary activity in his diocese because it caused tension with the Moslems.

From 1370 the Diocese of Morocco was formally attached to that of Seville, and the Bishop was a suffragan appointed in Seville. The Great Schism of 1382 in the Western Church saw the Castilians and Aragonese defecting from Rome and giving their loyalty to the antipope in Avignon, but this had little effect in Morocco. In the same year, the Franciscans returned to the episcopate in Morocco until 1409. When the Portuguese entered Ceuta in 1415, they began the practice, which we saw earlier, of appointing their own bishops for the enclaves they conquered.

The diplomatic and political action of the papacy, sorely tried by the schism, the Crusades, and the wars in Spain, slackened. However, Rome tried to keep at least a minimal ministry in North Africa. Pope Innocent VIII in 1487 ordered a Dominican named Pedro of Montemolin to take up his post without delay and to carry out no pontifical act outside his city and Diocese of Marrakesh. The last bishop claiming jurisdiction over all Morocco to visit his post was probably Sebastian of Obregon, who went to Tetuan and Fez to ransom slaves. Bishop Sancho Diaz de Trujillo (1534–1570) handed the goods of the "Moroccan" Church over to the Inquisition of Seville, first making sure he had guaranteed his own rents and revenues for a lifetime.

In the Franciscan tradition of Lull, though far inferior to the Catalan doctor in his intellectual gifts, was Andrea of Spoleto, an Italian Minor Friar from Umbria. After ministering to the sick in Corsica, he volunteered for service in Africa and landed in Ceuta about 1531. When he arrived in Fez he was the first priest many prisoners had seen in years.

Spoleto had been sure he would be able to preach to the Moslems. The Marinid sultan, Ahmed al-Watassi, quickly disillusioned him, informing him that his mission was only to console Christian captives and minister to them. Al-Watassi, considered relatively tolerant toward Christians, asked Spoleto why he had come. "To teach the truth and liberate the people from error," Spoleto retorted. As proof of the divine nature of his mission, he offered to resurrect the dead king, al-Watassi's father, or tame a wild lion, or resist the flames of the stake.

Taking Spoleto for a lunatic, the sultan advised him to stay in the reserved area with the rest of the Christians. Spoleto insisted several times on undergoing the trial by fire. The sultan then sent him to talk theology with the rabbis of the *mellah,* or ghetto. Spoleto, through the intermediary of Ibrahim, one of the royal ministers, finally managed to draw up a document signed by himself and witnessed by two other captives, certifying that he would face the fire of his own free will. The eyewitness accounts of the other captives, set down by a Portuguese Franciscan of Setubal, said Spoleto mounted the stake on February 9, 1532, calling on the Moslems to be baptized, and that the fire went out three times, despite the use of sulphur and gunpowder. When it finally burned, after another barrel of powder was thrown in, Spoleto emerged unscathed and smiling, walking like the Hebrews of yore among the flames. In a rage, the mob stoned Spoleto to death, tore his body to pieces, and threw it into the Fez River in which all of him disappeared but for a foot which was taken to Spain as a holy relic.

POLITICAL MISSIONARIES

By the sixteenth century, the spiritual tasks of some missionaries were augmented by others charged with missions of diplomacy or espionage. One such was the Spanish Redemptorist, Father Contreras, who arrived in Tetuan in 1539. During five years of ministering to the Christian captives—he reported in April, 1445, that there were five thousand in the town's prisons—Contreras worked on his own plan for a Spanish conquest of all North Africa. But the Cardinal of Toledo, mindful of the defeat of Charles V at Algiers only four years earlier, turned it down cold. Contreras persuaded both the sultan and the King of Portugal that a Jesuit mission to Morocco would be useful. The Jesuits redeemed more than two hundred prisoners during a five-year stay. They returned to Portugal with much valuable political information.

Another Dominican, Don Bautista, entered the Moroccan scene in the 1570's. After becoming friends with Sultan Mohammed al-Masluk, he lived to see the sultan killed in the Battle of the Three Kings at Al-Ksar in 1578. As a result of the Portuguese defeat, the Marrakesh prison filled up with priests and monks. The pastor of the slaves in Marrakesh at that time was Thomas of Jesus, an Augustinian who had been purchased by a fanatical *marabout* who had mistreated him and brought him to Meknes as a slave. Among his successors in Marrakesh was an Irish Dominican, Anthony, at the court of Mulay Zidan, a bibliophile. Anthony translated Latin authors into Castilian Spanish so that renegades could retranslate them into Arabic for the sultan. When Anthony left Marrakesh in 1622, he took a letter from the French prisoners to Louis XIII, petitioning for their redemption.

The political role of the missions continued to grow. In 1617, there were two-hundred French slaves in Marrakesh. Isaac de Rasilly, a Catholic nobleman, proposed to place in the sultan's service a troop of Frenchmen who would, after the manner of the old militias, be garrisoned in a fortified port. In compensation for their services, he hoped to obtain liberty for the slaves and guarantees from the sultan for free practice of the Catholic religion in the entire country. Already, as we have seen, there was some Protestant competition.

The Capuchin Order in France approved the project, and Richelieu urged it on the King. Rasilly and three apostolic "missionaries" arrived at Safi on October 3, 1624. The Caid of Safi promptly threw them into prison. Rasilly was sent back to France, but the mission of the two other Capuchins, themselves in capivity, ended as had so many others: in ministering to the other Christian captives, until they died natural deaths.

The papacy was greatly interested in the possibilities of the Capuchin mission. Cardinal Louis Ludovici (1575–1632) wrote in December of 1626 to Father Joseph, the Capuchin through whom

Richelieu hoped France would gain a foothold in Morocco, that he had high hopes for his work. He advised that missionaries be chosen who have "the simplicity and prudence which our Lord Jesus Christ seeks in such workers" and wrote that "the Holy Congregation awaits from time to time to have good news of the conversion of several souls. . . . There is great hope of profit in these Mohammedans, though they be strong in their false belief." [10]

Two years later, Father Pierre, another French Capuchin, arrived at the tolerant Mulay Zidan's court in Marrakesh. The sultan asked Pierre, "Does your law permit you to kill tyrants?"

"Far from it," Pierre replied. "It advises us to render them respect and obedience, not only through ceremony and civility, but through duty and the obligation of conscience, and recommends prayers for them." Pleased by this answer, the sultan offered to fill Pierre's hands with ducats. Pierre refused. The sultan was astonished until one of the court renegades told him that "these monks never handled money, and fled from women."

Pierre waited for his chance to talk of religion, and when it came he told Zidan that "there is one true religion, which is the Christian, Catholic, Apostolic, and Roman one." The sultan offered to arrange a debate between Pierre and a rabbi. Pierre agreed, and the debate was held. Then Pierre offered to endure trial by fire, as Andrea of Spoleto had. Here the sultan put his foot down and absolutely forbade it.

One night, Zidan went to the Marrakesh hostel where the Capuchin mission was staying and tried to persuade them to join him in some nocturnal revels. The concierge was wise enough not to open the door, and, fortunately for the Capuchins, the sultan changed his mind and left.[11]

THE NEW FRANCISCAN MISSION TO MOROCCO

To adapt missionary techniques to the age of discovery, Pope Pius V in 1568 set up a commission for study of apostolic problems. It renewed many of Lull's recommendations and tried to encourage

[10] Henry Koehler, *L'Eglise Chrétienne du Maroc* (Paris, 1934), p. 61.

[11] *L'Histoire de la Mission des Pères Capucins au Royaume du Maroc,* Bibliothèque Nationale, Paris Imprimes, OJ–63; in Castries, *Sources Inédites,* "France, Third Series," III, pp. 39–252, *passim.*

the study of Arabic. In 1630, the papacy sent a Spaniard, Juan de Prado, Apostolic Prefect of Missions, to Morocco. Prado, who had volunteered for this mission, was sixty years old and rather corpulent, which must mave made his ordeal far worse than it would have been for a younger man. While Juan was en route to Marrakesh, the tolerant Sultan Abd al-Malik, to whom his credentials were addressed, had died. He was replaced on the throne by Mulay al-Walid, who as we saw earlier was not averse to roasting prisoners at times.

The new sultan did not recognize the credentials addressed to his dead brother. After a few days of ministering to the prisoners, Juan de Prado and the other monks among the prisoners were suddenly arrested, slapped into irons, jailed, and put to work preparing gunpowder for mortars. A month later al-Walid called in Juan and questioned him, then personally shot him full of arrows. Juan, still alive, was tied to a stake, but a Moroccan ended his sufferings by crushing his skull with an iron bar. Two other Franciscan monks were spared and continued their ministry, and the next sultan, Mohammed al-Saghir, who liked Spaniards, set them free. In 1632, he even gave the Church of Notre Dame, which had been rebuilt, and an adjoining monastery to the Franciscan Order.

The Franciscans consider this the start of their new mission to Morocco. The two monks, Mathias and Julian, were not permitted to ring bells but took the signals for their own prayers from the muezzin of the nearby Koutoubia and Kasbah mosques. Earlier, the Marrakesh missionaries had called their small flock to Mass like an imam on a minaret, shouting *"Ave Maria,* brothers!"

The Franciscans instructed and actually baptized twenty Moroccans. When this attracted attention, later converts were given only a certificate and quickly whisked away to Christian territory where they were baptized and given jobs. Conversion of one Jewish family in the *mellah* (ghetto) caused a scandal: when other Jews complained, the sultan and his councilors ruled that to "change over from one false creed to another did not matter," since Koranic law was not affected.[12]

Later the Franciscans moved to the *mellah* where only two of

[12] Koehler, *op. cit.*, pp. 78–79.

them, a priest and a lay brother, lived on through famines and considerable mistreatment. When Ismail took the throne, the mission moved to Fez, leaving the house in the Marrakesh *mellah* to several Greek Christians. In Fez, they made permanent quarters for themselves within the enclosure of the prison, where in 1672 they found five hundred prisoners. They improvised a chapel and began to teach children, including some Moroccans who asked to be admitted. This may have been the first missionary school in North Africa.

After all manner of difficulties, including opposition from the Trinitarians who had now begun to arrive, they left Fez. By now, the main missionary activities centered around the redemption, as we have seen, of the Christian captives at Ismail's court in Meknes. Here the Franciscans had a church in the Spanish quarter. In June, 1686, a fresh contingent of Franciscans arrived from Spain and began work in Meknes with the Trinitarians and others.

Throughout such events as the fighting for the Spanish enclave of Larache in 1689 and various epidemics, Ismail protected the missionaries. The archives of the mission in Tangier contain over twenty letters addressed to Franciscans giving them privileged status. For a century, the mission in Meknes, attached to the Province of Santiago in Spain, had seventeen cells for resident monks. By 1712, the mission had four other churches besides the one in Meknes: two in Fez, one in Tetuan, and one in Salé. But when Philip V of Spain sent sixteen thousand reinforcements to Ceuta and attacked the nearby Moslem camp, Ismail ordered Father Diego, the Franciscan Superior, out of the country. Later, when the fighting was over, he asked him to come back. Diego returned with presents for Ismail, then left for the last time with twenty ransomed captives.

After Ismail's death, disorders broke out during which the Negro palace guard attacked the mission. Several friars were killed, and the pharmacy was wrecked. Ismail's son, Abd Allah, at first kept good relations with the Franciscans, who were able to help alleviate in Meknes the effects of the great earthquake that razed much of Lisbon in 1755. In 1775 and again in 1790, when hostilities broke out with Spain, expulsion orders were issued against the Franciscans, then later revoked.

The Portuguese missions in Tangier suffered from Europe's religious wars. When the British occupied Tangier, they sacked the city, not sparing the churches. Of the seventeen churches and chapels built by the Portuguese, the British left only one, with its convent, for the few Catholics who remained in the city. In 1790, when Sultan Mulay Yazid expelled all the missionaries in Morocco, the Franciscans left Tangier, only to return four years later under Sultan Sulaiman. In a treaty he signed with Spain in 1794, the sultan recognized that the missionaries, far from displeasing the Moroccans, were always appreciated by them because of their practical knowledge of medicine and their humanitarianism.

The Napoleonic wars hindered the work of the Franciscans, and no missionaries were sent during that time. The Spanish government ordered all its nationals in the missions to leave in 1822, and, by 1851, a single friar, Francisco Palma, constituted the entire mission.

In 1923, eleven years after the French military began the reconquest of Morocco, the French Franciscans arrived in Rabat. An apostolic vicarate and a French-type parish system were set up in Morocco. Once again, the sword had brought back the cross.

ST. VINCENT DE PAUL AND THE LAZARISTS

In 1581, a poor shepherd boy was born in Gascony who was profoundly to affect both spiritual and worldly things in North Africa. Vincent de Paul was ordained a priest in 1600. While on a sea voyage from Toulouse to Narbonne he was captured by pirates and, by his own account, was held in slavery in Tunis until he managed to make an adventurous escape in 1607.

Whether or not his own account was wholly true or partly imaginary, and historians disagree on this point, he was moved to found, in 1634, a new congregation in Tunis, intended to care for the poor. This was re-established in Paris at St. Lazare's College in 1832.

St. Vincent was canonized in 1737. The French consider him the father of orphan homes, and Tunisian Arab tradition remembers him as a "good *marabout*." His order was a secular one, called the congregation of Priests of the Mission, Lazarists, or Vincentians.

The new thing about it was that instead of proposing to convert Moslems or ransom Christians, the Lazarist friars took care of both the bodily and spiritual welfare of the Christian captives and also of whatever Moslems would accept their care. Often they had to mediate rivalries between the various Catholic orders then working in North Africa.

The Lazarists had much to do with the thorough penetration of religion and religious ideas into French politics in the Moslem world. They became powerful in the Maghreb, especially in Tunisia. Under their most distinguished grand master, Jean le Vacher, they acquired episcopal authority and control over the activities of the Italian Capuchins and Spanish Trinitarians working in Tunisia and sometimes in Algeria. In both ransom and diplomatic negotiations, many of them highly ticklish and secret, they started a French tradition of priests in diplomacy, which has not entirely disappeared today.

CHAPTER XIX

CARDINAL LAVIGERIE: THE CHURCH MILITANT

> Love the poor infidels. Do good to them. Heal their hurts. They will give you first their affection, then their confidence, and finally, their souls.
>
> CHARLES CARDINAL LAVIGERIE, 1874

The first French priests and missionaries who arrived with the expeditionary force in Algeria in 1830 were strictly forbidden to attempt any conversions. Baptisms were rare. The military frowned on them. One Frenchman who felt that Algeria's souls were yearning for Christ bitterly observed that the administration had left the Moslems "parked in their Koran and their barbarism" without any effort of either assimilation or conversion. In 1838, the Emir Abd al-Kadir is supposed to have told a French officer to hurry and build a church to prove that the French actually worshiped God and could be trusted.

The first bishops of Algiers found their episcopal activities hampered and their missionary designs frustrated by the anticlerical policies of Paris. Bishop Dupuch, the first incumbent, who was allowed five priests and later some nuns, had to order crucifixes removed from hospitals. His successor, Bishop Pavy, tried to open an orphanage for Arab boys, but this and a mission he established at Laghwat (Laghouat), on the edge of the Sahara, were ordered closed by the government.

One man, Charles Cardinal Lavigerie, was soon to change all this and for a brief moment to make a concerted effort toward the re-Christianization of all North Africa. His basic philosophy was simple: Christianity and Western civilization go hand in hand. It was the duty of the administration and the soldier to co-operate with the church militant in spreading the benefits of both; and the best form of political regime to assure this is a monarchy. Lavigerie was, in fact, the last prominent defender of the crusading and royalist tradition in religion, government, and politics.

THE MAKING OF A MISSIONARY CARDINAL

Charles Martial Allemand-Lavigerie was born on October 31, 1825, to a customs officer and his wife in Bayonne. Two family servants taught him the precepts of French Roman Catholicism, and he took the leadership of his class at the Larresore Minor Seminary. He won honors at a major seminary in Paris, then, at the age of twenty-two, he abandoned his plans to get married. When only twenty-three, he became the first doctor to graduate from the Carmelite Normal School, and the pope granted a special dispensation to ordain him a priest.

Lavigerie's commanding presence, husky physique, and great ambition, restlessness and academic brilliance were promising raw material for a great career in almost any field. In the French Church of his day, buffeted by the winds of anticlericalism and the socialistic tides of the 1848 revolution, they helped him in his role of militant cleric. When the Druses and Metualis massacred twenty thousand Christian villagers in the Lebanon in 1860—there would have been more victims, had not the exiled Abd al-Kadir intervened in their behalf—Lavigerie had his first contact with the Arab world. He worked tirelessly in the Middle East on behalf of the Christian refugees, and in raising funds for them in a personal campaign in Europe.

At thirty-seven, Lavigerie became Bishop of Nancy and the youngest bishop in France. He imposed the strictest discipline upon his clergy, both priests and nuns, within the living memory of Nancy. General MacMahon, Military-Governor of Algeria, invited him to become Archbishop of Algiers to replace Pavy, who had just died. But when MacMahon realized that Lavigerie intended to attempt the evangelization of Algeria, he tried to get Emperor Napoleon III to quash the nomination. It was too late. Pope Pius IX, who emphatically approved of Lavigerie, had also approved his appointment.

Lavigerie arrived in Algiers on May 15, 1867. In his first pastoral letter, he jubilantly spoke of Algeria as "the cradle of a great and Christian nation." To the Moslems, he announced that he would "claim the privilege of loving you as my sons, even though you would not acknowledge me as your father." [1] Perhaps it is unfair

[1] Glenn P. Kittler, *The White Fathers* (New York, 1961), p. 44.

to term Lavigerie's attitude toward them as pure, unadulterated paternalism, but it looked like this to the Moslems.

Lavigerie set out for Rome to win the support of Pope Pius IX, already the ally of Napoleon III because Napoleon had saved the papacy during the revolutions of 1848. On the return trip to Algiers, a storm tore off the ship's rudder. Lavigerie took charge. He told the seven hundred passengers to pray and submit themselves to the protection of the Mother of God. If they came through safely, they were to go to the new basilica of Algiers, Notre Dame d'Afrique, which Pavy had built, and dedicate themselves and all Mediterranean travelers to her. They were saved. Lavigerie's triumphal arrival at the head of a procession of the grateful passengers was the kind of dramatic gesture he loved.

With the support of Napoleon and the pope, Lavigerie plunged into his self-appointed task of evangelizing Algeria and eventually, he hoped, all of Africa, with fervent zeal. At the beginning, at least, his identification of the cross with the sword of France was as complete as that of St. Louis had been in 1270. He wrote:

> Like Europe of the fifth century, North Africa . . . was devastated by barbarian hordes and brought into this state of excess desolation. Its ruin has been consummated for eight centuries now and has grown more and more profound with the passing of the years. Everything disappeared from its soil, its magnificent cities, its eight hundred episcopal churches, its monasteries, its twenty millions of inhabitants. All this was replaced by hordes of savage conquerors whose destructive genius, incurable insouciance, sensual and fatalistic religion have all been covered with the dust of centuries and hidden away from the memory of men. . . . In the presence of this Barbary, we are watching the efforts of the great country which is ours and which for thirty-nine years has been calling upon all the live forces of contemporary civilization to give back to these countries the place which they once occupied.[2]

[2] Speech delivered by Lavigerie in 1869; in Lavigerie, *Instructions aux Missionaires* (1884); new edition (Maison Carrée: Imprimerie des Missionaires d'Afrique [Pères Blanc], 1939), pp. 18–19.

Lavigerie sensed that despite the good intentions of many of the French military men and colonizers, "what is lacking is a soul." Delighted with Lavigerie's ideas about rediscovering a Christian soul in Algeria and the possibilities of evangelization further south, Pius IX created the new Missionary Prefecture of the Sahara and the French Sudan, where French military penetration had already begun.

The novitiate of Lavigerie's new Missionary Order of Africa began in October, 1868, at the Algiers suburb of El-Biar, near the orphanage of Ben Aknun. The master of Lavigerie's three pioneer missionaries was Father François Vincent, a Jesuit. Lavigerie drove his staff workers and his priests relentlessly. He made them learn Arabic and Kabylie Berber. He asked impossible exertions from them. Only one of the original three, a *pied noir* named Pinateu, stayed on with three other newly arrived priests to live the truly hard life of poverty and study which Lavigerie decreed, sleeping only a few hours each night on the floor or ground, performing disinterested acts of charity, and eating such tasty fare as weed stew with dog meat.

Lavigerie opened several orphanages, which General MacMahon tried to close. When the orphans saw the white robes and red skull caps which Lavigerie ordered the members of his new order to wear, they are supposed to have remarked that unlike the other fathers, who are black fathers, "you are white fathers." The name stuck and has survived to this day.

The orphanages had more than a purely humanitarian aim. The bishop ordered his missionaries to aim at training the children with a view to "finding among them the elements of a *native clergy,* which, accustomed to the climate, will bear up under its conditions."

> This is the way in which all Christian lands have reached the Faith and one can hope, with the grace of God, to bring it to this great continent, still lost in the mists of error. It is therefore most important that as soon as they arrive at a mission, the Fathers should gather together and group around them the small children. . . . This should be all the easier for them because slavery exists everywhere in Africa and by this means

> [i.e., redemption of slaves] they will be able to obtain as many as their resources permit.[3]

Some of the orphans were to be sent to missions in coastal cities and given a basic schooling and, if possible, the rudiments of a higher education. During this time, they were to be "carefully watched for signs of ecclesiastical calling." But Lavigerie warned that it "would be neither opportune nor prudent to make them into secular priests." Some might enter the White Fathers themselves. All would need the discipline of some order. "For these children, who are destined for the religious condition, there will be a small seminary which will be run by missionaries." [4]

"A CENTURY OF PREPARATION"

Lavigerie's willingness to tackle the seemingly hopeless task of evangelizing Moslem North Africa becomes all the more difficult to comprehend when we realize that he seems to have fully appreciated its hopelessness. Unlike Ramón Lull, who had no centuries of fruitless missionary effort behind him, Lavigerie knew the historical position of missionary work in Islam and admitted it frankly. When the Superior of his seminary in France wrote to him in 1869 to ask his advice about training and prospects for missionary work in the Sahara and Central Africa, Lavigerie admitted in reply that "during the twelve hundred years of its establishment, Mahometism [sic] has opposed almost insuperable barriers to the Catholic apostolate. None of the missions founded in the countries where the Moslem religion reigns have produced appreciable results; no nation, no portion of any nation, has been converted or even shaken in its errors by our missionaries.[5]

Why, if Lavigerie realized this, did he go on?

The answer is clearly expressed in his life. He felt that French policy, to date, had brought only mismanagement and indifferent military successes against an adversary which he considered to be

[3] *Ibid.*, p. 12.
[4] *Ibid.*, p. 13.
[5] *Ibid.*, p. 14.

defending a fanatical pseudoreligion. France had brought no spiritual benefits to substitute for Islam. Civilization, for Africa as for the rest of the world, lay only in Catholic Christianity. It was his duty as a Christian, but also as a French prelate, to fight to the last ounce of his energy, his private means, and his faith for what he believed was the triumph of a just cause.

Besides, Lavigerie looked far ahead. Whenever MacMahon or another civil servant would force him to close a school or an orphanage for fear of stirring up trouble with the Arabs, Lavigerie would explain that he and his missionaries had not come to Africa to preach the Gospel, but to prepare the Algerians for "mass conversions," a preparation which "might take a century." The best preparation for future mass conversions lay in caring for children, schooling them, showing charity, setting Christian examples in all things but *not in individual baptisms* except those of his orphans.

Lavigerie and his new order saved about one thousand Algerian children from starvation in the famine of 1868 and gave them a start toward a useful life, even though it was a life outside their own society. When MacMahon demanded that he close the orphanages and turn the children back to Moslem friends or relatives, he refused. The children lost their fathers and their mothers, he said. "They belong to me because I saved their lives. If they are taken away, the cries of my bishop's heart will be echoed in the indignation of all those who still merit the name of men and of Christians." [6] When a combination of anticlerical measures in Paris followed the fall of Napoleon and new "hands-off-religion" edicts were issued by the army in Algeria, Lavigerie finally was forced to close the orphanages for good. He bought land in the Chelif Valley and arranged marriages for some of the older orphans whom he had earlier baptized. He gave each household a dowry of five hundred francs and sixty-eight acres of land and installed them in the new villages of St. Cyprian and St. Monique. In 1876, he solemnly inaugurated a new two-thousand-bed hospital built in Moorish architectural style. But the government had already stopped its annual subsidy of ninety thousand francs to the Algiers archbishopric in 1875, and the work could not go on. Eventually, in 1896, the cardinal moved some of

[6] Quoted in R. P. Lecanuet, *Les Dernières Années du Pontificat de Pie IX* (Paris, 1931), p. 52.

the orphans to St. Joseph de Thibar in Tunisia. There, they began a highly successful agricultural colony at which we shall look later.

There were precedents for the work Lavigerie undertook in the Kabylie Mountains. Despite opposition from the army, the Jesuits had already worked there with some success. In 1873, the White Fathers installed missions at the village of Tagmount Azouz and for the tribes of Banu Wadhia and Banu Arif. At first the tribes were defiant. The arrival of Christians in the mountains, previously inviolate, appeared to the Kabylie tribesmen as "the worst and the most unexpected of all evils," commented one eminent French Arabist.[7]

Lavigerie cracked down hard on all priests who might have been inclined to follow in the footsteps of Ramón Lull. In 1873, he forbade all Jesuits and missionaries of other orders to preach the Gospel in the Kabylie Mountains in public, and a bit later even privately. No boarding schools were to be permitted where Berber students "lived in," although he encouraged other schools where the children lived with their parents and came to class every day. All missionaries were ordered to speak only Arabic and Kabylie Berber *even among themselves* and never to use an interpreter in dealing with the Berbers, "even if this entails embarrassment at the beginning." They were not to visit or have contacts with purely French parishes, but if they needed anything from the parish priest, they were to send a Kabylie messenger with a note for the *curé*.

Obviously, the language provisions were hard on priests, no matter how well they had studied their Arabic and Berber lessons. It was actually a matter of forcing them to feel themselves Algerians, to become immersed in the cultural *paeduma* of Algerian life. "We must not make Europeans of them, we must make Arabs of ourselves," said Lavigerie. There were many lapses of linguistic discipline, and Lavigerie's faithful Father Superior, Deguerry, had to remind priests that violation of the linguistic rule was a "mortal sin."

Lavigerie absolutely forbade his missionaries in the mountains to "talk religion" or to baptize anyone, even a person in danger of death, except a child in the "last agony." He deprived one priest of the privilege of saying Mass for three years because he had baptized a sick, idiot child. "This is not the moment to convert, it is the

[7] Benabdallah, *op. cit.*, quoting M. E. Laoust, "Chants Berbères contre l' Occupation Française," *Publications de l'HEM,* XVIII, 9.

moment to win the hearts and the confidence of the Kabyles through charity and goodness," he wrote. "You should aim at nothing else. Anything you do to violate this will make us lose our cause." [8]

The army continued to be skeptical about Lavigerie's efforts, even when the Kabyles, moved by the missionaries' acts of charity and medical assistance, began to warm up somewhat toward them. Algerians respected the White Fathers because they took them for *marabouts,* commented General du Barail, "but if they induce one single village to abjure Islam, the entire French army could not prevent them from being massacred to the last man. One does not convert Moslems."

What, then, could the missionaries do? "First, pay visits to the neighboring tribes," Lavigerie told them, "presenting yourselves as men of prayer who are anxious to be helpful." Remedies and advice were to be supplied for the sick, so a missionary needed a good basic store of medical knowledge. Parents of sick children were to be invited to the mission to pick up medicines, "where they are to be received with great goodness and charity." Taking presents for the children during their rounds was not a bad idea, either.

Always, a devout example was to be set. Ostentatious praying, including the saying of the rosary, was always wise since "the Arabs will only think more of you as a result. The great cause of their revulsion toward Europeans is that they [believe them to] have no religion because they never see them praying." [9]

In 1878, when Lavigerie saw some of the White Fathers smoking and using strong liquor under the pretext of hospitality to guests, he warned them that while smoking or drinking moderate amounts of strong liquor were not sins in themselves, "for a missionary these are among the saddest marks he can give of the absence of one of the principal virtues of his condition: mortification. Among the Arabs, the best-known Moslem *marabouts* abstain from smoking out of piety. You know this. This wins them more respect from their fellow Moslems. And we, my dear children, can't we, for the sake of truth, do what these poor people do for the sake of error?" [10]

When cordial relations had been cemented, but only then, reli-

[8] Lavigerie, *op. cit.,* pp. 26–27.
[9] *Ibid.,* p. 9.
[10] *Ibid.,* p. 73.

gion could be brought up. "If they are among populations whose forebears were once Christian, as are nearly all the Berbers of North Africa, the best speech to make to them is to tell them of their ancient history; to tell them that their fathers were our brothers in faith and have never ceased to be, except as a result of the bloody persecutions which they suffered for centuries."

The next step was education. "One can then propose to them [the parents] to teach some of their children to read, to write, and to pray. If they agree, which sometimes happens, these children can be received in the presbytery, appropriately clothed, and a missionary will take charge of their direction and instruction. Soon these children will themselves be a sort of living ministry, and people will come to suggest to the missionaries that they take in others, especially orphans." Religious matters should be discussed only in answering specific questions. Answers should be in the form of stories or anecdotes, "which the natives always love to hear, concerning the life of Our Lord, the prophecies which He made, the marvelous events which followed Him, always stressing the enormous difference which exists between the Christian law and the other false religions as regards justice, the purity of life, respect for the truth, and especially charity. Little by little, you will see these speeches bearing fruit, but there should be no haste about plucking it. Neophytes should be seriously tested before believing their words or even their formal requests for baptism." [11]

After the French defeat in the Franco-Prussian War of 1870, Arab attacks upon the French forces increased in scope and power. Lavigerie tried to persuade the new military commander, Admiral de Guedon, to liberalize his policies and especially to halt mass reprisals against Kabylie villages. The current *mahdi,* Mokrani, was then operating from a base in the Kabylie Mountains. Father Charmetant, a priest who had treated Mokrani's daughter when she had been critically ill, tried to reach him for peace negotiations. He got past the roadblock at Alma, just east of Algiers, which marked the beginning of the insecure zone more or less held by Mokrani's forces, but never succeeded in reaching the *mahdi's* headquarters at Dra al-Mizan. Lavigerie became so discouraged at this point that he decided to disband the Fathers: the Council of the Order of

[11] *Ibid.,* p. 13.

White Fathers dissuaded him. He was heartened by the arrival of thirty-three new Fathers. With a dramatic flourish, he scrawled over their application forms: *visum pro martyrio* (approved for martyrdom).

BAPTISM AND WOMEN'S RIGHTS

Lavigerie's policy on baptism is important because he set norms which would probably come back into force if Catholic baptism were ever permitted again in North Africa. He confirmed a decree of 1763 by the Sacred Congregation of the Holy Office, which handles such matters in Rome, forbidding baptism of "infidel children" as long as they are still minors dependent upon their parents. Lavigerie also referred to the diocesan statutes which stipulate that "no Jewish or Moslem child will be baptized without express permission of his parents." In 1860, Lavigerie elaborated this to allow baptism of abandoned children or orphans, or those in imminent danger of death. In these cases, all precautions had to be taken to assure that orphans were really orphans and that any Christian parents adopting them—as French *colons* often did—would give them an adequate education. For adult baptisms, the permission of a bishop was necessary. Baptism had to be performed in secret—three Kabylie converts went to Rome for this purpose in 1888—unless it was proved that the convert would be going to live in a Christian community. For all prospective converts, including children, a four-year catechumenate of preparatory studies was required. These measures, with only slight variations, are still papal policy for most Islamic countries. Through them, Rome hopes to guard the welfare of converts' souls, protect them against backsliding, and defend them from the overwhelming social pressures which are brought to bear upon any convert who remains in Moslem society.

In at least one important field, Lavigerie was an important precursor of the Moslem nationalists of today, though his approach was decidedly different from theirs. He resolved to do something to lift Algerian women out of the servitude to which centuries of Islamic tradition had condemned them. He sent to France for some of the Sisters of St. Charles of Nancy and gave them a house at Kouba, on the heights of Algiers, some land to cultivate, and three hundred orphan girls. But the good nuns of Nancy were too genteel, well-educated, and delicate, in Lavigerie's view, to be up to the rough nature of their tasks. So he imported some husky farmers' daughters from Brittany. These were all right for the farming tasks but did not know sewing or child care. Next Lavigerie brought some Sisters of the Augustinians of the Assumption, a missionary order founded in 1843 at Nîmes to fight irreligion in Europe and bring back Oriental Christians to the Roman fold. The main task which Lavigerie gave them and the other nuns in Algeria was to supervise the orphanages. Later, when he sent them into Central Africa, their Algerian experience in nursing and teaching was useful in their work with adults.

LAVIGERIE AND COLONIZATION

From the beginning of his episcopate in Algiers, and long after he became cardinal in 1881, Lavigerie turned aside from theology and devoted all his energy to what he felt to be his life mission: establishing and consolidating a true African Christianity. One historian described his lackadaisical attitude toward the First Vatican Council in 1870, where he arrived "escorted by his Arab children, far more interested in his missionary affairs than in [papal] infallibility," [12] which was the chief item on the agenda.

Lavigerie must bear a large share of the responsibility for what has proved to be one of the most tragic dramas of our own time: the inadaptability and the uprooting, since 1962, of over one million Europeans who had made their lives and careers in Algeria but who were unable to live with Arab nationalism and so felt themselves forced to leave when Algeria became independent. His responsibility stems from the fact that he enthusiastically encouraged European settlement and the transplantation of the "French way of life" to Algeria after the Prussians defeated France in 1870–71. As a result of that war, France had to give up Alsace and Lorraine to the nascent German Empire. Thousands of refugees, who were fleeing the war's destruction or who preferred not to live under German rule, choked the highways of Western Europe. Lavigerie, in an appeal addressed to them, offered "land more fertile than your own"

[12] Lecanuet, *op. cit.*, p. 53.

in an "African" France where "you can form villages composed entirely of inhabitants of your provinces." [13] Perhaps never before had any prince or prelate been so generous with other people's land.

The appeal was heard. More than 100,000 Alsatians joined the flood tide of emigration from France. Upon the express demand of the Archbishopric of Algiers, they were given 100,000 hectares of land conceded by the administration. The village of Haussonwiller in the Issers Valley, Strasbourg and Duquesne near Jejelli, and Bitche near Constantine became the European communities which Lavigerie had envisaged. Many Alsatians, however, despite the cheap labor supply and the long growing season, found the soil too dry and arid, and they left the land for the industrial towns. Many others eventually joined the French Foreign Legion.

IN THE FOOTSTEPS OF ST. LOUIS

In 1881, the French military occupation of Tunisia opened that country to Lavigerie's action. He had already tried to shift the center of the White Fathers' activity eastward, sending missions to Tripoli, Ghadames, and Ghat in southern Libya as bases for a further push into the Sahara and to escape official French anticlericalism. In 1881, he became cardinal and three years later Bishop Primate of Tunisia. Despite his new interest in Black Africa, he was determined to push the work of the White Fathers in Arab Africa too. "I know not a single missionary who renounced the Arab mission. I will stick to it until my death," he told his associates in June, 1881.[14]

Perhaps, thought Lavigerie, Tunis and Carthage, the scene of the martyrdom of Sts. Cyprian and Louis and of all the infant victims of Baal in the olden days might be the seat of an African Church. French priests had guarded the tomb of St. Louis since 1875. Then, in 1884, the ancient See of Carthage was officially restored with the new cardinal archbishop at its head. During these years, Lavigerie had hundreds of churches built throughout Tunisia, including the Cathedral of Carthage and that of St. Vincent de Paul in Tunis. Once in Tunisia, he rarely left again. The French statesman Léon Gambetta said, "Lavigerie's presence in Tunisia is worth an army."

[13] *Ibid.*, p. 85.

[14] Lavigerie, *op. cit.*, p. 314.

Tunisia's excellent system of parochial schools, which was a chief subject of the accord signed between President Bourguiba and the Vatican in 1964, had its beginnings at this time. In November, 1880, Lavigerie had sent his instructions for the foundation of the new College of St. Louis at Carthage. Its purpose was to be "to train, through solid, moral and Christian education, the children belonging to the wealthy classes of the Regency of Tunis and to thus prepare for a better future for religion in this part of North Africa."

This, Lavigerie recognized, would be difficult because "the French and the Italians live in a state of perpetual opposition as a result of their national ambitions. The Moslems and the Jews have sectarian prejudices between each other and against the Christians, prejudices which it is hard to overcome. The effect of the instruction given at the College of St. Louis should be to fuse all these diverse and hostile elements in a true spirit of union, of mutual support, of charity, in a word, of a Christian spirit."

Religious toleration was a goal to be sought by all its teachers. "Their first concern," Lavigerie directed, "will be to wipe out, if need be with utmost rigor, the marks of aversion which the children have picked up as a result of family customs or from the population among which they live. They must never be permitted, for example, to call each other by the name of sects such as *Yudi* [*Yahudi,* the usual Arabic expression for Jews], *Rumi,* and the like, nor to treat each other with disdain." The Latin, Arabic, and Italian languages were to be taught in addition to French and the other usual modern disciplines.[15]

Aid to the farmer was an important part of the White Fathers' activities wherever they went. A new agricultural mission was set up at Thibar, seventy-five miles south of Tunis. There, near Roman Thibari, with its aqueduct, fourth-century basilica, and three-apse Byzantine chapel, a thriving agricultural community still remains. The White Sisters still operate a handicraft workshop for the grandchildren of the original Christian orphans brought in from Algeria. Bourguiba nationalized this under his agreement with the Church in 1964.

In 1896, Cardinal Lavigerie acquired several hundred acres of swampland. His missionaries drained it after long, hard work and

[15] *Ibid.*, p. 193.

built a model farm. A poisonous herb called St. John's wort had long been killing the livestock of the Tunisian farmers in the area. So that the new colony might prosper, and the surrounding Tunisian herdsmen benefit from its prosperity as well, a strain of sheep resistant to the herb's poison had to be developed. The White Fathers imported French and Algerian sheep which had black pigment in their wool and crossbred them. By 1925, this had produced the healthiest breed of sheep Tunisia had ever seen, called the "Black Race of Thibar." A sturdy breed of cattle was raised by similar scientific methods, and, in a country which always seems to have a shortage of dairy products, the resulting strain of dairy cattle was a godsend. It has been demanded by farmers and animal-husbandry specialists all over the world. The Thibar mission avoided adopting methods which would put Tunisians out of work and was one of the first enterprises to institute a liberal code of social legislation for its workers. Success of the Thibar colony, which also raises good Tunisian wines for consumption at home and export, greatly augmented the prestige of missionaries in Tunisia.

In 1963, President Bourguiba formally asked a special papal legate, sent to negotiate a general agreement on Church properties, to turn the Thibar enterprises over to the Tunisian state after a five-year period during which government technicians would be trained to run them. This was essentially the agreement reached in the summer of 1964.

THE SAHARA AND SOUTHWARD

Lavigerie was well aware of the phenomenal progress which Islamic missionaries were making in evangelizing Africa. Pope Pius IX had made him Apostolic Prefect of the Sahara and the Sudan as early as 1868. A year later, he sent some Jesuits to establish an advanced mission at Laghwat, which he later had to abandon. Lavigerie looked upon the distant city of Timbuktu, in the Sudan, with an almost literary romanticism. He regarded it as the heart of Islam and felt that, if his missionaries could reach it and evangelize it, his cherished dream of saving the soul of all Africa might some day be achieved.

In January, 1872, Lavigerie had sent Father Louis Richard to

Al-Golea at the head of the first missionary caravan to the Sahara. Richard found an explorer named Soleillet, who had been all the way to In-Salah, one thousand miles south of Algiers. Soon, the White Fathers had set up mission posts, in close collaboration with the French army, on the road southward.

Then a Berber bandit murdered another explorer on the road to Ghadames, in the southwest corner of Libya at the head of a crucial Saharan caravan route. By quizzing five Tuareg prisoners after the gang had been routed, one of Lavigerie's White Fathers learned how to organize desert caravans, how to use gifts in securing the help of tribes, and other useful information.

The veiled Tuareg warriors, feudal nomads living according to a strict caste system and using a language which apparently descended directly from the ancient Libyan, excited great curiosity in France at the time. Five Tuareg (singular: Targui) and two Arab tribesmen from the Sahara were given a warm reception in Algiers.

One of the Tuareg, Ida ag Guemmun, offered to guide Cardinal Lavigerie or his chosen emissary to Timbuktu. Though Lavigerie and the French military authorities were highly reluctant to let them go, three young priests, Alfred Paulmier, Philippe Menorat, and Pierre Bouchaud, were finally appointed. They left Metlili, the last French outpost, with four camel drivers, an Arab boy, and their Tuareg guides. When they were massacred by the Tuareg, the Paris newspapers called loudly for Lavigerie's recall.

Lavigerie's discouragement was short lived. Rather than evangelize the Sahara, he aimed further south. "It is the interior of Africa which is our objective," he told Father Charmetant. "It is there that we must bend all our efforts. I am confident that Our Lord will facilitate for you the means of entering into this promised land of our apostolate." [16] In 1878, Lavigerie sent a new caravan southward toward the equatorial regions and the central African lakes, where it was able to take up its activity.

Though the vast missionary activity of the White Fathers in Black Africa is outside our scope here, we should note in passing some of Lavigerie's ideas about how missions should act in countries where Islam was not yet an established faith and where there were

[16] *Ibid.,* pp. 24–25.

only pagans to convince and convert. As for preaching the Gospel, he reminded his followers that "we are no longer in Algeria and we do not need to hold ourselves back." When dealing with the "idolatrous blacks," as he termed them, "we must talk of religion beginning especially with the great truths which are accessible to the spirit of all men." A mistake often committed by European missionaries, he said, was to stress the rational and philosophical arguments: "Speak of the supernatural side of religion, its miracles, its prodigies, the marvelous effects of its prayers and sacraments." [17]

In all of his extensive campaigns against the slave trade, Lavigerie was obsessed by the idea of a "multi-national apostolate" in Africa, in which not only French missionaries but those of the other Christian powers would participate. He also spoke of the foundation of a "Christian kingdom in Central Africa, once the missionaries had done their work." The suppression of the vast slave traffic in Africa, some of which passed through southern Algeria, Morocco, Tunisia, and Libya on its way to markets there or in the Middle East, was a major objective of Lavigerie's later career. With papal sponsorship, he made a triumphal antislavery tour of Europe, everywhere raising money for the cause and attracting much favorable publicity. In a historical memorandum he prepared in 1888 on slavery for Pope Leo XIII, Moslems got the blame for a huge and lucrative slave trade which even in 1964 had not wholly disappeared in North Africa, despite its official suppression by the French and the independent governments that emerged from 1951 to 1962.

The White Fathers scrimped and saved and managed to free hundreds of African slaves, generally by paying their ransoms. One of Lavigerie's favorites was Adrian Atiman, a ransomed Negro child who had been raised near Timbuktu, caught by Arab raiders, and carried in a sack on camelback all the way to Algeria, where the Fathers ransomed him in the slave market of Metlili. In 1881, he was sent with nineteen others to Malta. Here he studied medicine with the Knights of St. John. In 1888, he went back to Africa with the White Fathers, this time to Tanganyika, where as a trained doctor and a largely self-trained and skillful surgeon he treated many fellow Africans and made numerous converts.

[17] *Ibid.,* pp. 80–81.

Lavigerie's last years were largely taken up with politics and diplomacy. Despite his earlier stand as a staunch royalist, Pope Leo persuaded him to help convince French Catholics that the Republic was, after all, the best thing for France. In 1890, the onetime royalist announced he had "rallied to the Republic." His concept of a secular government which would use the army and the navy to protect missionaries overseas was one ingredient in a great storm of controversy then sweeping over France. Lavigerie died in 1892 in Algiers. Great funeral processions were held for him there and in Tunis, and he was finally buried in the crypt below the sanctuary of the Carthage Cathedral. His remains are there today; his hat hanging over his grave, in keeping with tradition.

Lavigerie understood Islam far better than many of his predecessors. He had a knowledge of Arabic and the Koran and some idea of Islam as a social system. His attitude toward it seems to have varied between an early and impatient urge to see it swept into the background of Algerian society and a later understanding that neither he nor his contemporaries would ever live to see the conversion of any significant mass of North Africans, despite some success with the Kabylie tribesmen.

Lavigerie, like most militant Christian missionaries, thought of Islam as a monstrous mixture of error and half-truth. With great frankness and clarity of vision, he foresaw Islam's successes in Africa, and his lament of 1869 could almost be that of a Christian missionary of our own day:

> Nearly two hundred million human creatures are subjected by force to the yoke of the Koran. And, sad to say, the Mahometism [sic] which appears ready to founder in Europe along with the throne of the [Turkish] Sultans, continues its progress and its conquest at the gateway of our African possessions. Since the beginning of this century, nearly fifty million people have embraced Islam in the zone defined by the Sahara Desert and extending south to the Sudan. . . . These are considerable misfortunes, from the double viewpoint of the future progress of the Gospel and of those of civilizations in the north and center of Africa. We know from experience that our missionaries ordinarily find an easy reception among the idolators . . . but that

the obstinate and half-enlightened corruption of Mahometism, on the contrary, appears to defy all their efforts.[18]

Like Ramón Lull, Lavigerie was a firm believer in learning as a weapon against Islam. He encouraged Arabic and Islamic studies in Rome and among the other orders, as well as his own, working in Africa. He was also an advocate of stronger philosophy and theology, recalling that early Christians like Justinian, Cyprian, and Augustine used secular learning from the schools of their time to confound irreligion. He felt that modern missionaries had to be able to draw on modern learning, as well as traditional theology.

In 1963, there were thirty-five hundred White Fathers of twenty nationalities working in fifty-five different mission territories around the world. Lavigerie left a testament stressing the spiritual training of aspirants and novices in the great need to save souls, "principally the most abandoned ones. Everything, absolutely everything, depends upon this, and you will neither convert nor sanctify anyone if you do not convince yourselves above all of the need to work courageously toward your own sanctification."

All novices are required to pass rigorous courses in philosophy, Church history, African history and geography. To be admitted as a novice for priesthood in the order, an aspirant must have the prerequisite of two years' philosophy studies in one of the society's own institutions or come directly from a large seminary. The first year of training is devoted to the study of spiritual matters. There are language studies, chiefly in English and French, and silent spiritual exercises according to the method of St. Ignatius. Those who are to become friars undergo a two-year novitiate, with Bible studies as its principal feature. They undertake an engagement for two periods of one year each before taking perpetual vows.

The order emphasizes on-the-spot training in Africa. In 1963, it possessed nine large seminaries and thirty-four smaller ones between Carthage and Capetown. More than four hundred novices were distributed among colleges at Carthage; Louvain, Belgium; Totteridge, in London; Eastview, Canada; and Vals, near Puy, France. The missions operate some nine hundred charitable estab-

[18] *Ibid.*, p. 314.

lishments in all, and the Vatican newspaper *Osservatore Romano* reported that, in one unnamed year recently, their members paid some 9,229,000 visits to the sick. Since 1878, the order has been responsible for the Sanctuary of Saint Anne, in Jerusalem.

Though the White Fathers now publish little or nothing outside of tracts in the Arabic and Kabylie languages, apparently feeling that other fields are greener, in 1963 they published seven periodicals in Africa in French, English, Runyankola and Ruchiga (Uganda dialects), Meusizi (an East African dialect), and the main dialects of Ruanda and Burundi.

Throughout his or her training and career, a White Father or a White Sister is never allowed to forget Lavigerie's words that "the only important work is the apostolic one" and all else is only a means to the end. The profession of faith is there to remind him of her: ". . . I swear upon the Holy Scriptures to consecrate myself today and until my death to the work of the missions of Africa, in conformity with the constitutions of the Society of Missionaries, placed under the protection of Mary the Immaculate, the Queen of Africa." [19]

The Western military and political power which had made possible Lavigerie's pioneer work and the firm implantation of his order throughout Africa is shrinking and retreating now. The White Fathers and all the other missionaries will soon be totally on their own, separated from the protection of the Western power system which was logically their best friend, spiritually often their most terrible enemy.

[19] D. Martinez, *Osservatore Romano,* Weekly Edition (March 15, 1963).

CHAPTER XX

CHARLES DE FOUCAULD: A MODERN SOLDIER-MONK

> May God keep France! How has she reached her present state? The extreme decline of philosophical and religious studies has greatly harmed the Faith.
>
> CHARLES DE FOUCAULD, 1914

The year was 1878. The place was a room in the cadets' quarters of the military academy of Saumur. Under arrest for laziness, indiscipline, and general indifference to the military life, an overfed young man of twenty was enjoying his confinement to quarters. His name was Charles de Foucauld. A fellow cadet later recalled how Foucauld sprawled on a divan, watching the smoke clouds of a perfumed cigar.

This youthful gourmet, who had lost his Christian faith at the age of sixteen, and who at this moment had just inherited a fortune, was to become one of the most rigorous ascetics ever seen by modern Christianity. He was destined to bring a sort of military monasticism—scarcely seen since the Moslem warrior-monk of the eleventh century—back into the Sahara and with it a new kind of attitude toward the missionary's life.

Foucauld's family was old and distinguished. Among his ancestors was Bertrand de Foucauld, killed in the army of Louis IX at Mansurah, Egypt, during the Seventh Crusade. But the military life seemed to be the wrong life for Charles. He detested discipline almost as much as he scorned religion. When he was not out on such harebrained escapades as fleeing from confinement by wearing a false beard and posing as a peasant, or carousing with his fellow cadets, he was reading authors like Renan, Taine, Nietzsche, Anatole France, and Karl Marx. He had been thrown out of one Jesuit boarding school, and when he left Saumur in 1879, he ranked eighty-seventh in a class of eighty-seven.

Second Lieutenant Foucauld took up with a girl named Mimi,

and when his regiment was assigned to Algeria, he took Mimi along with him to Setif. His scandalized commanding officer gave him a choice: Mimi or the regiment. Foucauld chose Mimi. The War Ministry placed him on inactive status.

Then, on March 21, 1881, Foucauld read of the ambush of Colonel Flatters' column in the Sahara by four hundred Tuareg of the Kel Ahaggar tribe. The expedition against tribesmen in the Tunisian mountains, which launched the French protectorate in Tunisia, was just beginning. In southern Oran Department, nomads were attacking the new railroad line, after the tomb of one of their *marabout* holy men had been blown up. The Sanusiya had begun to spread its influence in southern Tunisia and back into Algeria, from whence it had come.

Foucauld made a snap decision: he forgot Mimi and asked for active duty again to fight against the nomads in southern Oran Department. He was suddenly seized with a desire to study and learn about the Moslems. He wrote his friend Henry de Castries, on July 8, 1901, that Islam had made a "fundamental change" in his life. The sight of Moslem piety vastly impressed him and set him to thinking about spiritual things.

Foucauld resigned his commission and resolved to explore Morocco, which was then a mysterious, unknown, and unmapped country for Europeans. Others had tried it before him, in disguise: René Caillie in 1828 had traveled through Morocco on foot, disguised as a Moslem student, and two Englishmen, Burton and Vambery, had done the same thing in *marabout* guise. But their accounts were fragmentary. An accurate journal of such a trip would be invaluable. It should be replete with the sort of geological, geographical, and scientific knowledge which Foucauld, in his new and seemingly insatiable thirst for knowledge, was acquiring, along with Arabic and Hebrew, in the Algiers library, where he was making up for the years lost in school.

The trip was highly dangerous and costly. With money supplied by his family, and a Jewish Rabbi named Mordecai Abi Serour, who had lived in southern Morocco, for a guide, Foucauld finally set out, in disguise. He wore the flowing robe and even had the accent of a Jew. Charles de Foucauld, for the journey, became Rabbi Joseph Aleman, supposedly from Moscow, since that was such a far-off and exotic place that it would silence embarrassing questions. They took the train for Oran. After sleeping in a synagogue the first night, they went on to Marnia where they boarded a ship bound for Gibraltar and Tangier, since the frontier area was not safe for travelers, especially Jewish ones. This was 1873, and Foucauld was twenty-five.

He and the rabbi managed to obtain letters of recommendation from the French minister in Tangier and the Sharif of Wazzan. But more than once, either Jews or Arabs penetrated their disguise. Near Chawen, east of Tetuan, they were almost massacred. On horseback, donkeyback, camelback, and foot, they trekked southward toward Fez. Foucauld had to conceal in his rabbi's habit the tiny notebooks in which he furiously scribbled notes as he rode. He also hid his barometer, thermometer, sextant, and a host of other scientific instruments which enabled him to draw the detailed maps and sketches later on for his famous book, *Reconnaissance au Maroc*.[1] For weeks, the two rabbis lived in the home of a wealthy Jew of Fez, Samuel Bensimhun, who supplied them with invaluable information. On the way they passed through Boujad, the sacred town of the *marabout* Sidi Dawd and center of the Cherkawiya brotherhood, which in 1963 was still one of Morocco's most powerful Sufi orders.

"He was a spy," was the scornful opinion of one young Moroccan of Boujad, a teacher in an Iraqi school in Casablanca with whom I discussed Foucauld. "Everyone remembers him. He came to our town to spy for the French army and to see whether he couldn't make some secret conversions." The fact that Foucauld scarcely considered himself a Christian at this time would probably have made no difference to my young friend, even had he known it. He probably summed up quite well the average educated North African's ideas about all European explorers.

Foucauld said he found the population living in "terror" and wondering when French forces would arrive to protect them from lawless tribes.[2]

After numerous more adventures, including an interlude in

[1] Published in Paris in 1883. For an excellent biography of Foucauld, see Anne Fremantle, *Desert Calling* (New York, 1947).

[2] René Bazin, *Charles de Foucauld* (Paris), pp. 46–47.

which Foucauld hid in a house in Mogador while waiting for money from France to pay bribes and Mordecai's salary, the two returned safely to Algeria, traveling far southeast of the Atlas Mountains. Mordecai collected the bonus which Foucauld's relatives, unknown to him, had promised for Charles' safe return. From his trip, Foucauld retained a lifelong fascination for Morocco. What seemed to be its extreme intolerance, he correctly concluded, "is not caused by religious fanaticism." For Moroccans, a European traveling in their country could be nothing but a spy. "One fears the conqueror much more than one hates the Christian." [3]

THE POINT OF NO RETURN

After considering marriage and being talked out of it by an aunt and a female cousin, Foucauld traveled some more in North Africa. Then, the Abbé Huvelin, vicar of the parish of St. Augustin in Paris, converted him and received his first confession since the age of sixteen.

North African Islam had changed Foucauld's life. He left for the Holy Land and walked the streets of Nazareth, wondering what to do. In 1880, at the age of thirty-two, he became a novice in the Trappist Order. Now "Rabbi" Joseph Aleman was "Friar Marie-Alberic" at the Trappist monastery in Akbes, Syria. After a long exile from his family and friends in France and years of inner struggle between a new humility and his old violent individualism, he was unable to take the final Trappist vows in 1891. Already, he was dreaming of founding his own community, *Les Petits Frères de Jesus,* and working out the rules—very strict ones indeed. His monks should live purely from manual labor, like Christ.

Finally, Foucauld decided to become, for the time being at least, a secular priest and to return to North Africa, which had never lost its fascination for him. In 1896, he arrived at the Trappist monastery at Staoueli, outside Algiers, which since its founding in 1843 had become a major agricultural colony. But almost at once he was ordered to Rome for two years of theology studies. The superior of the order absolved Foucauld from these at his own

[3] C. de Foucauld, *Reconnaissance au Maroc* (Paris, 1883), p. xv.

request. He preferred poverty and hard manual labor. His personal fortune was gone. He had reached the point of no return.

Next, as "Friar Charles," he worked as a common servant, performing the most menial tasks for a convent in Jerusalem. But he could not put North Africa out of his mind. He recalled that in Morocco, a country as big as France, there was not a "single priest" outside the coastal cities, while in the huge Sahara, there were only a dozen missionaries. Foucauld dreamed of evangelizing Morocco, as Lavigerie had wanted to evangelize Algeria, using a small hermitage somewhere near the border as a base. Impressed by the Sufi orders, "Friar Charles" seems to have intended a restoration of the pre-Moslem monastic life of the desert fathers of Egypt.

Not without strong opposition from much of the French military command, Foucauld, now signing his letters Frère Charles de Jesus, set up life as a hermit at the Oasis of Beni Abbes on the Algerian side of the Tafilalet Valley, part of the Diocese of the Sahara. Here, as he told a Trappist friend, he felt identification with the Hebrews, with St. John Chrysostom, and with Christ. His visitors ranged from French officers to Tuareg and Moroccan nomads and Negro slaves whom he ransomed whenever he could.

The first slave he ransomed, in 1902, he named Joseph of the Sacred Heart. He baptized a three-year-old slave child Abd Jesu (The Servant of Jesus). One of the ransomed slaves was Paul Embarek, whom Foucauld baptized at the age of fifteen and who later deserted him only to return to become his faithful companion after Foucauld moved to Tamanrasset, far to the east of Beni Abbes. Like Cardinal Lavigerie, Foucauld was bitter about the failure of the French authorities to take energetic measures to suppress slavery, for fear of offending the Tuareg slave owners and the Arab slave traders. Whenever he could scrape together a few francs, he would ransom some slaves, preferably children.

Throughout his monastic life in the Sahara, Foucauld drew upon his military training to write precise letters, which were virtual intelligence reports, to his lifelong friend, Commandant Laperrine, and other officers. Like Lavigerie and all his generation, he felt that French expansion in the desert automatically meant benefits to all its population. He admired men like General Lyautey, an old comrade-in-arms, whom he met again in 1903, and Laperrine. He thought they were combating Islam in a knightly manner, with respect rather than contempt for their adversary. He liked, too, their independence toward the fussy French bureaucracy, which he heartily shared.

Foucauld was fascinated by the veiled Tuareg, their feudal manners and mores, and their matriarchal society which granted women complete freedom and great political influence among the tribes. He heard that one Tuareg woman had prevented some of the men of her tribe from killing some wounded French taken prisoner in an ambush—for by now many Tuareg clans, under Sanusiya influence, had taken up arms against the French—and had cared for them herself, then sent them safely to Tripoli. He wrote a letter in which he asked her to pray for him.

The "White *marabout*," as the Moslems came to call Foucauld, resolved to move to the Tuareg country, the Hoggar Mountains. Perhaps the "people of the veil," as they called themselves, would prove more open to evangelization than the Moroccan nomads or the Arabs of the Algerian oases had been. In 1904, taking Paul Embarek with him, Foucauld trekked overland to Akkabli, in the Hoggar country, and began to finish the studies of Tamacheq, the Tuareg language, and the sociology of the strange people. He noted their division into classes: nobles, vassals, plebians, and the *haratini,* or free Negro farming people, and the slaves who lived in association with the Tuareg clans.

In 1905, one of the Saharan officers introduced him to Musa, the *amenokal,* or supreme chief of the Hoggar Tuareg, as "a Christian *marabout*" and "servant of the One God," who was eager to study the language and help the population in whatever way he could. The two became fast friends for the rest of Foucauld's life. Foucauld called Musa a "sincere and firm Moslem."

Foucauld settled at the outpost of Tamanrasset, where he built another simple retreat with a chapel. "I am doing my best," he wrote an officer friend, to make friends with the Tuareg. He found them "closer to us than the Arabs through their curious and open character and their morals." [4]

[4] Letter to General de Susbielle of September 25, 1865, in Georges Gorrée, *Les Amitiés Sahariennes du Père de Foucauld* (Paris, 1941), II, 113.

At Tamanrasset, Foucauld worked steadily at his grammar and lexicon of Tuareg and at translations of Tuareg poetry and songs. He finished them before his death. Musa called on him frequently for advice, and Foucauld saw to it that the contact was kept up: this had the effect of keeping the major part of the Hoggar Tuareg from succumbing to the anti-French propaganda of the Sanusiya, inspired by Turkey and Germany. In 1910, he built another hermitage, this time on the Assekrem Plateau, six thousand feet high in the Hoggar Mountains. A helper in his linguistic and ethnographic work was Ba Hammou, Musa's secretary, whom Foucauld suspected, probably justly, of being a secret agent of the Sanusiya.

When Foucauld, the onetime gourmet, fell ill from the effects of malnutrition during a period when French medical assistance was too far away to help him, local Tuareg cared for him. When the war broke out in 1914, he remained at Tamanrasset, after several brief trips to France. After the mass insurrection of the Tripolitanian tribes in 1915, he supplied Captain Duclos, commander of the Saharan company, with a steady flow of military and political information on the situation in the Hoggar and on the Moroccan and Sanusiya movements. On March 6, 1916, a powerful Sanusi column from Tripolitania, with artillery support, captured Fort Janet, Algeria. The "loyal" Tuareg began to defect. Foucauld considered the threat from Tripolitania as a threat to all Christianity, just as Lavigerie would doubtless have done had he still been alive.

The French built a fort to protect Foucauld. He moved his chapel into it. Instead of a *zawiya,* he now had a *ribat*—the stronghold of a soldier-monk. He kept arms on the premises, but was never given a chance to use them. On December 1, 1916, a small pro-Sanusi band arrived. No French garrison was present, only a few Tuareg. A traitor among them betrayed him, telling him to open his door to receive some mail. He was taken outside and shot before Embarek's eyes. Père de Foucauld was buried at Tamanrasset by Laperrine, who met his own end a short time later in an airplane crash in the same district of the Sahara and was buried beside Foucauld.

Foucauld, whose charitable and missionary orders of the Little

Brothers and Sisters of Jesus live after him, probably expected martyrdom. His lifelong friend, the late and eminent French orientalist, Louis Massignon, who shared much of his mystique, spoke in 1950 at Ghat, Libya, with the last surviving murderer of Foucauld. Then he went to Tamanrasset to keep a night vigil in Foucauld's chapel. He later said he felt Foucauld had given his enemies a "plenary dispensation to shed his blood in a legal immolation." If they were fighting a holy war, wrote Massignon, "they had enabled him to be a martyr." [5]

FOUCAULD, ISLAM, AND IMPERIALISM

Foucauld left an indelible impression on all who met him, Christian and Moslem. It is hard to tell whether his obsession with living the type of life Jesus led at Nazareth, which dominated his earlier monastic career, or the image of a soldier irrevocably committed to a national crusade is the picture that the Saharan Moslems retained of this extraordinary man. A French officer who first saw him in 1909 remembered his "very brilliant eyes" and his "humility." He saw something "supernatural" in Foucauld and found the Saharans prostrating themselves before him to kiss the hem of his robe. One said later, "So you do really have a religion and *marabouts,* and you don't live like dogs!" [6]

Whatever else he was, Foucauld was certainly a classic imperialist. From Tamanrasset, he wrote an officer friend in 1912 concerning a French plan for a trans-Saharan railroad: "What a marvelous empire! Provided we can civilize it—Frenchify [*franciser*] it and not be satisfied with keeping it subjected and exploiting it." [7] Otherwise, the subject peoples would turn against France.

Foucauld was also one of the theorists of the French Berberphile tradition. He saw Morocco as the key to power in North Africa, and the Berber population of Morocco as "full of vigor and capable of rapid progress." Morocco, he said, would rapidly become the "head of our magnificent northwest African empire which will be

[5] Lecture at the Sorbonne of March 18, 1959, in Louis Massignon, *Parole Donnée* (Paris, 1962), p. 71.

[6] Gorrée, *op. cit.,* II, 289, quoting General Gouraud.

[7] *Ibid.,* pp. 341–42.

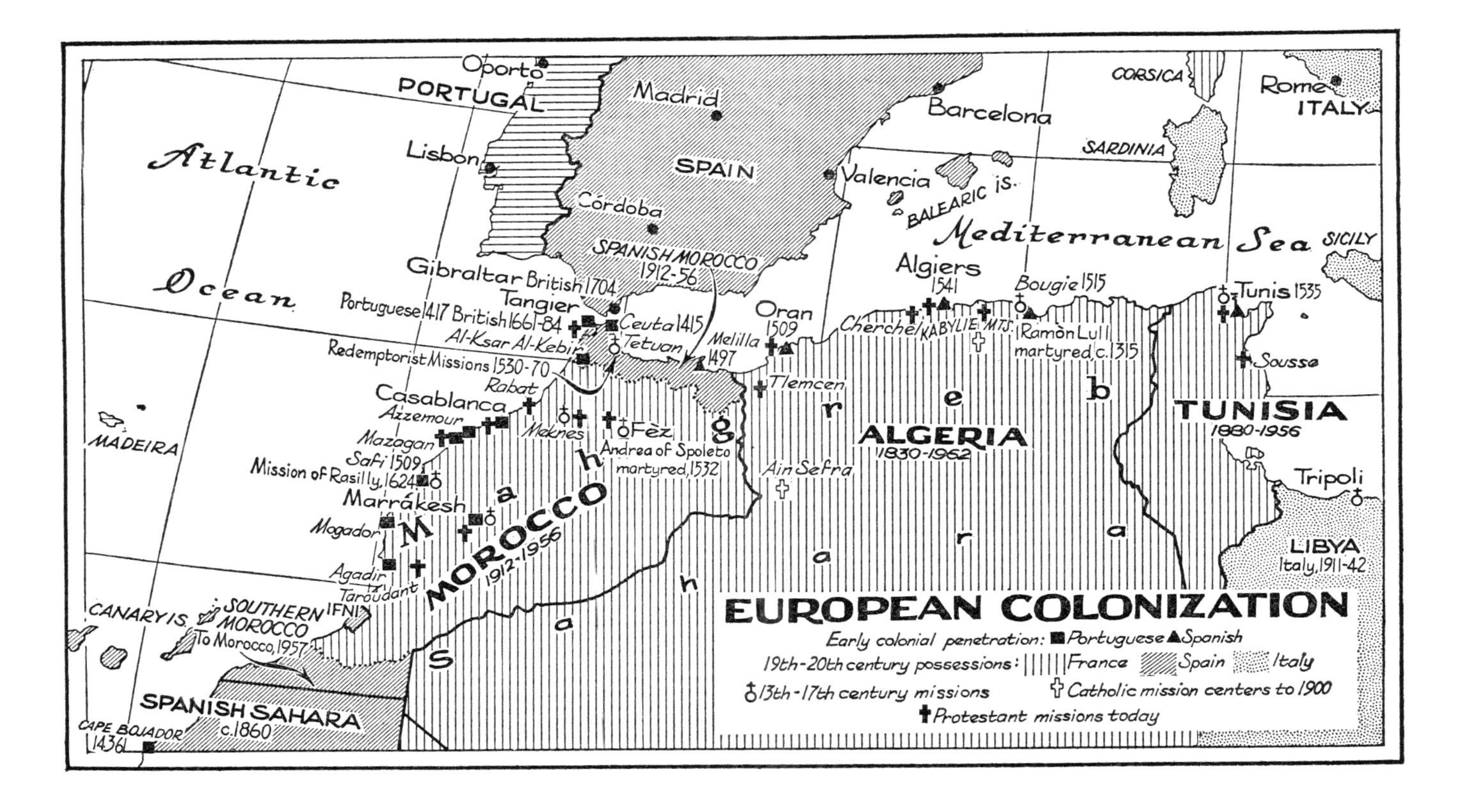
EUROPEAN COLONIZATION
Early colonial penetration: Portuguese Spanish
19th-20th century possessions: France Spain Italy
13th-17th century missions
Catholic mission centers to 1900
Protestant missions today
Atlantic Ocean
Mediterranean Sea
Oporto
PORTUGAL
Lisbon
Madrid
SPAIN
Córdoba
Barcelona
Valencia
BALEARIC IS.
CORSICA
SARDINIA
Rome
ITALY
SICILY
SPANISH MOROCCO 1912-56
Gibraltar British 1704
Tangier
Portuguese 1417 British 1661-84
Ceuta 1415
Tetuan
Al-Ksar Al-Kebir
Redemptorist Missions 1530-70
Rabat
Melilla 1497
Oran 1509
Algiers 1541
Bougie 1515
Cherchel
KABYLIE MTS.
Ramòn Lull martyred c. 1315
Tunis 1535
Sousse
Tlemcen
Casablanca
Azzemour
Meknes
Fèz
Andrea of Spoleto martyred 1532
Mazagan
Safi 1509
Mission of Rasilly, 1624
Marrákesh
Mogador
Agadir
Taroudant
MOROCCO 1912-1956
ALGERIA 1830-1962
TUNISIA 1880-1956
Ain Sefra
Tripoli
LIBYA Italy, 1911-42
MADEIRA
CANARY IS.
SOUTHERN MOROCCO To Morocco, 1957
IFNI
SPANISH SAHARA c. 1860
CAPE BOJADOR 1436
S a h a r a
g h a

one from the Mediterranean to the Chad. . . ." He urged that the policy of favoring the powerful Moroccan chiefs was wrong, recalling that the same policy in Algeria had been a mistake because the feudal class, continuing all its old abuses, built up a wall between the French and the Algerian people. Foucauld also gloomily predicted that if the Berbers in Morocco were not rapidly "Frenchified" and educated, they would educate themselves and form a vast nationalist movement with branches in Algeria, Tunisia, and the Sudan.

Foucauld's anti-Arab bias was typical of one that many missionaries working in North Africa still have today. The Arabs, he said, "are still at the same point they were in the time of Abraham," but the Berbers are people of another race "who can become like ourselves in a relatively short time." [8] This, then, was still the "Christian" ideal: to make the "others" as quickly as possible "like ourselves."

[8] Letter to Colonel Sigonney, June 23, 1912; quoted in Gorrée, *op. cit.*, II, 245.

CHAPTER XXI

ANGLO-AMERICAN PROTESTANT EFFORTS

> The calling of a Christian missionary is first and foremost to be "a witness," a living demonstration of the transforming presence and power of Christ in his own life. He is not a mere propagandist.
>
> REV. HAROLD W. STALLEY, FIELD DIRECTOR, NORTH AFRICA MISSION, 1963

On a soft spring day in London, May 17, 1880, a British couple, Mr. and Mrs. George Pearse, had a talk with a prominent British philanthropist, Dr. H. Grattan Guinness. It proved to be of crucial importance for the future of Christian mission work in the Maghreb. Their meeting, at which Dr. Guinness made an initial donation for missionary work, led to formation of the interdenominational North Africa Mission, the largest and most important of the Protestant groups working since then in North Africa.

The Pearses had been preaching the Gospel among French soldiers without success. The ingrown French mistrust of everything English and American, aggravated by the suspicion that Anglo-Saxon missionaries in French colonial territory were almost always political agents or spies, was to plague all of the Protestant missionary effort in North Africa, even more than Moslem indifference or hostility.

The Pearses visited Algeria in 1876 during a famine among the Kabylie tribes and resolved to help them, feeling that they were promising candidates for Christianity. Dr. Guinness himself went to Algeria in 1879 and agreed. Edward Glenny, a businessman of Barking, England, after reading an article in the *Daily Chronicle* about Algerian exports to Britain, concluded he might combine business with the Lord's work and decided with the others to found a mission to the Kabylie tribes.

Pearse proposed to several pastors and elders of the French Protestant Church of Algeria that they join them. Some of the

Frenchmen opposed the idea for political reasons—the Anglo-French rivalry in North Africa was beginning to grow more acute. Others thought the funds the Britishers had raised ought to be turned over to the French Protestants. This failure to agree at the beginning helped keep later Anglo-French missionary contacts to a minimum. One of the largest existing British mission organizations, the Church Missionary Society, also turned down Pearse's offer of collaboration.

The only thing to do was start a new mission on their own. Mr. Pearse and Mrs. Guinness published a pamphlet called *Mission to the Kabyles*. The Pearses had long missionary experience in the Far East, and they spoke French. They enlisted the aid of Salim Zaitun, a young Druze who spoke French and Arabic, and a Swiss named Mayor. Backed by a committee of prominent clergymen and philanthropists, they pleaded, incorrectly, that there was not a single missionary working anywhere from "Alexandria to the Atlantic." Besides, they argued, the French *colons* needed spiritual assistance which they were not getting from Catholicism, and it was desirable to circulate the Scriptures in Arabic. R. C. Morgan, editor of the missionary paper *The Christian,* backed them wholeheartedly.

As the site of their first station Pearse chose a lush plot of farmland near the large Kabylie village of Djemaa Sahridj, where there were many French-speaking Kabyles and where some Jesuits had worked earlier, before Cardinal Lavigerie's arrival. In pre-Moslem times, it had been a Roman settlement, Bida Colonia, the seat of a bishop. Pearse, Glenny, Zaitun, and Mayor arrived in Algiers in November, 1881, and set to work at once.

PROTESTANT MOTIVES

It was not difficult to arouse the interest of idealistic Anglo-Saxons in the new project. The moral incentive was paramount. Explorers and travelers had for years been writing gory accounts of the poverty, misery, official corruption, and "backwardness" of the North African "natives." The cities of the Maghreb were pictured as virtual sinks of iniquity. Tunis, for one English minister, the Reverend A. A. Bodly, was "a city which can scarcely be rivalled in its wickedness." The explorer Joseph Thomson found that Morocco was

> ... absolutely the most religious nation on the face of the earth, [but] also the most grossly immoral. In no sect is faith so absolutely paramount, so unweakened by any strain of skepticism, as among the Mohammedans of Morocco. Among no people are prayers so commonly heard or religious duties more rigidly attended to. Yet side by side with it all, rapine and murder, mendacity of the most advanced type and brutish and nameless vices, exist to an extraordinary degree. From the Sultan down to the loathsome half-starved beggar, from the most learned to the most illiterate, from the man who enjoys the reputation of utmost sanctity to the openly infamous opposite, all are alike morally rotten.[1]

Another missionary, Mrs. Haweiss, reported in *Travel* magazine in December, 1897, after attending the wedding of a sharif in Tangier, that she had "never realized the degradation of Mohammedan women till I saw the white bundles which represent the sister brides." A Moroccan woman was "subject all her life to that privileged sex to whom God sent her as a helpmeet, but who keeps her like his horse." Mrs. Pearse was impressed by the size of the Spanish and Jewish communities in Oran, which she found were living in squalor. "All these dark and benighted people are left to die in their sins," she noted.

Other English travelers, such as Kathleen Watson, who visited Algeria in 1897, were charmed by the exotic flavor of Islam, which in the Grand Mosque of Algiers she found to generate a "stern, sweet atmosphere." This, she discovered was "the glamour which non-Christian systems throw over us if we are not whole-hearted to the Lord Jesus Christ."

Rivalry with the Catholics was another motive for these missionaries, though perhaps a minor one. Glenny saw the French, Spanish, and Italian residents distributed from Casablanca to

[1] J. Rutherford and Edward H. Glenny, "Mission Work in North Africa," Part II of *The Gospel in North Africa* (London, 1900), pp. 160–161.

Tripoli, most of whom were Catholics, as "a wide field for evangelization." He felt that there was "a languid spirit oppressing the Christian Church," apparently meaning the Catholic one. The alliance between the Catholic Church and French military power was regarded as a mixed blessing. It had opened up the possibility of a Christian return to North Africa by removing Moslem control, but for this it had substituted French control. "God frequently removes political obstacles to the spread of Christianity by political means," observed Glenny, "and in the case of Algeria, He used Roman Catholic, freethinking France to break down this hitherto unsurmountable barrier to the progress of the Gospel." He found that the "moral condition prevailing among the Spaniards in Algeria, as elsewhere, is very low" and that this was "doubtless due to the centuries of Roman Catholic influence, which, as history proves, ever results in searing the conscience and depraving the character."

Pearse, Glenny, and Guinness also judged the political situation to be propitious for their effort. The echoes of the last serious uprisings of the 1870's were dying away, and there was real dissidence, for the moment, only in the southwestern part of the country. Lavigerie's Alsatian *colons* brought with them some relaxation of restrictions on preaching. The British were in somewhat less disfavor than usual because the Anglo-French rivalry over Morocco and Egypt had not yet grown acute. The Algerians, these Britons thought, had grown weary of seeing French bureaucrats and French priests and would welcome some British faces and ideas.

A final motive, perhaps the most decisive one, was the supposed susceptibility of the Kabyles to Christian doctrine. The familiar arguments of Lavigerie, Foucauld, and all the centuries of missionaries before them about the Christian heritage of the Berbers in general and the Kabyles in particular were all repeated. "Although Mohammedanism and sin have sadly damaged them" wrote Rutherford, "they are a race with many fine natural characteristics. . . . They are in many respects a noble race, and are not at all deeply imbued with Mohammedanism."

One of the French officials who tried to warn off the missionaries was Camille Sabatier, a local administrator who had worked in the Kabylie area for ten years when they arrived. His arguments only strengthened their resolve, especially since his judgment of the

Kabylie people, in a pamphlet entitled *La Question de la Securité,* corresponded with their preconceived notions:

> In comparison with the Arab the Kabyle is another being. To begin with, the Koran he does not know and has never known. In numerous regions he knows neither its rules nor its language; his "Kanouns" do not teach any of its prescriptions. The whole of his Islamic creed is confined to the hackneyed formulary [sic] "There is not a god but God, and Mohammed is the Apostle of God." As to morals, law, and the constitution of the family and property, his idea of political order and social justice, the Koran is outside it all.[2]

Since the Huguenots and English, such as Harrison, in the seventeenth century, few Protestants had come to North Africa to preach the Gospel or even to redeem captives. French Protestants, like the French Catholics, considered that the conquest of Algiers in 1830 had "opened up North Africa." The French Society of Evangelical Missions chose two young missionaries who were eager to go. The two studied Arabic and the Koran and followed other special courses at the Collège de France, but, when they were ready to leave in 1833, the military authorities opposed their trip. "The Berbers, descendants of the natives who had known Donatism, had not embraced Islam," commented one French Protestant bitterly. "And it was we French, who through complicity with the Mohammedans, facilitated their Islamization!" The two young missionaries went to South Africa instead.

By 1860, several British Protestants were trying to convert the North African Jews. The London Jews' Society was one group, with "missionary agents" in Tunis and Mogador. The British Jews' Society had a man working in Algiers. This later gave way to the Church Mission to the Jews, another English group, which in 1963 still had two representatives in Morocco, Miss M. Heroch in Marrakesh and Miss Benzaquen in Casablanca, both elderly ladies who were Moroccan converts themselves.

In 1880, there were about twenty Protestant pastors in Algeria to tend a small flock among the French settlers. Few, if any, were

[2] *Ibid.*, p. 163.

able to proselytize the Moslems because of French military restrictions. An English chaplain visited Algiers during the winters to minister to the small Anglo-Saxon colony, and in Oran a former Spanish Catholic priest turned Protestant was pastor to about twelve hundred Spanish Protestants there.

A Church of England clergyman, Furniss Ogle, found the climate in South America, where he lived, too much for him and went to Oran in 1858 to work among the Spaniards, hoping to reach the Arabs through them. He bought a farm and tried to preach to his Spanish and Arab farm hands. The farm lost money, and the French authorities gave him trouble. Ogle decided to return to England in 1865, but his ship was wrecked on the coast near Oran, and he and about forty other passengers and crewmen drowned. Wardlaw Scott, a ship broker, was inspired by his business contacts with Moroccans to persuade a married couple named Hoskins to work in Mogador. Their mission soon ended because Mrs. Hoskins' health failed.

THE NORTH AFRICA MISSION: FIRST YEARS IN ALGERIA

Before their mission house was ready for occupancy the Pearses and their companions lived for a time with a French *colon.* They found a Kabyle named Amrouche, who had had some instruction from the Jesuits, and completed his conversion. After they had moved into their new quarters, the Pearses began the distribution of pamphlets, books, and tracts from an Algiers center. Glenny, who had planned to found an industrial mission or farming colony, decided against the idea and returned to England instead to take over the administrative and propaganda work at home, while Mayor and the Druze, Zaitun, began classes for young people and an outpatient dispensary for the treatment of the sick. Their good friend and French government official, Monsieur Sabatier, warned them at this point that it was illegal to practice medicine without a French diploma, and also illegal to teach without a French teacher's license.

Gradually, other workers came from England and Scotland. When the English Congo Mission was dissolved, several members switched to the North Africa Mission. The Mission's "Principles and Practice" were drawn up, closely following those already used in China and the Congo by other Protestant groups. All candidates for field posts were required to agree on "the [Divine] Inspiration of the Scriptures, the Trinity, the Fall of Man and his state by nature, the Atonement, the Eternal Salvation of the Redeemed and the Everlasting Punishment of the Lost." All candidates were, and still are, required to consent not to depend entirely upon the Mission for financial support, as there are lean periods when allowances cannot be kept up. Missionaries were to "trust in God alone," a principle which the head offices in London, Glasgow, and Upper Darby, Pennsylvania, still stoutly defend. Private means, of course, are a big help.

An Alsatian field worker who joined them and the British consul in Algiers, Sir Lambert Playfair, took great pains to explain to Monsieur Sabatier that the new missionaries were not spies. Monsieur Sabatier was not convinced nor were many of his fellow countrymen. "The difficulties from Moslem fanaticism among the Kabyles," reported Glenny, "have been as nothing compared to those from the political nightmare of the French." [3]

The Mission next opened stations in Tlemcen and Tangier, hoping to reach the Rif mountaineers, who are also Berbers. To get at the Shawia, another Berber clan living between Biskra and Constantine, they established a post in the latter city, but, as in the west, they were diverted from their plan to seek out the mountain people because of the language problem and their deep interest in the Arabic townspeople close at hand. One advantage was the possession of a good translation of the Bible, published in 1865, though some missionaries, especially those working with the Jews, were still using the first known translation into Arabic: that of the Five Books of Moses by Saadia Gaon, who died as head of the Jewish Academy at Sura, Iraq, in A.D. 942. The Arabic Bible the Mission now uses is a translation of the Van Dyke version, called *Al-Kittabu Mekkadis*. In 1963, a new authorized Arabic Bible used by Protestant missionaries was under review by a committee appointed jointly by the British and Foreign Bible Society and the American Bible Society, with publication expected in 1966. A French-speaking Swiss, M. Cuendet, joined the North Africa

[3] *Ibid.*, p. 161.

Mission in 1884. He translated the New Testament and a number of hymns into the Kabylie language. He used the Roman alphabet and a system of phonetic transcriptions.

Several lady missionaries who arrived in the Kabylie country began to visit homes and tribes, teaching primary school classes and caring for sick children. The White Fathers set up a station near Mekla, a nearby French community, and attracted some of the children away from the Protestants. The local French authorities pretended to discover a "plot" to sell gunpowder to the Kabyles, but, wrote Glenny, "God graciously prevented them from stopping the work, though they made it much more difficult." [4]

Glenny also reported that

> Many cases of genuine conversion to Christ have taken place among the Kabyles. In Djemaa Sahridj, in 1897, quite a number of young men came boldly out from Mohammedanism and have remained true. One young Kabylie girl said to the lady missionaries, "I love Jesus; I believe in Him as my Saviour, I believe with all my heart," and when asked why she had forsaken the faith of Mohammed, replied, "His followers lie, thieve and sin; and if he cannot save us from our sins here, I do not think he is likely to save us hereafter." [5]

In western Algeria, especially at Tlemcen, a bastion of conservative Islam, the French authorities allied themselves with the local *ulama* and strictly enforced their rule against nursing and medical work without a French diploma. The medical mission was closed soon after it opened by special request of the French foreign minister. At Mostagenem, a seaport east of Oran, the local missionary was shadowed by plain-clothes police, and the local French press accused him of bribery, espionage, and other "anti-French" acts which were even discussed on the floor of the Chamber of Deputies in Paris.

One place where the Mission has kept up a nearly continuous effort is Cherchel, once the Roman Caesarea, about fifty miles west of Algiers. In 1964, this was the only other post in Algeria, besides

[4] *Ibid.*, pp. 164–65.
[5] *Ibid.*, pp. 38–39.

Algiers, which the Mission was able to staff, and it reported a successful summer camp program for boys.

Most converts, such as a young man named Hamami of Constantine, who was baptized in Tunis and then returned to Algeria as a Christian, found it impossible to profess their faith openly in their own home environment. The missionaries believed that a moral change for the better had been worked in their lives, even if they did "backslide" later on.

The McAll Mission and the British and Foreign Bible Society in Algiers concentrated largely on evangelizing among the French. An English couple, Mr. and Mrs. Moore, began to work in the French village of Mekla as part of a group called the Open Brethren. Similar "Brethren" organizations have operated in North Africa almost continuously since the 1880's. Some French and English members of the French Wesleyans began activity at Bougie in 1886, concentrating on Kabyles rather than on Arabs and moving afterward up to El-Mathen, a Kabylie village in a nearby valley where they founded a permanent mission station.

BEGINNINGS IN MOROCCO

The earliest English Protestant missionaries in the nineteenth century were interested mainly in Morocco's Jews. The London Society for Promoting Christianity among the Jews began operations in 1834, but their representatives were driven out of Mogador by the French bombardment of 1844 and by anti-Christian riots which followed. In 1858, a Jew whom the society had converted tried to evangelize the Tetuan Jews. He was beaten for his pains, and all his books were burned. The first serious and concerted effort of the society was an attempt by Pastor J. B. Crighton Ginsburg, a naturalized Englishman of Russian extraction and tempestuous temperament. He converted two Jews of Mogador in two months of effort, then he was replaced at the mission station by one of his neophytes, Zerbib.

In 1882, Mr. and Mrs. Mackintosh, British missionaries who had long experience among the Moslems of Syria and Egypt, volunteered to work for the British and Foreign Bible Society in Morocco. Interest in Morocco was then running high in British church circles as the result of a letter written to a London paper by Donald MacKenzie, an adventurous trader who had established a fortified trading post on the Saharan coast at Cape Juby, southern Morocco, later a stronghold of Spanish military colonization. MacKenzie announced that "the time has come for Christian missionaries to devote more attention to North Africa than they have done up to now." [6]

During their efforts in western Algeria, the North Africa Mission founders, especially George Pearse, had also become interested in the possibilities of Morocco. In 1883, they purchased an old house on Tangier's Marshan Plateau which European residents had nicknamed "Bleak House." Glenny and Mrs. Guinness decided to rename it "Hope House," and the name has survived. A small dispensary was attached. Within three years there were six missionaries working in Tangier and two at Arcila, a small Atlantic port about twenty-five miles to the south. Mr. and Mrs. E. F. Baldwin, an Englishman, and the daughter of an American physician, respectively, took charge and founded the nucleus of a medical mission, which in 1897, through the joining together of Hope House and the dispensary, became the Tulloch Memorial Hospital, named after a Scotswoman. In 1964, it was by far the North Africa Mission's largest medical activity in the Maghreb. Though the Moroccan government's public health services were improving, the dispensary was still badly needed.

A Miss Herdman began work among the Spanish Catholics, while Baldwin handled colportage operations, gradually moving into the hinterland. But the dispensary became the center of the Mission's activities in Morocco, since there were no restrictions on the practice of medicine in Morocco. After the French and Spanish moved into the rest of the country in 1912, the Tangier zone remained under a special jurisdiction which prevented any laws of France or Spain from interfering with the hospital.

The missionaries preached the Gospel to their patients. One Moroccan convert, Mehdi Kasara, now an American citizen, who worked at the hospital, has become an itinerant professional missionary. In 1963, he was still traveling between Tangier and other

[6] Ruth Stewart, "The New Algeria," *North Africa,* publication of the North Africa Mission (Sept.–Oct., 1963), p. 618.

principal Moroccan towns and cities, preaching the Gospel in private, often under considerable personal hardship and risk.

One of the Mission's leaders called the hospital "the key to our work in Morocco for decades." In 1963, it had three full-time doctors, eight full-time missionary nurses, and several other nurses in training, including two Christian Arab women who came to Tangier from Algiers. At various times the Mission has also operated dispensaries in Fez, Settat, and Azzemour. They suffered far less interference from the French authorities before independence than was experienced in either Algeria or Tunisia.

By 1889, a permanent North Africa Mission group was working in Tetuan, and, in 1890 and the following year, a Dr. and Mrs. Grieve, both English, had purchased for the Mission an old house in Casablanca and begun work there. By 1894, Casablanca had become nearly as active a center as Tangier. Regular work began in Fez in 1888, with Miss Herdman, a fluent Arabist, as the mainstay.

"The medical work," writes Glenny, "afforded an excuse for the men who were afraid to be known as enquirers. Miss Herdman used to read the Scriptures with these men and instruct them in their meaning almost every day, and when they were converted and more mature, send them out to disseminate Scriptures and teach others. Possibly in some cases they imposed on her sanguine disposition, but at the time of her death there were ten or a dozen men whom her fellow-laborers thought worthy to be still employed in this work." [7] One attempt to start a school ended when the first pupil's parents were imprisoned. There has been little school work done in Fez since.

A mission station was opened in Tetuan in 1889. Though its founders had ideas about preaching to the Rifians and the Andjera people of the surrounding countryside, the dispensary once again became the most popular and successful operation.

There was a new upsurge of missionary activity among the Tangier Jews in 1886 with the arrival of a British subject named Jacob Halbmillion, representing a group called the Mildmay Mission to the Jews. Halbmillion first concentrated on passing out Bibles. Then he and his wife took a house in Tangier and used it as

[7] Rutherford and Glenny, *op. cit.*, Part II, p. 185.

a base for field trips into the interior, until he died in 1888. Another missionary worked for the Mildmay group in Fez, Tangier, Marrakesh, and Demnat, in the High Atlas Mountains. Demnat is the site of an archaic community of "Palestine Jews," who claim descent from ancient Jewish immigrants. The North Africa Mission took over some of their work, and another Mildmay representative arrived in Tangier in 1895.

In 1885, an English Presbyterian Church Mission directed by a Dr. Kerr was established. He began the Lord's work in Rabat in 1886. Dr. Kerr learned Arabic from a renegade Scotsman, who called himself "Abdelkacem the Great," and got help from a family of Syrian converts. In 1894, Kerr broke with the Presbyterians and founded the Central Moroccan Mission which worked from a Rabat headquarters in Meknes and the Rharb Plain, stressing medical operations.

THE SOUTHERN MOROCCO MISSION

A Scotsman, John Anderson, head of the Ayrshire Christian Union, visited Morocco for his health in 1888. He was impressed by the work of the North Africa Mission. He returned to Scotland and spread the word that Morocco was a green field for action, then went back and moved into a house in Mogador with his family. At the end of the same year he was joined by Cuthbert Nairn, who was murdered in 1945 under circumstances never fully explained. He was first of a long line of Nairns concerned with missions and British consular affairs in Morocco. After solving their house-hunting and language problems, they founded the Southern Morocco Mission. In 1890, believing that the Atlas Berbers offered better raw material than Mogador's Arabs or Jews, Nairn and a Mr. Clark left for Marrakesh. They found the city even more closed to Europeans than was Fez: the passage of Ginsburg and his wife had made things difficult.

The only favorable factor they found in Marrakesh was the influence of an English protégé and house owner named Sidi bu-Bakr al-Ganjawi. Ma al-Ainin's influence had begun to grow in the south, and there was agitation and talk of an anti-Christian rising. The French and German legations at Tangier tried to persuade

Nairn and Clark to leave, and the "Caid" Maclean, at the sultan's court, heartily endorsed this view. But the British minister, Mr. K. Green, a pious Protestant, after visiting Marrakesh to see the situation for himself, persuaded the court to grant a temporary authorization to the mission, which the next British minister, Sir Evan Smith, managed to make permanent. Between 1890 and 1892, they extended operations to Al-Jadida (Mazagan), Mogador, and Safi and had sixteen missionaries in Morocco by the end of 1892. The chilling of Anglo-Moroccan diplomatic relations around the turn of the century arrested any further growth and made things difficult for nearly all of the British missionaries. In the crisis and rioting that followed Sultan Mulay Hasan's death, they had to abandon Azzemour.

THE AMERICANS

One of the first American Protestant organizations to show interest in Morocco was the World Gospel Union of Abilene, Kansas. In 1895, with their sponsorship, a Mr. Nathan, a Jew of Hamburg, Germany, who was a naturalized American citizen and a convert to Protestantism, arrived in Tangier with his wife and learned Arabic, with the help of personnel of the North Africa Mission. When the Nathans tried to set up shop in Meknes, the local authorities blocked them. Finally, after strong pressure by the United States consul general, the permission was granted. A French journalist says that missionary correspondence out of Meknes became a valuable source of political intelligence information to the Americans.[8] The World Gospel Union also set up a permanent office at Al-Ksar al-Kabir.

In 1901, the entire group was reorganized as the Gospel Missionary Union, with headquarters in Kansas City and twelve roving workers in Morocco, based in Meknes, Fez, and Tangier. The union has maintained an almost continuous presence in Morocco since then. Their most spectacular activity, in the 1960's, was the holding, with the co-operation of the North Africa Mission, of a camp meeting every year or second year, at Khemisset, where Moroccan converts attended divine services, sometimes in public.

[8] Jean-Louis Miège, "Les Missions Protestantes au Maroc (1875–1905)," *Hesperis,* XVII (1955), p. 165.

In May, 1963, sixty Moroccan Christians attended. They received unofficial "friendly" warnings that any Moroccans baptized in public might be "persecuted" and any of the baptizers might be prosecuted under a stringent new Moroccan penal code. So they performed their baptisms in private and, as usual, held their meeting on private property.

The North Africa Mission is now incorporated with the Southern Morocco Mission. In 1963, the Mission included Presbyterian, Methodist, Baptist, Brethren, and Anglican church groups, with a Canadian, Mr. A. J. Stewart, as Chairman of the International Council, its advisory board. One of the American publications most influential in the Mission's work is *The Evangelical Christian.* Some two-thirds of the younger field personnel were being recruited in the United States and one-third in Britain.

At its Casablanca field headquarters, the Rev. Harold J. Stalley, a long, rangy man, who radiates quiet strength and purpose, now runs the Mission throughout North Africa. In 1934, when he was twenty-two years old, he left the construction business and trained for the ministry in Glasgow, then decided to work abroad. At first he was associated with the Algiers Mission Band, a small independent group, from 1934 to 1943. The Vichy government of Marshal Pétain put him under house arrest in Algeria after the fall of France in World War II. In 1943, he returned to the United Kingdom for nine years. The Mission's council asked him to take over the field director's post in 1952. "One of the most extraordinary contacts I made," he told me, "was with a Spanish Protestant Missionary at Tolga Oasis, near Biskra, Algeria—with the honorable name of Señor Salvador Lull!" (Lull has since died, but his French wife and two children were still working in Tolga in 1963, assisted by two nurses.)

Stalley's assistant in Casablanca in 1963 was the Rev. Robert I. Brown, another career missionary. He is a genial, kindly, and scholarly man. He was first assigned to Tunis when he was twenty-five, in 1938. He too was arrested and interned during the war, by the Germans in Tunis in 1942. Brown has charge of field training and of the thorough language program under which all field workers, before assignment to their posts, must master classical and colloquial Arabic and French, with the emphasis always on practical conversation rather than on an academic approach. "This is one of the main differences between our approach and that of the Catholics, who emphasize scholarship," says Mr. Brown.

TRIAL AND ERROR

The toughest early problems which missionaries in Morocco, like those in Tunisia, Algeria, and Libya experienced, stemmed from old ingrown attitudes to Christians that are nourished in the local folklore. These, of course, apply equally to Protestants and Catholics. The Scottish anthropologist, Dr. Edward Westermarck, who spent many years in Morocco before 1930, found people who believed that Christians were not born like other human beings but grew up from seeds in the ground, had horns on their foreheads, and were capable of bringing all sorts of misfortune through possession of the evil eye. Barbers of the Andjera tribe, Westermarck discovered, maintained there was no *baraka* ("blessing," or some mystical or magical power or essence) in razors used by their colleagues in Tangier where so many Christians lived. Sultan Abd al-Aziz was supposed to have lost all his *baraka,* an indispensable attribute of any sultan, through too much association with Christians.[9]

MacIntosh translated the Bible into the Riffian dialect of Berber, while Nairn and Muir, another Morocco Mission worker in Marrakesh, translated it into Shleuh, the local branch of Berber.

Most of the Protestant workers, especially the younger ones, are constantly traveling, sometimes under hazardous conditions. The women emphasize cementing personal ties with families—person-to-person contacts are virtually the only way to accomplish anything in North Africa. One woman stationed in Safi, a Mrs. Badger, regularly visited eighty-seven Moroccan families, and this is still a favorite activity of the younger American women.

In their medical work, the missionaries are constantly struck by the fatalistic attitude about illness which exists among uneducated North Africans. *Maktub*—"it is written"—is often the verbal sigh of resignation with which people react to disease and death. Vaccinations that missionaries performed during Moroccan smallpox epi-

[9] Edward Westermarck, *Wit and Wisdom of Morocco* (New York, 1931), p. 128.

demics in 1895, 1901, and 1904, before there were any protectorate authorities, saved many lives. Nonetheless, Moroccan witches and witch doctors, called *tolabah* (singular: *talib,* not to be confused with the orthodox *talib* of Moslem theology who professes to look upon wizardry with horror) often spread vicious rumors about the missionaries, like one in Tangier that a "supernatural being" came in the night to devour woman patients at the Tulloch Hospital. This rumor was followed by a sudden upsurge in the number of new patients, apparently eager to see for themselves.

In their schools, the missionaries have often filled in gaps which governments could not or did not fill, and this has continued to be true since the North African countries became independent. As in baptisms, the Protestants are far less reticent than the Catholics about combining religious instruction, especially for orphan children, with academic subjects. Sometimes a "class" session ends up with the singing of hymns or recitation of Christian prayers in Arabic.

The missionaries' activities had political repercussions from the very beginning. During one debate at the turn of the century in the British Chamber of Commerce, foes of the missions claimed that "inopportune attitudes had developed xenophobia" in Morocco. The opposing view, voiced by Sir C. Evan Smith, was that "defense of the interests of civilization, including missions, coincides with British interests." We have already seen how systematic French hostility reinforced the instinctive early opposition of the Moslem authorities. A French deputy from Oran once touched off a debate in the French Parliament on "the machinations of the English Methodists." The French authorities suspected Mr. Lennox, a companion of Nairn in Marrakesh who became a consular agent after having been a missionary, of being a spy. This attitude has now been replaced by the Moslem suspicion, especially in Morocco, that missionaries are trying to undermine the state or the monarchy.

Among the classical errors committed since Protestantism began to proselytize in Morocco, a few have become almost legendary. Preaching to Moslem women in a Moslem cemetery in Rabat was one. But the balance has probably been positive. To many Moroccans, the Anglo-Saxon missionary was the first Christian who had not come to conquer, exploit, or profit from them. The nationalist political opposition to the missionary as a supposed representative of imperialism was latent but not strongly evident. It took the new national revolutions of 1930–1962 and the difficult period afterward, when independence was consolidated, to bring it back into the open.

THE NORTH AFRICA MISSION'S BEGINNINGS IN TUNISIA

The North Africa Mission had been warned by an English resident of Tunis that there was "more fanaticism" there than in Algiers. After a reconnaissance trip by a Mr. and Mrs. Bureau, who had worked among the soldiers of the French expeditionary force in Tunisia in 1881, Glenny reported that "the natives were more open" than in Algeria and "there were fewer French officials to hamper the work." They were also allowed to carry on medical work, which they had not been able to do except on a semiclandestine and catch-as-catch-can basis, in Algeria. By 1888, eight missionaries were working in Tunis and the Bureaus had broken ground at Sfax, two hundred miles south of Tunis. In 1896, a Dr. and Mrs. Leach were murdered, probably by the followers of a jealous *marabout,* shortly after they arrived in Sfax to begin medical work.

Work began at Sousse, a seaport one hundred miles south of Tunis, in 1895, and Sousse has been almost continuously "occupied" by the Mission ever since: in the fall of 1963, it was the only post left in Tunisia outside of Tunis. The Moslem holy city of Kairawan (1897) and the seaport of Bizerte (1898) were added to the list of stations; by 1900, the North Africa Mission had twenty-eight field workers in Tunisia.

In Tunis, the earliest work consisted largely of the sale of the Gospels in Arabic to those of the literate minority (about four per cent) whose interest was aroused by tracts handed them in the streets or in shops. Colportage remained a large part of the Mission's work in Tunisia down through the years. The French curbed this activity at various times by passing a law preventing the sale of "scurrilous literature" in public places and requiring official permission for the sale of Scriptures or religious tracts. The North Africa Mission never got such permission, but was allowed to sell literature in regular shops and give away samples. It soon opened bookshops in Tunis, Sousse, and Kairawan.

Tunisians or Europeans could meet each other or missionaries at the bookshops without compromising themselves too much, under the cover of looking over the literature. The shops usually had small, rather camouflaged halls at the rear where discussion groups, classes, or divine services could be held. Missionaries took turns as shop attendants, assisted by a Tunisian convert if possible.

Dr. and Mrs. Leach, the couple murdered in Sfax in 1896, had begun medical work in Tunis in 1893. Just as in Morocco, it seems to have been, for the missionaries as well as for the people they treated, the most satisfying and successful branch of their work. Patients, after treatment, would be told about the Gospel in informal conversations and were given literature if they could read. Glenny relates one interesting case of conversion:

> Si Ahmed al-Ghomati, a native, of one of the best families in the country, came to the Medical Mission as much from curiosity as for medicine. He was struck by the patience and grace of the lady missionary in dealing with his rather violent co-religionists, and was led to study the Scriptures, and ultimately to accept Christ as his personal Saviour. He has confessed Him both by baptism and by public testimony, and continues to lead his fellow-countrymen to Christ. He was imprisoned soon after his conversion for having become a Christian, but the French authorities, to their great credit, ordered his release on the ground of there being religious liberty.[10]

The Mission in Tunis also worked among the students, and still tries to today, distributing tracts and such books as *Why God Became Man,* translated by Mr. Mitchell, a fluent Arabist, from Latin into Arabic; Pfandner's *The Balance of Truth,* and al-Kindi's *Apology*. Around 1900, some French-speaking Jews attended the Mission's meetings in a hired hall. Among the European population the missionaries gave principal attention to the Italians, since there

[10] Rutherford and Glenny, *op. cit.,* Part II, p. 209.

was a British representative of the London Jews' Society and a French pastor for the French Protestant flock.

At Sousse, there were the usual French administrative roadblocks to overcome. A Dr. and Mrs. Churcher opened a successful dispensary in conjunction with a half refuge and half hospital, which came to be called the Baraka. They treated about twenty thousand people in four years. An itinerant physician paid regular visits to two branch dispensaries, in Kairawan and Moknine.

Mr. and Mrs. Cooksey, the first of the Mission's workers in Kairawan, found younger Moslems in the holy city to be "well educated" but "terribly entangled in the Mohammedan net." Just as in Morocco and Algeria, a few other Anglo-Saxon groups, including the British and Foreign Bible Society, began working in Tunisia about this time.

LIBYA: THE TRIPOLI MISSION

Like Cardinal Lavigerie, the Protestants of the North Africa Mission looked upon Tripoli as a likely steppingstone to evangelizing the southern reaches of the Sahara and Central Africa. Efforts were being made to penetrate them from the Congo and Nigeria, but in 1887 Glenny wangled permission from the Turkish authorities to visit Tripoli to assess the possibilities there. He found not a single Protestant missionary or even a Protestant consular chaplain in all Tripolitania. Though it was impossible to get permission to travel outside the coastal strip around Tripoli, Glenny felt that useful work might be done with caravans leaving Tripoli for the Sudan.

By 1889, the Mission's council had sent four missionaries, including Mr. Mitchell of Tunis and Mr. H. Harding, a druggist, who set up a successful medical mission in Tripoli. Though they had no qualified physician, they must have operated one of the most effective dispensaries in Libya. They had fifty thousand calls by 1900, and patients would even come up from the depths of the Sahara and from the Sudan, according to Glenny. A bookshop, and the visiting of cafés and stores was kept up by the men, while lady missionaries, as usual, tended to visiting homes and conducting classes.

By 1900, there had apparently been one true conversion of a Moslem farmer, but he lacked the courage to be baptized. In 1911, when the Italians conquered Tripoli, the Mission stayed open, but Mussolini closed it in 1937. The British military allowed it to reopen at the end of World War II, and it survived the first few years of Libyan independence under Sanusi rule.

Typical of the more extreme problems which the Mission has had in the new era of Arab independence was the experience of a Dr. and Mrs. McCarthy, who worked in Libya from about 1953 until 1960. In that year, their mission status was canceled by the Libyan authorities, but Dr. and Mrs. McCarthy were allowed to practice as doctor and nurse, since they had diplomas and were badly needed. They were told courteously, but firmly, by Interior Ministry officials that they were being allowed to "minister to the body only, not to the soul." The handful of converts they had made were spied on continuously by the Libyan police, and the mission finally closed in 1961.

An independent American missionary, Warren Bower, tried slipping into Libya about this time as a language student. Police in Derna searched his room and confiscated all his personal diaries, books, and recording tapes. When he came up for trial for "subversion," the prosecutor had to admit there was no case against him. He was allowed to leave the country quietly. Libya, as a recipient of American military aid and host country to the big American airbase at Wheelus field, would probably have been embarrassed by a repetition of such an incident. By 1963, Libya was virtually off limits to Protestant missionaries wishing to proselytize, though Italian and French Franciscans and Dominicans continued their usual works of scholarship and charity in Tripoli and Bengasi.

PART FOUR

CHRISTIANITY AND THE NATIONAL REVOLUTIONS

CHAPTER XXII

THE NEW NATIONAL REVOLUTIONS

> Missionary activity in its present form is one of the results of armed Christian fanaticism. It is one of the offspring of that oppressive force which labels freedom of religion or freedom of thought or freedom of trade everything that pleases it.
>
> THE ASSOCIATION OF ALGERIAN *Ulama*, 1935

On the evening of July 2, 1962, the riotous explosion of joy which celebrated Algeria's newly regained independence was reaching its height. I stood on the square next to the Algiers Cathedral. Mingled with the shouts of *Yahia al-Djazair* and *Yahia FLN* ("Long live Algeria," "Long live the FLN") were others of *Allah ihobb al-Djazair* and *Allah irh am shuhadda* ("God love Algeria," "God have mercy on the martyrs"). On that same night, a large statue of Joan of Arc in downtown Algiers was torn from its pedestal, probably because Joan held a cross pointed inward toward the land. Three days later, when the celebrating was over, several hundred Moslems entered the cathedral and walked through it, without any act of pillage or desecration. An imam mounted the pulpit and demanded the return to Islam of what had been, before 1830, the Ketchawa Mosque. At that point, a party cadreman of the FLN rose and told the crowd to leave the church at once. "All religions must be respected," they said. The crowd obeyed.

These events dramatized the distance Algeria had come since the reformist *ulama* first began seriously to turn the religious spirit toward national emancipation in the 1930's. They also helped place Algerian religion and the Moslem-Christian relationship, in all their complexities, into proper perspective among the contributing factors in the making of the revolution and the final, blood-washed rebirth of national independence.

THE THIRTIES: "FRANCE IS ME"

At the centennial of the conquest, in 1930, Algeria was already divided into two distinct communities. By their overwhelming acceptance of the Cremieux Decree, which permitted native peoples to accept French nationality, the Algerian Jews had in effect joined the European community. The Moslem community was now beginning to turn to the *ulama* and the political parties as its spokesmen. The younger generation already felt that official administrative Islam, the Islam protected and guaranteed by France, had become little more than a docile, domesticated religion.

The first important national party was the North African Star, started under Communist influence among Algerian students and workers in France and dominated after 1927 by Messali Hadj, who demanded Algerian independence and published in French a weekly paper called *Al-Umma.* Chekib Arslan, a Druze prince who was profoundly to influence all the North African nationalists, helped to talk Messali out of his Marxist ideas and to adopt Arab nationalist and pan-Islamic ones in 1936. This was the same year when Ferhat Abbas, later to play a decisive role in the revolution and then reject its socialist outcome in 1963, wrote his famous article called "France Is Me," saying, "I would not die for the Algerian fatherland because this fatherland does not exist. . . . I asked history, I asked the living and the dead, I visited the cemeteries, no one spoke to me of it." [1]

The political movement which Abbas and Dr. Mohammed Salah ibn Jallul of Constantine then directed was, in contrast to the Association of *Ulama,* a lay movement. It favored real integration with France, provided equal rights were granted to the "French Moslems" of Algeria. It did not stress religion.

The *ulama,* led by Ibn Badis, who had studied at the Zitouna Mosque in Tunis; by Tayeb al-Uqbi, who had lived in the Hidjaz; and by Bashir al-Ibrahimi, who had spent some time in Egypt and Syria, looked not to France and the West but to the East for reform and renewal. In April, 1936, the *ulama* answered Abbas in their review, *Al-Shihab,* published in Constantine: "We too have sought the Algerian nation, in history and in the present, and we have con-

[1] Ferhat Abbas, "La France, C'est Moi," *L'Entente* (February 23, 1936).

firmed that the Moslem Algerian nation has been formed and exists." The association opposed alcohol, smoking, the emancipation of women, and the other evils which it considered the Christian West had brought to Algeria. It denied the contention of Abbas and Ibn Jallul that the spiritual and the temporal could be separated, since under Islam all believers belonged to the *umma,* the nation. Because believers could not consent to being ruled by unbelievers, the ultimate goal of reformers must be the re-establishment of a Moslem society dominated by Moslems. This change should come about in an orderly manner. "This is the independence of which we conceive," wrote Ibn Badis, "and not bloody and criminal independence, as our criminal adversaries [the *colons*] envisage it. This is the independence we can count upon, with time and with the will of France."

To curb the political propaganda contained in the Friday sermons of the *ulama,* the French Secretary-General of the Prefecture of Algiers in 1933 banned all preaching in the mosques by any except members of the official administration of the Islamic religion, a measure which ran strongly counter to Moslem tradition. It led the *ulama* to found study groups and hold numerous conferences. One of these in Algiers in 1935 discussed Christian missionary activity in Algeria and produced one of the few comprehensive statements of the hostile, traditionalist reaction to missionaries as the allies of the colonial power:

> [Missionary activity] is a political instrument in religious garb and clerical form which polity *(siyasa)* promotes as its guide in conquest and colonization, supplying it [missionary activity] with aid, protection, and guidance. Missionary activity has so extended its scope that if one should cry out against it, polity would reply, "Keep quiet. Missionary activity is one of my deeds. It is free and I am the Protector of freedom. It is humanitarian and I am the humanitarian savior."
>
> This "humanitarian" Christian missionary activity realizes that its most dangerous enemies are the Moslem reformers, because they call for a purified Islam, and a pure Islam is not an object of missionary activity. This we have learned from Sheikh Rashid Reda . . . and his view on missionaries is perti-

nent. Cardinal Lavigerie laid the foundations of missionary activity in Algeria and founded its chief missions. Then the missionary orders finished what he had started. They are powerful orders to whom rich, free-giving Christians donate millions. Men and women of the clergy aid them in their work and "secular" governments extend assistance and support. . . .

For several reasons, it should be expected that missionary activity in Algeria should be more fruitful and have better results than in many other countries: (1) Its early beginnings, (2) The protection of imperialism, (3) Widespread ignorance, illiteracy, and poverty which are the prey of missionary activity, (4) The extent of Moslem [Sufi] orders which are the wet nurses and guarantors of missionary activity [because they weaken orthodox Islam], (5) The silence and inactivity of the *ulama* until the founding of the Association of *Ulama*.[2]

THE ENTRY OF THE COMMUNISTS

Like the Moroccan and Tunisian Communist parties, the Algerian Communist Party was founded by Europeans. It was a local section of the French Communist Party, rechristened Algerian Communist Party in 1935. Its program was not independence but assimilation, with equal rights and opportunities for Algerians and Frenchmen. Moslems never quite trusted it, partly because it had Christian and Jewish members. The tension and hostility between the different communities in Algeria was perhaps never demonstrated better than in 1934. A drunken Jewish soldier in the French army, who relieved himself against the wall of a mosque in Constantine, touched off anti-Jewish riots which caused the death of twenty-seven people and injured forty-eight others. The riots coincided with the beginning of the exodus of the German Jews to Palestine and were the first important manifestation in North Africa of the resulting Arab nervousness which was, in time, to crystallize into Arab anti-Zionism.

[2] *Shughe Mutamar al-Ulama al-Muslimin al-Jazairiyin* (Proceedings of the Algerian Association of *Ulama*), Moslem date: Jumadi II, 16–19, 1354 (Constantine, 1935). Translated privately by Professor Carl Brown, Harvard University.

On June 7, 1936, the "notables" of the French-sponsored corporative bodies, the *ulama,* and the Communists together sponsored an "Algerian Moslem Congress" in Algiers. It demanded full absorption of Algeria into France, with reform and separation of the Islamic religious establishment from the state machinery to which it had been subordinated and various social and educational rights, notably the teaching of the Arabic language. This was the first major Moslem political gathering since the conquest. The congress met again in August. Messali Hadj made an unexpected appearance and dramatically called for Algerian independence. The following year, he broke with the Communist Party; the North African Star was dissolved by the French authorities, and Messali founded the Algerian Peoples Party (PPA). This was dissolved in its turn as subversive in 1939, when the French feared it might support the Axis in World War II. It worked clandestinely until 1946, when a general amnesty briefly allowed all parties to work in the open again.

WORLD WAR II AND AFTER

After the French defeat of 1940, the Vichy administration of General Weygand appointed four Moslem members to the Council of Government for the first time, but the council never met. Ferhat Abbas, married to a French woman, worked for a time with the Pétain government. He suggested reforms which, once again, would narrow the social, economic, and political gap between Algerians and Frenchmen but which would not place in question Algeria's legal role as part of France. But the economic hardships of the war, the disaster of the Vichy fleet, sunk by the British in port with great loss of life at Mers-al-Kebir, and finally, the victory of the Anglo-American allies over Vichy resistance in the landings of November 8, 1942, "Operation Torch," raised hopes of the Algerian elite that the British and Americans might do something for them. After contacts with the Allies and in particular the American representative, Robert Murphy, which took place during bitter struggles between the various French factions, Abbas issued what he called a Manifesto of the Algerian People. He decried the opposition of the *colons* to all reforms, and continued:

> What does this mean if not that the Algerian problem . . . is essentially a *racial and religious one* and the discrimination against the autochtonic element [i.e., the native Moslem population] extends to all classes of society. . . . The hour has passed when an Algerian Moslem will ask to be anything but a Moslem Algerian.[3]

Abbas went on to demand civil liberties, equality of opportunity, universal and free public education for all children, freedom of religion, and separation of religion and state to be applied to all religions. In return, the Algerians offered to support the Allied cause. In May, 1943, Abbas spelled out in detail the structural reforms which would put into practice the demands of the manifesto. When General de Gaulle and the French Committee of National Liberation took power in Algiers, the French position toward the nationalists hardened: a few reforms were made, but they fell short of demands. The nationalists, including *ulama,* Communists, supporters of Abbas, and others drew together.

The political situation went from bad to worse, and rioting occurred during May Day labor parades in 1945. Then, on May 8, as the Western allies celebrated their victory over Hitler, spontaneous uprisings broke out when the Algerians turned victory demonstrations into nationalist ones, brandishing Algerian flags not seen since the days of the Emir Abd al-Kadir. Disorders turned to mass revolt in the Department of Constantine, especially at Setif. About one hundred Europeans were killed. The uprisings lasted until May 12, when sweeping reprisals by the French army, in which about ten thousand Moslem villagers were killed by French troops, succeeded in restoring calm. But this had been the worst revolt in Algeria since that of Mokrani in 1871, and it had, of course, roused the specter of the long-forgotten holy war for the first time since then.

Then French navy and air force took part in the repression, bombing and shelling villages. There were thousands of summary executions. The gross economic inequalities between the European and Jewish community on the one hand and the Moslem majority

[3] Roger LeTourneau, *Evolution Politique de l'Afrique du Nord Musulmane 1920–1961* (Paris, 1962), p. 320.

on the other had reaped a terrible whirlwind. One of the present Algerian national leaders told me, "The revolt of May, 1945, dug a ditch we could no longer cross between the two communities. It made us decide to take up arms." The result was the new and organized guerilla revolt of 1954, which finally brought independence in 1962 after lifting the Algerian imbroglio to a drama of world proportions.

The French authorities tried to cool the situation down with a political amnesty in 1946. In general elections held on November 1, 1946, the clandestine PPA, calling itself the Movement for the Triumph of Democratic Liberties (MTLD), won five of fifteen seats in the French parliament despite obstruction of the authorities. But in 1948, "arranged" elections for the Algerian National Assembly drove the MTLD out of effective existence: it became the overt wing of the now illegal PPA. Ahmed ben Bella, a former French army sergeant, Mohammed Boudiaf, Mohammed Khidder, and several of their friends, many from poor rural families, constructed a clandestine network, the OS, or *Mundama Siria* (Secret Organization), with ramifications in Egypt and the Middle East, to unleash an armed revolt and plan a secular, socialistic Algerian state for the future.

Many of independent Algeria's political and religious contradictions and disputes date back to this period of division in the PPA. Messali, with his messianic complex and strange blend of Trotskyism and pan-Islamism, was gradually discredited. He finished the revolutionary period as a virtual stooge of the French, in residence in metropolitan France. The "centralists," who believed in nonviolence, included such men as Benyusef ben Khedda, a mild-mannered intellectual and brilliant planner who was shoved aside by Ben Bella in his march to power in 1962, and Mohammed Yazid, well known to Americans because of his American wife, his long stay in the United States, and his important role as spokesman for the nationalist government in exile, the Provisional Government of the Algerian Republic (GPRA) in Tunis. The group that won out in the end was largely made up of the hard-core activists of the OS. One of these was Ahmed ben Bella, first premier, elected in September, 1963, first President of the "Socialist, Democratic and Popular Algerian Republic."

MOROCCO: THE BERBER DAHIR AND "DE-ISLAMIZATION"

Just as in Algeria, the theme of religious conflict in Morocco's twenty-five-year nationalist revolution—a quarter century that saw the ancient monarchy make gigantic strides into the twentieth century, while preserving many of the customs and institutions of the tenth—was usually subdued, though nearly always present. Economic inequalities, land-hungry peasants, a growing industrial proletariat were more strident themes, but the religious note was usually an insistent undertone.

In the early stages of Morocco's nationalist revolution, two religious positions are central: the Islamic reformers and their influence, and the great religious and political prestige of the sharifian throne.

Unlike Algeria, Morocco received the ideas of Sheikh Mohammed Abduh and the *Salafiya* very late. During the reign of Sultan Mulay Hasan, before 1894, a Moroccan scholar named Abdallah Sanusi traveled in the Middle East and brought back with him some of the reformist ideas. But he lacked the force of character or the didactic ability to spread them widely in Morocco. Sultan Mulay Hafid sympathized with the *Salafiya* and began his reign by cracking down on the Sufi orders. He asked the theologian Abu Shaib al-Dukkali, who was studying in the East, to come home and help in the reform of Moroccan Islam.

Dukkali accepted, and he found things in a bad state. The French colonization drive had begun. At the same time, study of the Koran and the *hadiths* had fallen off. There was even a popular belief that if a scholar began to study a commentary on the Koran, the sultan would die. Among Dukkali's principal students was a former member of the Tidjaniya Order, Mohammed bi al-Arabi al-Alawi, the Kadi of Fez, who became a teacher of many leading Moroccan nationalists.

Two nationalist study groups were formed. One was headed by Allal al-Fassi, a student of al-Alawi at the Kairouyine University in Fez. Ahmed Balafrej, a student from a wealthy bourgeois family of Rabat, with more interest and feeling for European civilization than al-Fassi, led another. The two joined forces in 1927. This was also the year when Sultan Mulay Yusef died. His third son, eighteen-year-old Sidi Mohammed ibn Yusef (later called Mohammed V), was chosen by the French authorities as a probably docile candidate and certified by the *ulama* as fulfilling the needed religious requirements for being both the temporal and spiritual ruler of Morocco.

In 1930, the protectorate authorities unwittingly provided a made-to-order rallying point for Moslem feeling and Arab nationalist sentiment. For years, French colonial administrators had favored encouraging the preservation of Berber customs and Berber law in the mountain areas. It was a way to keep them from being infected with the spreading ideas of Arabic nationalism and Islamic solidarity. On May 16, 1930, the residency got the young sultan to sign a *dahir* (law) officially removing the Berber tribes from the jurisdiction and the prescriptions of the Islamic law code, the *sharia.* To the young nationalists, this law, the Berber Dahir, indicated that France intended to remove the Berbers entirely, if possible, from the influence of Islamic society.

In the events that followed, the Catholic hierarchy in Morocco bears a share of responsibility. The French, Spanish, and Tangier zones of Morocco had been given an apostolic vicar in 1920 and placed directly under the Vatican's Sacred Congregation for Propogation of the Faith, like any other "missionary territory." In 1923, an apostolic letter separated the apostolic vicarates for Tangier and the Spanish zone, with its seat in Tangier, from that in Rabat, which had been given to the French Franciscans. Msgr. Henri Vielle was named second apostolic vicar in Rabat on June 8, 1927. Some of his advisers apparently felt, as had Cardinal Lavigerie and Charles de Foucauld, that the Berbers were good raw material for evangelization. These ideas were expressd openly in *Le Maroc Catholique,* official organ of the vicarate, and the nationalist-minded young Moroccans read them. They were all the more sensitive because in 1927 the son of one of the leading families of Fez and the brother of a man who was soon to play a leading role in the national movement converted to Christianity and entered a Franciscan seminary in France.

"French policy is to de-Islamize, to profane (*de-sacriliser*), and Christianize a considerable fraction of the Moroccan population which France should effectively and statutorally protect," wrote the nationalist newspaper, *Voix du Tunisien,* in Tunis on June 6, 1932.

To the Moroccan nationalists, it did indeed look as though the moral, political, and religious unity of the monarchy were being threatened all at once. Agitation began in Rabat on June 20, 1930, with the reading of a ritual prayer of mourning, called the *latif,* which is reserved for moments when the Islamic community, the *umma,* stands in great danger. Processions and demonstrations were organized by al-Fassi and other nationalist leaders, including Mohammed Hasan al-Wazzani, of the family of the Sharif of Wazzan, demanding revocation of the Berber Dahir. This was the first overt political opposition to the protectorate since the revolt of Abd al-Krim. It was not duplicated in the Spanish zone, since the Spanish authorities never took similar action. It became the center of attention in the Moslem world: Emir Chekib Arslan met Wazzani and Balafrej in Geneva, then came to Tangier and Tetuan where he contacted some of the other young nationalists.

With the co-operation of Arslan, who spread propaganda concerning Morocco throughout the Arab East, and a group of liberal and left-wing Frenchmen, Balafrej and Wazzani, who had studied in France, started the French-language magazine *Maghreb* in Paris. Backed by a weekly published in Fez and several other later papers, it became the chief organ of the new nationalist propaganda. It strove to keep alive the religious issue, reporting, for instance, in August, 1932, that six hundred Franciscan missionaries had arrived in Fez, whereas there were only about one hundred in the country at the time. In 1932, the apostolic vicar solemnly inaugurated the Church of Saint Theresa of the Infant Jesus at Khemisset, in Berber country. The ceremony was attended by some of the protectorate officials. A nationalist paper, *La Volonté du Peuple,* bitterly attacked the large subsidies given to the Catholic Church in Morocco and the building of many churches.

More and more, the nationalists sought the favor of the sultan—whom they were already calling *al-malik,* the king, to stress his role as a modern leader. Enthusiastic demonstrations on his behalf during a visit to Fez (Lyautey had moved the Moroccan political capital to Rabat) in 1934 caused the French authorities to suspend the nationalist papers. On December 1, 1934, Balafrej, al-Fassi, and a number of other nationalist leaders presented to the resident-general a comprehensive Plan of Moroccan Reforms, calling themselves the "Moroccan Action Committee."

They called for strict adherence to the Protectorate Treaty; an end to direct administration; Moroccan predominance in all government bodies and assemblies, with the participation of Moroccan Jews together with Moslems but not the European community; a unified judicial system based on the *sharia*; strict separation of powers; an end to the practice of giving away or selling for nominal cost the choicest farmland to the French colonists. Special reforms were sought, asking for an end to the "Berber policy," Christian proselytism, and suppression of the word "cross" from sharifian medals and decorations. Neither the residency nor the government in Paris acted on the demands.

As in Algeria, the nationalists took pains to found a network of private schools where Koranic and modern instruction would be mixed, to supplement the sporadic educational efforts of the protectorate authorities. The curricula included Moroccan history, stressed the French language and French philosophical and political ideals, and so naturally fanned the glowing sparks of an awakening national feeling. In Paris, Moroccans like Balafrej, Algerians like Ferhat Abbas, and Tunisians like Habib Bourguiba got to know one another and began talking and dreaming of a unified and independent Moslem North Africa, a Union of the Arab Maghreb. This idea was to persist when the focal point of North African émigré political activity shifted from Europe to Cairo in the 1950's. It is still a central concern of all the North African leaders today.

By 1937, rivalries between al-Fassi and Wazzani had led to a rupture. The same had occurred in the Spanish zone, where the vicissitudes of the Spanish civil war were affecting Moroccan politics and where an Islah, or National Reform Party, of Abdelhalek Torres was opposed by Mekki Nasiri, leader of the Moroccan Unity Party.

Al-Fassi's power grew rapidly in Fez, where he constantly invoked religious laws and canons, such as the desirability for shops to close on Friday instead of on the Christian day of rest, Sunday, as convenient themes of political action. The French resident-general, Nogues, reacted by dissolving the Moroccan Action Committee after trouble in Meknes over water being supplied to French *colons*. In October, 1937, he ordered the arrest of al-Fassi and other nationalist leaders, at Rabat. Demonstrations and popular uprisings followed in Fez, Rabat, Salé, Kenitra, and Marrakesh. Al-Fassi was exiled to Gabon, where he remained until 1946; the other prisoners were soon released. A period of uneasy calm and relative economic prosperity, at least for the French community and the wealthy Moroccan merchant class, followed until World War II.

THE WAR YEARS AND ISTIQLAL

When war broke out in 1939, Sultan Mohammed V pledged loyalty and support to France and the Allies against the Axis. The fall of France and the defeat of Vichy authorities in the American landings of November, 1942, weakened the French position in Moroccan eyes. During the Casablanca Conference of January, 1943, the sultan managed to hold a personal conversation with President Roosevelt without General Nogues' being present. This aroused hopes among the nationalists that perhaps Washington would support Moroccan independence after the war, and probably Roosevelt did make some such offer. This conversation, which Elliott Roosevelt related in *As He Saw It,* did much to strengthen a long tradition of anti-American and anti-British feeling among the French *colons* and administration in Morocco.

At the end of 1943, French control seemed to the nationalists to have weakened so considerably that Balafrej, Mohammed al-Fassi, the vice-rector of the Kairouyine, a relative of Allal, and a group of other Moroccans, many of whom had signed the Demand for Moroccan Reforms in 1934, decided to form the *Istiqlal,* or Independence Party.

Their manifesto, a historic turning point for Morocco, was submitted to the sultan, the resident-general, and the British and American consuls on January 11, 1944. It emphasized the nation's religious and political unity, declared that Morocco had earned its freedom through its aid to the Allied cause, and demanded Moroccan independence, adherence to the Atlantic Charter, and participation in the peace conference. It asked the sultan "to take under his high direction the reform movement which is necessary to ensure the progress of the country and leaves it up to His Majesty to establish a democratic regime comparable to the regimes of government adopted in the Moslem countries of the Orient, guaranteeing the rights of all elements and all classes of Moroccan society and defining the futures of each one."

French military intelligence agents arrested Balafrej and several other nationalist leaders, accusing them of co-operation with the Germans. They were never tried by a military court but were deported, Balafrej to Corsica. Uprisings of considerable violence erupted in Rabat, Fez, and many other cities. To force the submission of the old walled portion of Fez, the French authorities cut off its electricity and water supplies. The Kairouyine and most of the religious colleges were closed *sine die*. A deep split opened between the protectorate authorities and the nationalists. The Istiqlal militants still at liberty went underground, each swearing "by God before the Koran to remain faithful to my religion, my country, my King, and the Party, to observe discipline and keep party secrets." [4]

THE SULTAN AND THE *COUP DE FORCE*

The next important step in the unification of the national movement behind Mohammed V was the royal visit in 1947 to Tangier, under international rule again after occupation by General Franco's forces during the war years 1940–45. The king and his eldest son, Prince Mulay Hasan, intended to assert the territorial unity of Morocco and their rule over all three zones by short stopovers in the Spanish zone. Just before they left, on April 7, some Senegalese troops of a French detachment and a group of Arabs came to blows in Casablanca over the price asked by a prostitute. A massacre by the Senegalese ensued. Some nationalists claimed the incident was a premeditated provocation by the French. In any case, the sultan was so angry that in his speech at Tangier he omitted the ceremonial words of praise for French achievements in Morocco at the end. He clearly underlined Morocco's role as an "Arab nation, closely linked to the Arab East" and praised the Arab League.

[4] *Manifeste du Parti d l'Istiqlal* (*Hizb al-Istqlal*, Party Documents, Rabat, n.d.).

Prince Hasan and the Princess Aissha, who was already appearing in public unveiled to symbolize the emancipation of women, also made nationalistic speeches to enthusiastic crowds. Paris was horrified. The relatively liberal resident-general, Erik Labonne, was recalled and replaced by General Alphonse-Pierre Juin, the son of a French gendarme of Algeria who always felt that, if anything was needed in North Africa, it was more gendarmes.

The Maghreb Liberation Bureau, now reinforced by al-Fassi and Abd al-Krim, formed in Cairo. Intense propaganda began in the Middle East on behalf of North Africa. General Juin and the sultan played a game of hide-and-go-seek, Juin trying to maneuver Mohammed into signing numerous decrees which would have reformed the protectorate administration toward more Moroccan participation in some respects, but which also would have given political power to Morocco's French residents.

Religious tension sharpened: the most dramatic incident was the arrest of an imam of a Rabat mosque, Sheikh Abd al-Wahad ibn Abdallah, for having, in a Friday prayer, called upon Joan of Arc to help Moroccan Islam in its time of trial. Juin ordered his arrest, and he was sentenced to eighteen months in prison for having tried to exploit a Christian saint for subversive purposes. Al-Fassi alerted the Vatican: Msgr. Amadée Lefèvre, who had been apostolic vicar in Rabat since 1947, helped to intercede for the sheikh's release, which came after he had served four months of his sentence.

In 1951, Juin, backed by powerful economic interests in the French community and allied with some of the powerful chiefs, like al-Glawi, forced Mohammed V to sign some of the reform measures. Juin brought the mountain tribesmen to Rabat. He made it clear to Mohammed V that there would be a conspiracy to dethrone him if he did not sign. The king was forced to disavow the Istiqlal in writing; later he told a correspondent of the Egyptian newspaper *Al-Ahram* that he had acted under constraint. Islah and Istiqlal now formed a national front, pledging to fight for independence and agreeing not to collaborate with the Moroccan Communist Party.

The new solidarity of the Maghreb national movements was demonstrated in December, 1952, when the murder of Ferhat Hashed, a Tunisian trade-union leader, provoked labor demonstrations and riots in Casablanca. The local French administrator, Boniface, and the new French resident-general, Augustin Guillaume, used the occasion to arrest hundreds of Istiqlal leaders, especially those like Mahjoub ben Seddik and Abderrahim Bouabid, who had been concerned with trade-union matters, and some Communists. Bouabid, who became a cabinet minister under several of the post-independence governments and then, in 1960, a leader of the new socialist opposition movement, told me how American missionaries visited him in the Kenitra Prison and brought him copies of the Bible in French.

KITTANI AND THE SUFI ORDERS

The sultan, realizing that the Sufi orders were, largely speaking, a reactionary force, took strong action against them. Even before the Berber Dahir, the French had used them to weaken orthodox, "official" Islam which backed the throne. The protectorate authorities encouraged the building of new *zawiyas*. In 1946, the sultan forbade establishment of new orders or the construction of new *zawiyas* without royal permission. The learned and wealthy Sharif Abdelhai al-Kittani, chief of the Kittaniya Order, one of whose relatives had been put to death by the king forty years earlier, now took his revenge: he constituted a league of orders called the *Confréries d'Afrique du Nord.* Kittani worked closely with some of the most retrograde elements of the protectorate administration and the Glawi to remove the sultan. Just before the month of Ramadan, 1953, the alliance circulated a petition demanding the sultan's dethronement for "crimes against Islam." It got hundreds of signatures.

Many of the Sufi orders were more or less compromised in this plot. On August 11, when the conspiracy was already far advanced, Kittani and the Glawi gave it a pseudo-religious flavor by sacrificing two black bulls at the sacred mountain of Zerhoun and swearing an oath on the tomb of Mulay Idris to depose the sultan. Military force and a military flavor were added by a great mass rally of the Berber tribes on the Middle Atlas Plateau of Tiz'n Tretten.

On August 15, the Glawi, Kittani, and their allies met in Marrakesh and proclaimed Mulay Mohammed ben Arafa, the sultan's uncle, "Imam of the Faithful," just a step short of anti-sultan. Nationalist protests against this grave rupture of Moroccan religious unity degenerated into riots in Casablanca, Rabat, Marrakesh, and other towns. Near Oujda, the entire tribe of the Banu Snassen revolted, provoking major French military intervention. In Paris, Foreign Minister Georges Bidault first forbade General Guillaume to depose the sultan, then changed his mind.[5] The arrest and forcible deportation of the sultan and his family, first to Corsica, then to Madagascar, took place August 20, 1953. To make matters worse in Moroccan eyes, this happened to be the date of the Id al-Adna, Islam's most important feast, commemorating the Biblical and Koranic sacrifice of Abraham. France, bound by international treaty to defend the integrity of the throne and the state religion, had instead violated both. The *ulama* of Fez recognized the succession of the puppet sultan, Ben Arafa, though some of them had to be locked up for several days before they would sign the *beya,* or act of submission.

Most of the known Istiqlal leaders were in prison. When, within a few months, armed terrorism began, it was the work of lesser known or unknown individuals, sometimes acting on their own, such as one killed by a palace guard as he tried to stab Ben Arafa, or of small clandestine cells under Istiqlal or sometimes Communist influence. The brilliant Tangier lawyer, Abderrahman Yusefi, and Mohammed Basri, nicknamed "the teacher," organized resistance from bases in the Spanish zone.

The Spanish authorities had never recognized the sultan's deposition. A guerilla Liberation Army in the Rif, the Atlas Mountains, and the southern desert was formed and its cadremen trained at Nador, Spanish Morocco. In August, 1955, as the French administration began to realize the extent of the terrible error it had committed and to seek a formula to bring back Mohammed V, now a national martyr and almost a saint in popular eyes, some of the Atlas Berbers revolted. At the same moment, the FLN in Algeria launched major attacks that took many French lives.

Liberal French journalists and intellectuals like François Mauriac and Louis Massignon exerted continual pressure on the

[5] The secret official telegrams concerned were cited by the Paris newspaper *L'Express* of August 20, 1955.

French government, which tried to set up a Regency Council. Then, after a consultation with Moroccan nationalists and others at Aix-les-Bains, King Mohammed V, as he was soon to be called, was flown back from Madagascar by the French government. After being treated with honors in Paris—during which al-Glawi humiliated himself in public and asked Mohammed V for pardon—he returned to his throne in Rabat, amid scenes of mass rejoicing that were singularly free from anti-European violence. France revoked the Protectorate Treaty and, on March 2, 1956, recognized Moroccan independence and the end of the Treaty of Fez. After some hesitation and tough negotiations with Mohammed V, General Franco did the same for the Spanish zone on April 7, 1956. The sovereignty and political unity of the Sharifian Empire had been restored: cultural and economic unity, though not real economic independence, came gradually during the years that followed, as the long revolution in Algeria raged next door.

INDEPENDENCE: THE MONARCHY CONSOLIDATES ITS POWER

The story of Morocco's first decade of new-found political freedom—economically Morocco remains closely tied to French and to other Western business and financial interests—belongs to political history. It has been well told in some of the newspapers and by such writers as Nevill Barbour and Rom Landau. But a word is in order here about the coexistence of the various religious communities and some of the ethnoreligious problems which Mohammed V and his son, Hasan II, who succeeded him in March, 1961, have had to face.

The "Berber question," as French journalists and historians like to call it, has reappeared at various times since 1956. It began mainly as Berber opposition to the traditional elite of Fez, which made up a large part of the predominantly Istiqlal administration during the first years of independence. Addi Ou Bihi, the Berber governor of Tafilalet, with some encouragement from a few French officers, led one short-lived revolt against Istiqlal control in 1957. Other rebellions erupted in the fall of 1958 in the Rif Mountains and among Berber tribes of Rabat province. Another local insurrectional movement broke out in the Beni Mellal region in 1960. This was the same year that the new socialist party, the National Union of Popular Forces, was first accused of plotting against the monarchy. In none of these cases was Morocco's religious unity an issue.

Morocco's Jewish population, which shrank through emigration from over 300,000 to about 60,000 in 1964, posed a different sort of problem. Favored in educational and economic matters by the French, only a few Moroccan Jews took part in the independence movement. To carry out his promise that Moroccan Jews would enjoy complete equality with the Moslems, Mohammed V appointed a Jewish physician of Casablanca, Dr. Léon Benzaquen, as his first Minister of Posts and Telegraphs. But Morocco's adherence to the Arab League in 1958, despite considerable Moroccan mistrust of Nasserism and the United Arab Republic, brought anti-Zionism into favor as official doctrine, and Jews gradually left or were weeded out of high posts. There were occasions when the Istiqlal party press, generally under the direct influence of Allal al-Fassi, would attack clandestine emigration to Israel or other matters as examples of the "ingratitude" of Moroccan Jews for their good treatment. At such times, the border line between anti-Semitism and anti-Zionism often became quite thin indeed. Such was the case, for example, during the Moroccan parliamentary elections of May, 1963, when Istiqlal, then in strong opposition to the regime of King Hasan, "warned" its followers that "Moroccan Jews have been told to support the FDIC" (the official royalist party).

THE CHRISTIAN CHURCHES AND MOROCCAN INDEPENDENCE

The Vatican saw Moroccan independence coming. On September 14, 1955, two months before Mohammed V returned from exile, the Holy See appointed Louis Amédée Lefèvre archbishop, placing him directly under the authority of Rome. Lefèvre, who was still archbishop in 1965, was well liked by Mohammed V, the royal family, and many of the nationalists because of his frequent reminders to French Christians that they had Christian duties toward their neighbors and his disapproval, expressed in several pastoral letters, of the "counterterrorism" of some lawless European elements, mainly Corsicans and others of the poorer, lower-class European settlers. Archbishop Lefèvre kept intact the parish structure, which consisted of about fifty parish churches, that existed before independence. However, with the total Catholic population of all European nationals down to about 220,000 at the end of 1964, the problem of adapting Morocco's relatively large clergy to the new situation became more acute, especially since priests were urgently needed in other places, such as Latin America.

Whereas some of the Protestant missionary groups still dream of establishing a "native Moroccan Church," the Catholics, as in Algeria and Tunisia, now have abandoned all attempts at evangelization. Baptisms of Moroccans, even those seeking it, are forbidden by episcopal order. The Catholic Church now concentrates on charitable, educational, and, above all, social work among young people in maintaining a "Christian presence." Toumliline Monastery, a Benedictine priory founded in 1952 in the Middle Atlas Mountains, has become an outstanding example of this new "Christian presence" by means of its encouragement of interfaith contacts and its patient work with needy or knowledge-hungry Moroccan youth. At its summer courses, scholars, writers, and artists from all over the world have gathered to meet and discuss the world's problems with each other, with the monks led by Prior Dom Denis Martin, and with the Moroccans who attend.

In August, 1957, King Mohammed V received participants in the Toumliline summer course, telling them

> Morocco is a country which has always practiced religious tolerance permitting numerous religions to enjoy liberty and dignity. In particular, Christianity and Islam live side by side in Morocco, working together in a climate of co-operation, friendship and serenity and collaborating for the well-being and happiness of humanity, spreading everywhere the Divine prescriptions and preaching the attachment to sacred, humanitarian principles and to higher moral values. The pursuit of this work constitutes the best guarantee of humanity's safeguard.[6]

[6] Quoted in *Images de Toumliline*, a special brochure published in Rabat (July, 1950).

In 1963, shortly after passage of a new penal code which allows the government to imprison anyone from three to six years for "seducing" a Moslem to abandon his faith and which might some day be used to suspend all missionary activity in Morocco, a European visitor asked Dom Denis Martin whether Toumliline ever "made Christians" out of its many Moslem visitors. "No," replied Dom Martin, "but many of them go away better Moslems than they were."

The first years, during which Dom Martin and some of the other monks often visited Europe and the United States, seeking support for Toumliline, were fruitful ones. The priory became nearly self-supporting by cultivating some four hundred acres of orchards, by beekeeping, and by raising chickens originally donated by the Homeland Foundation in the United States.

At Dom Martin's request, Toumliline's jurisdictional ties to its French order were broken, and it now comes under the direct control of the Subiaco congregation. When participation of young Moroccans in its courses fell off in 1958 and 1959, Dom Martin asked Abderrahim Bouabid, then vice-premier, if Toumliline should continue the summer course. After all, he recalled, the Benedictines were Morocco's guests. If their services were not wanted, they should not impose them. Bouabid assured them that their work was valuable and should continue, and even helped to plan the following summer's session.

In 1958, such varied speakers as Princess Aissha, Mulay Ahmed Alaoui, the effervescent Minister of Information and Tourism, and the socialist leader Mehdi ben Barka—convicted in 1963 of being the "brains" of a plot against Hasan II—all took part in the summer session, together with such visitors as Professor Daniel MacCall of Boston University, the late Father John La Farge, the Jesuit scholar, and Jesuits and Dominicans from the Middle East. Visits of Protestant clergymen or laymen were also frequent.

TUNISIA: FROM ISLAMISM TO BOURGUIBISM

Of all the North African revolutions, the one in Tunisia has had the fewest religious overtones. This has been due to the secular mindedness of most of the Tunisian leaders and also to the restraint and a dislike of religious conflict on both the French and Tunisian sides. Nevertheless, just as in Algeria and Morocco, the Tunisian revolution began about 1930 on a strongly religious note.

In 1930, Archbishop Lemaître of Carthage, former chaplain to Negro troops in a Senegalese unit of the French army and a brigadier general in the reserve, decided to hold the Eucharistic Congress at Carthage, with great pomp and circumstance. Thousands of European children were dressed up in uniform, and some of the participating priests added to the general crusading atmosphere by wearing crosses. When Moslem students of the Zitouna Mosque and the Saddiki College protested the holding of the congress by a strike and demonstrations, the police made arrests. More than one hundred Tunisians signed a protest which alleged that the congress was the start of "a violent Crusade against Islam in North Africa." [7] A sense of resurrecting the North African Christian past, at least some Moslems thought, was also to be found in the archeological work being done at Carthage and at other early Christian sites and in the historical work of such scholars as Stephen Gsell, who wrote about the power and prosperity of Africa's pre-Moslem days.

The Eucharistic Congress gave young nationalists like Habib Bourguiba, the lawyer son of an army officer, who, like Ferhat Abbas, had studied in Paris and later married a French woman, a weapon against the religious traditionalists. Since the Mufti of Tunis had been invited and had accepted, and a few of the Moslem dignitaries had gone so far as to march in the procession with the bishops, Bourguiba's attacks bore a sharper sting. The Vatican replaced Archbishop Lemaître with his coadjutor, but the damage was done.

Added to this was the naturalization question. Since before World War I, many Tunisians had the possibility of acquiring French nationality if they wished. Many had served in the French army or had married French women. Some had requested that they remain subject to the *sharia* even after naturalization. The French did not permit this. The Moslem Congress in Jerusalem had just decided to fight against naturalization of Moslems in French-ruled territories. Trouble started when a naturalized Moslem, the husband of a French woman, died at Bizerte. The Mufti of Bizerte, who

[7] *As-Sanab* (Tunis, May 16, 1930).

was looking for a way to get out of his job, forbade the burial of the man in the Moslem cemetery. But when the French authorities insisted, a demonstration took place at the cemetery: the naturalized man was called a renegade. There was a wave of such incidents in the year 1933, and the nationalists feared that France planned to "assimilate" Tunisia.

Habib Bourguiba, born at Monastir on July 3, 1903, and educated in Tunis and Paris, now came to the forefront of the Destour, the Tunisian nationalist party. With Mahmud Materi, a physician, he led a revolt against the old guard of the party and founded the Neo-Destour in 1934. It was far more secular minded and modern in outlook than the old Destour, of which Sheikh Taalbi became the principal spokesman and which drew upon the wealthy bourgeoisie of Tunis and the conservatives of Kairawan and the Zitouna Mosque University for its support. The Neo-Destourians came from families of artisans, fishermen, merchants, small farmers, schoolteachers, and civil servants.

The Popular Front government in France brought a liberalization of the protectorate for a time. In 1936, Bourguiba suggested in a note to Pierre Vienot, a Tunisophile in the French foreign ministry and, in a public speech several weeks later, that Tunisia should be given her independence, following which she would sign a treaty guaranteeing French interests their position in the country. Much of Bourguiba's later career was spent in trying to reassure both the French government and the French and Jewish communities of Tunisia that the Neo-Destour did not intend to throw the country into the arms of the Axis. He proved his sincerity in this during the war.

Sheikh Taalbi returned from exile in 1937, but Bourguiba and his friends had assured the Neo-Destour's supremacy. When the Popular Front government fell, French policy got tough and, accordingly, so did the Neo-Destour's. After demonstrations and repression, there was a serious riot in Tunis in April, 1938. Bourguiba and other principal Neo-Destourians were arrested and court-martialed. Bourguiba began a long imprisonment and exile which finally ended only after World War II. In 1939, Tunisia found itself in the forefront of Mussolini's designs on the Mediterranean coastal areas. Tunisia was under the rule of a new bey, Moncef, who sympathized with the Destourians. Moncef managed to avoid becoming too closely involved with the Axis troops, and few Tunisians collaborated actively with the Axis. But the Tunisians were dismayed when the Allied victory brought the return of French troops in force, the departure of the other Allies, and, seemingly, the end of hopes for independence or even a genuine Tunisian administration.

The Germans had liberated Bourguiba from prison in Marseilles and sent him to Rome. The Italians tried unsuccessfully to get him to make radio broadcasts in support of the Axis. They let him return to Tunis in 1943. The French deported Moncef Bey, just as they were to deport Morocco's Mohammed V ten years later, for acting too independently. The nationalists were disorganized and discouraged. Bourguiba left for Egypt and toured the world, trying to stir support for the Tunisian cause. This was the period when Egyptian and Arab League distrust for Bourguiba began, since he was always ready to make a compromise or a tactical retreat when he felt it suited his cause. The chief advocate in the Neo-Destour of a tough anti-French and pan-Arab policy was Bourguiba's old friend, Salah ben Yusuf.

After French Premier Robert Schumann promised Tunisia internal autonomy in 1950, carrot and stick succeeded one another rapidly in French policy. In 1952, Bourguiba was arrested and deported again. But under liberal French governors, the Destour was able to make gains and secure reforms, especially new opportunities for Tunisian civil servants. Upon many occasions, Father André Demeerseman, director of the White Fathers' Institute of Belles Lettres Arabes (IBLA) at Tunis, gave important assistance to the Neo-Destour. Archbishop Maurice Perrin, from his seat at Carthage, encouraged contacts between the nationalists and the French community and administration whenever he could, just as many of the Catholics under Archbishop Lefèvre were doing in Morocco. Some of the die-hard "ultras" in the French community demanded Demeerseman's expulsion for his "pro-Arab political activity."

Terrorism against French police and Tunisians who collaborated with the French arose just as it had in Morocco. French "counter-terrorists" and organized Tunisian guerilla bands in the mountains (the *fellagha* or "bandits," which later became a title of honor in

Tunisia) now appeared. Upon this troubled scene, the visit of the liberal French Premier Pierre Mendès-France in July, 1954, worked like a soothing balm: negotiations were to begin immediately for internal autonomy and a new convention to regulate French interests. The talks were long and complicated. Bourguiba was released and allowed to follow its latter stages in Paris. He made a triumphal return to Tunis at the beginning of June, 1955, just before agreements were signed. Salah ben Yusuf, who had fled to Egypt, returned to lead a violent campaign against both the conventions and Bourguiba, whom he called a "traitor." His followers even assassinated some of Bourguiba's associates and organized another armed guerilla movement which co-operated with the rebels in Algeria. After France granted Morocco its independence in March, 1956, the position of Bourguiba and of the Tunisian Premier, Tahar ben Ammar, very soon became so difficult that they prevailed upon the socialist government in Paris to sign another protocol granting Tunisia full independence.

On July 25, 1957, Bourguiba, then premier, and the Tunisian National Assembly, which was controlled by the Neo-Destour Party, deposed Lamine Bey, the successor of Moncef, and abolished the monarchy. Under the constitution promulgated June 1, 1959, Tunisia became a republic. "Its religion is Islam, its language Arabic. . . . The Republic," says Article Two, "constitutes a part of the Greater Maghreb, for the unity of which it works in the common interest." Article Five lays the basis both for religious liberty and for measures which are taken, from time to time, against the Christian missionaries: it "guarantees the dignity of the individual and liberty of conscience and protects the free exercise of cults, under the reservations that they do not disturb public order." Only a Moslem can be President of the Republic: Bourguiba, the only candidate, was elected by 91 per cent of the registered voters in November, 1959, and re-elected in November, 1964.

Just as in Morocco, the Algerian war brought suspension of most French financial and technical aid and its replacement by American assistance. It also brought frequent crises in Tunisian-French relations, the gravest being three days of fierce warfare over the French air and naval base at Bizerte in July, 1961. This resulted in a mass exodus of French and Italian residents and even of Tunisian Jews, who previously had shown little inclination to emigrate, even though they were free to do so. The resulting disruption of the large French educational establishment and of French technical assistance, which was beginning to resume, set back Tunisia's economic and cultural progress considerably. The tension eased, and the Bizerte affair was completely settled by the French evacuation in December, 1963, which Presidents Bourguiba, Nasser, and Ben Bella celebrated in lavish ceremonies at Bizerte.

CHURCH-STATE RELATIONS SINCE INDEPENDENCE

It was in Tunisia that the Roman Catholic Church in North Africa held its largest material stake. It faced a government which in general was better disposed toward it than it was toward the Protestant missionaries.

The rapprochement between Bourguiba and the Catholic Church began in 1956, immediately after independence. As in Morocco, the Holy See removed the Archbishop of Carthage from the French hierarchy and put it under Rome. Archbishop Perrin, Father Demeerseman, and Bourguiba agreed that it was time to begin detaching the Catholic Church from French secular power. Father Demeerseman approached Bourguiba with the idea, which was Archbishop Perrin's, of quietly removing the statue of Cardinal Lavigerie, for Tunisians the symbol of the old attachment, from its strategic position at the gateway to the Tunis *medina,* the old Arab quarter. Bourguiba, who has a house next door to the White Fathers' Mission in Tunis, agreed wholeheartedly. On a dark April night in 1956, the statue mysteriously disappeared, removed to seclusion on church property on the Hill of Byrsa, in Carthage.

As far back as 1948, Tunisians had been working with Demeerseman and his colleagues in a study group at IBLA. A nucleus of three Tunisians swelled to two hundred and fifty. Yvon Hamel, a Canadian pilgrim on his way to Palestine, volunteered to teach, and entered the White Fathers' seminary at Carthage. IBLA keeps religion out of its classes unless one faith asks questions about the other. In line with Catholic policy throughout the Maghreb, there is no proselytizing.

In 1964, one of the countless delicate tasks facing Pope Paul VI in improving relations with the non-Catholic world was completion of talks which began in 1963 on a new status for the Catholic Church in Tunisia. By now, Tunisia had only about 60,000 communicants as against 225,000 in 1953; yet there were hundreds of churches and many empty parishes. Bourguiba had met Pope John XXIII early in 1959, and it was tacitly agreed that old accords between the Vatican and the French protectorate authorities ought to be replaced.

In 1959, Bourguiba said he intended to conclude an agreement "defining the method of appointing the chief of the Catholic community, the status of church property and of its educational institutions." Tunisian leaders objected especially to continuance of French government subsidies to the churches in Tunisia. In June, 1961, just before the Bizerte crisis, the Tunis weekly newspaper *Afrique-Action* published an unsigned article entitled "The Failure of Saint Augustine," posing the question of the past association between Catholic Christianity and Western imperialism in strong terms. The writer of the article was Father Alfred Berenger, the Algerian secular priest who at that time, with permission from Rome, was a sort of chaplain to the FLN leaders and military forces based in Tunisia. Later he became a deputy in the Algerian National Assembly and a confidential adviser to Premier Ahmed ben Bella.

The Bizerte conflict interrupted contacts. Then, in 1962, Bourguiba saw Pope John again. In February, 1963, Tunisian Foreign Minister Mongi Slim reached agreement with the pope on the opening of talks. The Vatican sent Msgr. Luiggi Poggi, a special counselor, to Tunis. The Tunisians made it known that they wished to nationalize the Thibar agricultural colony within five years of the signature of the agreement.

Agreement was finally reached in June, 1964. A large majority of the churches in smaller towns or villages were turned over to the control of the Tunisian government, which expected to turn them into libraries or museums. All properties, such as the Thibar estates, were ceded "courteously"—in the phrasing of the agreement—to the Tunisian state. Some thirteen Catholic schools and colleges, with 14,000 students including 6,500 Moslems, were not affected. They already had a legal existence under Tunisian education laws.

CHAPTER XXIII

RELIGION AND REVOLUTION IN ALGERIA

> Algeria, conscious of its economic, cultural, and political vocation, will be a democracy which will admit diversity of races, religions, and opinions.
>
> THE FLN, May, 1956

From the first uprisings in the Aurès Mountains on November 1, 1954, All Saints' Day, down to the first year of independence in 1962–63, a curious dualism marked the attitude of the Algerian nationalists concerning religious matters. While frequently speaking their propaganda of "the holy war for liberty" and even calling their official newspaper *Al-Moujahid* (*al-Mudjahid,* "fighter for the faith"), virtually all of the leaders of the National Liberation Front (FLN), which in 1963 became Algeria's official ruling party and the only legal one, have steadily insisted that the war had nothing to do with religion and that all faiths would be respected in the new Algeria.

The Islamic flavor of the FLN's program is strong throughout. In the first comprehensive statement of its goals, it spoke of the need to "realize North African unity within its natural Arabo-Moslem framework." *Al-Moujahid,* especially in its Arabic-language edition, repeatedly mentioned what Algerian nationalists whom I met in their places of exile in Morocco and Tunisia liked to call Algeria's "national Islamic culture."

At the same time, the FLN did its best to reassure the Christian and Jewish minorities that this was not a religious war or an "outlaw" movement, as the official French propaganda was painting it. In an open "Letter to the French," in 1956, the FLN reiterated that "the Algerian resistance movement, which is holding in check a half million soldiers of a modern army, cannot be the work of a few 'bandits' with no other popular credit than the terror which they are supposed to inspire. Nor does it have anything to do with the odious imagery in which a specifically Moslem religious fanaticism is supposed to be multiplied by an all-consuming will to power and by the dream of an Algeria breaking away from Western control in order to be dissolved into a vast and conquering Arab Empire. No: the Algerian revolution is not a holy war, but a campaign of liberation."[1]

The most important basic text of the revolution was the "Platform" drafted mainly by the late Abban Ramdane. It was adopted at a secret FLN congress held in the Valley of the Soummam, in the Kabylie Mountains, on August 20, 1956. On religion, it said:

> Our revolution is not a civil or a religious war. The revolutionary demarcation line is not drawn between the religious communities which make up Algeria, but between the partisans of liberty, of justice, and human dignity on the one hand and the colonialists and their backers on the other, regardless of their religion and special condition.[2]

The Evian peace agreements signed by France and the FLN on March 18, 1962, solemnly pledged Algeria to guarantee "the liberty of the Catholic, Protestant, and Jewish religions." And when the independent Algerian state adopted its first constitution by popular referendum in September, 1963, it consecrated both Algeria's Arabic and Moslem character and the freedom of religion. Though President Ben Bella has taken a very strong stand against Israel and all but thirty thousand Jews had left for France, Israel, or elsewhere by 1963, the regime has nearly always made a distinction between the Algerian Jewish community and the Zionist state.

Like the constitutions of practically every new state in Africa and Asia, the Algerian one reflects the memory of Algeria's colonial past. Among the fundamental objectives in Article Nine are "Elimination of all vestiges of colonialism, defense against all discrimination, especially that founded on race and religion." Some of the memories of a century of French domination will be long in dying.

[1] "Lettre du FLN aux Français," mimeographed tract, Algiers (?), 1957.

[2] The Soummam Platform, printed clandestinely in an undated tract in French and Arabic (1957).

Article One, after stating Algeria's fundamental nature as a "democratic and popular republic" and "an integral part of the Arab world and of Africa," says that "Islam is the state religion. The republic guarantees to everyone the respect of his opinions and his beliefs, and the free exercise of cults."

The basic texts would thus seem to bear out what the Abbé Berenger told me in February, 1962, a few months before independence: "The churches have a unique chance to meet Islam on equal terms in Algeria. The possibilities for a real Moslem-Christian dialogue are immense."

But how immense are they, really? And how will the chances look after the first difficult years are over and the first agonizing reappraisals, the first judgments of the tiny Christian minority, have been made? Before trying to answer this, we ought first to look at the role which both Islam and Christianity played in the revolution.

CHANGING ISLAM: THE RELIGIOUS REVIVAL

Everyone who spent any time in Algeria during the war years knows the very large part Islam played in arousing national feeling. It crystallized the vast but vague discontent of the mass of people into the precise national pattern which the FLN leaders—a tiny minority at the outset—wished it to take. From 1955 on, and especially as the revolution gained support in certain rural districts that had been indifferent or hostile to it at the outset, mosque attendance noticeably increased. As a young student, a member of the FLN underground network who was constantly risking capture, torture, and imprisonment, told me in Orléansville in 1958, "Certainly I go to service on Fridays. Everyone in the family says their prayers, whereas we rarely did before. Prayers are part of our civic duties."

Though the French authorities systematically blocked all legal entry of the literature and periodicals of the Arab countries, millions of Algerians listened daily to radio broadcasts from Cairo, Damascus, and other Arab capitals. The Arabic and Kabylie-speaking programs of Radio Algiers, including the official Friday prayers said by the French-installed imam or mufti, were listened to in many places as before the war. But any listeners' poll would probably have shown very low audience ratings for the programs of news and propaganda. People listened to the news programs from Arab capitals instead. French development of Algerian television during the last two years of the war partially offset this, but only in the case of the tiny minority of Algerian Moslems—perhaps a few hundred—who could afford this expensive plaything of the Europeans.

The prospect of Algeria's return to the Arab family of nations was a source of excitement to the younger generation. They listened to the foreign broadcasts and disseminated the clandestine FLN propaganda in cafés, shops, and classrooms. Despite constant persecution and eventual economic strangulation by the French authorities, the Association of *Ulama* managed to open several new schools in the early war years. One was the Dar Al-Hadith College in Tlemcen, which began classes in 1956.

The mosques, where the faithful were sometimes safe from police spies, were often the gathering places for nationalists who dared not risk meeting in public anywhere else. As a result, the French administration was usually unwilling to meet a tremendous increase in requests for funds to finance the building of new mosques. "They pretend to keep out of politics," said one French official about the Moslem "clergy" in 1961, "but they are really the very heart of the rebellion."

Though the *khutba,* or political sermon, was forbidden practice which could land its author in jail or a concentration camp, many an imam took the risk. After the Bizerte tragedy in Tunisia in August, 1961, one preacher in the mosque of Tebessa, near the Tunisian border, abjured his flock to "pray for the Moslem victims." The imam of the Grand Mosque of Algiers, in September, 1961, summoned the faithful after some particularly murderous deeds by the Secret Army Organization (OAS) against Moslems in Oran to "pray for our brothers, killed in cowardly fashion in Oran . . . they will be avenged sooner or later, by God or by men." Members of the official religious hierarchy who were too open in antinationalist propaganda or who had compromised themselves gravely with the French administration were killed by the FLN. One was the Mufti of Bône, shot in the Grand Mosque of Bône on August 15, 1961.

An FLN acquaintance assured me that the preachers in the mosques gave valuable help in keeping the Moslem populace of Algiers from undertaking a mass insurrection which would have resulted in great loss of life in April, 1961. This was during the anti-de Gaulle *putsch,* when a junta led by Generals Maurice Challe and Raoul Salan, later the chief of the OAS, took and briefly held power in Algeria, hoping to topple President de Gaulle from power in France.

Especially during the early years of the war, the FLN frequently ordered boycotts, based on both national and religious motives, of such French-produced and -controlled products as tobacco. One prominent Moslem citizen of Constantine showed me a tract he had received in the mail forbidding him to play cards or dominoes (both made in France); to use "discs of dishonesty" (phonograph records of "profane" popular music, recorded in France: Egyptian jazz records, if they could be obtained, were all right); to drink alcoholic drinks (revival of the traditional Koranic prohibition); or to frequent cafés, cinemas, or football games managed by Europeans. The possible penalty was well known: death from a grenade or a bullet fired by one of the *fidayeen* (redeemers), the official FLN term for its terrorists.

At the same time, the countercampaign waged by the famous "Fifth Bureau," or Psychological Warfare Service of the French army, was capable of such feats as printing up entire fake numbers of *Al-Moujahid* or issuing false boycott orders. One of these, against bottled lemonade made by Mozabites, was described in a tract published by Wilaya (District) IV of the Army of National Liberation (the ALN, military arm of the FLN) as "false, against the national interest, and designed to turn the different ethnic and religious groups against one another." The same French services, of course, constantly magnified and exploited to the full some very real dissensions between Berber and Arab leaders inside the FLN and the ALN. "The struggle between the Kabylie and the Arab clans" was a constant theme of French propagandists.

One politicoreligious prescription which the nationalists enforced whenever they could was the closing of shops on Friday, the Moslem sabbath. Many a shopkeeper, even one who considered himself a devout Moslem, would complain that closing both on

Friday and on the obligatory official holiday, Sunday, was ruining a business to which the war had already dealt critical blows.

THE ROLE OF THE SUFI ORDERS

We have already seen how a leader of the Sanusiya Order, instead of preaching the holy war against France as of old, had turned about and supported French policy. Some of the other Sufi brotherhoods disobeyed nationalist orders and more or less actively supported the French administration. Occasionally they would brave FLN orders against "maraboutism" and make a pilgrimage to a sanctuary or the tomb of a saint. While in Oran in the summer of 1961, I remember seeing a few of the thirty thousand pilgrims leaving for the tomb of Sidi Mohammed ibn Awada at Tiaret, in the southern part of Oran Department. The reward which these pilgrims got for their observance—a vestige, perhaps, of pre-Islamic paganism—was the explosion of an FLN grenade which left three dead and twenty wounded.

Besides the Sanusiya, the Rahmaniya, another Algerian order, especially its *zawiya* at Biskra, backed the French. The Darkawa Order assassinated its pro-French sheikh, a Moroccan named Si Ali al-Kabir and moved firmly into the FLN camp, as did the Amariya, the Kadiriya, and the Alawiya. The Taibiya, an order whose principal influence was around Nedroma in Oran Department, tried to stay neutral and preach a reconciliation between the Moslem and European communities. In Biskra, the largest remaining community in Algeria of heretical Ibadites, the anti-FLN minority faction which owed allegiance to Messali Hadj, the so-called Algerian National Movement (NMA), had its major stronghold. It was reduced by armed ALN action at the end of the war.

Since independence, the Sufi orders have been the first Islamic institutions to suffer from the wave of secularism which is sweeping over Algeria. But they have not been alone. The orthodox Islamic "hierarchy" (officially there is none in Islam, but the term is convenient to denote the government-supported imam or mufti), as well as the nationalist religious leaders themselves, have also suffered great losses of prestige and influence. Some of this loss may stem from the lack of enthusiasm shown by many of the leaders of religious thought, such as they were, for the revolution. A great deal of it, in my opinion, comes from the vast amount of Marxist propaganda, some of which has been made official doctrine, imported by the political leaders of the "exile army," the sixty thousand men who spent much or all of the war in Morocco or Tunisia, unable to cross the French mine fields and electrified frontier barriers defended by crack French army units and who spent much of their time infusing their troops with the teachings of Marx and Mao Tse-tung. I saw copies of writings of both men when I visited the mountain headquarters of one guerilla chief south of Algiers in June, 1962.

The only member of the Association of *Ulama* who still remained in a position of power or responsibility in 1963 was Tewfik al-Madani, the Algerian poet and religious philosopher who had represented the FLN at Arab League headquarters in Cairo during the war years. "Conditions have changed now," he told me during a conversation in Algiers. "The reformist *ulama* have done their job. We woke up the nation in the thirties and the forties. Now there is a regular Algerian government and our main role has ended." Madani was a cabinet officer in Ben Bella's government—the Minister of Habus (religious properties).

Religion, both traditional and otherwise, has been tremendously, perhaps critically, weakened by the war and its aftermath. In villages of southern Oran Department, the same ones in which Charles de Foucauld was so struck by Moslem piety, the local *marabout,* who usually lived a peaceful life on local charity, is now often an object of scorn and ridicule. Children throw stones at him, and troops of the ALN—now called the ANP (The National Peoples' Army)—have been known to set the example for them in this.

Young Algerians have told me that the education the *ulama* propagated boomeranged. During its studies in the *madrasas,* the younger generation forgot the superstitions of its parents. In the early thirties, the younger generation of students came mainly from the homes of the more well-to-do peasants. These same peasants are among those who have rejected Ben Bella's socialist measures the most fiercely, especially the agrarian reform measures that took away their land.

Destruction of entire villages and vast tracts of farmland by the FLN, the French army, or the OAS during the war helped speed a rural exodus toward the cities, which mass rural unemployment and hunger in the postwar era have further aggravated. The old fatalism of the typical farmer, toiling his life away in scratching a precarious living from Algeria's arid, rocky soil, is being replaced by an officially inspired will to self-improvement, instilled by the socialist slogans and the encouraging words, sometimes backed by distribution of new seeds and farm machinery, of the FLN political commissars and the chairmen of peasant "management committees" or the nationalized farms. The amount of time spent in prayer is likely to decrease as the time given over to co-operative farm activities—or political indoctrination—increases.

Algeria's annual observance of the Ramadan fast in 1963 was an ideal time to watch the growing tug of war between Islam and secularism. Whereas during the war for independence, breaking the fast was a rupture of civic discipline which occasionally brought terrorist reprisals, some Algerians publicly refused to observe it in 1963. Some offenders were publicly punished. One man stabbed another in Algiers for having accused him of breaking the fast. The official FLN newspaper, *Al-Shaab* ("The People"), defended the orthodox tradition of observing the fast. Mohammed Khidder, who was then secretary-general of the FLN's political bureau, reminded Algerians in a radio broadcast on July 2, 1963, that "Ramadan is the best tradition that Islam has given us to teach us endurance, patience, perseverance, so as to lift the voice of the Moslems and the Arabs."

This was in sharp contrast with President Bourguiba's regular annual discouragement of Ramadan, which he believes saps national energies and productivity. *Al-Shaab,* on the contrary, reminded its readers on February 2, 1963, that "the fast is obligatory for every Moslem adult, man or woman, in full possession of his or her physical and mental faculties." Adolescents were obliged to begin it as soon as they reach puberty. "From a moral point of view, fasting has as its objective to acquaint the wealthy with the rigors of hunger and thirst, to have him suffer the same sufferings as the poor, to let him understand him who is hungry or thirsty"—numbering in the hundreds of thousands in postwar Algeria, despite food-relief aid from all over the world—"in order to render justice to him."

Dissenting voices were raised in the Communist newspaper, *Alger-Republicain* on February 13, 1963. "A pregnant woman—poor child, poor mother—" wrote a group of four students, "after a very hard month and a hard delivery, what state will they be in? . . . Is this a way to develop the country? Whether in a construction site, a factory, an office, or a school, it is exactly the same problem."

Just plain irreligion, even atheism, has also made its appearance in Algeria's cities. Some students at Algiers University will tell you frankly that they no longer believe in God or even in marriage and the home. The breakup of tribal life in the countryside has its parallel in the cities in the decay of the family, the fundamental social unit in any Islamic, as in any Christian, society. Adolescents who have acquired the worst habits and tastes of Western society from their nodding acquaintance with French culture are likely to pass these on to their younger brothers and sisters now in school.

There was scarcely a single family in Algeria that did not lose one of its male breadwinners during the war. This forced women into jobs and speeded their escape from the traditional Islamic restraints on their sex. In some ALN units, women took part in the fighting along with their men. Algerian women are going into the professions and into politics, and several became deputies in the first parliament. Islam in the cities will scarcely keep any hold on many of these unveiled women unless it can quickly adapt, as it is trying to do in such other Arab cities exposed to Western ways as Casablanca, Tunis, Beirut, and Cairo, to the rapid changes in manners and mores.

ISLAM AND ONE-PARTY RULE: AN ALGERIAN CONCEPTION

Ben Bella and the other Algerian leaders frequently insist that their one-party constitution is a sort of twentieth-century version of the Islamic *umma,* or mother society, inspired by tribal conditions adapted to city life and directed by the will of God. This, they say, is why Algeria will not "go Communist," despite their admiration for Fidel Castro, their fascination for the Chinese revolution, and their growing dependence on Soviet economic aid. This is also why Algeria, under its 1963 constitution, became not a lay state but an

Islamic one. The idea of its founders was that it should represent the spiritual, economic, and moral "consensus"—called in Arabic *idjma*—of the elite in the Islamic community which makes it up.

This is where Ben Bella draws his theory of the FLN as a party of the "advance guard." In this concept of the ideal Islamic state, the vote of the majority rules, but it is a majority guided by an "enlightened" minority—in Algeria's case, the Party: the FLN. "Contested elections," according to one of the early nationalist theorists, cannot be permitted, since Islam "does not believe in the collective infallibility of the incompetent nor in the majority of the ignorant." Contrary to the situation in Western democracies, "the Moslems . . . only ratify the choice" already made by the elite "or they denounce it." No organized opposition in the sense of a rival political party is tolerated. This concept was unsuccessfully challenged by conservative Moslems at the FLN's first party congress held since independence in April, 1964.

There are opposition parties in Morocco, though there, in 1963, the king crushed the socialist opposition after discovery of a "plot." The one-party system prevails in Egypt and in Tunisia, to say nothing of the other one-party Arab states of the Middle East—multi-religion Lebanon being the outstanding exception. Libya's monarchy permits no political parties at all.

CHRISTIANS AND THE REVOLUTION: THE VATICAN AND CATHOLIC HIERARCHY

Perhaps in no colonial war or national revolution has Christianity been invoked by so many people in so many different ways as in Algeria. In the name of Christianity, Catholic and Protestant priests and laymen backed positions ranging from outright support for the FLN through every shade of hesitation and compromise all the way to the other end: frank and militant support for the preservation of a "French Algeria" and its most extreme and terror-inspiring partisan, the OAS.

Fortunately for Catholicism's future in Algeria, the Vatican and the Archbishop of Algiers, Léon-Etienne Duval, nicknamed "Mohammed Duval" by the French colonists, took a firm stand, at first in favor of peace with justice, later on behalf of the new Moslem nation that emerged from the war. By breaking away from the temporal power in time, Archbishop Duval, always backed by John XXIII and Paul VI, has kept the good name of Christianity alive among the Algerian elite.

In Pope Pius XII's Christmas message of 1954, a few weeks after what France officially presented to the world as a "minor outbreak" by some "bandits" in the Aurès, the pontiff noted "explosions of nationalism . . . unforeseen conflagrations . . . which are, at least in part, the fruits of Europe's bad example." A year later, Pope Pius told Archbishop Duval's parishioners that "a just and progressive political liberty should not be refused to these people," something which the archbishop was already saying. By way of encouragement, the Papal Secretariat of State on July 11, 1956, expressed Pope Pius' concern about the "fatherland of Saint Augustine, where in our time, Your Excellency [Duval] and his colleagues are trying to promote . . . a life fully in conformance with the Spirit of Christ." [3]

During the generals' *putsch* of April, 1961, when civil war threatened in France, Pope John cabled his personal encouragement to Archbishop Duval—who received the telegram only after the de Gaulle government had re-established control, since the junta had cut all communications between Algeria and Europe. The Archbishop spoke out indignantly against the widespread use of torture and "psychological warfare" methods by the French army and some of the police services under the often-heard pretext that the FLN was "pro-Communist." During the Lourdes pilgrimage, on June 30, 1959, Duval said that those who copied Communist methods "prove that they themselves are contaminated by Communism." He hit out strongly at the "usurpation of Christian symbols as emblems of political groups"—some of the proto-Fascist groups which hoped to profit from the Algerian war by seizing power in France were using crosses.[4]

When the anti-Moslem terrorism of the OAS reached a crescendo in March, 1962, just before signature of the Evian accords, Duval publicly attacked the OAS leaders, including General Salan, who frequently pretended that the OAS defended "Christian civilization."

[3] Léon-Etienne Duval, *Messages de Paix* (Bruges, 1962), pp. 7 f.; 12.
[4] *Ibid.*, pp. 14; 149 f.

In a pastoral letter he said that "it is odious to pretend that such procedures [of terrorism] can serve to defend the values of civilization. They are the negation of the Christian ideal and of all human morals." [5]

I spoke with Archbishop Duval, a gentle-mannered man of about sixty, in January, 1963, in his quiet office of the unobtrusive building where he had moved the archbishopric after turning over the cathedral—once again the Ketchawa Mosque—and the archbishop's palace to the Moslem authorities. This move had earned him some reproaches from Paris, which felt that he should have consulted first with the French government, since the palace was state property. He recalled how his own life had been threatened by the OAS, which had planted three bombs in and near the cathedral. "I had to find a different route to drive from home to the office every day," he recalled with a rather tired smile.

He told me how two missions of White Sisters had been ordered by the OAS to leave the Algiers kasbah just before the OAS had begun the all-out slaughter of Moslems venturing into European quarters. After the Moslems had all been forced out of the European city, the FLN came to the White Sisters—who had defied OAS orders and continued their charitable work among the kasbah's poor—and explained apologetically that it would, after all, be safer for them to leave. Most did, but there were at least two nuns on duty in the kasbah all through the final, apocalyptic days of terror which preceded the "armistice" between the OAS and the FLN in June, 1962.

What changes had he made in the clergy since independence? "Very few," Archbishop Duval told me. "Only one priest was transferred. Twenty-three others left, but some of these were normal rotations." At the moment I talked to him, the archbishop was mildly annoyed—by Protestant missionaries.

"Some of them began passing out tracts on the day Ben Bella made his first trip into the Kabylie Mountains," he told me. "The Moslems still tend to confuse the Catholics—who are doing no proselytizing—with the Protestants, who are. Tewfik al-Madani telephoned to the nearest mission of the White Fathers and said he held them responsible!"

Archbishop Duval was highly appreciative, he said, of the relief

[5] *Ibid.*, p. 223.

effort in Algeria carried out by the National Catholic Welfare Service of the United States. He also spoke of efforts to teach the Europeans about Islam. During the week of our conversation, the principal event listed on the diocesan calendar had been a lecture by Father Jacques Jomier of the Dominican Institute of Oriental Studies in Cairo, who spoke on "The transcendence of God in Islam and Christianity," and "Naguib Mahfouz, a great novelist of modern Egypt."

Most, though not all, of the French cardinals more or less approved of Duval and supported him in varying degrees. In a pastoral letter published in February of 1962, one of the last before peace, the French cardinals and archbishops warned that "violence produces violence. To seek to create a climate of civil war is to become responsible for civil war oneself." Some French intellectuals, not all of them on the far left either, felt that such pronouncements were too lukewarm and were intended to soothe the feelings of the "national Catholics," French right-wingers such as George Sauge, an ex-Communist who helped found the Cité Catholique movement and the so-called Centre d'Etudes Supérieur de Psychologie Sociale in Paris. In March, 1962, rather late in the game, the Cité Catholique finally disavowed the OAS.

During the chaotic months that followed independence, some Algerians, acting on their own, committed atrocities and reprisals from which FLN discipline had earlier held them back. Six priests were among those kidnaped or killed during 1962. Archbishop Duval now spoke out loudly in favor of the Europeans and permitted those who felt themselves in special danger to enter convents and monasteries for refuge. As a visiting Catholic journalist, Gunnar Kumlien, noted, "the voice of the Archbishop was more respected by the Moslems than it had been by the Christians when he fought the OAS." [6]

PRIESTS FOR ALGERIAN INDEPENDENCE

In the face of overwhelming obstacles, a small group of French priests in Algeria took an active stand on behalf of the FLN. This group became, in fact, a small team that worked during the war to

[6] Gunnar D. Kumlien, "The Challenge of Islam," *The Commonweal* (November 9, 1962), p. 172.

prepare a place for the Church in independent Algeria. Among its most famous supporters was the Abbé Jean Scotto, the parish priest of Bab el-Oued, the poor quarter *par excellence* of Algiers and a stronghold of the OAS.

Abbé Scotto, a down-to-earth man who would have found a place in the worker-priest movement if it had survived, narrowly missed being assassinated by the OAS because he dared remind his parishioners of their Christian duties toward the Moslems. During the worst days of the spring of 1962, when the OAS in Bab el-Oued was shooting not only the Moslems but also the draftee troops of the French army, Scotto learned that several of his parishioners, some of whom came to church regularly on Sunday, had been among a group of European thugs who had pushed a number of Moslem dockworkers into the harbor the day before. At Mass the next day, he asked for a special collection to aid the victims of their families. He got a big collection. "It was partly 'conscience money,'" he said afterward. "But there was more than that to it too." Archbishop Duval publicly congratulated the Abbé on Christmas Day, 1962, when he dedicated the new Cathedral of Algiers, Our Lady of Africa.

One of the most picturesque of the priests who threw total support to the FLN and one who—unlike other such priests—was fortunate enough to escape going to a French prison is Father Alfred Berenger, a *pied-noir,* born in Oran. He was parish priest in the village of Mamet St. Croix, in western Algeria, when an FLN detachment ambushed a French patrol, killing the young lieutenant who commanded it.

A French colonel in command of the sector, who is now a general in the French army, rounded up all the adult males of the neighboring village, about eighty in all—according to Father Berenger—and had them shot in reprisal. At Mass the next day, Father Berenger spotted the colonel among the congregation. "One of the officers here has blood on his hands," said Berenger. There was a shocked hush in the church. "I won't continue this Mass," Berenger went on, "unless that officer leaves this church at once." After a tense silence of about a minute, the colonel stalked out of the church.

Several days later, Berenger received a letter from the supreme commander in Algeria, General Raoul Salan, later the chief of the

OAS, ordering him to leave Algerian territory. In Paris, a cardinal offered to intercede with Salan so that Berenger could return. "No thanks," said the Abbé. "I've had enough." With that, he was off to Rome. He saw some of the pope's highest advisers and explained that he felt himself from now on to be an Algerian, not a Frenchman, and would apply for Algerian citizenship after the war. (He is, in fact, now an Algerian citizen.) What was more, he intended to work for the creation of a purely Algerian Church. Despite the anger of some French members of the hierarchy, he went to Tunis and became a sort of informal chaplain, adviser, and priest-of-all-work to the FLN. As the only European in the Algerian Red Crescent Organization—the Moslem equivalent of the Red Cross—Berenger reorganized its nursing and medical services and spent much of his time visiting the Algerian wounded and sick in Tunisian hospitals. With Benyusef ben Khedda, the former premier of the nationalist government-in-exile, he visited Latin America to raise funds on behalf of the Red Crescent. An old friend of Ben Bella, he became a parliamentary deputy. His fluent Spanish stood both him and Ben Bella in good stead during Ben Bella's headline-making trip to see Fidel Castro in Havana in October, 1962.

"The Algerian Church should throw off all French ties, adopt an Oriental rite, and become a truly national church," Berenger told me. "There is a marvelous opportunity for the Catholic Church to enter a dialogue with Islam here in Algeria, but most of the Catholics don't see it yet. We must get priests of other nationalities than French to come and serve in a new Christian presence. And, whether they like it or not, they will have to learn to say Mass in Arabic."

Needless to say, Abbé Berenger's ideas have not found favor among the French hierarchy.

Some of the steadiest journalistic support to all the North African nationalist movements, including the FLN, came from the distinguished liberal French Catholic weekly, *Temoignage Chrétien* ("Christian Testimony"). This had been founded as an organ of religious resistance to the Nazi occupation of France in 1940. During the Algerian war, such pre-eminent French literary men as François Mauriac, Catholic scholars like André Mandouze, and journalists like Robert Barrat waged a vigorous campaign on behalf of Algerian independence, denouncing terrorism on both sides and the abuses committed by the security forces. *Temoignage Chrétien* did not hesitate in 1963 to attack the Moroccan monarchy, which it had campaigned to restore a decade earlier, when it began to use strong-arm police methods against the Moroccan opposition parties.

For its one-thousandth issue, published on September 5, 1963, Ben Bella sent the paper his best wishes, writing, "The Algerians know of the part played by the real Christians in our liberation struggle. . . . I do not think that Christians fail to understand that Algeria is trying to restore dignity to the poor." He reiterated this a few weeks later in an interview with the Arabic-language service of Vatican Radio. Habib Bourguiba, in the same issue, observed that the voice of *Temoignage Chrétien* had been lifted "in the most critical hours of our national struggle and we will always keep a grateful memory. It was to rally precious support for our cause, support which had hesitated to show itself."

PROTESTANTS: FRENCH AND OTHERS

French Protestants were just as divided as were Catholics on the Algerian issue, if not more so. Most Protestants in Algeria belonged, before independence, to the Reformed Church of France. The Reformed Church of France took a big part and still does—as the Reformed Church of Algeria, separated by its own request from the mother church in France in 1963—in an active inter-denominational relief organization, the CIMADE. French Protestants, like their English and American brethren and the White Fathers, had made a few conversions in Algeria, mainly of Kabylie tribesmen. These Algerian Christians all attended the church at Rue de Chartres in the Algiers kasbah.

Like the Catholics, the great majority of Protestants among the European settlers felt that France and especially General de Gaulle, whom an army revolt originating in Algiers in May, 1958, had brought to power, had abandoned them. In their synods, however, most of the French Protestant churches, Reformed and Lutheran, began opposing the colonial system as far back as the Indochina war of the forties. They continued to do so after the outbreak of the conflict in Algeria. Like the Catholics, they took strong stands in metropolitan France against the torture of prisoners and the adaptation, by the French army and the French security services, of the Communist methods of "subversive warfare" to the situation in Algeria. Pastor Marc Boegner, President of the Protestant Federation of France, interceded against such methods with Premier Guy Mollet, shortly after the kidnaping in October, 1956, of Ahmed ben Bella in a Moroccan aircraft had offended the sense of hospitality of King Mohammed V and torpedoed prospective peace negotiations. Councils of the Protestant churches in France also showed some sympathy for French conscientious objectors who refused military service, but never gave them wholehearted support, any more than did the Catholics.

A few Protestant clergymen and laymen in Algeria deplored the timidity of both the Reformed Church and the Lutherans, and some also went to prison for their acts of charity or support for the FLN nationalists. But the Protestants had their right-wingers and supporters of a "French Algeria" just as did the Catholics. Just as *Verbe,* bearing the pontifical colors, became the organ of the Catholic "ultras" and was avidly read by the psychological warfare officers in Algeria, a Protestant monthly called *Tant qu'il fait jour* ("As long as daylight is here"), was first issued in 1959 by a group of Protestants determined to defend "French Algeria." It opposed President de Gaulle's policy of leading Algeria toward independence, though it also objected to the terrorism of the OAS. When Protestant young people in France in the Federation of Student Christian Associations and the Council of the Alliance of (Christian) Youth Movements came out for the FLN, another body of French Protestants formed a countergrouping favorable to the ideas of *Tant qu'il fait jour.* Never was the old saying, "Get three Frenchmen together and you'll have nine different opinions," more true than in the case of churchgoing Frenchmen and the Algerian war, a drama which shook France, mentally and morally, to its very foundations.

Experiences of the British and American Protestant missionaries during the war would fill several books. One which came to world attention was that of the Rev. Lester E. Griffith, Jr., a slim, bespectacled Methodist from Cleveland, Ohio. Throughout the war, the

Methodist missions in Algeria and Tunisia kept a staff of about thirty in the field. On August 18, 1958, Griffith, who was in charge of the field staff, was driving through a lonely stretch of the Kabylie Mountains. Suddenly, just as the road dipped into a wood, three armed ALN partisans waved him to a halt. Later he learned they had simply been told to stop the first European they met. They took him prisoner. He marched and camped with them for forty days and nights. The ALN detachment was constantly on the move. It was commanded by a Berber, Colonel Amrouche, who was killed later. The French considered him a "chivalrous" adversary.

Earlier, Amrouche had been misled by Colonel Yves Goddard, one of the "psychological warfare" experts, who later joined the OAS, into thinking that four hundred of his own men had betrayed him. Amrouche had them shot. Griffith, whom I talked with in Algiers the day after Amrouche had released him into the custody of a mission of White Fathers, told me they had treated him with "great respect." He found the ALN men to be "convinced souls, with a marvelous sense of discipline. They feel they are fighting for independence and are prepared to die for it." They also had a polite, though rather abstract, interest in hearing about Christianity. Griffith was faithful to the promise he had given Amrouche not to answer military questions which reporters asked him about the ALN organization. The Methodist mission continued its work of charity and education throughout the war and into the beginning of independence. Like the White Fathers and Sisters, it was always ready to care for the wounded, whether French or FLN.

THE "NATIVE" CHRISTIANS AND THE OTHERS

In 1954, there had been close to six thousand "native" Christians—those of Arab or Kabylie descent—in Algeria. Many were converted by the White Fathers during or after Lavigerie's time. This was a far higher figure than that for Tunisia, where only a few score of the offspring of Lavigerie's Thibar mission still keep their faith, or in Morocco, where there are perhaps no more "native" Catholics than one could count on the fingers of one hand and about five hundred Protestants, converted through the efforts of the

North Africa Mission and the Gospel Missionary Union. The Catholics in Algeria use the Latin rite but say two masses in Berber; the Protestants are still experimenting with Arabic as a liturgical language.

When the war broke out, the pressures generated by the Arabo-Islamic majority in the FLN and ALN became irresistible for many of the Kabylie Christians. Some left the country, others embraced Islam. By 1963, only about fifteen hundred remained who would give public testimony of their faith. I met several Moslem officers in the ALN who assured me that one or more Christians had served in other units than their own. One of the most distinguished Kabylie Christians, who went into public administration and has remained, is Ismail Marrough. In 1963, he was secretary-general of the economic planning service in the Ben Bella government. He left Algeria after the outbreak of the war and came to Morocco, where he became a close friend and associate of both French Catholics and Moslem National leaders. He helped to launch La Source, a group of Catholics in Rabat interested in a rapprochement with Islam. Under the government of Premier Abdallah Ibrahim, whom King Mohammed V placed in power with a progressive pro-labor program in 1958, Marrough worked closely with Abderrahim Bouabid, at that time Vice-Premier and Minister of National Economy, and had a large share in preparing Morocco's Five-Year Economic Plan. Marrough returned to Algeria to become a precious link between the various Christian groups remaining after independence and the Moslem authorities. He filled this role, often at the cost of much personal hardship and misunderstanding arising from the hostility of some Moslems.

A Kabylie Christian author who dramatically presented his people's dilemma was Jean Amrouche. I met him in Tunis, in 1960, while we were both covering the peace negotiations, just then beginning, between France and the FLN. Two years later, he died, just before the return of the peace he had sought, his heart broken by what he called "the brothers' war." Amrouche wrote in French. His most interesting literary work, which regrettably has never been translated into English, is *Chants Berbères de Kabylie*. But his name came before the French and Algerian publics chiefly as a publicist and journalist, working steadily for the peace and understanding between all of Algeria's communities which Albert Camus, and all his generation of *pieds-noirs,* had also sought.

There was a gentle, reassuring air about Amrouche which allowed him to rise above the polemical or controversial side of any discussion. It hid a troubled soul. But his was always a voice raised in hope, not in anger, and he remained a foe of violence and terror. After his death, the Algerian poet and playwright Kateb Yacine recalled, in an article written for *Jeune Afrique* in July of 1963, his first encounter with Amrouche at the offices of his magazine *L'Arche,* in Paris in 1946. "This first contact was glacial for me," said Yacine. "Amrouche represented, for me, the worst image of French Algeria: a Christianized Kabyle. Because of my extreme leftist nationalist convictions, I believed him hopelessly corrupted."

The next meeting between the two Algerians, the Moslem, who had enlisted his pen in the cause of the revolution, and the Christian, who at that time was running the Kabylie-language program of the French State Radio, came a decade later. The Algerian war was approaching its most violent phase. Amrouche revealed to Yacine his own inner dilemma, caused by the painful knowledge that some Frenchmen were fighting his people in the name of his own Christian faith and that most Algerians then regarded Christianity as simply part of the colonial system. Yacine relates that Amrouche told him that he sympathized with the FLN, "while still conscious of the paradox of calling himself Amrouche and also Jean; of being simultaneously Berber and French, Christian and Algerian far above the ordinary."

In June, 1963, Professor Giorgio la Pira, the Mayor of Florence, where the annual "Mediterranean Colloquia," a gathering of artists and men and women of letters and of good will from North Africa, Europe, and the Middle East is held, invited Yacine to Florence to receive the first Jean Amrouche literary prize. The committee awarded it, announcing that Yacine had been their choice because of all his work, including *Nedjma, Le cadavre encerclé* ("The Surrounded Corpse"), *La Femme Sauvage* ("The Wild Woman"), and another work published in late 1963, *Le Polygone Etoilé* ("The Polygon of Stars"). In accepting the prize, Yacine named Amrouche, together with the Martinique Negro, Franz Fannon, whose *Les*

Damnés de la Terre ("The Damned of the Earth") had been a major inspiration to the Algerian revolutionary leaders, as Algeria's "second great literary name."

After a Requiem Mass and presentation of the prize to Yacine, Amrouche's widow, Suzanne Amrouche, read from some of her husband's unpublished letters in which he spoke of the agony it had cost him "to nourish a double loyalty and that he could be nothing other than a bridge between two peoples locked in a struggle."

THE ISLAMIC CONVERTS

Today, Amrouche's personal drama is that of many another Christian of North Africa, native as well as European. It is that of any convert and holds true for the Christians who have gone over to Islam, too—and there are at least as many of these in North Africa, if not more, than there are Moslems who have become Christian. Nearly every month, the Algerian papers, and sometimes the Moroccan or Tunisian ones, list the names of Europeans who have decided to become naturalized in their host country. Nearly always, though the letter of the law does not require it, this involves pronouncing the *shahada* (profession of faith) and entering the *umma* of Islam. At least one American whom I know well, a teacher, found the peaceful existence he wanted in North Africa. He chose this course. He changed both religion and nationality and has even made the pilgrimage to Mecca. Despite his mastery of Arabic and the great attraction the new way of life held for him, I know that he has moments of doubt and regret.

The Algerian Catholic Church is doing the best it can to ease for Europeans the process of adaptation to the new conditions, doubtless in the hope that not too many will choose to become Moslems. Archbishop Duval started an organization called the Association d'Etudes in Algiers, publishing periodically a bulletin intended for the diminishing Christian flock. Some of its recent directives and counsels point up the Christian dilemma dramatically.

"Do we," it asked, "agree to be the envoys sent by Christ to these men whom He loves, to be the Church of Christ among the Algerians? A minority, certainly, but a minority in the Lord, who made Himself a Jew among the Jews, a Greek among the Greeks, and may make Himself an Algerian among the Algerians."

These dedicated Christians seem to suspect that they may be fighting a lost cause, but they intend to keep on fighting it. They recognize that "even if this or that pastor or layman is accepted . . . we should have no illusions. . . . The Algerians reject the Church, because it is the Church of the West. Even if the standard of living of the West is attractive to them, this movement is simultaneously a repulsion."

In March, 1963, at Camp du Maréchal, Kabylie, some fifty European and Algerian Christians met to discuss "how to bring the message of the Gospel to a community where we are only an infinite minority." The answers given were clear and stark. First, the individual Christian can set an example in his or her professional life and patiently and disinterestedly pass on to the Algerians the technical skills, the knowledge they need. "Christian testimony," in this context would be repairing a Moslem's automobile for him, but at the same time showing him how to do it himself. If a *colon* decides to leave his farm—many thousands have left and many more will doubtless be leaving in 1964 and 1965 and afterward as Ben Bella's agrarian reform measures take full effect—the Christian approach, decided the Camp du Maréchal meeting, would be to organize everything before leaving so that one's workers do not suffer from his departure: "Don't wait until the tractors are requisitioned: offer them beforehand!"

The Association d'Etudes is especially worried about isolated Christians. Like those in the ancient diaspora, it feels they should always be attached to some parish or some community, though not proselytizing, always prepared to answer questions for Moslems, "Why do you do things this way?" or "Why are you a Christian?"

One obstacle to real integration of the Christian Europeans into the new Algeria is the wording of the law on naturalization. Though it provides for naturalization of non-Moslems and does not require them to embrace Islam, it grants Algerian nationality without naturalization to "every person who has at least two ancestors of the paternal line born in Algeria and enjoying a Moslem status." As the Abbé Berenger himself observed in the Algerian parliament, this unfortunately creates two classes of Algerian citizens and has been hardly reassuring to the Christians.

PART FIVE

THE CHALLENGE OF THE FUTURE

CHAPTER XXIV

DIALOGUE OR DIATRIBE?

> Israel has its roots in Hope; Christianity is devoted to Charity; Islam is centered upon Faith.
>
> LOUIS MASSIGNON

The Christian churches in North Africa and elsewhere are now beginning to take a serious interest in learning about Islam and meeting it on its own ground. Islam, however, is generally far less interested in learning about Christianity. This is because Islam, especially in Africa, has found Christianity's Achilles' heel, its old secular links with the West, which it exploits mercilessly in making 9,000,000 new converts in Africa each year.

The relations of North Africa's Islamic establishment, with its minority of economically powerful Christians, have entered a period of new crisis. Algeria is the crucial testing ground. There, the "Christian presence" of the Catholics and the aggressive proselytizing of the Protestants will either show that Christianity does have something to offer besides charity—or both will be completely submerged, as is now happening in such other African countries as the Republic of the Sudan.

ROMAN CATHOLIC STRATEGY

How is Christianity organized to cope with the challenge? The Roman Catholics are striving to keep in step with the times. Administratively, all of the North African Roman Catholic churches in Morocco, Algeria, Tunisia, and Libya are placed, like many other mission territories, directly under the jurisdiction of the Sacred Congregation of the Propagation of the Faith in Rome. Their prefect is Cardinal Agaganian, who is constantly urging the missionary bishops everywhere to maintain their independence from secular powers. The local archbishops have far more administrative power than they had when attached to the French, Spanish, or Italian churches. The Commission for Extraordinary Affairs informally examined the problem of relations with the Moslems during the consideration of general ecumenical matters at the first session of the Vatican Council in the fall of 1962.

Before the 1963 session of the council opened, the commission was dissolved. A small committee, which included such relative "progressives" as Cardinal Liénart of Belgium, had already met during the first council session to try and agree on a text which would extend a hand toward Islam—some gesture, perhaps, which could be included in Chapter Seventeen of the council's declaration, "The Church and the Modern World." Neither this attempt nor another in the fall of 1963 were successful.

In a letter addressed to Eugène Cardinal Tisserant in September, 1963, Pope Paul VI announced he was nominating four cardinals of the council's co-ordinating committee to study relations with non-Christian faiths and perhaps to set up a new secretariat to deal with these relations.

During the final days of the third session of the Vatican Council in 1964, a statement on the need for dialogue with non-Christian religions was released to the world. It said, "The Church also considers with respect the Moslems who adore the Living and Subsisting God, All-Powerful Creator of the heavens and the earth, whose decrees are sometimes hidden, but to Whom one must submit with all one's soul, as Abraham submitted to God, Abraham to whom the Moslem faith refers. . . ."

After referring to the Moslem usages of prayer, charity, fasting, and morality, the statement added, "If, in the course of the ages, numerous dissensions and enmities have manifested themselves between Christians and Moslems, the council exhorts both to forget the past and sincerely seek mutual comprehension and to keep and cause to advance together social justice, moral good, and also peace and liberty for all men."

This concern at the Vatican, if we exclude the medieval contacts already discussed, is of a relatively recent date. The first real official diplomatic relations between the Vatican and Arab states in modern times were opened in Morocco in 1888, when Sultan Mulay Hasan sent Mohammed Torres as his ambassador to Pope Leo XIII, accompanied by a Spanish Franciscan, Father Lerchundi.

The Middle Eastern Arabs began regular contacts with the Vatican when King Fuad of Egypt saw Pius XI in 1927. Just before the outbreak of World War II in 1939, Pius XII directed the major institutes of higher ecclesiastical learning to give more attention to the languages and institutions of Moslem lands. The intention of the Holy See was to end controversy between Catholicism and Islam, if possible, over the Scriptures and the Koran. Gradually, the Jesuits, the Franciscans, Dominicans, Carmelites, Augustinians, and White Fathers have improved their Islamic study programs. The object was not the proselytism of the ages of Lull or Lavigerie, but rather an attempt of the Church to make a friendly approach to the world's second largest faith, which claimed 430,000,000 believers in 1960 throughout the world, nearly half of Christianity's approximately 915,000,000.

In North Africa, many priests are now striving to learn Arabic, either on their own, with local teachers, or in the institutions set aside in Beirut or in Tunis. Even before the 1963 council decision to authorize use of local languages in liturgy, experiments in this direction were under way. In Rabat, for example, a convent of Poor Clares, the Franciscan order of nuns, decided in 1960 that their European rule was too strict to allow them to do social work among Moslem women. The Vatican gave them permission to take a new rule. As the Sisters of the Resurrection, they follow an Oriental rule which enables them to work with Moroccan women. In their churches, the Malekite liturgy is used and Mass is said in Arabic. They are in close contact with a similar chapter of nuns in Nazareth, though they remain under the jurisdiction of the Archbishop of Rabat.

The former Spanish zone of Morocco is still kept separate, because both Europeans and Moroccans still use the Spanish language there. Archbishop Aldegundo, whose see was in Tangier in 1964, was considered one of the small group of relatively progressive and socially conscious Spanish bishops.

Curiously enough, the Algerian Sahara, which was an apostolic vicarate in Lavigerie's time, is a separate archdiocese, completely separate from Algiers. The incumbent in 1964, Archbishop Mercier, had one of the largest and most sparsely populated parishes in Africa. His see was in the Oasis of Ghardaia, heart of the Mozabite country. In Libya, an Italian archbishop cares for the souls of his countrymen who remain, as well as the many other foreigners, especially Germans and Americans, who have arrived with the oil boom which the country has been enjoying since 1961.

What can the Catholic and Protestant clergy do to keep their presence "discreet but effective," as they want it? Regrouping more of the clergy in the cities where most of the Europeans now live—Casablanca, Rabat, Tangier, Oran, Algiers, Tunis, Tripoli—and thus releasing priests who serve only tiny handfuls of Europeans in small village parishes was advocated by many at the Vatican Council. "This would provide priests for areas where they are critically needed, like Black Africa and Latin America," one monk urged.

While the Benedictines, for example, say they intend to stay on at Toumliline in Morocco "as long as we are welcome," they have curtailed some of their medical activities, especially child care. Moroccans were coming to their dispensary instead of to the local government hospital in Azrou. This risked stirring up bureaucratic sensibilities and straining the ties of personal friendship and sympathy which make it possible for them to stay on in Morocco. Dom Denis Martin, the prior, was already devoting more time in 1963 to the two brother institutions at Bouake (Ivory Coast) and Ougadougou (Upper Volta), where the missionary opportunities, as elsewhere in Black Africa, are still considerable but where "competition" of Moslem missionaries is serious as well.

THE ANTI-MISSIONARY MOVEMENT: ALGERIA

Of the former French-ruled Maghreb countries, Algeria is the one where Christian missionaries have so far found the least official interference. This is partly because of Moslem gratitude for the work of the White Fathers and some of the Protestants during the war for independence, but also because the Ben Bella government was very well aware of Algeria's vast need for the social welfare work and above all the precious medical care which the Christian groups in Algeria have provided.

In October, 1962, the North Africa Mission started an intensive campaign in Algeria for its Bible Correspondence Courses. From the standpoint of tangible results, this is the Mission's most successful project. Giving something away is so unusual in North Africa that when the Mission's field workers show up at country fairs or in village squares with the bright-colored pamphlets and books—anything with printing or writing on it holds a special interest for the peasants in many back-country areas—both children and adults often flock around them and sign up. At the end of a variable period of weeks, the student can sign a paper, if he wishes, "acknowledging Christ as his Saviour." This may or may not be followed by baptism, depending upon how serious the Mission judges the would-be convert's intentions to be and whether his family and social circumstances are all relatively favorable or not. The Mission claimed some twenty-five thousand students in Morocco in 1963 and another eight thousand in Tunisia at the moment when the Tunisian government ordered the program suspended.

In Algeria the number of enrollments rose from five hundred in November, 1962, to thirty-five hundred in early February and five thousand in the summer of 1963. A mobile group of eleven Americans and Europeans, which the Mission called the "Send The Light Team," opened a hall in Oran and toured Algeria. The mission station in the Kabylie Mountains continued its work: five weekly classes, taught by Miss Kay Castle, who arrived there in 1954; visits to homes; and the medical ministry.

Muriel Butcher, one of the missionaries, described her arrival in a small town in Oran Department:

> We open the back of the station wagon and take out our baskets and briefcases, already stacked with the . . . (Arabic) Gospels and New Testaments—discuss briefly how to divide up the village, and set out. Already, every pair of dark eyes on the square is upon us, eyes turned lazily and curiously in our direction. Why should four strangers visit their village? . . . Our Arabic greetings receive surprised and delighted rejoinders, suspicion dies out of their eyes, and we are welcomed with a wide grin.
>
> "Can you read?" is the first essential question. "No, Achti (sister)," says one, "Neither Arabic nor French. I am just a donkey; I never went to school." . . . A group of proud, high spirited young men tell us confidently that they are studying philosophy

at college. One of them, surprisingly, buys a New Testament in Arabic.

An old man in flowing beard and white robes approaches. Someone says "The Sheikh," and they respectfully make way for him. "The Gospel, eh! What do we want with these books? Our own books are far superior." The old arguments begin, and the crowd prick up their ears. We politely point out that this is the Book which speaks of Eternal Life, of pardon from sin and peace with God.[1]

"In general, the health and educational authorities are with us," one of the Mission's executives asserted, "but we are having trouble from elsewhere." The "elsewhere" was chiefly Tewfik al-Madani, Minister of *Habus,* who told me that he considered distribution of any kind of Christian tracts or brochures aimed at conversions "intolerable."

MISSIONARIES IN MOROCCO

All of the basic documents on the structure of the monarchy, including the constitution of December, 1962, stress Morocco's predominantly Islamic nature. "Islam is the religion of the state, which guarantees the liberty of sects," the constitution says.

In Morocco, the anti-missionary drive since independence in 1956 has been sporadic but at times intense, at least in some of the Arabic press. Its prime movers have been the *ulama* and Allal al-Fassi, both in his capacity as President of the Istiqlal Party and "grey eminence" of "reformed" Islam in Morocco, especially while he was Minister of Islamic Affairs, from 1961 until January, 1963, a post originally created for him. In 1963, King Hasan II turned the Istiqlal Party out of the government.

Many missionaries in Morocco have made extremely good names for themselves and their work. One was Father Jean-Marie Peyriguere, a follower of Charles de Foucauld, who worked the last thirty-six years of his life among the Berbers of Al-Kbab, a village in the Middle Atlas. Another is the Rev. C. F. Green of the Bible

[1] Muriel Butcher, "A Day's Colportage in Algeria," *North Africa* (July–August, 1963), pp. 147–48.

Churchmen's Missionary Society, minister of the English church in Casablanca, who has worked in Morocco since 1934.

Mr. Green has told me that in many ways he has found missionary work in Morocco far easier since independence than before it, when the French authorities periodically sent the police to ask him not to baptize and when, on one occasion in 1948, they tried to turn the English church in Mogador into a police station.

Mr. Green's experience was typical of that of many other Protestant missionaries. In 1959, a Moroccan law had required all associations to register. Mr. Green registered his mission and got a receipt for his documents. He was assured that this constituted permission for the small private school he runs in his own house in Casablanca and which about one hundred young people attend every week. Nothing further was said by anyone until April, 1963. Then Moroccan police asked Mr. Green whether he was responsible for all missions in Morocco. "No, only the Episcopal ones," he told them. The questioning was thorough but courteous. Mr. Green went on with his school, occasionally making a convert or two.

In 1959, al-Fassi protested about some sensational articles which had appeared in the French-language press about the supposed appearance of the face of Christ on the inside walls of a house at Meknes. He used this as the occasion to attack the missionaries as "a destructive group which is seeking to create a spiritual vacuum among youth and the popular masses." He also confused suppression by Pope John of the phrase "perfidious Jews" in the liturgy with a supposed phrase, "bring the idol-worshipers and the Moslems into the Kingdom of Heaven"—a phrase which never existed. "If the Pope is trying to be tolerant," said al-Fassi, "he should aim at recognizing Islam as a revealed religion, as we recognize the Christian and Jewish religions. We doubt whether the Christian religion is ripe for such recognition." [2]

The anti-missionary drive began in earnest in 1961. In June, the *ulama* of Fez formed the *Rabitah Ulama al-Maghreb* (League of Moroccan *Ulama*). Among its avowed purposes, according to Abderrahman al-Kittani, one of the founders, was to summon the nation back to God and the fundamentals of the faith, "combat

[2] *Al-Ayam* (Rabat, October 2, 1959).

moral and social decline, promote and sponsor instruction in the Moslem religion, and to *oppose all Christian missionary efforts in Morocco.*" [3]

Six months later, al-Fassi created his new ministry, arousing criticism of some of the *ulama,* who claimed there was no need for it. Among other things, it was supposed to watch over the organization of Islamic education at all levels, supervise religious personnel, and publish various periodicals and books to encourage an interest in Islam.

Perhaps the most concerted and serious printed theological attack ever made against the missionaries in Morocco came from the pen of Professor Abul Abbas Ahmed Tidjani and was published by the Ministry of *Habus* (religious properties). It was replete with anti-Trinitarian arguments and the classical Moslem objections to the divinity of Christ. He also gave his version, doubtless a highly imaginative re-creation, of a debate he had held with Dom Denis Martin, the Prior of Toumliline Monastery, which he called the "main center of evangelization installed in the Atlas":

> I asked him how many persons composed God before the birth of the Messiah, for instance in the time of Noah. . . . After a moment of silence, the Superior answered me: "Religion insists that we have faith and that we obey the prescriptions of the Church, without having to make researches or efforts at reflection." [Replied Tidjani:] "We live in a century when science is spreading everywhere among men and women. Your own scholars have published works on this subject which, if they were divulged in all circles, would ruin Christianity down to its very foundations." He answered me: "The Church is informed of that. It fights this movement by regularly publishing a list of works placed on the Index." I did not insist further . . . recalling this verse of Nebhani: "I do not see how I can make a blind man understand certain notions which are familiar only to beings who can see." [4]

[3] *Al-Alam* (Rabat, June 9, 1961). My italics.
[4] *Dawat al-Haq* (Rabat, November, 1961).

Some of al-Fassi's political enemies taunted him with the "existence in all corners of Morocco of bureaus charged with propagating the Christian faith." *Maghreb al-Arabi,* the newspaper of the Agrarian Popular Movement, illustrated such a concern in attacking the Bible correspondence courses, in an article of December 4, 1961:

> Even the new League of *Ulama* has not reacted and has done nothing about this violent attack against the religion of the Islamic nation, the religion of the Moroccan state, the religion of Arabism. . . . This literature . . . constitutes the worst of poisons. . . . We are in the presence of a vast and well organized network of evangelization, the purpose of which is to deviate and confound the African populations. And Morocco occupies, in this regard, a chosen place. . . . What we especially want is to oppose the neo-colonialist intellectual and moral infiltration which shows itself in the religious missions! These missionaries do not, it seems, seek to work for peace and tolerance, as did Christ—may He be saved—but, on the contrary, they work to sow error in spirits, to light fires of sedition in the hearts of children and youth. These, by the way, constitute favorable ground, because their religious instruction is generally poor.

Other press attacks at the same time were directed against activities of the Bahai faith in Morocco, against the nondenominational, private American School in Tangier, and against Morocco's Jewish schools, whose teachers had already been the object of discriminatory police measures when President Nasser visited Morocco to attend the Casablanca Conference of January, 1961. In the face of this campaign, al-Fassi assured his critics in a ministerial communiqué that he would make "energetic decisions." But these decisions were never announced. It seemed likely that the king had blocked them.

The bookstores run by various Protestant groups and the annual camp meeting conducted by the Gospel Missionary Union for Protestant Moroccan converts were also under heavy attack in the Arabic press during 1962. The Mission had already decided to suspend its practice of running a stand at the annual Casablanca Trade Fair because an independent Protestant missionary of Hungarian nationality was murdered there in April, 1961, while distributing tracts.

Repeatedly, al-Fassi and some other Moroccan politicians have used religion as a political weapon. By attacking Jewish emigation to Israel, Zionism, and the Christian missionaries, al-Fassi was demonstrating that he was the leading defender of state institutions. When I discussed religion with him in May, 1962, he told me, "Certainly we are in favor of Christianity. It is one of the revealed religions. But we are not in favor of evangelizing Morocco, any more than the pope or the Italian authorities are in favor of Islam when they prevent a group of Moslems from building a mosque in Rome."

One of the reasons for the anti-missionary outcry had been the brief return to Morocco in 1961 of Friar Jean Abd al-Jalil, a convert and Franciscan. Al-Fassi and several of Friar Jean's relatives locked him into a room in his ancestral home in Fez, then announced to the news agencies that he had "returned to Islam." Friar Jean returned to his residence in France soon afterward, denying that he had done anything of the kind. The next major impetus was the strange case of the Bahaists. A court in Nador in December, 1962, sentenced three members of the Bahai faith to death and twelve others to long prison terms for "subverting the state." Some of them were foreigners. The official version was that they had been infecting the minds of Moslem school children in Nador with Bahai propaganda, and the protests of parents had caused demonstrations which threatened public order. The trial of the luckless defendants was, in fact, a trial for heresy: the prosecution, inspired by al-Fassi, contended that the Bahai religion, founded in 1862 in Iran by the self-styled prophet, Bahaullah, was not a true religion at all but a heretical sect of Shiite Islam.

"This is not a religion at all, but an *ersatz,*" said King Hasan when asked about the Bahai in a "Meet the Press" television interview for the National Broadcasting Company news on April 1, 1963, while on a visit to New York. "It is as though you were to permit someone to walk stark naked in the streets of Washington." He then said he would pardon the prisoners if the Supreme Court upheld the original sentence. One of al-Fassi's associates who had joined the campaign against the Bahai told me that the new Moroccan penal code "will enable us to get rid of the missionaries and expel the Bahai." In December, 1963, the Supreme Court quashed the sentences and set all the prisoners free.

The penal code, promulgated on June 5, 1963, gave the monarchy a powerful weapon to use against the Christian missionaries if it decided to do so. Six months to three years in prison and fines of up to one hundred dollars could be imposed on "anyone who employs means of seduction with the aim of shaking the faith of a Moslem or converting him to another religion, either by exploiting his weakness or his needs, using institutions of education, health, asylums, or orphanages." [5]

If the government chose to interpret this literally, it could have ended the activities of virtually all the approximately three hundred and fifty Protestant missionaries who worked in Morocco in 1963. It could also close some thirty-four Catholic private schools where, in the summer of 1963, 5,368 Moroccan Moslems were getting a Western-type education. All were ordered in September, 1963, to include Arabic in their curricula.[6]

What do the missionaries accomplish now, and what can they expect? The experience of one North Africa Mission couple, the Rev. and Mrs. Harris (Scottish Presbyterians) in Al-Jadida (Mazagan) may be typical. When Mr. Harris first arrived in Morocco, police refused to extend his residence permit in Mogador. He and Mrs. Harris then moved to Al-Jadida, into a house purchased there by the Mission. There they installed a small private chapel. One day, he was unexpectedly arrested and taken to Casablanca. Here he appeared before a French magistrate—there were still many among the thousands of French civil servants who bolstered King Hasan's regime—who dismissed his "case." Three years later, he was again arrested and taken before the same magistrate, who dismissed his case again, closing his "dossier."

Mr. Harris says that he has made about thirty Moroccan converts in Al-Jadida, though not all of these were baptized. He finds that Christianity has "a good chance" in Morocco and "is growing."

[5] Official Bulletin of the Kingdom of Morocco, No. 2640, June 5, 1963.
[6] Figures supplied by French Embassy, Rabat.

Moroccans complained to him of the "decadence" and the "lack of satisfaction" they find in Islam. Mr. Harris and his wife care for numerous children of poorer families who come to them. They teach them hymns, including "Lead, Kindly Light," in Arabic, played on a tape recorder.

The Harrises, when I talked to them, were planning to start a trade school to teach carpentry, metalworking, and other crafts to their Bible pupils. Mr. Harris introduced me to one of his young converts, Ali, in the street, outside their house. "Yes, I am a Christian and so is my mother," Ali admitted openly in front of our group and numerous passers-by. "So is one of my classmates at the Lycée." Ali smiled wanly, shook hands, and left us. I wondered to myself: What will become of Ali if the missionaries leave for good?

TUNISIA: THE BOURGUIBIST APPROACH

Bourguibism, which its author has defined as reacting flexibly to each given situation, has been applied to missionary activity in Tunisia with curious results. Generally, as in Morocco, the transition to independence was reasonably smooth. Father Demeerseman's work for the Neo-Destour and the reputation of Archbishop Perrin among the Tunisian leaders stood the Catholic Church in good stead. Unlike Morocco, Tunisia had no major opposition movements which could make religion a political issue. Up to the time the Tunisian talks began with the Vatican, the only serious problem of the Catholics had been the closing down, in 1959, of a shelter for the poor of all denominations run by the Petites Soeurs des Pauvres. Under the terms of a law enforced in 1959, all foreign missions had to register and deposit copies of their statutes with the authorities. They would then be approved or disapproved. But the Petites Soeurs were never able to get approval, and the government confiscated their shelter. Only upon intervention of the World Council of Churches were they allowed to keep some penniless Russian refugees on a private basis.

One of the North Africa Mission's bookshops, which had been broken up by an excited mob shortly after celebrations of Tunisian independence in 1956, had to close in 1959 after Tunisian police had a careful look through its Bibles and tracts. In January, 1964, the Mission announced that the bookshop had been closed, the Bible correspondence courses discontinued, "and we are no longer welcome in this land." While officially the Tunisian Education and Interior Ministries had reproached the missionaries for "influencing the masses," the public health service had generally shown delight with their medical efforts and have encouraged them.

The outlook for the tiny handful of converts in Tunisia is just as bleak as that in Morocco, Algeria, or Libya. "About five young people came into the store each year and asked about how to become Christians," one of the American missionaries in Tunis told me. "Many others, of course, came simply to browse. In four years, we converted three Tunisian students. They converted three others. One of the original converts was flunked in his exams, even though he was sure he had really passed them. He managed to get a job teaching in a Jewish school and doing translations. But he has been boycotted by his friends, interrogated by the police, and called a 'traitor.' "

A few Christians in North Africa, virtually all Protestants, still dream, as certain Catholics did a generation ago, of reaching and converting some of the Moslem elite. "It is only in this way that we can ever hope to found a real native church, with native clergy," one missionary said.

CHAPTER XXV

CHRIST, MOHAMMED, AND MARX

Judaism, followed by its younger brothers, Christianity and Islam, made the first attempt to demystify man. . . . This was a decisive step in the emancipation of the human spirit.

MOHAMMED AZIZ LAHBABI, 1961, DEAN OF THE FACULTY OF LETTERS AND SOCIAL SCIENCES, UNIVERSITY OF RABAT

After looking back at the battle of god against god in North Africa through the centuries, the non-Moslem may pause and ask—and the Moslem will never agree with him more wholeheartedly than on this question: Are all the efforts, past, present and future, to win souls for Christianity really worthwhile? From the strict viewpoint of conversions, have the expenditure of thousands of human careers, of vast amounts of blood and treasure in Christian missionary ventures of all types, really been worth the meager returns?

Certainly they have constituted "Christian testimony." But the only practical result has been to create a tiny handful of native Christians, isolated in their own society, nearly all of modest stations in life, where they are unable to influence large numbers of people, and who are constantly subject to all sorts of pressures.

The heart of the problem, however, lies neither in continuing missionary efforts nor in ceasing them. It lies in divining what kind of new society lies ahead, for North Africa as well as for the rest of the Afro-Asian world. What contributions can Christianity, a largely discredited faith of a minority in North Africa, and Islam, which is growingly complacent about its own superiority, each make to this new society?

Before the "new" Afro-Asian countries won their independence, the "Christian" European communities living in them were largely self-sufficient. They were preoccupied with their own jobs, their own love affairs, their own families, their own advancement. Rarely did their lives seriously touch those of the Moslems (or Hindus, or Hottentots, etc.) in whose country they were living. Nearly always the relationship was that of the colonizer and the colonized, in all the good and bad senses of both words. It was as difficult for a Frenchman in Algeria to really understand and to love, in the Christian sense, the Moslem in the Moslem world at his doorstep, as it still is for a South African white to appreciate a Zulu. Indifference, suspicion, politics, and religion lay between. If the "native" became too much like the "master," might he not want to get the upper hand himself? And if the "master" approached the "native" on too familiar a basis, might not the "native" seize the occasion to wipe out, if he could, the huge economic gap between them?

Fortunately, there were members of each society who refused some of the premises upon which their fellow members were living and sought others in the other society. We have seen who some of these were on the European side in North Africa: Charles de Foucauld, Louis Massignon, André Mandouze, some Quakers, and many others. On the Moslem side, there are Habib Bourguiba and Abderrahim Bouabid. There is Mohammed Aziz Lahbabi, who met leading European philosophers, then returned to Morocco to work out his own doctrine of "realistic personalism," in which he calls on Moslems to give more sympathetic attention to Christianity.

With independence and the mass departure of Europeans, there has come a change in the type of European resident. Instead of the rich *colon* or factory owner or the modest European artisan, the outsider now tends to be a skilled specialist, the *assistant technique,* as the French call him, who works as a salaried employee for the new government. Or, he may be a volunteer for a relief organization or a member of the American Peace Corps. Many of these arrive, interested in getting to know the "natives," and are astounded when they see the indifference and ignorance of the old-style Europeans.

At the same time, independence, especially in Algeria, has brought about profound social changes in the Moslem population.

These changes are chiefly expressed by secularization and a deep interest in the practical techniques of the West, but also in foreign socialist experiments, such as those in Yugoslavia, the Soviet Union, China, and Cuba. This often, though not always, involves a simultaneous weakening of religious faith. "What can either Allah or the Christian God offer us, when their followers are so hypocritical? What do their teachings have to do with crop rotation or steel plants?" a Tunisian university student once asked me.

Despite efforts of some Arab publicists, notably those serving the Nasser regime in Egypt, to show socialist ideas as not incompatible with Moslem religion, young people in the Maghreb are usually skeptical about such arguments. They find the close association of the temporal and the spiritual in their fathers' Islamic society, its rigidity and class consciousness, is outmoded. Women and girls, especially, have grown impatient with traditional religion because they suffered too long from their relegation to the status of playthings, beasts of burden, and the bearers of children.

The agrarian experiments of the socialist countries, especially China, hold a vast fascination for North Africans, as I have personally seen time and time again in talking with the young and middle-aged men who aspire to tomorrow's leadership in the Maghreb: men like Abderrahman Yusefi, an opposition leader in Morocco, or Ahmed ben Salah, Finance and Planning Minister of Tunisia. Their thinking relegates formal religion to a less than secondary role. It will not be religion, but practical experience in the secular things of life, which will finally determine whether they "go Communist" or work out their own destiny based on their own imperatives, though the second eventuality is far more likely than the first. This does not preclude a dialogue between the faiths. It actually strengthens the need for it.

But will Christian overtures be met with understanding from the Moslem side? The Moslem position on this as presented to me by leaders in Morocco, Algeria, and Tunisia, is simple: In the past, every colonialist enterprise was backed by literature and propaganda of a "Christian" nature. Now the past is dead. The new competition will be not between East and West but between national ambitions and secular ideologies of socialism, capitalism. All of these claim to have the foolproof means of developing economies and leading the "new" societies, which are really loaded with archaic baggage, down the road to a happier life.

"True Christianity is almost the same thing as true Islam," Allal al-Fassi told me. "Christianity is a confirmation of the Mosaic Law. Christian moral and ethical values have common roots with ours. Islam preserved the balance between Judaic materialism and Christian spiritualism. This is why Islam is easier for the peoples of Africa to embrace than either Christianity or Judaism, and this is why they are embracing it.

"In ancient times, the Christian and Islamic religious authorities were often in close touch with one another. Politics and greed spoiled these contacts. Christianity itself perhaps did irreparable historical harm by not condemning colonialism. What we can do now is try to repair the damage by resuming contacts. This time they must be on an informal basis, but this does not mean they cannot be close. One of the requirements for a dialogue, however, is that the missionaries cease to trouble our society with their preaching. We can have a fruitful alliance with Christians and with Jews, if we all respect that which is common to all of us—the One God and the Law—and cease trying to change one another.

"The points of contact between us are three: our monotheism, our charity, and *our doctrine of Islamic socialism.*"

Islamic socialism—a phrase to conjure with in the Moslem world today! Nearly every Moslem government, from that of Gamal Abdel Nasser to that of Ayub Khan in Pakistan, uses this cliché to justify the most secular aspects of its policy. Theorists of the Algerian Popular Democratic Republic see in it a formula to reconcile material and spirit: Marx and Mohammed.

Some of the most incisive statements of Islamic socialism have come from the pen of the late Sheikh Mahmud Shaltut, the former Rector of Al-Azahr University, who saw mutual assistance and charity as the basis of Moslem life:

> Social solidarity proceeds from the awareness that men are responsible for each other. Each individual supports the failings of his brother. If he commits evil, he does so for himself

and for his brother. If he is righteous, he is righteous for himself and for his brother. . . .

Islam has a universal character. Not only does it determine relationships between man and his Master [God], but it also establishes the rules which govern human relations and public affairs with the aim of assuring the well-being of society.

Members of the human society cannot be considered independently of one another. Quite the contrary, as a result of their existence in this world and the very conditions of their life, they render each other mutual services and co-operate to satisfy their needs. . . . Social solidarity under Islam takes on a larger sense and a more complete one. . . . In Islam, the link [with faith] is the religious fraternity of the Moslems. It is within this fraternity that social rights and duties are expressed in the most sincere way. Social solidarity under Islam takes on a larger sense and a more complete one . . . it extends to five rights which are the rights of man: to conserve his religion, his life, his children, his property, his reason.[1]

Few Christians would contest Sheikh Shaltut's propositions, though they would amplify several of them, notably on the natural rights of man, for Christianity, after all, still does identify itself with the good points as well as the bad ones of Western culture. The crucial points of difference between the best in Islamic principles and the best in Christian principles are theological, not social or political. But theological discussions should be undertaken only between people who know one another well. Most Christians and most Moslems do not know one another at all. Vast programs to get better acquainted, programs of educational and cultural contacts on a scale beyond any yet seen, are one way to remedy this. Such exchanges could accomplish far more than the most ambitious program of evangelization.

The secular context of today, the population explosion, the insistent outcry of man's material needs, and the widening gulf between "developed" and "underdeveloped" countries may decree that no organized religion, in its narrow theological terms, will have much to offer the North African, or the Afro-Asian world, of tomor-

[1] *Al-Gumhuriya* (Cairo, December 22, 1961).

row. By contrast, the broad doctrines and the concept of each man as his brother's keeper, which the Western faiths all share, have everything to give. Religion, in a revolutionary world, must join the revolutionary current, not swim against it.

APPENDIX

THE VOICE OF ISLAM AND THE VOICE OF THE GOSPEL

Every day, millions of words are beamed at the African continent over the air waves. Peking, Prague, and Moscow bombard an estimated 12,000,000 radio sets in Africa—about one-sixth of which are in the Maghreb—with appeals, counterappeals, and harangues of all sorts. These are heard by an average of four listeners to each set. Much of the radio propaganda, especially since the ideological division between Peking and Moscow, is carefully adapted in language and content to local listeners of each land. Cairo's powerful Voice of the Arabs has been supplemented since 1962 by the Voice of Islam, religious programs transmitted from Alexandria, often with an amalgam of political propaganda stressing Islam as a "pure" or "liberated" religion.

For years, missionaries felt that there ought to be a strong Christian voice to answer back. Such a voice was heard for the first time in February, 1963. Called the Voice of the Gospel, it is broadcast from Addis Ababa, Ethiopia, by the World Lutheran Federation, co-operating with a committee of representatives of the Christian Conference of East Asia, the Conference of Churches of all Africa, the Christian Council of the Middle East, and the Ecumenical Council of Churches. Half of the air time, between 6 and 10 A.M., is devoted to religion; the other half to educational and cultural subjects. "The Voice of the Gospel is not going to be just an anti-Communist voice or anti-anything else," predicted the British Broadcasting Corporation in a program welcoming the new station. "It is to be a witness for the Christian faith and its programs will be positive and practical."

While covering the Addis Ababa African summit conference in May, 1963, I was able to talk with some of the program's producers. They were pleased with the results. They had received interesting listeners' reports from many areas, including North Africa. Broadcasts each day were in English, French, Arabic, and Swahili, starting first in Ethiopia, swinging south to Madagascar, East Africa, then over to West and North Africa, and including South Africa. Programs are prepared by natives of each region to suit local tastes.

By 1964, only in Algeria did local government radios in North Africa permit broadcast of Christian religious services; in this case, Catholic Mass. Attempts by some of the Catholic missionary orders to arrange for small private radio stations along the southern coasts of Europe to beam religious programs to North Africa met resistance from the Church hierarchy.

GLOSSARY OF ARABIC TERMS

amir. *See* emir.

Amir al-Muminin (*lit.* "prince of the true believers," or "commander of the faithful"). A title of the Caliph [*q.v.*] or any religious and temporal leader of a Moslem community, e.g., the King of Morocco.

baraka (*lit.* "blessing"). Blessing or beneficence; also in North African folklore, a quality or essence inherent in certain holy men, rulers, animals, objects, especially white ones; a kind of white magic.

cadi. *See* kadi.

caid. A military commander or the chief of a tribe or clan with paramilitary functions; used mainly in Morocco.

Caliph (*lit.* "successor"). The representative of God on earth and therefore the successor of the Prophet Mohammed. The title was first held by Arab and then by Ottoman rulers until the final overthrow of the Ottoman Caliphate after World War I.

dhimmi. A non-Moslem living under a "covenant" (*dhimma*) with, or under special obligation to, a Moslem government. Within Moslem society he enjoys protection and certain rights in exchange for payment of a special tax.

al-Djamaa (*lit.* "gathering"). Friday, the Moslem day of worship; the Day of Assembly.

djihad. Moslem holy war against nonbelievers, whether pagan, Christian, or Jew. It is considered a duty of Moslems in general, though not necessarily one of the fundamental duties of an individual Moslem.

emir. Prince, or commander. *Also spelled* amir.

fatwa. A legal advisory or opinion concerning Moslem religious law issued by a Moslem jurist.

fonduk. A hostelry, inn, shelter, or refuge; also, in medieval times, a protected portion of a North African city where European merchants lived and traded.

fukaha (pl.). Theologians or religious savants.

habus. Religious property or real estate held by the state.

hadith (*lit.* "communication" or "narrative"). The body of verbal or written traditions concerning the words and deeds of the Prophet

Mohammed and his companions; also a single one of these traditions.

Hidden Imam. *See mahdi.*

Hidjaz. The holy province of southern Arabia which includes the cities of Mecca and Medina and their environs. *Also spelled* Hejaz.

hidjra (*lit.* "breaking of relations" or "emigration"). The Prophet Mohammed's flight from Mecca to Medina in A.D. 622; the date from which the Moslem era is counted. *Also spelled* Hegira.

Ifrikiya (from the Latin "Africa"). Africa; especially Tunisia.

imam. The temporal and spiritual ruler of Islam; a title of the caliph [*q.v.*]. Also, the leader in prayer at mosques.

Islam (*lit.* "submission to the will of God"). The belief in one God and in the role of Mohammed as His messenger.

kadi. A judge in a court of religious law. *Also spelled* cadi.

karamet. Miraculous gifts or graces given by God to chosen individuals or saints; divine favor.

khutba. The ritual Moslem sermon given in mosques on Friday; often it has a political content or political overtones.

khuwan. A senior brother of a religious order; often the man in charge of a *zawiya* [*q.v.*], or monastery.

Koran (*lit.* "reading," or "recitation"). The holy book of Islam; revealed to the Prophet Mohammed by an angel.

madrasa. A secondary school where Islamic studies are pursued; in contemporary North Africa, secular subjects are often included in the curriculum.

mahdi (*lit.* "guided one"). Name taken by various Islamic leaders who claimed divine enlightenment. In an eschatological sense, it refers to the Hidden Imam, who will appear on earth at the end of time.

makhzen. In Morocco, the government or administration; used pejoratively by Moroccan nationalists to indicate the French Protectorate and its Moroccan co-workers.

marabout. A holy man or saintly man; often a Sufi holy man.

medina (*lit.* "city"). Term used to indicate the Arab quarter of a North African city as distinct from the European quarter.

mellah. The Jewish ghetto of a North African city.

Mozarab. A Christian Spaniard converted to Islam. *See mustaribun.*

mudjahidun (sing. *mudjahid; lit.* "fighters for the faith"). Originally, the fighters in holy wars; in contemporary North Africa, nationalist guerrilla fighters.

mufti. A canon lawyer of high standing in the Moslem community who may issue opinions concerning the application of religious law to personal and religious life.

mustaribun (*lit.* "arabicized"). Originally, the non-Arab tribes converted to Islam; in Spain, Christian Spaniards converted to Islam. (In Spain, corrupted to Mozarab.)
nabi. Prophet.
Ramadan. The ninth month of the Moslem lunar calendar in which the Koran [*q.v.*] was first revealed to Mohammed; observed by fasting and abstinence during daylight hours.
rasul. Messenger.
ribat. A fortified monastery where religious discipline, Islamic values, and warrior virtues were inculcated; found especially in the Sahara and along the Mediterranean coast of Tunisia in medieval times.
Rumi. Originally, any Greek or Byzantine; later, and in contemporary North Africa, any Christian.
al-sawm. The rite of fasting, usually during the month of Ramadan [*q.v.*].
shahada (*lit.* "testimony"). The Moslem profession of faith: "There is no God but God and Mohammed is the apostle of God."
sharia (*lit.* "clear path"). The canon law of Islam.
sharif. Sing. of *shurafa* [*q.v.*].
Shiite (*lit.* "partisan"). A follower of a Moslem denomination which rejects the first three Caliphs and the authority of the *sunna* [*q.v.*].
shurafa (pl. of sharif). Direct descendants of the Prophet Mohammed; also a title of honor.
Sufi. A follower of a system of Islamic contemplative life.
sunna (*lit.* "custom," "usage," or "statute"). The orthodox code of Islamic practice transmitted through Mohammed's immediate successors.
sura. A chapter of the Koran.
talib (pl. *talabah*). (1) A learned man, scholar, or student. (2) In Maghreb vernacular, a sorcerer, magician, or soothsayer.
tarik. A pathway or system of Islamic contemplative life; hence a Sufi order.
tarika. (1) A method of moral psychology used by medieval Islamic philosophers. (2) A contemplative, or Sufi order, which follows a certain rule or rite.
ulama (pl.). Canonists and theologians who rule on weighty religious and political matters.
umma. The Islamic community of believers.
zawiya. A monastery or place of learning and devotions for members of an Islamic religious brotherhood or order.
zindik. A heretic whose heresy is theoretically punishable by death.

SOURCES AND BIBLIOGRAPHY

In compiling materials for this book, I drew heavily on my own experience in reporting events in North Africa in the late 1950's and early 1960's. In addition to the files of my own dispatches and broadcasts, I was fortunate in having access to a wide range of North African newspapers and periodicals which touched on the special problems that concerned me. Among them were: *Al-alam,* Rabat; *Al-Ayam,* Rabat; *Bulletin de l'Association d'Etudes,* Algiers; *Dawat al-Hag,* Rabat; *Al-Gumhuriya,* Cairo; *Maghreb al-Arabi,* Rabat; and *Al-Shaab,* Algiers, as well as the French press of Paris and North Africa.

Two unpublished lectures also proved informative and helpful. One, a lecture by Allal al-Fassi, entitled "The Role of the Islamic Ulama," given in Fez in October, 1959, was made available to me through the lecture notes of Stuart Schaer; the other, a lecture by Sir Hamilton Gibb given at Toumliline Monastery, Morocco, on August 13, 1960. I also had access to a translation of the "Proceedings of the Algerian Association of Ulama, 16–19 Jumadi II" (1935), thanks to Professor L. Carl Brown.

In studying the history of the Maghreb, the Arabic collection of the Bibliothèque Nationale, Paris, was also very helpful.

The following is a list of published books, articles, and collections of documents which I have either cited in the text or found useful in preparing this work.

Abbas, Ferhat. "La France, C'est Moi," *Entente* (February 23, 1936).

Abul Hasan ibn Abu Bakr. *Extraîts Inédits Relatifs au Maghreb.* Algiers, 1924.

Africanus, Leo (Hasan ibn Muhammed al-Wazzan). *Description de l'Afrique,* trans. Apaulard. Paris, 1956.

"A.M." "Regards sur l'enseignement des Musulmans en Algérie," *Confluent* (June-July, 1963).

Algerian Constitution, in *Al-Shaab* (August 29, 1963).

Andrade, Antonio Alberto de. *Many Races—One Nation.* Lisbon, 1961.

Annuaire de l'Archdiocèse de Rabat. Rabat, 1962.

Archives Marocaines. 38 vols. Rabat, 1926.

Ashford, Douglas. *Political Change in Morocco.* Princeton, 1961.

Atkinson, William C. *A History of Spain and Portugal.* London, 1960.
Augustine. *The Confessions of Saint Augustine,* trans. E. B. Pusey. New York, 1961.
Bakri, al-. *Kitab al-Masalik.* 2nd ed. Algiers, 1912.
Barbour, Nevill (ed.). *A Survey of North West Africa.* London, 1959.
Bayan, al-. *Histoire de l'Afrique et de l'Espagne,* trans. E. Fagnan. Algiers, 1901.
Benabdallah, Abdelazziz. *Les Grands Courants de la Civilisation du Maghreb.* Casablanca, 1958.
———. "L'Islam et la structuration de l'Etat Marocain," *La Nation Africaine* (October 7, 1962).
Benumeya, Rodolfo Gil. *España y el Mundo Arabe.* Madrid, 1955.
Berenger, Alfred. "L'Echec de Saint Augustin, *Jeune Afrique* (June 19, 1961). (Article was unsigned.)
Berque, Jacques. *Le Maghreb entre Deux Guerres.* Paris, 1962.
Blunt, Wilfred. *Black Sunrise.* London, 1951.
Briggs, Lloyd Cabot. *Tribes of the Sahara.* Cambridge, 1960.
Brockelmann, Carl. *History of the Islamic Peoples,* trans. Joel Carmichael and Moshe Perlmann. New York, 1960.
Brunel, Camille. *La Question Indigène en Algérie.* Paris, 1906.
Burckhardt, Jacob. *The Age of Constantine the Great.* Garden City, 1956.
Carcopino, Jerome. *Le Maroc Antique.* Paris, 1943.
———. "Volubilis Regie Jubae," *Hesperis,* XVII, Fasc. i (1933).
Castelloni, G. *Tunisi e Tripoli.* Torino, 1911.
Castries, Henry de, and Pierre de Cenival. *Les Sources Inédites de l'Histoire du Maroc.* 20 vols. Paris and London, 1918.
Cenival, Pierre de. "L'Eglise Chrétienne de Marrakech au XIIIe Siècle," *Hesperis,* VII (1937).
Charles-Roux, François, and Jacques Caille. *Missions Diplomatiques Françaises à Fez.* Paris, 1955. (Publications de l'Institut des Hautes Etudes Marocaines.)
Chaudru, Raynal de. *De la Domination Française en Afrique et des Principales Questions que fait naître l'Occupation de ce Pays.* Paris, 1832.
Chouraqui, André. *Les Juifs d'Afrique du Nord.* Paris, 1952.
Cintas, Pierre. *Amulettes Puniques.* Vol. I. Tunis, 1946.
Courtois, Christian. *Les Vandals et l'Afrique.* Paris, 1956.
Cragg, Kenneth. "Africa: The Challenge of Islam," *The Christian Century* (February 7, 1962).

Dahir partant organisation de Ministère d'état chargé des Affaires Islamiques. Rabat, Rajeb 13, 1381 (December 21, 1961).
Daraul, Arkon. *Secret Societies*. London, 1961.
Daniel, Norman. *Islam and the West*. Edinburgh, 1962.
De Madariaga, Salvador. *Spain, A Modern History*. New York, 1958.
Dermenghen, Emile. *Muhammad and the Islamic Tradition,* trans. Jean M. Watt. New York, 1957.
Des Allues, Elisabeth. *Toumliline à la Recherche de Dieu au Service de l'Afrique*. Paris, 1961.
Drague, Georges. *Esquisse d'Histoire Religieuse du Maroc, Confréries et Zaouias*. Paris, n.d.
Driss, Abdelazziz. *Treasures of the Bardo Museum*. Tunis, 1962.
Duprée, Louis. "The Arabs of Modern Libya," *The Muslim World* (April, 1958).
Duval, Léon-Etienne. *Messages de Paix*. Bruges, 1962.
Fassi, Allal al-. *Hadith al-Maghreb fil Mashrek*. Cairo, 1956.
Frazer, James. *The Golden Bough*. Abridged edition. London, 1954.
Fremantle, Anne. *Desert Calling*. New York, 1947.
———. *A Treasury of Early Christianity*. New York, 1953.
Foucauld, Charles de. *Lettres à Henry de Castries*. Paris, 1923.
Gagigas, Isidoro de los. *Minorias Etnico-Religiosas de la edad Media Española*. 2 vols. Madrid, 1947–48.
Gautier, E. F. *Le Passé de l'Afrique du Nord*. Paris, 1952.
Gibb, Hamilton. *Studies on the Civilization of Islam,* ed. S. Shaw and W. Polk. Boston, 1962.
Gibbon, Edward. *The Decline and Fall of the Roman Empire*. 6 vols. London, 1960.
Gorée, Georges. *Les Amitiés Sahariennes du Père de Foucauld*. 3 vols. Paris, 1941.
Gsell, Stephan. *Histoire Ancienne de l'Afrique du Nord*. 10 vols. Paris, 1921.
Harm, Sylvia G. *Arab Nationalism and Religion*. Berkeley and Los Angeles, 1962.
Hashaishi, ben Othman al-. *Voyage au Pays des Senoussia,* trans. V. Serres. Paris, 1903.
Hassan, Hassan Ibrahim. "The Idea of the Caliphate," *La Pensée* (March, 1963).
Hitti, Phillip K. *Islam and the West*. Princeton, 1962.
Ibn Batuta. *Voyages*. Paris, 1942. (A bilingual French-Arabic edition.)
Ibn Khaldun. *Histoire des Berbères,* ed. M. de Slane. Paris, 1933.
———. *Muqadimma,* trans. Franz Rosenthal. 3 vols. London, 1958.

———. *Prolegomena,* trans. M. de Slane. Paris, 1934.

Julien, Charles-André. *Histoire de l'Afrique du Nord.* 3 vols. Paris, 1961.

Kittler, Glen P. *The White Fathers.* New York, 1961.

Koehler, Henry. *L'Eglise Chrétienne du Maroc.* Paris, 1934.

Kritzeck, James. *Peter the Venerable and Islam.* Princeton, 1964.

———. "Pierre le Vénérable et l'Islam," adapt. by Dom Placide Pernot in *Images de Toumliline* (January, 1962).

Kumlien, Gunnar D. "The Challenge of Islam," *The Commonweal* (November 9, 1962).

Lanczkowski, Gunter. *Heilige Schriften.* Stuttgart, 1956.

Lavigerie, Charles (Cardinal). *Instructions aux Missionaires.* Maison Carrée: Imprimerie des Missionaires d'Afrique (Pères Blancs), 1885. (Reprinted 1939.)

Lecanuet, R. P. *Les Dernières Années du Pontificat de Pie IX.* Paris, 1931.

Leenhardt, M., *et al.* (eds.). *Protestantisme Français.* Paris, 1945.

Lesourd, Paul. *La Vraie Figure du Père de Foucauld.* Paris, 1925.

LeTourneau, Roger. *Evolution Politique de l'Afrique du Nord Musulmane, 1920–1961.* Paris, 1962.

Levy-Provençale, E. "La Foundation de Fez," *Annales de l'Institut d'études Orientales,* IX (1938).

Llorca, Bernardino. *Nueva Visione de la Historia del Christianismo.* 2 vols. Barcelona, 1956.

MacBurney, C. B. M. *The Stone Age of Northern Africa.* London, 1960.

Manifeste du Partie de l'Istiqlal. Hizb al-Istiqlal. Party Documents. Rabat, n.d.

Martinez, D. "Les Pères Blanc d'Afrique," *Osservatore Romano,* weekly edition (March 15, 1963).

Massignon, Louis. *Parole Donnée.* Paris, 1962.

Meynier, R. "Les Sanoussiyah en Libye," *Cahiers Charles de Foucauld,* no. 16. Paris, n.d.

Miège, Jean-Louis. "Les Missions Protestantes au Maroc (1875–1905)," *Hesperis,* XVII (1955).

Mones, H. "Le Malekisme et l'échec des Fatimides en Ifriquiyah," in *Etudes d'Orientalisme dédiées à la mémoire de Levy-Provençale.* Paris, 1962.

Monteil, Vincent. *Maroc.* Paris, 1962.

Nabhami, Kouriba. "L'Algérie: la Terre et les Hommes," *Confluent* (June-July, 1963).

Paillat, Claude. *Le Dossier Secret de l'Algérie*. Paris, 1961.

Peers, A. *A Life of Ramón Lull*. London, 1927.

Penrose, Boles. *Travel and Discovery in the Renaissance, 1420–1620*. New York, 1962.

Picard, Gilbert-Charles. *Les Religions de l'Afrique Antique*. Paris, 1954.

Pionset, L., and R. Lancere. "Un Sanctuaire de Tanit à Carthage," in *Revue de l'histoire des religions*. Paris, 1923.

Pirenne, Henri. *Mohammed and Charlemagne*. New York, 1962.

Previte-Orton, C. W. *Shorter Cambridge Medieval History*. Vol. VI. Cambridge, 1953.

Quirtas, Roudh el-. *Histoire des Souverains du Maghreb et Annales de la Ville de Fes,* trans. Beaumier. Paris, 1860.

Ricard, Prosper. *Maroc* (Les Guides Bleus). Paris, 1951.

Ronart, Stephan and Nancy. *Concise Encyclopedia of Arabic Civilization*. Amsterdam, 1959.

Runciman, Stephen. *Byzantine Civilization*. New York, 1956.

Rutherford, J., and Edward H. Glenny. *The Gospel in North Africa*. London, 1900.

Schroeder, Eric. *Muhammed's People*. Portland, Maine, 1955.

Slawi, Ahmed ben Khaled en-Naciri es-. *Kitab El Istiqça Li Akhbar Dawal El Maghreb el-Aksa,* trans. A. Geraille. 3 vols. Paris, 1923.

The Soummam Platform. Printed clandestinely by Front de la Liberation Nationale in French and Arabic, 1957.

Southern, R. W. *Western Views of Islam in the Middle Ages*. Cambridge, Mass., 1962.

Speight, R. M. "Islamic Reform in Morocco," *The Muslim World* (January, 1963).

Steele, Francis R. "Tolerance and Truth," *Cross and Crescent* (June, 1963).

Stewart, Ruth. "The New Algeria," *North Africa* (September-October, 1963).

Suffert, Georges. "Les Evêques de France de l'OAS," *France Observateur* (February 15, 1962).

Tabari, Abu Jafar Mohammed ibn Jarir al-. *Chronicles,* trans. Herman Zotenberg. Vol. III. Paris, 1958.

Talbi, M. "Kairouan et le Malekisme espagnol," in *Etudes d'Orientalisme dédiées à la Mémoire de Levy-Provençale*. Paris, 1962.

Terasse, Henri. *Histoire du Maroc*. 2 vols. Casablanca, 1954.

Tisserant, Eugène (Cardinal), and G. Wiet. "Une lettre de l'Almohade Murtada au Pape Innocent IV," *Hesperis,* VI (1926).

Toynbee, Arnold J. *A Study of History*. London, 1949.

Treece, Henry. *The Crusades*. London, 1962.
Van der Meer, F., and C. Mohrmann. *Atlas de l'Antiquité Chrétienne*. Paris, 1960. English edition: *Atlas of the Early Christian World*. Nelson, 1958.
Von Grunebaum, Gustave E. *Medieval Islam*. Chicago, 1958.
Waddell, Helen. *The Desert Fathers*. Ann Arbor, 1957.
Watt, W. Montgomery. *Muhammed at Mecca*. Oxford, 1953.
———. *Muhammed at Medina*. Oxford, 1956.
———. *Muhammed, Prophet and Statesman*. London, 1961.
Westermarck, Edward. *Wit and Wisdom of Morocco*. New York, 1931.
Wiebe, Abe. "A Saviour of Life and Death," *North Africa* (September-October, 1963).
Zeraffa, Michel. *Tunisie*. Paris, 1955.
Zerecki, es-. *Chronique des Almohades et des Hafsides,* trans. E. Fagnan. Constantine, 1895.

INDEX

JOHN K. COOLEY

For the past seven years, John K. Cooley has been correspondent for *The Christian Science Monitor,* based in Casablanca, Morocco. He covered the Algerian war for his newspaper and for the National Broadcasting Company, and he has also served as a correspondent in the same region for United Press International, the Canadian Broadcasting Corporation, and the foreign news service of the London *Observer.* Articles by Mr. Cooley have appeared in such magazines as *The Reporter, The New Republic, Commonweal,* and *This Week.*

Born in 1927 in New York City, Mr. Cooley grew up in Mount Vernon, New York. After serving in the United States Army in Europe, he received his A.B. degree in 1952 from Dartmouth College, where he wrote for the *Daily Dartmouth* and other campus publications. For five years, Mr. Cooley was based in Vienna, where he studied, served with the U. S. Departments of Army and State, and occasionally covered Central and Eastern European affairs as a free lancer for the *New York Herald Tribune.*

He first went to North Africa in 1953 to work with a construction company in Morocco, then resumed writing for the *Herald Tribune.* After a brief stint in New York as an editorial writer for this newspaper, he returned to North Africa to do public information work with the U. S. Army's Corps of Engineers. In 1957 he left government service to become a full-time newsman.

Mr. Cooley has studied at the New School for Social Research, Columbia University, and the Universities of Zürich and Vienna, in addition to informal studies and research at various institutions in North Africa. In 1964 he was awarded the annual resident fellowship for an American foreign correspondent by the Council on Foreign Relations in New York.

PORTUGAL
SPAIN
Madeira
Strait of Gibraltar
Tangier
Algiers
Rabat
Oran
KABYLIE
Casablanca
Fez
SAHARAN ATLAS
MOROCCO
MIDDLE ATLAS
Atlantic
Marrakesh
HIGH ATLAS
Canary Islands
IFNI
Colomb-Béchar
Ocean
A L G E R I
Villa Cisneros
SPANISH SAHARA
In-Salah
S
a
h
Tropic
Atar Oasis
MAURITANIA
MALI
Dakar
SENEGAL
Timbuktu
GAMBIA
Niger
PORTUGUESE GUINEA
UPPER VOLTA
GUINEA
SIERRA LEONE
NIMBA
MTS.
IVORY COAST
GHANA
TOGO
DAHOMEY
Niger
Ibadan
Monrovia
LIBERIA
Accra
Lagos
Gulf of Guinea
Equator
10°
20°
30°
40°
0°